The Mortgage Originator Success Kit

The Mortgage Originator Success Kit

Darrin J. Seppinni

McGraw-Hill

New York   Chicago   San Francisco
Lisbon   London   Madrid   Mexico City
Milan   New Delhi   San Juan   Seoul
Singapore   Sydney   Toronto

The **McGraw-Hill** Companies

3 4 5 6 7 8 9 0   DOC/DOC   0 9 8 7 6

ISBN 0-07-146481-6

This publication is designed to provide accurate and authoritative information in regard to the subject matter covered. It is sold with the understanding that neither the author nor the publisher is engaged in rendering legal, accounting, futures/securities trading, or other professional service. If legal advice or other expert assistance is required, the services of a competent professional person should be sought.

> —*From a Declaration of Principles jointly adopted by a Committee of the American Bar Association and a Committee of Publishers*

McGraw-Hill books are available at special quantity discounts to use as premiums and sales promotions, or for use in corporate training programs. For more information, please write to the Director of Special Sales, Professional Publishing, McGraw-Hill, Two Penn Plaza, New York, NY 10121-2298. Or contact your local bookstore.

 This book is printed on recycled, acid-free paper containing a minimum of 50% recycled, de-inked fiber.

Library of Congress Cataloging-in-Publication Data

Seppinni, Darrin J.
   The mortgage originator: the quick way to a six-figure income/by Darrin J. Seppinni.
     p. cm.
   Includes index.
   ISBN 0-07-146481-6 (alk. paper)
   1. Mortgage brokers—United States. I. Title.

HG2040.5.U5S46 2006
332.7'2068—dc22

                  2005032471

CONTENTS

PART TWO
Educational and Licensing Requirements for the Loan Originator

ACKNOWLEDGMENTS

I would like to give a special thanks to my wonderful wife, Jayne, for her unwavering love, support, and input to this project. I would also like to acknowledge with deep appreciation the efforts and superb work of my staff, who stood by this project no matter what obstacles we encountered. I want to thank my agent, Meredith Bernstein, for guiding me through the book publishing business. I'd also like to extend a thanks to our publisher, McGraw-Hill Trade, and our editor, Mary Glenn, for their interest in my project.

INTRODUCTION

The secret is out about the mortgage business. It is the only industry that allows anyone the capability of earning a six-figure income without an educational degree. The opportunity is the same for women, minorities, and individuals with no college background. You are paid on the work you put out.

Have you noticed on some of the reality shows on TV lately how many participants are mortgage brokers? Sarah on *Joe Millionaire*, Bob on *The Bachelorette*, and the more notable Troy McClain on *The Apprentice*—all were mortgage brokers.

Becoming a loan originator is a job requiring competence, interpersonal skills, honesty, and integrity. Whether your customers are purchasing a home or refinancing their existing loan, they are encountering one of the most stressful and important decisions of their lives. Your role as a loan originator is to guide them through the complex process of residential mortgage lending.

There has never been a better time to enter into the mortgage industry. The mortgage industry in 2003, with its historical low interest rates, reached a record-level mortgage production of $3.8 trillion. New construction and home sales (at an all-time high) continue to create a huge demand for mortgages. Real estate experts have identified a new market yet to embark into first-time homeownership: minorities and the echo boomers, or Generation Y. The echo boomers are the largest generation of young people since the 1960s. They are considered to comprise a third of our population at 80 million strong. Currently spending $120 billion a year, these young people are just starting to purchase their first cars. Generation Yers will certainly have a powerful impact on the real estate market when they prepare for homeownership.

In addition, the mortgage industry's growth can be attributed to a wider range of mortgage loan products available to the loan originator today. Most notably are the no- and low-down-payment mortgage programs that have made homeownership available to millions of people who might not otherwise qualify for a loan. The future growth and demand for mortgage loans will continue to create unlimited career opportunities.

However, there is a significant lack of *qualified* individuals available to handle this growth. Most loan originators learn the business the hard way, the sink-or-swim method—on-the-job training that can be painful and can take several years. You would be surprised to discover that there are many "experienced" loan originators who lack a thorough knowledge of some very important mortgage principles. My hopes are that you read carefully Part One of this book, gaining vital information that you can reference time and time again throughout your career.

The Mortgage Originator Success Kit offers invaluable information on an extremely financially rewarding industry. Each chapter builds upon the prior one, so that the reader has an opportunity to learn about all facets of residential mortgage lending. With this training manual you will have a complete understanding of the mortgage business, from the inception of a mortgage loan to the selling of that loan in the secondary market. You will also find priceless information on customer service and sales techniques that, if applied correctly, will ensure a successful career as a mortgage loan originator. This book lays out a doable strategy in an easy-to-learn format that anyone can use immediately to start a career or take his or her existing career to the next level.

To save you time and to help you get better results as quickly as possible, you will be provided with tips and suggestions that have been distilled from years of experience. The knowledge and understanding of the mortgage industry that you will have after reading this training manual will give you an unquestionable edge as you enter into the mortgage business.

Job Opportunities and Earning Potential

This book is for ambitious people who want to get ahead in life and want a real opportunity to become financially independent. The earning potential with a career in the mortgage industry is truly unlimited, and loan originators and mortgage brokers are fast-moving entrepreneurs. A mortgage loan originator is basically a sales position; therefore, you earn commission on each loan produced. How much money you will earn is determined by your personal initiative, salesmanship ability, and tenacity.

In order to succeed as a loan originator, it is important to obtain the proper training. *The Mortgage Originator Success Kit* will provide you with all the necessary training and education to start your career immediately, with the potential of earning *$100,000 to $1 million-plus in income per year*.

The following example reflects what a top originator can produce: he or she can originate 456 loans in one year with an average loan amount of $110,994 and fund a total of $50,590,751, generating the loan originator an annual income of approximately $1 million. In fact, according to the latest Executive Compensation Survey by Inside Mortgage Finance Publications, the highest-paid executive in the 2003 survey was a male first vice president working at a mid-size mortgage banking firm. He took home $6,690,000 in total pay—most of it in stock options.

Although *The Mortgage Originator Success Kit* is focused on how to start your career as a loan originator, there are many other job opportunities: in "retail" there are positions such as loan processors and underwriters, and in "wholesale" there are positions such as account managers and account executives.

My Reasons for Developing this Manual

My career started in the mortgage business 24 years ago at the ripe age of 21. I wanted a career in a business where I could provide a service that would benefit people. At the same time I was seeking an opportunity in a career where I would be rewarded with unlimited income potential in return for hard work and determination. I had the eye of the tiger, and I wanted to utilize my sales skills, competitive nature, and burning desire to get ahead in life. The mortgage business gave me the ability to grow my knowledge and experience to become an independent entrepreneur, first as a successful loan originator, then a mortgage broker, and eventually a national mortgage banker.

When I first started my career as a loan originator, I looked around for a training book such as this but found only books on how to succeed in the real estate industry. I needed a book that would guide me in how to succeed as a loan originator. I was forced to start my career with absolutely no knowledge of mortgage lending. I learned how to become a loan originator, as most people do, from on-the-job training. This can be extremely difficult, especially the first few years in the business, and it requires much determination and persistence.

As my career progressed, I counseled and trained many a loan officer and mortgage broker. I started compiling all my knowledge and experience and began the development of *The Mortgage Originator Success Kit*. I felt that this was the right time for me to pass on this valuable information to aspiring professionals seeking an opportunity in the mortgage business.

The most important part of this book, however, is not just what you read or learn. It is also what you actually *do* with these practical and proven concepts. Action is everything! I look forward to assisting you in the best decision of your life and welcome you into the mortgage industry.

MORTGAGE FUNDAMENTALS

PART ONE

CHAPTER 1

INTRODUCTION TO THE MORTGAGE BUSINESS

The greatest thing a man can do in this world is to make the most possible out of the stuff that has been given him. This is success, and there is no other.

—Orison Swett Marden

Before we launch into the basics of the business, it's helpful to be familiar with, essentially, who's who and what's what.

WHO'S WHO

Account Executive

A person who represents a specific banker or *wholesale lender*. This individual has detailed information, including guidelines and rates on the loan programs the lender offers. The account executive is the contact person for the mortgage loan originator or broker. Account executives are responsible for initiating and maintaining relationships with local mortgage brokers, Realtors, builders, and other business partners as a referral source for the origination of home loans.

Appraiser

An individual who provides an opinion of the property's fair market value based on specific market data. A person who conducts routine appraisals of residential, industrial, and commercial properties.

Borrower (Mortgagor)

A person who applies for and receives funds in the form of a loan and is obligated to repay the loan in full under the terms of the loan.

Builder or Developer

A person or company that is actively involved in the building of homes for sale. A developer prepares raw land so that it can be built upon.

Credit Reporting Agency

An agency that compiles, maintains, and provides credit and other personal information to creditors. This information includes bill-paying habits, credit account references, balances, and place of employment. There are three major credit bureaus that provide nationwide coverage of consumer credit information in the United States: Equifax, Experian, and TransUnion.

Escrow

A procedure in which a third party acts as an intermediary for both the buyer and the seller, carrying out both parties' requests and assuming responsibility for handling all the paperwork and distribution of funds.

Lender

The institution or individual (in the case of a private lender) who provides the funds when a mortgage loan is made. Lenders typically have warehouse lines (lines of credit) to fund loans before they are sold to the secondary source. Brokers typically do not have warehouse lines and therefore cannot fund loans.

Loan Originator

A person who, for a commission or fee, takes the borrower's application and finds the best loan program to fit the borrower's needs.

Loan Servicer

A company that works with the customer after the loan closes to provide customer service by collecting mortgage payments and to provide an escrow account if necessary. If an escrow account is established, the servicer pays the property taxes and insurance payments.

Mortgage Banker

A direct mortgage lender who originates and funds loans in his or her own name for resale in the secondary mortgage market (Fannie Mae, Freddie Mac, Ginnie Mae).

Mortgage Broker

Also known as a *broker.* A person or company that arranges mortgage loans through a mortgage banker or lender (also known as a *wholesale banker* or *lender*). The broker establishes a relationship with this banker or lender and acts as the intermediary between the borrower and the banker or lender. Typically, the broker has a relationship with more than one banker or lender, allowing the broker to shop the loan in order to find the best rate and term available to suit the borrower's needs. The broker does not fund loans (or lend money).

Mortgage Insurance Company

A company that insures the lender for higher-risk loans. These insurance policies protect the lender by paying the costs of foreclosing on a house if the borrower stops paying the loan. Mortgage insurance (MI) is typically required for conventional loans with a down payment of less than 20% of the sale price. To avoid MI, a second mortgage at a higher interest rate can be obtained.

Processor

A person working with the loan originator who gathers information provided by the originator, applicable to the loan file, and submits the loan for a decision to the lender. The processor gathers information needed to meet all the conditions requested by the lender in order to fund the loan.

Realtor

A person licensed to negotiate and transact the sale of real estate on behalf of either the borrower or the seller, and in some cases can represent both parties.

Real Estate Agent

A person who is licensed to negotiate and transact the sale of real estate property. This person can represent either the seller or the buyer or both.

Real Estate Broker

A person who supervises agents with less experience to effectively run a real estate office. Brokers have high levels of knowledge and experience in the areas of advanced real estate practice, law, finance, appraisal, economics, property management, escrow, and/or real estate office administration. Many brokers own the firms they work in; others work with national real estate franchises.

Surveyor

A person or company that measures the boundaries of a parcel of land, including any improvements. The surveyor prepares a report known as a *survey*. Most lenders require a survey of the property in a purchase transaction.

Settlement Company

Also known as the *settlement agent*. A company that acts as the go-between in coordinating the closing between the buyer, seller, and lender. The settlement company usually is an escrow company or a settlement attorney, depending on the state where the property is located. The settlement company serves as the meeting place between the related parties of the mortgage where the mortgage documents are executed and the property ownership is transferred to the buyer on a purchase transaction. The settlement company collects all money in the transaction and disburses the money to the proper parties.

Settlement Attorney

A lawyer or attorney who specializes in real estate. Settlement attorneys are not required in every state. They will perform the same duties as an escrow or settlement agent.

Title Company

The company that provides a title policy and title exam. The title company is also responsible for the recording of the deed and all other legal documents. Title companies specialize in doing title searches and insuring title to property.

Underwriter

An individual who works for the lender and reviews the loan file for the purpose of making a decision on the loan. The underwriter is responsible for reviewing a loan application and determining whether to make a loan based on credit, income, debt, appraised value of the house, and other factors. An underwriter is responsible for evaluating the loan to determine the risk involved for the lender. Many loans are also underwritten via automated systems such as Freddie Mac LP (Loan Prospector) and Fannie Mae DU (Desktop Underwriter).

Wholesale Lender

A lender that typically works only with mortgage brokers. Wholesale lenders accept completed loan packages and underwrite them. They offer mortgage brokers discounted pricing in return for the up-front work done by the mortgage broker.

Definitions

Loan Officer

Also known as a *loan agent, loan originator, loan solicitor,* and *salesperson.* The loan officer plays an important role in the loan process. The loan officer can work as an independent contractor for or as an employee of a mortgage broker or lender. Loan officers may or may not need to be licensed, depending on state laws. Either way their role is primarily the same. They work hand in hand with Realtors, builders, lenders, and the borrowers themselves. The main duties and responsibilities include, but are not limited to, taking a complete and accurate loan application, qualifying the potential borrower with a suitable loan program and lender, obtaining all necessary documentation, and working with processors, underwriters, title, escrow, and lenders to ensure that the loan process goes along smoothly and closes on time with few or no surprises.

Mortgage Banker

A loan company that originates, services, and sells loans to investors. It typically has a servicing department and will monitor the payments, taxes, insurance, and other services associated with the mortgage after it is closed. Mortgage bankers will finance the loan and can make a profit by either selling the loan on the secondary market at a premium or collecting the loan fees and interest that the customer pays on the loan. See Figure 1.1.

FIGURE 1-1
Mortgage Banking Firm
This is a general overview of a mortgage banking firm. It is used for illustration purposes and does not reflect a specific company.

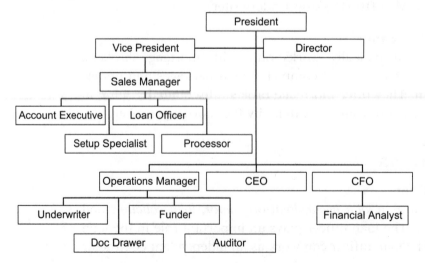

Mortgage Broker

A real estate professional whose main focus is on originating residential and/or commercial loans. Mortgage brokers enable mortgage lenders to provide financing on loans originated nationwide without having to incur the cost of having an actual physical presence. Typically the common mortgage broker office will have a very small support staff, anywhere from one to five employees. See Figure 1.2.

Net Branch

The "net branch" concept was created to give the broker or originator the ability to, in a sense, own his or her own business but have the support and backing of a big company. Support may include processors, underwriters, funders, human resources, and licensing. Having this backing allows the broker to focus on originations and keeping clients happy, as opposed to having to be concerned with the day-to-day operations of running a big company. There are actually two types of net branch operations: one consists of mortgage bankers, and the other consists of mortgage brokers. There are no requirements that specify how big or small a net branch can be. The most common approval requirements to become a net branch include having at least three to five years of strong management experience, being a top producer with a large referral base, and having good business rapport with lenders, Realtors, builders, and other professionals.

FIGURE 1-2
Mortgage Broker Firm

This is a general overview of a mortgage broker firm. It is used for illustration purposes and does not reflect a specific company.

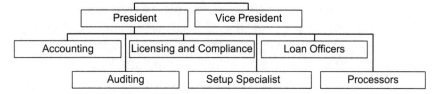

LOAN LINGO

1003

Another term for a loan application. It refers to the Fannie Mae form number, 1003.

Commercial Loan

A loan for a business or commercial property.

Key Note: An apartment building with fewer than four units is considered a residential property.

Conforming

A loan that conforms to the standards of Fannie Mae or Freddie Mac.

Conventional Loan

Any mortgage that is *not* insured or guaranteed by a government agency such as HUD, FHA, VA, or Farmers Home Administration.

Department of Veterans Affairs (VA)

A government agency that guarantees a portion of the mortgage loan to qualified veterans and active military personnel.

Federal Home Loan Mortgage Corporation (Freddie Mac or FHLMC)

A government-sponsored enterprise (quasi-governmental) that exists for the same purposes as Fannie Mae. See *Federal National Mortgage Association (Fannie Mae)*.

Federal Housing Administration (FHA)

An agency of the U.S. Department of Housing and Urban Development (HUD), whose main activity is to insure residential mortgage loans made by private lenders. FHA sets standards for construction and underwriting but does not lend money or plan or construct housing. It is typically easier to qualify for an FHA loan in comparison with conventional loans. FHA loan limits vary by geographic region.

Federal National Mortgage Association (Fannie Mae or FNMA)

Fannie Mae is a private, shareholder-owned company that is the largest supplier of home mortgage funds. This government-sponsored enterprise's (quasi-governmental) main purpose is to facilitate the sale of conventional loans in the secondary market. Fannie Mae does not lend funds directly to home buyers. The current conforming loan limit is $359,650.

Good Faith Estimate

A good faith estimate must be provided to the applicant within three days of the application. The good faith estimate itemizes the costs and expenses that the borrower will encounter with the processing and closing of the loan.

Home Equity Line of Credit (HELOC)

Typically, a second mortgage with an open line (similar to a credit card) that the homeowner can draw upon for cash.

Nonconforming

Any loan that does not fit Fannie Mae or Freddie Mac guidelines. Typically a subprime or jumbo loan program.

Preapproval

The process in which a borrower completes a loan application and provides debt, income, and savings documentation and an underwriter reviews the application and approves it. A preapproval is usually done for a certain loan amount and makes assumptions about what the interest rate will be at the time the loan is actually made, as well as provides estimates for the amount that will be paid for property taxes, insurance, and other costs. A preapproval applies only to the borrower. Once a property is chosen, it must also meet the underwriting guidelines of the lender.

Purchase Financing

A mortgage loan obtained to finance the purchase of a home.

Refinance Financing

A mortgage loan for someone who is seeking to reduce his or her costs on an existing home by finding a loan with a lower interest rate, by cashing out on the equity, or simply by changing the loan type—for example, changing from an adjustable-rate mortgage to a fixed-rate mortgage loan.

State-Specific Predisclosure

Mortgage loans require the lender to provide the borrower with several government-required disclosures. Some of these disclosures are specific to the property state and are required by both state and federal regulating agencies.

Streamline Refinance

A loan refinance with modified government loan processes that require no income verification or appraisal.

Subprime Loan

A mortgage loan with B-D credit or one that does not conform to normal guidelines.

STEP-BY-STEP LOAN PROCESS

Purchase Transaction

This is the process in which a purchase money loan is exchanged for real estate. A purchase money loan is a new loan for the purchase of real property. The sales price minus the down payment is the new loan amount. For example:

Sales price	$100,000
Down payment	− 5,000
Loan amount	$ 95,000

In a purchase loan the borrower will need to come up with the down payment plus the closing costs in order to complete the transaction. For the example above, if we assume that the closing costs are $2,500, then the borrower would need to bring to escrow or the settlement company a total of a $5,000 down payment plus $2,500 closing costs.

Steps in Obtaining a First Mortgage

Prequalification. Prequalification is a process in which a prospective home buyer works with a loan officer to find out how much the home buyer is eligible to borrow prior to the application of a loan. The duty of a loan officer is to prequalify a borrower by reviewing his or her credit and income and finding the program that is best suited for that borrower.

Key Note: Not all borrowers get prequalified before shopping for a home.

Finding the property. A potential borrower will work with a Realtor to find a property within the borrower's price range. Once a property is found, an offer to purchase is made to the Realtor representing the seller.

Application stage. If the offer is accepted, then all involved parties will sign the purchase agreement. The loan officer (if the borrower is not already prequalified) will take the loan application, obtain authorization to order a credit report for the borrower, provide required predisclosures, request a credit report, and provide a preapproval letter to the Realtor. An escrow or settlement company will be selected to collect all deposits and documentation for the sale.

Key Note: In conventional loan programs, a loan officer can take the loan, submit the loan through an automated underwriting system, and obtain an approval. The borrower then has an option to lock in the rate at this application stage. If the borrower chooses not to lock in the rate, it is considered "floating." The rate lock is in effect for a certain number of days, for example, 30 days. (The longer the rate lock, the higher the interest rate.)

Processing stage. The loan officer works with the processor to gather all necessary documentation for loan approval. An appraisal, title, and survey report will be requested. If required, a termite or pest report will be ordered. The processor will order all required verifications (employment, assets, mortgage or rental history).

Lender approval. If the loan officer is working for a mortgage broker, the processor will submit the loan to the lender for approval. If the borrower is working with a lender directly, the loan will begin the underwriting stage (see step 6).

Key Note: Mortgage brokers typically send the loan to a lender and work as the intermediaries between the lender and the borrower. This is referred to as *wholesale*. However, lenders may also have originators (loan officers) making loans directly to the consumer. This is referred to as *retail*. The lender (note the embedded word *lend*) actually provides the money for the loan through a warehouse line.

Underwriting stage. The underwriter working for the lender will underwrite the loan file and provide a decision on the loan.

Conditional approval or denial. The processor receives either a conditional approval (this means that the lender will approve the loan if the broker can provide the additional conditions requested) or denial from the underwriter. The processor will review the items requested and advise the loan officer. The loan officer will notify the borrower and Realtor of this status.

Final approval stage. If all conditions are satisfactorily met, then the lender will issue a final approval.

Loan doc stage. The loan processor coordinates the deliverance of the loan documents between the lender and the escrow or settlement company. The lender will either prepare the loan documents or order them through an independent loan doc preparation company.

Signing stage. The loan processor coordinates the date and time of the signing of the loan documents between the borrower and the escrow or settlement company. Once signed, the loan documents are returned to the lender.

Key Note: Round table closing is used in most states and is the most common kind of closing. In a round table closing, all parties appear at the closing table to sign the loan documents. In an escrow closing (used most notably in California), the closing takes place separately between the parties.

Review. The lender receives the loan documents and reviews them to ensure that all necessary documents have been received and signed properly. The lender will then prepare to release funds on the day agreed to by both the buyer and seller as defined in the purchase agreement. In a roundtable closing, the funds are released upon signing of the loan documents.

Funding stage. The lender releases funds (will wire the funds) to the escrow or settlement company. The escrow or settlement company receives and disburses the funds to the appropriate parties as indicated by both lender instructions and HUD-1 (settlement statement). The escrow or settlement company will instruct the title company to record the mortgage or deed of trust with the local public county recorder. (In California, recording must occur prior to the releasing of funds.) The loan is funded and recorded, and all parties are notified.

Servicing stage. The lender will set up the loan for servicing; this means setting up an account to begin collection of the mortgage payments. Lenders who do not service their own loans will sell the servicing rights to an outside company. The borrower makes payments to the servicing company.

Steps in Refinancing

Refinancing is the process of paying off one loan with the proceeds from a new loan secured by the same property. Generally the closing costs are financed into the new loan.

Considering the benefit. The prospective borrower works with the loan officer to evaluate the benefit of refinancing a new loan on the prospective borrower's home. The prospective borrower could be interested in refinancing in order to lower monthly mortgage payments, take some cash out of the equity, or just change loan types (e.g., from an adjustable-rate mortgage to a fixed-rate loan). A refinance transaction must offer an identifiable benefit to the borrower, such as a lower interest rate, lower payment, debt consolidation, or cash for home improvement.

Application stage. The loan officer will take the loan application, obtain authorization to order a credit report, provide the required predisclosures, order a credit report, and ask for the necessary documents to begin the processing of the loan.

Gathering documentation. The loan officer works with the processor to gather all necessary documentation. An appraisal will be ordered. An escrow or settlement company will be chosen, and a title report will be ordered.

Key Note: FHA, VA, and conforming loans offer streamline refinances, which may not require any income verification or appraisal.

Processing stage. The processor, if working for a mortgage broker, will submit the loan package to the lender for approval or will run the loan through DU or LP for automated underwriting. If the loan is originated with a lender, the processor submits the loan to the in-house underwriter for a decision on the loan.

Underwriting stage. The underwriter, working for the lender, will review the loan file and provide a decision on the loan. The underwriter will issue a conditional approval or denial.

Review by processor. The processor reviews the decision and notifies the loan officer of the decision. If additional documentation is requested, then the processor will provide this information to the underwriter.

Final approval stage. If all conditions were satisfactorily met, the lender will issue a final approval.

Loan doc stage. The loan processor coordinates the deliverance of the loan documents between the lender and the escrow or settlement company.

Signing stage. The loan processor coordinates the date and time of the signing of the loan documents with the escrow or settlement company and the borrower. In some cases the escrow or settlement company provides a traveling notary public service to bring the loan documents to the borrower for signature. Once signed, the documents are returned to the lender.

Review by lender. The lender receives the loan documents and reviews them to ensure that all necessary documents have been received and signed properly. The lender will then prepare to release funds on the fourth day after the right of rescission.

Key Note: On an "owner-occupied" refinance, the funds are not released until a three-day right-of-rescission period is over. This period gives applicants three days to change their minds and is required by the Truth in Lending Act. The right of rescission is applicable to refinances and home equity loans (second mortgages), but it does not apply when *purchasing* or refinancing an investment property. In addition, the three-day right of rescission is not required in some states, known as wet-funding states.

Funding stage. The lender wires the funds to the settlement company. The settlement company receives the funds and disburses them to the appropriate parties. The settlement company will instruct the title company to record the mortgage or deed of trust with the local public county recorder. (In California, recording must occur prior to the releasing of funds.) The loan is funded and recorded, and all parties are notified.

Servicing stage. The lender will set up the loan for servicing, set up an account, and begin the collection of mortgage payments. If the lender does not service its own loans, the loan is released to a servicing company. The borrower makes payments to the servicing company.

Mortgage Terms Quiz

1. What is a conforming loan?
   A. A subprime or jumbo loan
   B. A mortgage that is insured or guaranteed by a government agency
   C. A loan that fits into the standards of Fannie Mae and Freddie Mac

2. What is FHA?
   A. A government agency guaranteeing mortgage loans to qualified veterans
   B. A HUD agency whose main purpose is to insure residential mortgage loans made by private investors
   C. A private, shareholder-owned company that is the largest supplier of home mortgage funds

3. What is a streamline refinance?
   A. A loan refinance with modified requirements such as no income verification or appraisal
   B. A loan refinance on a commercial property
   C. A loan refinance on an equity line of credit

4. What does an underwriter do?
   A. Works with the loan originator to gather information applicable to the loan file and submits it to the lender for a decision
   B. Sends out the loan documents and schedules the loan signing with the escrow company
   C. Works with the lender and reviews the loan file for the purpose of making a decision on the loan

5. A mortgage broker originates the loan, finds the appropriate loan program for the borrower, and lends the money to the borrower to close the loan.
   A. True
   B. False

6. A three-day rescission is required on which transaction?
   A. A purchase money loan
   B. A refinance on an investment property
   C. Neither A nor B

7. What is a 1003?
   A. A uniform loan application
   B. The number representing the real estate agent
   C. The final settlement statement

8. What is the process called when a potential borrower works with a loan officer to see how much the potential borrower can afford to borrow?
   A. Prequalification
   B. Preapproval
   C. Presubmission

9. What is a survey report?
   A. A report specifying the measurement of the boundaries of a parcel of land
   B. A report of the insurance given on the title of the property
   C. A report, based on market data, that gives the property's fair market value

10. What is the procedure in which a third party acts as an intermediary for both the buyer and the seller, carrying out both parties' requests and assuming responsibility for handling all paperwork and the distribution of funds?
    A. Loan servicing
    B. Escrow
    C. Surveyor

Answers to the quiz can be found at the end of Part One.

CHAPTER 2

MORTGAGE BASICS

Always bear in mind that your own resolution to succeed is more important than any other one thing

—Abraham Lincoln

WHAT IS A MORTGAGE?

Let's begin this chapter by defining what a mortgage is. A *mortage* is a legal contract that grants a lender an interest in the property of the borrower and protects the lender. The recordation of a security instrument (deed of trust) places a lien on the property. The lender holds the title to the property until the debt is paid back in its entirety. If the monthly mortgage payments are not made on time, the lender can sell the property (foreclose) in order to get back its money.

The Down Payment

The *down payment* is the lump sum paid up front that reduces the amount financed. Borrowers can put as much money down as they want, or as little as 3% (for FHA loans) or no money down (for an 80/20 nonconforming loan). The more money that can be put down as a down payment, the less that has to be financed and the lower the monthly payments will be.

The Mortgage Payment

The *mortgage payment* is made up of:

Principal. The total money borrowed from the lender. It is the amount being financed.

Interest. The money the lender is charging to make the loan. It is a percentage of the total amount of money borrowed.

Taxes. Refers to property tax. Money to pay the taxes is often put into an escrow account (meaning that the money is placed in the hands of a third party) until it is time to pay or certain conditions are met. When taxes are escrowed, a portion of the property tax is added to the monthly mortgage payment and held in escrow until the property taxes are due.

Insurance. Several types of insurance can come into play with a mortgage. Hazard insurance is required to protect against losses from fire, storms, etc. If the property is in a flood zone, then flood insurance will also be required. If the mortgage being obtained is higher than 80% of the value of the property, private mortgage insurance (PMI) will also be required. This can become pretty expensive, and so many times a second mortgage will be obtained to avoid this fee. For example, if you are seeking a 100% loan program, you can offer your borrower an 80% first mortgage lien and a 20% second lien. Even though the second lien carries a higher interest rate, there is still a considerable savings.

These four pieces of the mortgage payment are referred to as *PITI*.

History of Mortgages

In the old days when someone wanted a home loan, he or she would walk downtown to the neighborhood bank. If the bank representative knew the customer and considered the person a good credit risk, then the customer would get the loan. Mortgage loan terms were not customer-friendly in those days. Loan terms were limited to 50% of the property value, and the repayment schedule was spread over three to five years and ended with a balloon payment. America consisted primarily of renters, and only four in ten households owned their own homes. It wasn't until 1934 that the Federal Housing Administration (FHA) played a critical role in helping the country out of its economic depression. FHA initiated a new type of mortgage aimed at those folks who did not qualify under the existing loan programs. FHA lengthened the loan terms from the traditional 5- to 7-year loan to 15-year loans and eventually to the 30-year loan term, which is so common today. FHA started a program that lowered the down payment requirements. It set up programs that required a 20% down payment, a 10% down payment, and lower. This forced banks and lenders to change their loan terms, creating many more opportunities for average Americans to make their dreams come true and own their own homes. FHA also started the trend of qualifying people for a loan based on their actual ability to pay back the loan, rather than the old way of simply knowing someone.

Another trend that FHA enforced was to ensure the quality of the home's construction.

FHA set standards that homes had to meet to qualify for the loan that are still enforced to this day.

Before FHA, traditional mortgages were interest-only payments that ended with a balloon payment that amounted to the entire principal of the loan. That was one reason why *foreclosures* (see Chapter 6) were so common. FHA established the *amortization* of loans, which means people got to pay an incremental amount of the loan's principal amount with each interest payment, reducing the loan gradually over the loan term until the loan was completely paid off.

Table 2-1 provides a look back at average interest rates for the last 33 years.

TABLE 2-1
History of 30-Year Fixed-Rate Mortgages and Points per Freddie Mac

Year	Rate	Pts.	Year	Rate	Pts.
2003	5.92	0.6	1986	10.89	2.3
2002	7.00	0.8	1985	13.08	2.5
2001	7.03	0.9	1984	13.37	2.3
2000	8.21	1.0	1983	13.25	2.2
1999	6.79	0.9	1982	17.48	2.2
1998	6.99	1.4	1981	14.90	2.0
1997	7.82	1.8	1980	12.88	1.6
1996	7.03	1.8	1979	10.39	1.5
1995	9.15	1.8	1978	9.01	1.3
1994	7.07	1.7	1977	8.72	1.1
1993	7.99	1.6	1976	9.02	1.1
1992	8.43	1.8	1975	9.43	1.2
1991	9.64	2.1	1974	8.54	1.0
1990	9.90	2.1	1973	7.44	1.0
1989	10.73	2.1	1972	7.49	0.9
1988	10.38	2.0	1971	7.31	N/A
1987	9.20	2.2			

HOW MORTGAGES WORK

What Is the Secondary Market?

When one applies for a mortgage loan—whether at a commercial bank, savings and loan, or mortgage or finance company—the institution is known as the *primary originator* of the mortgage. Mortgage brokers will use the funds of a mortgage banker or commercial bank to close the loan, and this is done in the form of a warehouse line. Companies that purchase mortgages from primary originators are called *secondary originators*, as they sell these loans in the secondary market. Primary originators

FIGURE 2-1
Generating Cash for Mortgages—Made Simple

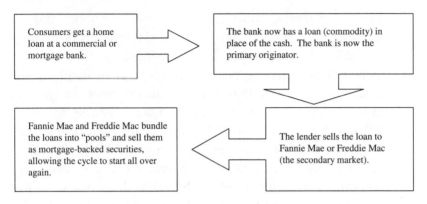

(mortgage bankers and lenders) group a large number of mortgages together into a "pool" and then sell them off to one of the three main purchasers of mortgage loans: Fannie Mae (FNMA), Freddie Mac (FHLMC), and Ginnie Mae (GNMA). Once these groups purchase the pools, they break them down into smaller ownership parcels. The principal and interest payments made by individual mortgage holders are then combined to create *mortgage-backed securities*, which are then sold on Wall Street. By selling these bonds, FNMA, FHLMC, and GNMA replenish their funds in order to buy new pools so lenders can get more money to lend to new borrowers. (See Figure 2-1.) Now, not all loans conform to FNMA and FHLMC guidelines, which is why those loans are known as *nonconforming*. Nonconforming loans are pooled together in a process called *securitization* and are sold as mortgage-backed securities as well.

Who's Who in the Secondary Market

Government National Mortgage Association (Ginnie Mae or GNMA). A government agency that facilitates the sale of government-insured loans. Ginnie Mae was created in 1968 by Congress and is the primary buyer of insured government loans. GNMA is a part of the Department of Housing and Urban Development (HUD), the same department that houses FHA. Government-insured loans are programs developed by the Federal Housing Authority and the Department of Veteran's Affairs.

Federal National Mortgage Association (Fannie Mae or FNMA) and Federal Home Loan Mortgage Corporation (Freddie Mac or FHLMC). Government-sponsored enterprises (GSEs) whose primary purpose is to facilitate the sale of mortgages that are *not* government mortgages; rather, they are conventional mortgages. Fannie Mae was created by Congress in 1938 and became private in 1968. Freddie Mac was created by Congress in 1970 and is a congressionally chartered corporation. The president appoints the members of the board of directors, who also oversee the operation of 12 Federal Home Loan Banks. Both Fannie Mae and Freddie Mac are corporations that are traded on the New York Stock Exchange.

Categories and Types of Loans

There are two categories of loans: conventional loans and insured government loans.

- *Conventional loans* include:
  - *Conforming loans.* These are available under the guidelines of Fannie Mae and Freddie Mac.
  - *Nonconforming loans.* These are loans that do not meet Fannie Mae or Freddie Mac guidelines. Nonconforming loans are also referred to as *jumbo loans* and *subprime loans*.
- *Insured government loans* are mortgage loans insured by either the FHA or the VA. The FHA was created after World War II to stimulate investing in housing. The VA Guaranty Program was created to stimulate the interest of veterans in owning their homes.

Fannie Mae and Freddie Mac

The largest purchasers of mortgages on the secondary market are Fannie Mae and Freddie Mac. Because Fannie Mae and Freddie Mac are GSEs, their debt obligations are backed by the credit of the U.S. Treasury, which reduces the credit risk for investors and allows these loans to carry a lower interest rate. These GSEs were created by Congress in order to make mortgages available to more people with low to moderate incomes. Since 1968, Fannie Mae has helped more than 63 million people achieve homeownership. Freddie Mac, since its inception 35 years ago, has purchased more than 35 million mortgages. These impressive numbers are the reason these are the two largest procurement companies in the United States. America's housing financing system is envied throughout the world.

The loan limit for both Freddie Mac and Fannie Mae loans is $417,000 for single-family homes in the United States. This is what defines the "conventional" loans you hear about. Fannie Mae and Freddie Mac purchase almost all mortgage loans under $417,000. Loans higher than that amount are called *jumbo loans* and usually have higher interest rates. These limits change annually and are based on the October-to-October changes in the average home price, published by the Federal Housing Finance Board.

Fannie Mae and Freddie Mac establish the basis for interest rates charged to consumers. Fannie Mae and Freddie Mac set guidelines that mortgages must meet in order to be eligible for purchase. These guidelines specify:

- Loan size limits and property specifications

- Down payment requirements

- Qualification specifications of the borrower(s)

If a mortgage meets these guidelines, the loan is a conforming mortgage. Conforming mortgages typically carry a lower interest rate than nonconforming mortgages because the conforming mortgages are easier to sell. Nonconforming mortgages, as noted earlier, are mortgages that do not meet Fannie Mae or Freddie Mac guidelines.

What Happens When a Mortgage Is Sold?

Most lenders that originate loans in order to sell them off quickly are referred to as *direct lenders*. When a lender keeps and services the loan, the lender is referred to as a *portfolio lender*. When a loan is sold, the lender has two commodities: the loan itself and the servicing rights of the loan.

A banker who sells a loan will make a certain amount of points on a package of loans. Let's say, for example, he has a package of loans worth a million dollars. If he makes 1 point (1% of $1 million), he would make $10,000. Not only does he make an immediate profit, but he has just freed up $1 million that he can turn around and use to fund more loans. If he sells $1 million a month, the banker or lender would be making $10,000 × 12 = $120,000 annually.

The servicer is paid a monthly fee for collecting and processing the monthly payments from the consumer. The fee is typically 3/8 of a percent (0.375%), or 37.5 basis points. (A basis point is 1/100 of 1%.) This does not sound like much, but servicers usually service billions of dollars in home loans. Let's look at an example with an average of 37.5 basis points:

$$\$100,000 \times 0.00375 \ (0.375\% \text{ or } 37.5 \text{ basis points})$$
$$= \$375 \text{ annually}$$

Certainly, $375 annually may not seem like a lot of money for all the functions a servicer performs. However, as just mentioned, servicers typically service billions of dollars annually. Suppose, then, that a servicer services $5 billion a year. Do the math, and you get

$$\$5,000,000,000 \times 0.00375 \ (0.375\% \text{ or } 37.5 \text{ basis points})$$
$$= \$18,750,000 \text{ annually}$$

It is easy to see why large mortgage lenders tend to make their money servicing loans. The origination fees of a large retail mortgage lender are usually consumed by the high overhead expenditure.

What Is a Rate Lock?

A *rate lock*, or rate commitment, is a lender's promise to hold a certain interest rate and a certain number of points on a mortgage loan for a specified period of time while the loan application is being processed. When a consumer applies for a mortgage loan, he or she has the choice to lock in a rate at application, to let the rate float between application and closing, or to choose a float-down program.

A *rate float* is a delay of the decision to fix the interest rate. Keep in mind that if the interest rate changes 1/8 to 1/4%, for most people this is a difference of $10 or $20 per month in interest— a difference, but not a great difference. It is the borrower who is applying for a larger loan who would significantly benefit from floating the interest rate.

A *float-down option* is the ability to lock in a rate today and take advantage of any drop before the closing. The cost for this feature and all rate lock policies varies greatly by lender. So it is important for the loan originator to be knowledgeable about the rate lock policies of the lenders he or she will be working with.

Remember that the longer you want to lock in a rate, the more risk the lender takes, and, therefore, the more expensive the rate is. Although rates are often stable, in an active market the rates can literally change by the hour. Interest rates tend to move down slowly but increase quickly. The cost for a rate lock is relatively small when compared to the cost of an interest rate increase. Most lenders charge an additional 1/4% on a 90-day rate lock.

Is it better to float or lock in a rate? Let's look at an example:

On a $100,000 loan amount 30-year term	
1/4% additional fee for a 90-day lock	$250
If interest rate increases by 1/4 of 1%	$16 per month
Interest rate increase over the life of a 30-year loan	$4,000 in a higher payment

What Determines a Rate?

Many factors determine the rate, but basically interest rates are a function of risk:

- The risk that the investor will not get paid back. (This is why D credit mortgages cost more than A credit mortgages.)

- The risk that inflation will cause rates to go up. Remember, when rates go up, the value of the asset created goes down. This is why adjustable-rate mortgages are cheaper than fixed-rate mortgages. (The further you lock in a rate, the more expensive it is.)

- The risk that the servicer will get paid back too quickly. (If a servicer paid a certain number of points for servicing rights to a loan and the loan is refinanced in a few months, then obviously the servicer is unable to recapture his investment. This is why above-market, or no-closing-cost, loans are more expensive.)

How Do Mortgage Companies Make Their Money?

Mortgage brokers make their money from origination fees, rebates or yield spread premiums, and miscellaneous fees (such as processing and application fees). Mortgage bankers and lenders make their money from the following principal sources:

1. *Origination fee.* The origination fee is typically 1% of the mortgage amount. For example, if the mortgage loan amount is $100,000, the loan origination fee (1%) is $1,000. The origination fee is a fee to compensate for the costs of originating the loan. These costs include:
   - Commissions paid to the loan originator
   - Salaries for the operations staff (receptionist, processors, underwriters, funders, and managers)
   - Office overhead (rent, utilities, phones, equipment, etc.)

2. *Miscellaneous fees.* Lenders may also charge third-party fees (fees that are paid directly to a third party and that include document preparation fees, underwriting fees, and tax service fees). These fees can make the mortgages more profitable to service in the long run and supplement the income from the origination fee.

3. *Overage.* The difference between the lowest available price and any higher price that the borrower agrees to pay is an overage. Many lenders allow their loan originators to sell mortgages with overages. The overage is part of the commission paid to the loan officer. Not all lenders allow overages.

4. *Servicing income.* As we discussed earlier, servicing income can be quite lucrative for the lender. Another benefit is the fact that servicing is a year-round source of income.

5. *Sale of servicing rights.* The earnings made in the sale of the servicing rights can be quite significant. On most mortgage loans, the servicing rights can be sold for anywhere from 1 to 2% of the mortgage amount. If a mortgage lender loses one point on the origination fee (one point in commission fee and overhead), the lender will still be at a profit if it receives 2 points for the servicing rights.

   Key Note: The servicing released premium (SRP) is the amount a wholesaler is willing to pay for the servicing value of a loan.

RENTING VERSUS HOMEOWNERSHIP

Is it better to rent or own a home? This is a complicated question that requires an understanding of leverage and rental equivalency.

Understanding Leverage

Leverage is the use of borrowed money to increase the potential return on an investment. For example, suppose you purchase a home for $170,000 with a down payment of $17,000 and your home appreciates at the average rate of 6% a year. In 10 years your home would be valued at more than $304,000. That means your down payment of $17,000 would have grown to $151,000 in home equity.

$170,000 purchase price − $17,000 = $153,000
New value of $304,000 − $153,000 = $151,000

The growth in your home equity represents a return of 24% on your original investment.

Another factor to consider is the principal reduction. Remember, as homeowners continue to make their mortgage payments, they continue to pay down the mortgage balance, which can be added to the leverage principle.

Understanding Rental Equivalency

Mortgage interest and real estate taxes are still the only major write-offs available for the majority of Americans. These deductions are itemized on the federal 1040 tax form, Schedule A. To calculate how nontaxable income (such as rent) equates to a taxable mortgage payment is difficult, as there are several tax implications to deal with. Table 2-2 compares $900-a-month rent

TABLE 2-2
Rental versus Owning

$900 rent versus mortgage payment for $150,000 purchase price with 3% down and a loan amount of $142,000 at 7% interest on a 30-year term:			
Principal and interest	$948.52	Interest	$806.24*
Property taxes	150.00	Property taxes	150.00
Homeowner's insurance	30.00	Total tax and interest	$956.24
Private mortgage ins.	58.19		
Total PITI	$1,186.71	Total tax and interest	$956.24
		Borrower tax bracket	× 28%
		Total tax savings	$267.75
	Total PITI		$1,186.71
	Less total tax savings		267.75
	Rental equivalency		$918.96

*Assuming 85% of the P&I payment is applied to interest.

to the monthly mortgage payment for a house with a $150,000 purchase price. In the example in the table, we assume that 85% of a typical mortgage payment is tax deductible and that the borrower falls in the 28% tax bracket.

Note that Table 2-2 does not include the portion of income that is not tax deductible, the amount of the payment that is going toward paying down the principal mortgage balance. Keep in mind, though, that as the principal is paid down, equity builds up. This is a kind of forced savings, and if you add that portion to the tax savings, this would further reduce the rental equivalency. As well, this does not include any appreciation gain from an increase in property value. In recent years many homeowners have experienced a significant increase in their property's value.

Mortgage Basics Quiz

1. What option would allow the borrower to lock in a rate but still have the advantage of a lower rate?
   A. Lock
   B. Float
   C. Float-down

2. What is the principal of the mortgage payment?
   A. The borrower
   B. The total money borrowed from the lender
   C. The money the lender is charging to make the loan

3. Which of the following is *not* a third-party fee?
   A. Document preparation fee
   B. Tax service fee
   C. Origination fee

4. What is the current conforming loan amount for a single-family home in the United States?
   A. $333,700
   B. $417,000
   C. $300,650

5. Fannie Mae and Freddie Mac are government-sponsored agencies whose main purpose is to purchase FHA and VA loans.
   A. True
   B. False

6. Who collects the monthly mortgage payment from the borrower?
   A. The servicer
   B. The escrow company
   C. The broker

7. On a conventional conforming mortgage, private mortgage insurance, known as PMI, is required when the mortgage being obtained is over 70% of the value of the property.
   A. True
   B. False

8. Which type of loan listed below is *not* an insured government loan?
   A. FHA loan
   B. VA loan
   C. Conventional loan

9. Any loan that is *not* insured by the government is known as a conventional loan.
   A. True
   B. False

10. The amount of the mortgage payment that a borrower can use as a tax deduction is
    A. The principal
    B. The taxes
    C. The interest

Answers to the quiz can be found at the end of Part One.

CHAPTER 3

MORTGAGE LOAN TYPES

*Many men fail because they quit too soon. Men lose faith
when the signs are against them. They do not have the
courage to hold on, to keep fighting in spite of that which
seems insurmountable. If more of us would strike out
and attempt the "impossible," we very soon would find
the truth of that old saying that nothing is impossible.
Abolish fear, and you can accomplish anything you wish.*

—Dr. C. E. Welch

The last 20 years have brought many changes in the mortgage
finance system. The variety of products offered today allows
home buyers an assortment of loan options. There are terms,
points, fees, and other factors to consider. Understanding these
mortgage products is vital to a loan officer. Finding the specific loan program that is best suited to a customer's needs is
one of the most important tasks you will undertake as a loan
officer.

In this chapter, we will review:

- Fixed-rate mortgages (30-year, 20-year, and 15-year term)

- Fixed-rate hybrids (balloon loans and graduated-payment
  mortgages)

- Adjustable-rate mortgages

- Second mortgages (equity lines and reverse mortgages)

FIXED-RATE MORTGAGES

A *fixed-rate mortgage* is the simplest and the most common of all mortgage products. During the past few years, fixed-rate mortgages have risen because of the historical low mortgage interest rates. With lower interest rates, payments of fixed-rate mortgages are more affordable, and therefore the borrower is able to qualify for a larger mortgage loan. The only difference among fixed-rate mortgages is the length of the mortgage term. The *term* is the amount of time it takes to pay off the loan. Fixed-rate mortgages have two distinct features:

- The interest rate and payments must be fixed over the term of the mortgage.

- The mortgage must be paid off completely at the end of its term.

Amortization

A *fully amortized* loan is a mortgage that is paid off completely by the end of its term. To *amortize* is simply to decrease the principal balance on the mortgage by a monthly payment of principal and interest calculated to pay off the mortgage at a fixed period of time.

An amortization schedule can be produced for any mortgage, laying out the payments over the life of the mortgage. There are several Web sites available that can provide an amortization schedule; all you need to provide is the principal loan balance, interest rate, loan term, and starting month and year.

As a loan officer, it is important to know how an amortization schedule is calculated. Figure 3-1 presents an example of an amortization schedule.

As we can see from Figure 3-1, the amortization is calculated for a $100,000 loan amount with a 7% fixed-rate

FIGURE 3-1
*Annual Amortization Table for a 30-Year Term $100,000
Loan with a 7% Fixed-Rate Mortgage*

Year	Total Monthly Payments	Total Annual Principal	Total Annual Interest	Remaining Balance
1	$7,983.60	$1,015.78	$6,967.82	$98,984.22
2	$7,983.60	$1,089.21	$6,894.39	$97,895.01
3	$7,983.60	$1,167.95	$6,815.65	$96,727.06
4	$7,983.60	$1,252.38	$6,731.21	$95,474.68
5	$7,983.60	$1,342.91	$6,640.69	$94,131.77
6	$7,983.60	$1,439.99	$6,543.61	$92,691.77
7	$7,983.60	$1,544.09	$6,439.51	$91,147.68
8	$7,983.60	$1,655.71	$6,327.89	$89,491.97
9	$7,983.60	$1,775.41	$6,208.19	$87,716.56
10	$7,983.60	$1,903.75	$6,079.85	$85,812.82
11	$7,983.60	$2,041.37	$5,942.23	$83,771.44
12	$7,983.60	$2,188.94	$5,794.66	$81,582.50
13	$7,983.60	$2,347.10	$5,636.42	$79,235.32
14	$7,983.60	$2,516.86	$5,466.74	$76,718.46
15	$7,983.60	$2,698.80	$5,248.80	$74,019.66
16	$7,983.60	$2,893.90	$5,089.70	$71,125.76
17	$7,983.60	$3,103.10	$4,880.50	$68,022.66
18	$7,983.60	$3,327.42	$4,656.18	$64,695.23
19	$7,983.60	$3,567.96	$4,415.64	$61,127.27
20	$7,983.60	$3,825.89	$4,157.71	$57,301.38
21	$7,983.60	$4,102.47	$3,881.13	$53,198.91
22	$7,983.60	$4,399.03	$3,584.57	$48,799.88
23	$7,983.60	$4,717.04	$3,266.56	$44,082.84
24	$7,983.60	$5,058.03	$2,925.57	$39,024.80
25	$7,983.60	$5,423.68	$2,559.92	$33,601.12
26	$7,983.60	$5,815.76	$2,167.84	$27,785.36
27	$7,983.60	$6,236.18	$1,747.42	$21,549.18
28	$7,983.60	$6,686.99	$1,296.61	$14,862.19
29	$7,983.60	$7,170.40	$813.20	$7,691.79
30	$7,983.64	$7,691.79	$294.85	$0.00

mortgage. Using a financial calculator or loan origination software program, we find that the monthly payment for this loan is $665.30.

Next, we need to find the monthly interest rate by dividing the annual rate by 12 (7% divided by 12 = 0.583%). Since this is a fixed-rate mortgage, these numbers will not change during the life of the loan.

To perform the amortization calculation for the first month, we take the loan amount and multiply it by the monthly interest rate ($100,000 × 0.583% = $583.33). Thus, $583.33 of the first month's payment goes to pay the interest.

Subtracting this amount from the payment reveals the portion that goes toward payment of the principal ($665.30 − $583.33 = $81.97). We now subtract this amount from the original loan amount to find how much principal remains at the end of the first month ($100,000 − $81.97 = $99,918.03).

Key Note: An amortization schedule is provided to every borrower. It is included in the loan documents.

30-Year Fixed-Rate Mortgage

A 30-year fixed-rate mortgage gives the maximum tax advantage by having the greatest interest deduction. The 30-year term is attractive to some homeowners who are seeking the lowest monthly payment, especially if they do not think their income will increase dramatically. The 30-year fixed-rate mortgage has the following attributes:

- The monthly payments are constant (the same amount) during the term of the loan.

- Each payment reduces the principal (slightly at first).

- The previous month's interest is paid with the current payment. This results in a gradual:
  - Decrease in the interest charged each month
  - Increase in the principal amount credited

- The principal payment will increase dramatically in the last several years of the loan.

What are the benefits?

- The monthly payment is always the same amount.

- Spreading the payment over a 30-year period results in the lowest monthly payment of the fixed-rate mortgage options.

A disadvantage is the slow growth of equity. The equity in the home does increase as more principal is paid. But with a small principal amount paid monthly, especially in the first years of the loan, equity does not increase much.

20-Year Fixed-Rate Mortgage

A 20-year fixed-rate mortgage is the same as a 30-year fixed-rate mortgage except that the term of the loan is shortened by 10 years. Table 3-1 compares the two. As you can see from the table, there is a savings of about $58,000 in interest paid. That is a major reason why 20-year fixed-rate loans are becoming more popular. Demand for this product has increased dramatically since 1990. Still, only a fraction of the loans originated are 20-year mortgages.

15-Year Fixed-Rate Mortgage

A 15-year fixed-rate mortgage is basically the same as the 20- and 30-year mortgages. A 15-year mortgage calls for a higher monthly payment and results in a significant reduction of the principal annually. Table 3-2 compares the three types. Note the savings in interest. If the borrower is comfortable with the higher monthly payment compared with that for 20- and 30-year loans, the savings in interest paid and the quicker amortization of the loan are beneficial to the borrower.

TABLE 3-1
20-Year versus 30-Year Fixed-Rate Loan

	30-Year Fixed-Rate	20-Year Fixed-Rate
Principal amount	$100,000	$100,000
Interest rate	7.5%	7.5%
Payment	$699.21	$805.59
Total interest and principal paid	$251,717.22	$193,342.37

TABLE 3-2
30-Year, 20-Year, and 15-Year Mortgage Comparision

	30-Year Fixed-Rate	20-Year Fixed-Rate	15-Year Fixed-Rate
Principal amount	$100,000	$100,000	$100,000
Interest rate	7.5%	7.5%	7.5%
Payment	$699.21	$805.59	$927.01
Total interest and principal paid	$251,717.22	$193,342.37	$166,862.22
Interest savings compared with a 30-year fixed-rate mortgage		38%	55%

Like 20-year mortgages, 15-year mortgages are also gaining in popularity as baby boomers desire at retirement to have:

- Lower fixed costs
- Their homes paid for

As loan terms decrease, the interest rate charged on the mortgage generally decreases.

Prepayment

One of the most popular features of a fixed-rate loan is the ability to *prepay*, or reduce, the principal balance of the mortgage, without a penalty. Be prepared to have your borrowers ask whether they can prepay their mortgage without incurring some form of prepayment penalty. The penalty is a sum of money that must be paid if the mortgage is paid off before the term or even paid down faster than the amortization schedule requires. Conforming, FHA, and VA loans generally do not carry a prepayment penalty.

The Biweekly Mortgage

This is a relatively new program that allows the borrower to make one-half of the monthly mortgage payment every two weeks, which equals one extra monthly mortgage payment a year. This is because making a mortgage payment *every other week* is equal to *26 mortgage payments or 13 months,* and of course there are only 12 months in a year.

There are pros and cons to this loan program. First the facts: On a $100,000 30-year mortgage at 6.50%, $127,544 is paid in interest. Add the $100,000 principal for a total of $227,544. Paying biweekly will result in interest of $97,215, a savings of $30,329! Obviously the larger the mortgage, the more dramatic the savings.

The disadvantages of biweekly mortgages are:

1. There is a greater potential for incidence for late payments (because you now have twice as many payments).

2. Biweekly mortgages are more likely to be priced as 30-year mortgages rather than as 15-year mortgages.

3. Most mortgage companies offering a biweekly option will require that the mortgage payment be made by *direct deposit*. With direct deposit every two weeks, you do not have the flexibility of making the payment during the 15-day *grace* period after which a mortgage is due.

Interest-Only Programs

In recent years, interest-only (IO) loan programs have become very popular, specifically in nonconforming loans, such as jumbo and subprime loan programs. Interest-only programs are designed to offer the lowest payment possible, because the borrowers are not paying anything toward the principal in their monthly payment. The major advantage of these programs is obviously a lower payment.

As an example, suppose you have a mortgage for $100,000 with an interest rate of 6.50%. The regular monthly payment—one that includes principal and interest—is $632.07. To determine the interest-only payment, take the principal balance, multiply it by the annual interest rate, and divide by the number of payments in a year. For our example; we would get

$$\$100,000 \times 6.5\% = \$6,500/12 = \$541.66$$

Generally, these types of loans will have a fixed-rate payment for the first 3, 5, or 10 years and the remainder of the term fully amortizing.

Benefits of this type of loan are:

- Reduced payment for the first 3, 5, or 10 years
- Maximum tax deduction in the 3-, 5-, or 10-year period

FIXED-RATE HYBRID

Hybrid loans are a combination of a fixed-rate loan and an adjustable-rate mortgage (ARM). Typically, a hybrid starts out with a fixed rate for a certain length of time and then later converts to an ARM. These loans carry less risk than a 1-year ARM, and the interest rate is generally lower than that for a fixed-rate mortgage. Since many homeowners remain in their homes an average of 7 to 10 years, hybrid loans are a good choice, allowing the borrower to take advantage of a lower interest rate in the first few years of the mortgage.

Hybrid mortgages include:

- Balloon mortgages
- Graduated-payment mortgages
- Growing equity mortgages
- Temporary buydowns
- The Flex ARM program

Balloon Mortgages

Balloon loans are short-term mortgages that have some features of a fixed-rate loan. They offer an initial interest rate that is lower than that for fixed-rate mortgages. The balloon mortgage keeps this low fixed rate for 5 to 7 years and then requires a "balloon" payment. The balloon payment is the final payment of the loan and pays off the entire balance. Balloons are also called *bullets, demands,* or *calls,* referring to the one-time payment. Monthly payments are low because the payments for those first 5 to 7 years are amortized at a low interest rate over the total length of the loan, which is usually a 30-year term.

The benefits of this type of mortgage product are:

- The lower interest rate and payment, which means that the mortgage payments are more affordable, which means that the borrower can qualify for a larger mortgage

Having a balloon payment is a gamble; this type of loan program does carry risks. To address the risks, FNMA and FHLMC developed a feature for converting the loan to a fixed-rate loan after the balloon; this is referred to as a *conditional refinance*. It is important for your borrower to know that a balloon mortgage is not an ARM—that a conditional offer to refinance at maturity does not guarantee financing. This feature is the same as the provisions contained in ARMs with a conversion option— the ability to convert to a fixed rate. The right to refinance is called *conditional* because certain conditions, or requirements, must be met to give the borrower a right to convert to a fixed rate. Those requirements are:

- Mortgage payments must be current. No payments can be more than 30 days late during the past year.

- The property must be owner-occupied.

- There can be no second mortgage liens on the property.

- The rate of conversion can be no more than 5.0% over the current note rate, or the lender can refuse conversion.

- A written request must be made to the mortgage holder within 60 days of the maturity date.

Graduated-Payment Mortgages

A *graduated-payment mortgage (GPM)* is a type of flexible-payment mortgage where the payments start off low, gradually increase at predetermined times, and then level off. The difference between a GPM and an ARM is that the borrower who takes out a GPM will know what the payments will be through the life of the loan, even though the payments are changing.

The initial lower payments are not sufficient to amortize the loan, and the interest is not sufficient to cover the interest due on this loan. The result is that the interest that is not paid throughout the course of the loan is added to the initial principal amount of the loan in a process known as *negative amortization* (which is discussed below).

Negative Amortization

Negative amortization occurs when the minimum monthly payments are not large enough to pay all the interest due on the loan. This unpaid interest (excess interest) is added to the unpaid balance of the loan. The danger of negative amortization is that the home buyer can end up owing more than the original amount of the loan.

There are two types of negative amortization:

1. *Scheduled negative amortization*, knowing from the beginning of the mortgage term that there will be a negative amortization (such as in a GPM)

2. *A potential for negative amortization*, not knowing the future rate on an ARM and thus not knowing whether there *is* negative amortization

There is usually a limit by which the loan balance can increase over the life of the loan. This limit typically ranges from 110 to 125% of the loan balance. For example, if the original mortgage balance is $100,000 and the limit of increase is 110%, then the loan balance can never exceed $110,000.

Negative amortization loans are best suited to borrowers who have large cash reserves and who want the flexibility of lower payments during certain parts of the year but plan to pay off their loan in large chunks during other parts of the year.

The benefit of this type of loan:

- The small monthly payment in the first few years. In fact, the payment is even smaller than the monthly payment for an interest-only mortgage.

The disadvantage of this type of loan:

- Should housing prices fall, then the borrowers would find themselves in "negative equity," meaning they would owe money to the lender if they sold their homes.

Growing Equity Mortgages

One type of GPM is the *growing equity mortgage* (*GEM*). In contrast to an ARM, a GEM has a fixed-payment schedule, so the additional principal payments reduce the term of the loan. The GEM's additional payments avoid the negative amortization, and the payments decrease while the term of the loan remains constant.

The monthly payments for the GEM increase annually. It is the increased amount that is used to reduce directly the principal balance outstanding and thus shorten the term of the loan.

The benefits of this program are:

- The mortgage starts with a 30-year term but is frequently paid off in 15 years.

- The higher payments are delayed for future years.

This program *eases* a borrower into a higher housing expense, so it is a great choice for the borrower who seeks the equity buildup of a 15-year loan but who may not initially qualify. This is a type of forced savings, and it is obviously not for everyone. Borrowers with fixed incomes would not be good candidates for this loan.

Temporary Buydowns

In a *temporary buydown*, the borrower prepays the interest in exchange for a lower rate for the first two to three years of the loan. The mortgage itself is *not* changed; the buydown agreement and funds are collected at closing and placed in escrow during the term of the temporary buydown, and the funds are used to offset the monthly payments as required by the terms of the note.

The most common buydowns are the 2-1 and 3-2-1 buydowns.

Let's look at an example of a 2-1 buydown for a $100,000 fixed-rate mortgage. We will lower the permanent interest rate of 8.50% to 6.50% for the first year and to 7.50% for the second year:

- At 6.50% for the first year the payments will be $632.07 a month. The difference monthly is $136.84 × 12 = $1,642.08.

- At 7.50% for the second year the payments will be $699.21 a month. The difference monthly is $69.70 × 12 = $836.40.

- At 8.50% for the third year to 30 years, the monthly payment is $768.91.

The total buydown cost for the above example is $1,642.08 plus $836.40, for a total of $2,478.48. This cost is expressed in terms of points: $2,478.48 divided by $100,000 = 2.47 points. The benefit of using a temporary buydown is often the builder, seller, or lender—all who want to make this loan—may pay for the cost of the buydown.

Flex Arm

A new loan product is the *flex-arm mortgage.* This loan product is structured in a manner that offers a borrower the flexibility of three payment options. Each month the lender sends the borrower a payment coupon that calculates the three payment options:

- The negative amortization amount

- The interest-only amount

- The fully amortized amount

This program is particularly attractive to self-employed and commissioned borrowers who have sporadic income. These options allow the borrowers to adjust monthly payments to match their income fluctuations. This is a good choice for borrowers who like options and have large cash reserves they can call on when payments increase in the later portion of the loan.

The benefit of this type of loan:

- The bank does all the work. Each month the lender recalculates the balance and tells the borrower how much he or she would owe under different scenarios.

The disadvantage of this type of loan:

- Borrowers could end up owing more on the mortgage than what they could get if they sold their home.

ADJUSTABLE-RATE MORTGAGES

An ARM (or variable-rate loan) has an interest rate that changes based on changing market rates and economic trends. This kind of mortgage usually offers an initial interest rate that is two to three percentage points lower than that of fixed-rate mortgages, but it doesn't offer the stability or assurance of a known mortgage payment in the years to come.

With the long period of low interest rates that followed World War II, there was no reason to take a mortgage other than a 15- or 30-year fixed-rate loan when purchasing a house. However, when interest rates soared into the double digits in the early 1980s, people could not afford to buy a home. The lenders' answer was a loan with an interest rate tied to a variable index, allowing them to offer interest rates below conventional low rates by sharing the risk of rate fluctuation (up or down) with the borrower.

An ARM has the following attributes:

- It usually offers a lower initial interest rate (start rate) than fixed-rate loans.
  - The interest rate is typically 2 to 3% lower than prevailing interest rates on a 30-year or 15-year loan.
  - Most ARMs qualify the borrower's payment ability based on the start rate.

- The interest rate on an ARM is adjusted periodically based on an index that reflects changes in market interest rates. (See "The Index" below.)
  - The interest rate can increase or decrease based on the index plus a certain percentage for "margin."
  - The percentage added for margin can vary from 2 to 3.75%.

- ARMs have defined adjustment periods that determine how frequently the interest rate can change.
  - The initial fixed period before the first adjustment can be short (1 month) or quite long (10 years).
  - After the initial interest rate adjustment, the interest rate on most ARMs adjusts every year.

Typical adjustable-rate mortgages are 1/1, 3/1, 5/1, 7/1, and 10/1. What exactly do the numbers mean?

- The first number represents the period for which the adjustable rate of the mortgage is guaranteed.

- The second number is the length by year of subsequent adjustments. So, for example, the interest rate on a 10/1 ARM will not change for the first 10 years but can then change annually.

What are the benefits?

- Lower payments for a specified time result in significant savings.

- Most ARM programs qualify for the start rate, allowing borrowers to qualify for a larger loan amount.

- Often borrowers choose an ARM program knowing they will sell or refinance the property before the interest rate adjustments begin (in fact most mortgages are held an average of 5 to 7 years).

The Five Features of an ARM

ARMs are more complex than the fixed-rate loan programs we have previously discussed. What makes one ARM different from another is how the interest rates change in the future. Five major features are involved:

- Index

- Margin

- Adjustment period

- Rate caps

- Conversion feature

To better understand how an ARM works, you will have to learn how each feature works.

The Index

An index is a statistical indicator or reference published by financial institutions to reflect changes in market interest rates. At adjustment time, the lender will add the index rate to a fixed margin to determine the new rate.

Some of the most common indexes are:

- *Cost of fund index (COFI).* This index represents the weighted-average cost of funds determined by a combination of savings, checking, money market, and short-term CD accounts from the 11th District Federal Reserve Bank (California) and is derived monthly.

- *Treasury bill constant maturity (TCM).* The index used for all U.S. Treasury ARMs is the weekly average yield of U.S. Treasury securities adjusted to a constant maturity of one year as published in the *Wall Street Journal.* Securities are issued by the federal government to raise capital. These securities are offered in various denominations or length (three months, six months, one year, two years, etc.). Short-term securities are known as *T-bills*. Medium-term securities (i.e., three-year securities) are known as *T-bonds*.

- *London Interbank Offered Rate (LIBOR)*. This index is the interest rate charged by banks in the foreign market for short-term loans to one another. The LIBOR is available as of the first business day of the month, as published in the *Wall Street Journal*. It is the average of rate quotes from five major banks: Bank of America, Bank of Tokyo, Deutsche Bank, Barclays, and Swiss Bank.

- *Monthly Treasury average 12-month (12-MTA)*. This index is based on the average annual monthly yields of U.S. Treasury securities (T-bills) adjusted to a constant maturity of one year, as made available by the Federal Reserve. The index is determined by adding together the most recent 12 months and dividing by 12. Since it's an average, higher yields in some months are offset by lower yields in others. It's considered a sound choice since interest rate increases take longer to affect the 12-MTA.

The Margin

The margin is the lender's profit. To ensure that the lender's expenses are included in the payment, the lender adds a margin to the index. Margins run between 2 and 4%. The margin doesn't change throughout the life of the loan. When you add the index and the margin, you get the new interest rate:

$$\text{Index} + \text{margin} = \text{new rate}$$

The new rate is the "true" interest rate of the ARM. This rate is also known as the *fully indexed accrual rate* (FIAR). It is simply the present value of the index plus the margin. Therefore, if the index is presently at 3.00% and the margin is set at 2.750%, the FIAR will be 5.75%.

Of course if an ARM were introduced with a FIAR, it would probably be close to a fixed-rate mortgage and would not be attractive to a potential borrower. This is the reason that the "teaser rate" was introduced. To make the ARM attractive to the customer, a low beginning interest rate is offered; then through periodic changes the rate is increased in order to equal the FIAR. The teaser rate is typically the *floor* of the adjustable rate, or the lowest rate an ARM can achieve.

SAMPLE TEASER RATE	
Index	3.00%
Margin	2.75%
FIAR	5.75%
Teaser rate	3.50%

Key Note: The APR (discussed in Chapter 8) will vary on ARMs, but the payment schedule provided to the borrower is always based on the current FIAR, taking into consideration any rate caps.

Adjustment Period

The most significant variable among the adjustable-rate mortgages available today is the adjustment frequency or adjustment period. The mortgage-payment adjustment period is the agreed-upon interval at which the payments of the principal and interest are changed. The day the interest rate changes is also known as the *reset date* or *anniversary date*. The adjustment period often appears in the program's name. For example:

- *One-year ARM.* The rate changes every year.

- *Three-year ARM.* The rate changes every three years.

- *Three/one ARM.* The rate is fixed for three years, and then it changes annually.

The less often the loan adjusts, the more financial risk the lender is accepting and thus the higher the initial rate or the higher the margin.

Rate Caps

Now that you understand how ARM rates can change, you can understand why this type of mortgage can be a risky option for your borrower. For this reason, ARMs carry a feature known as a *rate cap*. A rate cap is the maximum allowable interest rate the lender can charge on a loan. The rate cap limits how much the interest rate can change per adjustment period. The most common is a 2% cap per adjustment period. For example, if the start rate is 5%, then the first adjustment period could result in an interest rate of 7%.

Another kind of cap is also involved with an ARM—a *lifetime cap*. The lifetime cap limits the maximum and minimum interest rate that can be charged by the lender. Most ARMs carry a 5 or 6% lifetime cap. For example, if a lifetime cap on a loan is 6% and the starting rate is 5%, then the interest rate can never exceed 11% on the loan. With this kind of cap, the frequency of adjustments in conjunction with the maximum rate changes will be the customer's focus when deciding on an ARM.

When the rate caps come into play, your formula *may* change from:

$$\text{Index} + \text{Margin}$$

to

$$\text{Rate} + \text{Cap}$$

This will depend on which is a smaller change.

Therefore, when comparing ARMs, you need not only to compare the fully indexed rate (FIAR), but also to compare the impact of the caps. This comparison is referred to as the *worst-case scenario*, which is discussed below.

Worst-Case Scenario

The worst-case scenario occurs when the interest rate on a loan increases to its maximum capacity based on the interest rate caps. To find the worst-case scenario, you need to compare the rate of an ARM with that of a fixed-rate mortgage, and to do this you must add the interest rate for (a period of time) and achieve the average interest rate on that loan.

EXAMPLE

Mortgage type	1-year ARM
Annual cap	2%
Lifetime cap	6%
Initial interest rate	4%
Year 1	4.0%
Year 2	6.0%
Year 3	8.0%
Year 4	10.0% (lifetime cap—6%)
Total interest	28.0%
Divide total interest by 4 years	7.0% (average interest rate)

This comparison is usually performed when interest rates are increasing. The average interest rate will increase the longer the ARM is kept.

Let's take another look at the average rate on an ARM, compare it with that of a fixed-rate mortgage, and determine how long it will take the average rate to reach the same fixed rate. In our example (on page 54), we shall compare the same one-year ARM with an annual cap of 2%, a lifetime cap of 6%, and an initial interest rate of 4.0%.

In the example, it may appear that the borrower begins to pay more for the mortgage at year 4 when the interest rate reaches 10% (the maximum allowed by the rate cap). However, the average rate of 8% on the one-year ARM is not reached until year 6. Therefore the borrower does not begin to pay more for the one-year ARM compared to a fixed-rate mortgage of 8% until year 7 when the average rate becomes 8.28%.

COMPARING A ONE-YEAR ARM AGAINST A FIXED-RATE MORTGAGE AT 8.0%		
	Worst-Case Scenario Rate	**Average Rate**
Year 1	4.0%	4.00%
Year 2	6.0%	5.00% (4% + 6%, divide by 2 yrs = 5% avg.)
Year 3	8.0%	6.00% (4% + 6% + 8%, divide by 3 yrs = 6% avg.)
Year 4	10.0% (reached cap)	7.00% (4% + 6% + 8% + 10%, divide by 4 yrs = 7% avg.)
Year 5	10.0%	7.60% (4% + 6% + 8% + 10% + 10%, divide by 5 yrs = 7.6% avg.)
Year 6	10.0%	**8.00%** (4% + 6% + 8% + 10% + 10% + 10%, divide by 6 yrs = 8.0% avg.)
Year 7	10.0%	8.28% (4% + 6% + 8% + 10% + 10% + 10% + 10%, divide by 7 yrs = 8.28% avg.)
Year 8	10.0%	8.50% (4% + 6% + 8% + 10% + 10% + 10% + 10% + 10%, divide by 8 yrs = 8.50% avg.)

When does the rate cap keep the interest below the FIAR rate?

We already learned that the fluctuation of the interest rate on an ARM is based on the formula *index plus margin* (taking into consideration the rate cap and whichever is a *smaller* change) *equals the new rate*. We have also just seen what will happen if the interest rates increase to the maximum capacity (the worst-case scenario—this is generally the main concern for a borrower). However, the rate does not always increase to the maximum capacity. Sometimes the FIAR (index plus margin) increases more than the rate cap. We now take a look at the past performance of a one-year TCM index to see how the activity of the ARM is affected.

Here are the particulars of the mortgage:

Mortgage	5/1 ARM
	5% initial rate
	2/6 caps
	2.75 margin
Date of mortgage	January 1, 1998 (anniversary date)
Index	1-year TCM index
Index at closing	7.0%

Now let's view the track record.

EXAMPLE OF A TRACK RECORD	
Year 1 interest rate	5.00%
Year 2 interest rate	7.00%
	January 1999 index value: 4.51 + 2.75 = 7.26%
	FIAR of 7.26% is higher than 2% than annual cap allows; rate to stay at 7%
Year 3 interest rate	9.00%
	January 1, 2000, index value: 6.12 + 2.75 = 8.87%, or 9% (*rounded up* to nearest 0.125%)
	FIAR is the same as 2% annual cap
Year 4 interest rate	7.50%
	January 1, 2001, index value: 4.81 + 2.75 = 7.56%, or 7.50% (*rounded down* to nearest 0.125%) FIAR lower than 2% annual cap, dropping the rate
Year 5 interest rate	5.00% January 1, 2002, index value: 2.16 + 2.75 = 4.91%, or 5.00% (*rounded up* to the nearest 0.125%) FIAR is lower than 2% *annual* cap, dropping the rate again
Average rate 6.70% = 6.75%, less than the 8.0% 30-year fixed-rate mortgage	

Mortgage rates are commonly limited to a percentage increase of *1/8 (0.125)%*. Therefore, when we take our formula of index + margin = new rate, as we did in the example above, for year 3, we get

$$6.12 + 2.75 = 8.87\%$$

We need to round the rate to the nearest 1/8%, which would require rounding up to 9%. For year 4 we get

$$4.81 + 2.75 = 7.56\%$$

Rounding the rate to the nearest 1/8%, would require rounding down to 7.50%.

Conversion Feature

Many ARMs today come with a conversion option feature. This allows the borrower to convert the ARM to a fixed-rate mortgage sometime during the lifetime of the ARM. Conversion features vary, as well as the associated fees and cost of conversion. The current rate will determine the interest rate; however, if a dip in the interest rate occurs, the borrower would be able to take advantage of the lower rate by converting to a fixed rate without the need to requalify for a loan. The benefit of a conversion is the fact that the conversion fee is lower than the cost of refinancing.

SECOND MORTGAGES

Private Mortgage Insurance

Before we begin discussing second mortgages, we discuss conventional mortgage insurance (MI). Both Fannie Mae and Freddie Mac require coverage from a private mortgage insurance company if the down payment is less than 20%. Mortgage insurance protects the lender in the event the borrower defaults on the loan.

Generally, the cost of this insurance will vary according to the loan-to-value (LTV) of the mortgage (see Table 3-3), the type of mortgage product, and the mortgage insurance company chosen. The highest cost would be for a 100% loan-to-value mortgage and for an adjustable-rate mortgage.

TABLE 3-3
Sample MI Factor Chart

LTV	Factor
80.01–85%	0.27% × loan amount divided by 12 = monthly MI payment
85.01–90%	0.45% × loan amount divided by 12 = monthly MI payment
90.01–95%	0.73% × loan amount divided by 12 = monthly MI payment

Private mortgage insurance (PMI) is required on loans that exceed 80% loan-to-value unless the borrower chooses a self-insured program (in which the borrower pays a higher interest rate to avoid MI). Borrowers can cancel their PMI when:

- The PMI has been in force for over 24 months. The property must still be owner-occupied.

- No late monthly mortgage payments were made in the last 24 months.

- The loan-to-value reaches 80% or lower.

Other than making a down payment of 20% or more, the only other way to eliminate the need for private mortgage insurance is to obtain a second mortgage.

What Is a Second Mortgage?

A second mortgage is any loan made in addition to another mortgage, with priority settlement of claims given to the earlier mortgage. This means that in the case of default the second lien holder receives proceeds after the *first mortgage* lender's claim has been met. In addition, foreclosure proceedings *cannot* be initiated without the consent of the first mortgage lien holder. As a result, second mortgage loans are considered a higher risk and thus carry a higher interest rate.

At some point, some homeowners may wish to borrow against the equity in their home (take out a second mortgage) to:

- Get cash

- Educate their children

- Make home improvements

- Consolidate personal debts

A second mortgage comes in two options:

- One option is a traditional second mortgage. This option is available in one of two forms:
  - A stand-alone second. In this case, a second mortgage lien is placed after a first mortgage lien already exists.
  - A concurrent second. In this case, a first and second lien are placed simultaneously.

- The other option is a home equity line of credit (HELOC).

Second mortgage loans are different from first mortgages in several ways. They often carry a higher interest rate, generally carry a fixed rate, and are for a shorter time period (20 years or less). However, a 30/15 is also available (the payment is amortized over 30 years, but the loan is due in 15 years).

Combo Loans

Second mortgages may be taken out simultaneously with first mortgages in order to reduce private mortgage insurance and/or allow a borrower to buy a home with a smaller down payment. Here is a sample of concurrent loans:

80/20 (100% loan)—an 80% first mortgage lien and a 20% second mortgage. For example:

$80,000	First mortgage
$20,000	Second mortgage
$100,000	Total sales price

80/10/10—an 80% first mortgage lien, a 10% second lien, and a 10% down payment. For example:

$80,000	First mortgage
$10,000	Second mortgage
$10,000	Down payment

Are two mortgages better than one? Table 3-4 presents a comparsion. The example in the table reflects a savings in

TABLE 3-4
Comparing a Single Loan to a Combo Loan

Sales price	$250,000	**Mortgage plus PMI**	
Down payment	$25,000	Primary mortgage	$225,000.00
	(10%)	P&I payment	$1,277.53
Loan term	30 years	First trust PMI	$97.50
Interest rate	5.50%	**Payment on one loan**	**$1,375.03**
		Combo loan—first and second mortgage	
		Primary mortgage	$200,000.00
		First trust deed payment	$1,135.58
		First trust deed PMI	
		Second trust deed rate	6.875%
		Second trust deed amount	$25,000.00
		Second trust deed payment	$164.15
		Payment on combo loan	**$1,299.73**

payments of $75 a month when utilizing a combo loan. Keep in mind, though, that even without a monthly payment savings, the combo loan would still be a better choice since PMI is not tax deductible, whereas the second mortgage interest rate is.

Equity Lines

Equity lines (also known as HELOC) are revolving lines of credit using real estate as collateral. The lender establishes a loan amount based on the equity in the property. When the funds are needed, the borrower has the option to draw on the line of credit.

Equity lines:

- Operate similarly to a credit card

- Are accessed by checks or drafts

- Provide for floating interest rates

There are many benefits to using a line of credit versus a traditional second mortgage:

- Interest is charged only on the outstanding balance.

- The rate is usually based on the prime lending rate,* which can change day to day. Interest is charged per month on the outstanding balance only. This differs from a traditional second mortgage that has a fixed interest rate.

- Typically HELOCs do not carry any up-front costs; some second mortgages do.

- Like second mortgages, the interest rate on a HELOC *may* be tax deductible. (Keep in mind when discussing tax advantages with a borrower that you are not a tax adviser, and so *always* use the word *may* and *always* refer your borrower to a tax consultant for details.)

- There are many HELOCs designed for self-employed individuals with limited or no income documentation.

These benefits vary from lender to lender.

Reverse Mortgage

A *reverse mortgage*, also known as *reverse annuity mortgage* (RAM), is a mortgage enabling older homeowners (62+) to convert the equity in their home into tax-free income without having to sell their home, give up title, or take on a mortgage payment. The loan is repaid when a borrower becomes deceased or permanently (generally 12 consecutive months is considered permanent) moves away.

Introduced in the late 1980s, reverse mortgages allow homeowners to receive a lump sum of cash, open a line of credit, or receive monthly income on this loan. The amount a homeowner can borrow depends on the person's age, the equity in the home, the value of the home, and the interest rate.

---

*The prime rate, which is published in the *Wall Street Journal*, is an average of the rates charged by the largest banks in New York.

Reverse mortgages have gained in popularity as baby boomers continue to reach retirement age. To qualify for a reverse mortgage:

- The borrower must be at least 62.

- The borrower must have paid off all or most of the home mortgage.

- The borrower must undergo free mortgage counseling from an independent government-approved "housing agency."

The benefits of a reverse mortgage are:

- The income is tax deductible.

- This type of mortgage allows the borrowers to remain in their home.

Mortgage Loan Types Quiz

1. Fixed-rate mortgages have two distinct features. One feature is that the interest rate and payments must be fixed over the term of the mortgage. What is the other feature?
   A. This type of mortgage delays the higher payments for future years.
   B. The unpaid interest is added to the unpaid balance.
   C. The mortgage must be paid off completely at the end of its term.

2. Which fixed-rate mortgage gives you the maximum tax advantage by having the greatest interest deduction?
   A. 20-year fixed-rate mortgage
   B. 30-year fixed-rate mortgage
   C. 15-year fixed-rate mortgage

3. If a borrower is only going to be in her home for five years and she wants the lowest payment available and the maximum tax deduction, which loan program would you recommend?
   A. 30-year fixed-rate mortgage
   B. Interest-only mortgage
   C. 15-year fixed-rate mortgage

4. A balloon mortgage can be an attractive loan program for a borrower who wants to qualify for a larger mortgage, because there is a conditional refinance option at the end of the maturity that guarantees financing.
   A. True
   B. False

5. What is the advantage of a temporary buydown over an adjustable-rate mortgage?
   A. The payment will adjust based on market conditions.
   B. The long-term interest rate can adjust based on changing market conditions.
   C. The long-term interest rate and payment are fixed.

6. To calculate the fully indexed accrual rate (FIAR) on an ARM, you will need to add the index plus:
   A. Margin
   B. Cap
   C. APR

7. When comparing different products with different point options, you can easily adjust for each point by adding *what* to the starting rate for each extra point?
   A. 1%
   B. 1/2%
   C. 2%

8. Second mortgages are different from first mortgages in what way?
   A. They carry a lower interest rate.
   B. They carry a higher interest rate.
   C. The loan typically has a longer term than a first mortgage.

9. Why would a borrower prefer a 15-year fixed-rate mortgage over a 30-year fixed-rate mortgage?
   A. He wants a low monthly mortgage payment.
   B. He wants to have his home paid for more quickly.
   C. He does not want a prepayment penalty.

10. With a loan that carries a prepayment penalty, a person can incur the prepayment penalty if she pays down her loan faster than the amortization schedule requires.
    A. True
    B. False

11. When does negative amortization happen?
    A. When the monthly payments are not large enough to pay the interest due on the loan
    B. When a loan is fully amortized
    C. When the initial monthly payments are lower but eventually graduate and catch up to what is required to amortize the loan

12. The first number of an adjustable-rate mortgage determines the period for which the adjustable rate of the mortgage is guaranteed—for example, 3/1, 5/1, or 10/1. What does the second number signify?
    A. The length by year of subsequent adjustments
    B. The length by month of subsequent adjustments
    C. The amount by which the adjustments will be made

13. If your borrower wants a 15-year loan because he wants to pay off his home more quickly but he does not initially qualify for the larger payment, which loan program should you offer him?
    A. 15-year fixed-rate loan
    B. Growing equity mortgage
    C. Biweekly mortgage

14. Why are rate caps important to an ARM?
    A. They specify when the interest rate can increase or decrease.
    B. They specify how much the interest rate can increase or decrease.
    C. They specify how often the interest rate can increase or decrease.

15. Which of the following is *not* of a HELOC?
    A. It is a second mortgage.
    B. It is an equity line of credit.
    C. It is a type of ARM.

16. What is the difference between a fixed-rate hybrid and a fixed-rate loan?
    A. A fixed-rate hybrid is a fully amortized loan.
    B. A fixed-rate hybrid has a fixed-rate payment throughout the course of the loan.
    C. A fixed-rate hybrid does not have a fixed-rate payment throughout the course of the loan.

17. There are five basic features of an adjustable-rate mortgage. Which of the following is *not* a feature?
    A. Index
    B. LIBOR
    C. Frequency of change

18. When is an adjustable-rate mortgage beneficial?
    A. When rates are at a historical low
    B. When the borrower qualifies for a low fixed-rate mortgage loan
    C. When the interest rates are rising

19. On a $100,000 loan amount, your borrower has two options: a 30-year fixed-rate loan at 8.25% interest with 0 points or a 30-year fixed-rate loan at 7.75% interest with 3 points. Your borrower intends to stay in his property with no plans of moving. Which loan program would you recommend?
    A. 8.25% interest with 0 points
    B. 7.75% interest with 3 points
    C. Neither A nor B

20. A look at our amortization table on a fixed-rate 30-year loan (see Figure 3-1) reveals that the major portion of the mortgage payment for the first few years is applied to:
    A. The interest
    B. The principal
    C. The balance

Answers to the quiz can be found at the end of Part One.

CHAPTER 4

PROGRAM GUIDELINES

To get profits without risk, experience without danger,
and reward without work is as impossible as it is to live
without being born.

—A. P. Gouthey

Now that you are familiar with all the different *types* of mortgages, you are ready to learn about the individual specifications for these mortgage products. All mortgage plans can be divided into two major categories:

- Conventional loans
  - Conforming loans
  - Nonconforming loans

- Insured government loans
  - FHA
  - VA

CONVENTIONAL LOANS

A conventional loan is *any* loan *not* insured by the government. Under conventional loans there are two subcategories: conforming and nonconforming. We begin the chapter by looking at conforming loans.

Conforming Loans

Conventional conforming loans are loans that follow the guidelines of and are eligible for purchase by Fannie Mae (FNMA) and Freddie Mac (FHLMC). Fannie Mae and Freddie Mac are government-sponsored enterprises (GSEs) created by the government but exist in the private sector. These two stockholder-owned companies purchase mortgage loans that conform to these guidelines from mortgage lenders and sell the loans in the secondary market. Fannie Mae and Freddie Mac establish the maximum loan amount, borrower credit and income requirements, down payment, and property requirements (see Figure 4-1). The new conforming loan amount is announced at the end of every year.

Who is eligible for a conforming mortgage?

Eligible borrowers include U.S. citizens, permanent resident aliens, and nonpermanent resident aliens with verification of two-year employment and residency history.

What is the maximum mortgage amount for a conforming mortgage?

The maximum conforming loan amounts for the current year (2006) are as follows:

		Alaska and Hawaii
• One-unit properties	$417,000	$ 625,500
• Two-unit properties	$533,850	$ 800,775
• Three-unit properties	$645,300	$ 967,950
• Four-unit properties	$801,950	$1,202,925

The conforming loan limit for second mortgages is $179,825 (and in Alaska and Hawaii it is $312,750).

What types of properties are eligible for a conforming mortgage?

The types of properties eligible for conventional conforming mortgages include:

- One- to four-unit residential properties

FIGURE 4-1
FNMA/FHLMC Conforming Matrix

Loan Amounts		
Property Type	Loan Amount	(Alaska/Hawaii)
Single Family, Condo	$ 417,000	$ 625,500
2 Unit	$ 533,850	$ 800,775
3 Unit	$ 645,300	$ 967,950
4 Unit	$ 801,950	$1,202,925

LTVs						
Standard Eligibility – Fixed Rate Mortgages						
Loan Purpose	Occupancy	Units	Max. LTV	Max. **CLTV	Max. **HCLTV	
Purchase and Limited Cash-Out Refinance	Primary	1	95%	95%	100%*	
		2	90%	90%	95%	
		3–4	80%	80%	85%	
	Second Home	1	90%	90%	95%	
	Investment	1–4	75%	75%	80%	
Cash-Out Refinance	Primary	1–4	70%	70%	80%	
	Second Home	1	70%	70%	80%	
	Investment	1–4	70%	70%	75%	
*Requires a minimum FICO score of 680 (700 if self-employed)						
Refinancing	Streamline or limited qualifying to 95% LTV if current loan is FNMA–Serviced – > 90% cannot include closing costs or prepaid items. Existing 2nd mortgage must be "seasoned" for 12 months or payoff is considered "cash-out"					
Multiple Properties	Owner-occupied no limit investment / 2nd – max 10 and limited to $2 million max combined loan balance.					
Mortgage Insurance	Conventional private mortgage insurance required for all owner-occupied properties and second homes with loan-to-values greater than 80%.					
Documentation Types	Full/Alternative – Income verification may be waived by DU/LP					

Income/Borrower Restrictions	
Qualifying Ratios	95% LTV – 28/36 or DU/LP ARMs Qualify at 2nd Year rate. 75% LTV – 33/38 or DU/LP Buydowns qualify at start rate.
Employment History	Minimum 2 years history, 2 years in same business for self-employed
Non-occupant Co-Borrower(s)	Max LTV for using non-occupant co-borrower(s) income for qualifying is 95% LTV. Occupant borrower's debt ratio is limited to 43% and must have 5% of own funds invested unless LTV/CLTV ≤80%.

Asset Restrictions	
Seller Contributions	95% LTV – 3% 90% LTV – 6% Investor – 2% 75% LTV – 9%
Cash Reserves	95% LTV – 3 months PITI 2 months – may be waived under affordable 90% or less – 2 months Gold, community home buyer
Gift Letters	80.01 – 95% LTV borrower must have 5% of own funds invested into transaction. <80% LTV – No limit. Source, transfer, and receipt must be documented. Donor must be "family" member.
Secondary Financing	Payments must cover at least the interest due Neg, am not permitted, No pre pay penalty allowed, 2nd mortgage maturity must be at least 5 years.
Borrowed Funds	Must be secured/counted for qualifying

Credit Restrictions	
Credit Score	Bureau scores are applied. With two scores, take the average, with three scores, take the middle. Scoring regimen is not absolute but follows the following guideline: Eligible for enhanced criteria Over 700 Cautious 660–620 Not eligible for max financing Below 620
Mortgage History	0 × 30 day late in last 12 months
Major Derogatory Credit	Must have 2 years re-established history. Required time elapsed for: bankruptcy — Chapter 7, 11, 12 , and 13—4 years; Foreclosure 4 years.

TABLE 4-1
FNMA and FHLMC Condo Requirements

FNMA Type A/FHLMC CLASS III—Existing Project
1. 100% complete; no additional phasing
2. Owner's association has been in control for one year
3. 90% sold, 60% owner-occupied
4. No entity owns 10% or more
5. Hazard, flood, liability insurance coverage must be maintained
6. Lender can warrant compliance
FNMA Type B/FHLMC Class II—Existing Project Not 100% Sold Out
1. Complete; no additional phasing
2. 70% sold, 70% owner-occupied
3. Developer no longer in control of association
4. Hazard, flood, liability insurance coverage must be maintained
5. Addendum B (budget adequacy)
6. No single entity owns more than 10% of the project
FNMA Type C/FHLMC Class I—New Project   FNMA Form 1028 Project Acceptance Letter accepted   Form 1027 is conditional project approval
Requirements are:
1. Developer must still have control
2. 70% of units within a phase must be sold or under contract to settle. Unit appraisals must include Addendum A and Addendum B
3. Attorney's opinion letter addressing condominium documents
4. Condo coversions require engineering structural survey within last three years

- Planned unit developments (PUDs)

- Condominium projects (must be approved by FNMA and FHLMC—see Table 4-1)

- Manufactured homes

- Modular, prefabricated, panelized, and sectionals

- Leaseholds (not permitted with balloon mortgages)

- Cooperatives (Type 1 must have 80% ownership; Type 2 projects must appear on FNMA approved list)

What are the qualification guidelines for a conforming mortgage?

The debt-to-income qualification must be met. The most common ratio method is 28/36. Higher ratios are tolerated when submitted through the automated underwriting systems—Loan Prospector (LP) or Desktop Underwriter (DU).

Ratio methods are discussed in further detail in Chapter 5. The debt-to-income ratio is calculated by dividing monthly minimum debt payments by monthly gross income. In the ratios 28/36, the first figure—28%—represents the maximum housing ratio, and the second figure—36%—represents the total debt-to-income ratio.

What are the cash requirements for a conforming mortgage?

Most conventional conforming loan programs require that the borrowers invest at least 5% of their own cash in any purchase transaction with a loan-to-value (LTV) greater than 80% *and* have the equivalent of two months' mortgage payment (PITI) in reserves after closing. (The 5% can be borrowed, as long as the purchaser can qualify for the additional debt and an owned asset secures the loan.) On loans below 80% LTV, the entire down payment may be a gift. The gift must be from:

- A spouse or child

- An individual related by marriage or adoption

- The borrower's fiancé or fiancée or domestic partner

To satisfy the cash requirement (aside from the obligatory 5% cash), the following options are allowed:

- A gift from an immediate family member for closing costs. The gift letter must document specifically that this is a gift and that there is no requirement of repayment. Also in some cases you may need to prove that the donor has the ability to give, and you must be able to establish a "paper trail" of funds.

- The seller can pay closing costs. This is known as *seller contributions*. However, there are limitations:

For 90% LTV or higher	3% maximum seller contribution
For 90% LTV or below	6% maximum seller contribution
For 75% LTV or below	9% maximum seller contribution
For investor transactions	2% maximum seller contribution

Note: The seller's maximum contribution is based on sales price or appraised value, whichever is less (not the mortgage amount).

What about credit?

The minimum credit score for a conforming loan is 620. Most lenders determine the credit score by using the middle of three scores or the lower of two scores. For example, suppose your borrower's scores are:

656 on Experian

666 on TransUnion

686 on Equifax

The lender will use the 666 credit score.

Fannie Mae requires four years to elapse from the discharge date of a Chapter 7, 11, or 12 bankruptcy; four years from the date the repayment plan was completed and discharged for a Chapter 13 bankruptcy; and four years from the foreclosure date and the date a deed-in-lieu was executed.

For a borrower with a two-year-old bankruptcy, foreclosure or deed-in-lieu exceptions will be made if the borrower can provide verification that the incidence was a result of extenuating circumstances (or a nonrecurring event)—for example, divorce, severe medical issue, or, in some cases, job loss. In addition, the borrower must have reestablished credit. Reestablished credit requirements are:

- A minimum of four credit references (one must be a rental or mortgage history, and the other three must have a 24-month active status).

- No debt can have more than two 30-day late payments in the last 24 months.

- No 60-day late payments in the last 24 months are allowed.

- No housing debt may be delinquent since the time of the bankruptcy or foreclosure.

What about seconds?

Second mortgages are permitted, but the first mortgage may be limited to 80% LTV, and a minimum 10% down payment may be required. Secondary financing is not allowed under most balloon first mortgage programs. In addition, seconds must meet the following requirements to be considered a *conforming* second mortgage:

- No negative amortization loans are allowed.

- No prepayment is allowed.

- The payments must be regular and cover at least the interest due.

- The mortgage must not balloon in less than five years.

What about coborrowers?

If your borrower plans to use a coborrower who does not intend to live in the property, then the *LTV will be limited to 90%,* and the minimum debt ratio requirement for the occupying borrower is 43%. In addition, the occupant must make the first 5% down payment from his or her own funds unless the loan-to-value is 80% or below.

Nonconforming Loans

There are many mortgage products that are not purchasable by FNMA and FHLMC. Examples include:

- Subprime mortgages (less than perfect credit)

- Jumbo loans (loans that exceed FNMA and FHLMC loan limits)

- Alt-A loans (generally stated income or ARMs with 640 and above credit score)

- Negative amortization mortgages

- Second mortgages with higher loan-to-values and lower credit scores

Here we focus on subprime and jumbo loans.

Subprime Loans

Subprime mortgages emerged with rapid growth in the 1990s, with lenders seeking increased profits. Regulatory changes, significant technological innovations, and liberalization in some mortgage programs allowed lenders to extend credit to millions of borrowers who would otherwise have been denied the opportunity of homeownership.

Nearly 9% of the total mortgages made in 2003 were subprime. That's up from 4.5% in 1994. In terms of volume, $388 billion in subprime mortgage loans were originated in the first nine months of last year (2004). According to Inside Mortgage Finance Publications, that is more than triple the amount made 10 years ago.

Subprime lending can be defined simply as lending that involves elevated credit risk. Subprime loans are made to borrowers who are credit-challenged, who may have deficiencies in demonstrating the capability of repaying the loan (for example, a high debt-to-income ratio), and who may have a limited down payment, therefore requiring a loan with a higher loan-to-value.

It is general knowledge that a credit score below 620 represents a subprime loan. However, about half the subprime mortgages originated carry credit scores above this threshold, indicating that a good credit score *alone* does not guarantee a prime loan. A subprime loan may include:

- A self-employed borrower with less than two years at his or her business

- A borrower (self-employed or wage earner) seeking a "no income verification" loan program

- An investor with many properties

- A property with partial commercial use

- A property with excessive acreage (rural property)

- A high land-to-value ratio

A borrower will fall into one of five categories: A, A−, B, C, or D (see Figure 4-2). The more serious the credit problems, the lower the grade and the higher the interest rate and fees that the loan will carry. Lenders justify the higher rates and fees because of a higher risk of default.

Subprime loans are more likely to include a *prepayment penalty.* Prepayment is the payment of all or part of the mortgage debt before it is due. Prepayment-protection mortgages (PPMs) restrict the right to prepay the loan without penalty in its early years. A prepayment penalty is a fee charged by the lender to the borrower who wishes to repay part or all of the loan in advance of the regular schedule. Mortgage companies introduced prepayment penalties on mortgage loans as a way to offer lower interest rates to borrowers who do not expect to prepay. The risk of prepayment probably is higher in the subprime mortgage market than the prime market, because it is more likely for the borrower to improve his or her credit or financial situation and thus seek another mortgage loan with a lower interest rate.

Most mortgages with prepayment penalties have an interest rate 1/4% to 1% below those without penalties. The lower interest rate charged for PPMs allows borrowers to reduce the cost of purchasing a home. Many borrowers who couldn't be qualified for market-rate mortgages could be qualified for a lower-rate PPM mortgage.

What is the maximum mortgage amount for a subprime loan?

The maximum mortgage amount allowed varies, depending on the lender. Currently loan amounts are between $750,000 and $1 million. Keep in mind that the credit grade and loan-to-value will determine the maximum loan amount.

FIGURE 4-2
Subprime Matrix

	Mortgage 12 Mos.	Credit Score	Doc Type	Loan Limits		Owner Occupied					Investment			
				Owner	Investment	SFR	2 Units	3-4 Units	Condo	MFG	SFR	2 Units	3-4 Units	Condo
AA	0X30	640	Full Doc	$500K	$400K	95%	90%	85%	95%	85%	90%	80%	80%	85%
			Limited	$500K	$400K	95%	90%	85%	95%	80%	85%	80%	75%	85%
			Lite Doc	$500K	$400K	95%	90%	85%	95%	80%	80%	75%	70%	80%
			Stated Inc	$400K	$300K	95%	85%	85%	95%	80%	80%	70%	70%	75%
A	1X30	600	Full Doc	$500K	$300K	95%	90%	85%	95%	80%	85%	80%	80%	85%
			Limited	$400K	$250K	95%	90%	85%	95%	75%	85%	80%	75%	85%
			Lite Doc	$400K	$250K	90%	90%	75%	90%	75%	80%	75%	70%	80%
			Stated Inc	$350K	$200K	90%	85%	75%	90%	75%	75%	70%	70%	75%
A-	2X30	580	Full Doc	$400K	$300K	95%	85%	80%	95%	80%	80%	75%	75%	75%
			Limited	$400K	$250K	90%	85%	80%	90%	75%	80%	75%	75%	75%
			Lite Doc	$400K	$250K	90%	80%	75%	90%	75%	80%	75%	70%	75%
			Stated Inc	$350K	$200K	80%	75%	75%	75%	75%	75%	70%	70%	70%
B+	3X30	550	Full Doc	$400K	$250K	85%	80%	80%	80%	75%	75%	70%	70%	70%
			Limited	$400K	$200K	85%	80%	75%	80%	70%	75%	70%	65%	70%
			Lite Doc	$350K	$200K	80%	75%	70%	75%	70%	70%	65%	65%	65%
			Stated Inc	$333,700K	$200K	75%	70%	70%	70%	70%	65%	65%	65%	65%
B	1X60	500	Full Doc	$400K	$250K	80%	75%	75%	75%	70%	70%	65%	65%	65%
			Limited	$350K	$200K	80%	75%	70%	75%	65%	70%	65%	65%	65%
			Lite Doc	$333,700K	$200K	75%	70%	70%	70%	65%	65%	65%	60%	65%
			Stated Inc	$333,700K	$200K	70%	70%	70%	70%	65%	65%	60%	60%	65%
C	2X60 1x90	500	Full Doc	$333,700K	$250K	75%	70%	70%	N/A	70%	60%	60%	60%	60%
			Limited	$333,700K	$200K	75%	70%	70%	N/A	60%	60%	60%	60%	60%
			Lite Doc	$333,700K	$200K	70%	65%	65%	N/A	60%	60%	60%	60%	60%
			Stated Inc	$333,700K	$200K	70%	65%	65%	N/A	N/A	N/A	N/A	N/A	N/A

MATRIX NOTES

GENERAL

All owner occupied refinance transactions must benefit borrower.
Second homes subject to same first mortgage LTV restrictions as grades;
AA, A, A–, & B+. Second homes are treated as N/O/O for grades B&C.
For Stated Income, a complete and signed 1003 must be received prior to
ordering docs.
Incomes disclosed on 1003 must be consistent with profession and
experience.

DOCUMENTATION REQUIREMENTS

Full Doc – 2 years W2's with current pay stubs and tax returns
(if applicable) OR 24 months bank statements.
Limited – W2 covering 1 year employment and a current pay stub
OR 12 month bank statements.
Lite Doc – a current pay stub covering at least a 6 month history with
year to date calculation OR 6 months bank statements.
Stated Inc – Income stated on 1003 is used for calculating DTI &
employment is verified. Tradeline activity and credit history must support
bureau score and level of income.
Bank statements – 100% of deposits from personal bank statements OR 50%
of deposits from business bank statements is used to calculate income for
DTI purposes.

RESERVE REQUIREMENTS

2 MONTHS PITI
Over 90% LTV/CLTV on stated income (S&S).
New primary residence is purchased and current residence is retained on
stated income only (S&S).

DEFINITIONS
　　Sourced & Seasoned (S&S): PITI and funds to close must be held in
borrowers' account disclosed on 1003 for a minimum of 60 days.

Disposable Income
$500 for primary borrower and $150 for each additional household member.
Fixed income borrowers must have disposable income to maintain housing
and living expenses on non-grossed up income.

First Time Home Buyers
2 year minimum credit history required and 4 reported accounts.
Minimum 12 month housing history verified via canceled checks or
institutional VOR.
Closing costs may be a gift up to 90% LTV/95% CLTV

Appraisals
On loan amounts over $500, a second appraisal is not required.

What are the ratio qualification guidelines for a subprime loan?

A subprime loan does not consider the housing or front-end ratio. The guidelines for a subprime loan are more liberal when it comes to debt-to-income ratios; the maximum allowable range is between 50 and 55%.

What are the cash reserve requirements for a subprime loan?

Generally, there are no cash reserve requirements on a subprime loan, with the exception of some 100% financing with "stated income."

What about income documentation?

Subprime loan products include full income documentation, limited income documentation, and stated income. Self-employed borrowers benefit with this type of loan product because of the flexibility regarding income documentation. Most lenders will allow the use of business bank statements in lieu of full tax returns and will price the loan as a full-income documentation loan. The lender will take the total amount of deposits and use the average amount of deposit income as the eligibility income for qualification purposes. For limited income, typically the lender will use the average deposits of the last 12 monthly bank statements. This is a great opportunity for a self-employed individual to obtain better pricing and a higher loan amount if he or she can provide proof of earnings. Stated income programs carry a higher rate and restricted loan amounts, but the programs allow the borrower the opportunity to "state" what his or her gross earnings are for qualification purposes. Copies of either a business license or a letter from a certified public accountant, which verifies that the borrower has been in business for a minimum of two years, are required.

What about credit?

As you might imagine, credit guidelines are more liberal when it comes to the subprime loan. Primarily the credit score is reviewed to determine the credit grade. Standard guidelines require a minimum credit score of 500. The mortgage history for the last 12 months is reviewed to determine the credit grade, which determines the maximum loan amount and pricing. For example:

> No mortgage or rental payments made late in the last 12 months = A grade

> A mortgage payment that was 120 days late in the last 12 months = D grade

What about bankruptcies and foreclosure?

A borrower can be one day out of a Chapter 7 bankruptcy or foreclosure and qualify for a subprime loan with a loan-to-value restriction, typically up to 70%. Consumer credit history generally is not considered unless it affects the title of the property, i.e., judgments or tax liens.

Jumbo Loans

As discussed earlier, conventional conforming loan amounts are set by Fannie Mae or Freddie Mac. These limits change annually. As of January 2005, a conventional loan can be up to $359,600. Loans that are above that limit are called *jumbo loans*. Because jumbo loans don't offer the same Fannie Mae– and Freddie Mac–backed safety to investors as conventional loans, their interest rates tend to be higher by about 0.25 to 0.50%.

In today's market with home prices at an all-time high, jumbo loans are prevalent. Jumbo loans are available with fixed interest rates and a variety of adjustable-rate mortgages.

INSURED GOVERNMENT LOANS

Government-insured loans help lower the costs of mortgages so that more people can afford to own their own homes. There are three government agencies that insure mortgages: the Federal

Housing Administration (FHA), which is part of the U.S. Department of Housing and Urban Development; the Veterans Administration (VA); and the Rural Housing Service (RHS), which is a branch of the U.S. Department of Agriculture. Ginnie Mae is an agency within HUD that guarantees the investment quality of mortgage-backed securities made by approved lenders. Ginnie Mae ensures that adequate funds are available for mortgage loans that are insured or guaranteed by the FHA and the VA.

FHA

FHA is not a lender—it does not lend money. Rather, it is regarded as an *insurance program*. Lenders are merely protected, or *insured*, against default by the borrower. This protection comes in the form of mortgage insurance. The FHA borrower pays for this insurance in what is known as *mortgage insurance premium*, or *MIP*. Because FHA provides insurance backed by the federal government, it is able to provide more lenient qualification standards, such as allowing lower down payments and allowing more flexibility when it comes to calculating household income and payment ratios. (See Table 4-2.)

Only approved lenders can offer these loans, and there are required standards that the property has to meet in order to qualify. There is a *Direct Endorsement (DE) program* that allows these approved FHA lenders to use the automated system to obtain case numbers and to utilize staff appraisers; this in turn speeds up the process. With DE the lender is permitted to approve not only the borrower but the property as well.

One of the advantages of an FHA loan is the eligibility process: the FHA allows two or more borrowers, or *coborrowers,* to finance a house under this program. These coborrowers need not be related. FHA limits one FHA mortgage per borrower to be outstanding at any one time.

Another advantage is that an FHA loan is assumable, allowing a person to take over the mortgage without the additional cost of obtaining a new loan. There is only a $500 buyer qualification fee.

TABLE 4-2
Types of FHA Financing

203(b), 234(c)	Fixed-rate mortgage on an owner-occupied property. This loan can be a purchase transaction, rate reduction, or FHA streamline or cash-out refinance. 234(c) is for condos.
251	Adjustable-rate mortgages—1-year ARM with 1/5 caps.
203k	Rehabilitation mortgage. These mortgages are used for the purchase of an existing one- to four-family owner-occupied property that needs repairs. The cost of rehab can be included in the mortgage amount, with no additional down payment required. The construction costs must be at least $5,000 under this program, and construction plans must be approved by an FHA consultant (estimator). Other costs that can be included are up to six months PITI, permit, consultant, inspection, and title update fees—and, if needed, architectural or engineering fees. The lender loans enough money to cover the purchase of the property and places the excess necessary to complete the repairs in escrow. The repair money is then released as the work is completed.

What types of properties are eligible for FHA financing?

The properties allowed include:

- One- to four-unit properties. The maximum mortgage amount is increased for multiple-unit properties. (See Table 4-3.)

- Planned unit developments (PUDs).

TABLE 4-3
National FHA Maximum Loan Limits

	1 Unit	2 Units	3 Units	4 Units
Base loan limits	$200,160	$256,248	$309,744	$384,936
Maximum high cost	$362,790	$464,449	$561,411	$697,696
Check with the FHA regional offices for individual city and county loan limits. https://entp.hud.gov/idapp/html/hicost1.cfm				

- New homes must have plans and specifications approved by FHA.

- Condominiums—must be on the FHA-approved list.

- Manufactured homes—must be on permanent foundation.

When FHA and VA approve a condominium unit, it appears on their "approved list." For FHA approval a condominium unit must have 51% owner occupancy.

If an existing project is not FHA-approved, it is possible for that individual unit to qualify for "spot-loan" financing. To qualify for spot-loan financing, the condominium project must meet the following requirements:

- It must be 100% complete—no additional phases.

- 90% of the units must be sold.

- 51% must be owner-occupied.

- The association must have control for at least one year.

- No legal action is pending against the association.

- No more than 10% of the units (20% for projects with 30 units or less) are eligible for spot financing.

What are the closing costs and mortgage amounts for an FHA loan?

The determination of the maximum mortgage amount for an FHA loan is made by a loan-to-value formula. High-cost areas are regions that levy taxes in a mortgage transaction. As noted in Table 4-4, smaller transactions and higher-cost areas were accorded more leverage (higher LTVs).

The required down payment is 1.25 to 2.85%, depending on the sales price. The borrower must invest at least 3.0% in the transaction (including the down payment according to the maximum loan-to-value as specified in Table 4-4). The FHA allows the 3% contribution to be a gift from a blood relative or to come from a nonprofit organization.

The greatest disadvantage of FHA home loans is the up-front mortgage insurance premium. All FHA mortgages must have

TABLE 4-4
Closing Costs and LTVs

LTV	Loan Amount	Applicable States and Territories
	Low Cost	
98.75%	Less than $50,000	Arizona, California, Colorado,
97.65%	$50,000–$125,000	Guam, Idaho, Illinois, Indiana,
97.15%	Over $125,000	New Mexico, New York, Oregon, Utah, Virgin Islands, Washington, Wisconsin, Wyoming
	High Cost	
98.75%	Less than $50,000	All other states
97.75%	Over $50,000	

mortgage insurance, regardless of the amount of the down payment. FHA collects mortgage insurance up front and monthly (except for condominiums 203k, which have no up-front premium. Condos are only subject to a monthly insurance cost).

- *The up-front premium* is 1.5% of the mortgage amount. For example, suppose the FHA loan amount is $100,000 (base mortgage amount).

   The mortgage insurance premium would be $1,500 ($100,000 × 1.5%).
   The mortgage amount including MIP would be $101,500 ($100,000 + $1,500).

- The amount of *monthly mortgage insurance* (MMI) depends on the amount of down payment applied to the mortgage,

FHA Monthly Insurance Chart

	Up-Front MIP	MMI Down Payment		
		10% or More	**5–10%**	**4.99% or Less**
30-year loan	1.50%	0.50%	0.50%	0.50%
15-year loan	1.50%	None	0.50%	0.50%

as shown in the FHA Monthly Insurance Chart on page 80. A 15-year term with 10% or more down payment does not carry MMI.

Key Note: Any unused portion of the up-front MIP may be refunded if the loan is paid off early. Furthermore, the MMI payment will automatically be canceled when the outstanding balance reaches 78% of the original purchase price (providing MMI payments have been made for a minimum of 5 years for 30-year loans).

FHA Rules

1. *Nonallowable FHA closing costs.* The borrower *cannot* be charged certain miscellaneous lender fees, for example, tax service, underwriting fees. If the lender charges these fees, the *seller* must incur these costs at closing. While this is not an all-inclusive list, nonallowable fees include:
   - Application fee
   - Processing fee
   - Document preparation fee (unless the documents were prepared by a company other than the lender)
   - Flood certification fee
   - Inspection fee (only FHA appraisal compliance inspections are permitted)
   - Tax service fee
   - Underwriting fee

   Allowable fees include the following. Again this is not an all-inclusive list.

   - Appraisal fee
   - Credit report fee (actual cost)
   - Compliance inspection fee
   - Cost for title exam and title insurance
   - Endorsement fee (related to title insurance only)
   - Escrow fee (one-half of the total transaction fee and not more than what the seller pays)
   - Home inspection fee (up to $200)
   - Notary fee
   - Origination fee (a maximum of 1% of the loan)
   - Recording fee, transfer stamps, and taxes

These fees are allowable in a refinance (this is not an all-inclusive list):

○ Beneficiary statement
○ Courier fee
○ Wire transfer fee
○ Payoff of other bills
○ Reconveyance fee

2. *Seller contributions.* The seller is allowed a maximum of 6% of the sales price toward *contribution* for the borrower's closing costs. Seller contributions may include any temporary buydowns, prepaids, up-front MIP, and discount points.

3. *Subsidy program.* A mortgage credit certificate (MCC) is allowed with county approval. First-time home-buyer counseling may be required; counseling must be from a HUD-approved nonprofit agency.

4. *FHA prepayments.* When paying off an FHA mortgage, it is important to schedule the closing toward the end of the month because FHA has the right to collect interest on a loan until the end of the month regardless of when the payoff is made. This is unique to FHA. Conventional mortgages stop interest collection the day the lender receives the payoff amount.

What about credit?

The main advantage of an FHA home loan is that the credit criteria for a borrower are not as strict as the FNMA's or FHLMC's criteria. The following is a brief synopsis of the credit guidelines for the FHA:

- *Lack of credit history.* If a borrower does not have a minimum of two trade lines on his or her credit report, alternative forms of credit may be used. This would include items such as auto insurance payment history and utility bills.

- *Included credit obligations.* Any installment loan (e.g., student loans, car loans) with less than 10 months remaining does not need to be included when qualifying for an FHA home loan. However, consideration is given if the debt affects the borrower's ability to make the mortgage payment immediately after the loan closes. Payments on auto leases with less than 10 months *must* be included in the qualifying ratios. The minimum payment on all revolving accounts (i.e., credit cards) must be factored in. If minimum payment is not reflected on the credit report, then 5% of the balance is used for qualifying purposes. If the borrower has an open revolving account with a zero balance, then $10 is applied for each open account—again, for qualifying purposes.

- *Chapter 7 bankruptcy.* FHA requires a minimum of two years since the *discharge* of the bankruptcy. An explanation of the bankruptcy will be required. Furthermore, the borrower should have reestablished credit (i.e., a secured credit card) with no late payments.

- *Chapter 13 bankruptcy.* FHA will consider a borrower still paying on a Chapter 13 bankruptcy if the payments to the court have been made satisfactorily for a minimum of one year. Verification and approval from the court trustee will be required.

- *Federal debts.* All student loans, SBA loans, property tax liens, or any other debt guaranteed by the government (such as HUD or VA mortgage) must be brought current (generally a three-month history will be required), or payment in full is required for eligibility.

- *Judgments.* Judgments must be paid in full prior to closing.

- *Collection accounts.* If a collection account is minor in nature ($100 or less), it generally does not have to be paid off as a condition of loan approval.

- *Foreclosure.* A borrower with a foreclosure or deed-in-lieu of foreclosure within the previous three years is generally not eligible for an FHA home loan. However, if the foreclosure was the result of extenuating circumstances beyond the borrower's control (such as the death of a spouse, loss of employment, or serious long-term illness) and the borrower has since reestablished good credit, an exception may be granted. In addition, an applicant with a prior foreclosure may be limited to owner-occupied properties only.

- *Cosigned obligations.* If the individual applying for an FHA loan is a cosigner on a car loan, student loan, or any other obligation, including a mortgage, then the debt must be counted in the borrower's credit obligations unless verification can be provided demonstrating that the primary obligator has been making the payments on a regular basis (12 consecutive months) and does not have a history of delinquent payments on the loan.

What are the qualifying requirements for an FHA loan?

FHA's qualifying ratios are a 29% housing ratio and a 41% debt ratio. However, FHA has specific compensating factors that you may use should you need to exceed these limits. Those compensating factors are:

- The down payment is larger than the minimum required.

- There is less than a 10% increase from the old rent or house payment to the new housing expense.

- The borrower has shown the ability to accumulate savings (for example, savings accounts, IRAs).

- The borrower has three or more months' cash reserves (PITI after closing) that are not part of a gift.

- The borrower has demonstrated a conservative use of credit.

- The borrower has potential for increased earnings.

- The borrower has additional income that cannot be used as qualifying income.

- The dwelling is energy efficient.

Funds to Close

The borrower's cash investment in the property must equal the difference between the amount of the FHA mortgage, excluding any up-front MIP, and the total cost to acquire the property (to include prepaid expenses, closing costs, etc.). All funds must be verified from acceptable sources. These sources include:

- *Earnest money deposit.* Satisfactory documentation is a copy of the borrower's canceled check or verification of deposit (VOD) from the bank. However, if the amount of the earnest money deposit exceeds 2% of the sales price or appears excessive based on the borrower's history of accumulating savings, the deposit amount and source of funds must be verified.

- *Savings and checking accounts.* The lender must verify these accounts with a VOD. A copy of the borrower's last three bank statements will also be required. If a large increase in deposits is present or the account was recently opened, an explanation of the source of the deposit must be given and verification established. Nonsufficient funds, bounced checks, or account overdrafts will need to be reasonably explained.

- *Gift funds.* A gift for the down payment and closing costs is acceptable from a family member. The gift letter must specify the dollar amount given, signed by both borrower and donor. The letter must state that *no repayment* is required, and it must include the donor's name, address, phone number, and relationship to the borrower. In addition, the letter must state that the funds were not contributed from any parties involved in the transaction. Verification of transfer of funds from the donor to the borrower's account must be provided (for example, the borrower's deposit slip or bank statement).

- *Sale of an asset.* Sale of an asset is considered an acceptable source of income if the borrower provides (1) a copy of the bill of sale or HUD-1 settlement statement (for the sale of a home), (2) a copy of the check or verification of funds transfer from the buyer of the asset to the borrower, and (3) a copy of the borrower's deposit slip or bank statement showing the deposit of the funds into the borrower's bank account.

- *Cash on hand.* Cash on hand is an acceptable source as long as the borrower can demonstrate the ability to accumulate such savings. The lender must determine the credibility of the savings based on the borrower's income, spending habits, and history of using financial institutions, as well as considering how long it took to accumulate the funds. The cash on hand will need to be deposited into a financial institution or held at an escrow or title company.

- *Lease option.* If the portion of a borrower's current rental payment is to be used to purchase the property the borrower currently occupies, the borrower will need to provide a copy of the rental or lease agreement. The rental or lease agreement must include the clause allowing an option to purchase and specify the amount of rental payment that is to be used as a rent credit.

- *Trade equity.* The borrower may agree to trade his or her property to the seller as part of the cash investment. The amount of the borrower's equity contribution is calculated by subtracting all liens against the property being traded (along with any real estate commissions) from the property's appraised value or sales or trade price (whichever is less).

Figure 4-3 summarizes the requirements for FHA loans.

The Department of Veterans Affairs

The VA guaranty program was established under the GI Bill in 1944 to provide a special homeownership benefit for veterans returning from World War II. Since then, more than 17.5 million veterans, including servicemen and servicewomen who served in Korea, Vietnam, and other conflicts, have used this benefit, some more than once.

FIGURE 4-3
FHA Matrix

LTV Matrix								
Transaction	LTV	CLTV			Property Type	Loan Amount	High Cost (87% of FNMA)	
Purchase or Rate and Term Refinance	97.75 Low Closing Cost States				Single Family / Condo	$200,160	$362,790	
					2 Unit	$256,248	$464,449	
	98.75 High Closing Costs States (<50,000)				3 Unit	$309,744	$561,441	
					4 Unit	$384,936	$697,696	
Cash Out	85%	N/A			SFD, Condo			

Programs Offered	30, 20, 15, 10 year fixed (Sections 203b & 234c). 1 year ARM with 1/5 caps (Sec 251). Rehabilitation/Construction Permanent loan (Section 203k)		
Assumability		Mortgage Origination Date	Assumability Feature
		12/15/89 – present	Assumable by owner/occupant only for $500

Mortgage Insurance	Loan Term		Up-Front MIP	Monthly Premiums Based LTV		
				90 % or Less	90.01 – 95%	Over 95%
	30 Year		1.5	None	.5 to .78LTV	.25 to 78%
	15 Year		1.5		.25 to 78%	

Automated Approval	FHLMC-Loan Prospector, FNMA-DU for FHA, and pmiAURA System for FHA.
Refinancing	Streamline Refinance – With 12 month mortgage payment history and payment reduction, borrowers do not need to re-qualify. Loan amount can only be increased for closing costs with new approval.
Eligible Properties	SFD, 2-4, Condo, & PUD units must be approved – http://entp.hud.gov/idapp/html/condlook.cfm

Income Restrictions	
Qualifying Ratios	29/41. ARMs and Buydowns Qualify at 2nd year rate if LTV is > 95%
Documentation Types	Full and Alternative Documentation
Non-Occupant Co-Borrowers	No restrictions – may not be used for qualifying on 2–4 family properties
Self-Employment	Minimum 2 years
Trailing Spouse	Not allowed

Asset Restrictions	
Cash Reserves	Although cash reserves after closing are not required on FHA insured mortgage transactions (except on 3–4 unit purchase transactions), cash reserves are considered in the risk assessment of all automated underwriting systems.
Gift Letters	Acceptable from any source. Must verify gift, and paper trail. Donor may borrower (secured) funds for down payment.
Seller Contributions	6% of Sales Price, including: buy downs, up-front Mortgage Insurance Premium and mortgage payment protection ins.
Required Contributions	Borrower MUST invest 3% cash in Transaction, including closing costs of down payment.
Borrowed Funds	Must be secured/counted for qualifying

Credit/Borrower Restrictions	
Credit Scores	Not considered
Non-Residential Aliens	The borrower must have a social security number and be eligible to work in the U.S.
Major Derogatory Credit	Significant Derogatory credit may be tolerated with documented extenuating circumstances. Bankruptcy Chapter 7 – 2 years from discharge; Chapter 13 – 1 year from discharge. Foreclosure – 3 years from discharge

Loan amounts vary depending on jurisdiction. See https://entp.hud.gov/idapp/html/hicostlook.cfm for current list.

The VA program acts as a guarantor against foreclosure for eligible veterans. The VA program *guarantees* only a portion of the mortgage against default, as opposed to the FHA loan program, which is 100% insured. The lender still is at risk if the loss in a foreclosure process exceeds the amount of the VA mortgage guaranty.

VA home loans are fixed-rate mortgages with terms of either 15 or 30 years. Since the VA guarantees the mortgage, there is no mortgage insurance. However, the VA requires the borrower to pay a funding fee ranging from 0.5 to 3% for the mortgage (this fee is waived for qualifying disabled veterans). In addition, VA home loans are fully assumable by a qualifying borrower. Assumptions are freely assumable at the same rate and terms, with a credit check; however, the veteran will not receive his or her eligibility back without a substitution of entitlement. For processing assumptions, the lender can charge a $300 fee, and the VA charges its 1.0% funding fee.

Who qualifies for a VA mortgage?

The following table shows what type of service (and for what duration) is required in order to be eligible for a VA loan:

WARTIME		
Service during:	World War II	09/16/40 to 07/25/47
	Korean War	06/27/50 to 01/31/55
	Vietnam	08/05/64 to 05/07/75
	Persian Gulf	08/02/90 to (not yet determined)
PEACETIME		
Service during:		07/26/47 to 06/26/50
		02/01/55 to 08/04/64
		05/08/75 to 09/07/80 (enlisted) to 10/16/81 (officer)

The veteran must have at least 90 days on active duty. Plus he or she must have been discharged under other than dishonorable conditions. If the person served less than the standard 90 days, he or she may be eligible if discharged for a service-connected disability.

If on active duty, the veteran is eligible after having served on continuous active status for at least 90 days. If the person is separated from the service, he or she needs to have had 24 months of continuous duty to be eligible.

A veteran may also be eligible if he or she:

- Was discharged for a service-connected disability

- Is an unremarried spouse of a veteran who died while in the service or from a service-connected disability, or is a spouse of a serviceperson missing in action or a prisoner of war

- Is a commissioned Public Health Service officer, cadet or midshipman at a service academy, officer of the National Oceanic and Atmospheric Administration, or merchant seaman with World War II service

- Has completed a total of at least six years in the Reserves or National Guard.

There is no limit to the number of VA mortgages a veteran can obtain. However, she or he must have remaining *guaranty* for each mortgage.

What types of properties are eligible for VA financing?

The types of properties eligible for VA financing are:

- One- to four-unit properties

- PUDs in approved projects

- Condominiums in approved projects

- New homes

- Manufactured homes

The following items make VA financing different from FHA financing:

- The maximum mortgage amount is not increased for multiple-unit properties.

- Condominiums do not have to have the 51% owner occupancy and do not require an environmental assessment.

- VA appraisals are called *certificates of reasonable value*, or CRVs.

Another notable difference between the FHA and the VA is the selection process of the appraiser. FHA allows the lender to select the appraiser as long as the appraiser is FHA certified, and any state-certified appraiser in good standing is allowed to become FHA certified. In comparison, with VA financing the lender must order an appraisal directly from the VA. The order request can be performed online through The Appraisal System (TAS) at tas.vba.va.gov. The VA then selects an appraiser on a rotating basis from an approved list of appraisers and assigns the appraiser the loan. This process can be problematic resulting in slow and low-quality appraisals. Poor appraisers continually receive assignments because removal of an appraiser can be a lengthy process that can involve appeals. However Rep. Adam Smith (D-Wash.) introduced a bill into Congress entitled the Veterans Appraiser Choice Act (H.R. 1500) allowing the veteran to choose an appraiser from the VA's list of appraiser. A hearing on this legislation was held in June 2003, and unfortunately to date, there is no evidence that Rep. Smith's bill has received traction in Congress. In the interim the VA recently announced that it would add 2,000 new appraisers to its fee panel.

What is the entitlement and maximum loan amount?

Each eligible veteran is given a loan guaranty designated on a form called a *certificate of eligibility*, or COE. This form is obtained through each regional VA office by completing VA Form 26-1880, Request for a Certificate of Eligibility, along with proof of military service. The lender may request a COE online through ACE, the automated certificate of eligibility system. In either case, the veteran *must* have this original form in order to close on a new VA loan.

Full Entitlement

The amount of entitlement has been increasing over the years. The maximum loan guaranty is $36,000 for loan amounts above $56,251 and below $144,000. However, in an attempt to keep pace with home prices, the VA loan program was recently modified with VA bill S.2486, which was enacted January 2005. The bill provides for increasing the maximum VA loan guaranty amount and indexing it annually to 25 percent of the conforming loan limit. For 2006, the conforming loan limit was $417,000; therefore, the present full entitlement is $104,250 for loans in excess of a $144,000 sales price. This means that qualified veterans can obtain a no-down-payment VA loan of up to $417,000.

Although there is no maximum loan amount mandated by the VA, GNMA requires that its exposure be limited to 75% LTV. Therefore, most lenders require that a combination of the guaranty entitlement and any cash down payment equal 25% of the reasonable value or sales price of the property, whichever is less.

The beauty of this loan program is that the entitlement is never exhausted. It may be utilized to guarantee a loan on a veteran's home, but as soon as that home is sold and the loan is paid off, the veteran has that portion of entitlement back to use again. The only way to restore eligibility is to sell the home or have the loan assumed by a qualified veteran who is willing to substitute his or her eligibility for that of the original veteran. On a one-time basis, if the veteran has repaid the prior VA loan in full but has not disposed of the property purchased with the prior VA loan, his or her entitlement can be restored.

Partial Entitlement

If a veteran has already used a portion of his or her eligibility and the existing VA loan will not be paid off, any partial remaining eligibility would be available for use. The amount of guaranty available is the difference between the originally used entitlement and the current maximum of $36,000 for loan amounts up to $144,000.

For example, a veteran obtained a VA loan for $25,000 in 1974. He or she would have used a $12,500 guaranty entitlement (the maximum available at that time). In this case the veteran's partial entitlement would be $23,500.

Remember, lenders require the guaranty to be 25% of the property value or sales price. In this case the veteran would qualify for a $94,000 loan amount with no down payment.

Key Note: The law requires a veteran obtaining a VA guaranteed loan to certify that he or she will be occupying the property. In the example above, the veteran would have to intend to occupy the new property.

One exception to the owner occupancy law is the Interest Rate Reduction Refinancing Loans (IRRRLs).

What are the closing costs for VA loans?

There is a one-time charge (or funding fee), which the veteran pays to reimburse the VA for administrative costs. The VA allows the funding fee to be financed, or added to the base maximum loan amount up to the Ginnie Mae loan limit, or $417,000. Veterans using their VA eligibility for a second time must pay a higher fee. In addition, newly eligible borrowers— specifically, reservists—pay a higher premium than do normal veterans. Disabled veterans are exempt from payment of the funding fee.

The cost of the funding fee stated as a percentage of the mortgage amount is as follows:

Funding Fee	Transaction Type
2.00%	Purchase with less than 5% down or refinance
3.00%	Purchase with less than 5% down with restored eligibility
1.50%	Purchase with less than 10% down
1.25%	Purchase with 10% or more down
0.50%	Streamline refinance
2.75%	Reservist—purchase with more than 5% down
2.25%	Reservist—purchase with 10% or more down
0.75%	Reservist premium (except streamline)

Nonallowable Fees

Like FHA, the VA does not allow the veteran to pay miscellaneous fees above and beyond the origination fee. Therefore, lender fees such as tax service fees, lender inspections, and other fees are typically paid by the seller. These fees cannot be charged on refinances.

There is a limit of 4% of the sales price that the seller can *contribute* toward the borrower's costs in the transaction; however, normal discount points and closing costs do not count toward the 4% limitation.

What are the benefits of the VA loan program?

There are several advantages to the VA loan program:

- *Higher ratios.* The VA debt ratio is 41%, compared with the conventional 28/36% debt ratio.

- *Residual income*. Residual income may be utilized if the ratio is higher than 41%. (We discuss residual income in more detail in Chapter 5.)

- *Cash requirements*. The VA has the following cash requirements, which are clearly less than those of any other major mortgage source:
  1. The down payment is zero.
  2. The funding fee can be financed.
  3. The seller is allowed to pay up to 4% toward closing costs and an additional 4% to the benefit of the borrower.
  4. The veteran can receive gift funds for any and all cash requirements.
  5. There is no requirement for cash reserves after closing.

What about credit?

Another significant benefit of the VA loan program is the aggressive credit standards. The VA loan program is not credit score–driven, like most traditional loan programs today. Currently, the general guidelines require the borrower to have no late payments on credit debt and no collections or judgments in the previous 12 months. At the time of application, there can be a balance on collections or judgments so long as the actual debt was incurred more than 12 months prior and the balance is paid to zero before the closing of the loan. The benefit of this program is that if the veteran has debt that needs to be paid off prior to closing the loan, the allowable 4% from the seller (benefit of the veteran) can be used to pay for this.

Chapter 7 Bankruptcy

The bankruptcy must be discharged for two years. If a Chapter 7 was discharged within one to two years, a borrower *may* qualify if *both* these conditions are met:

1. The borrower has obtained consumer items on credit subsequent to the bankruptcy and has made payments satisfactorily over a continued period of time.

2. The bankruptcy was caused by circumstances beyond the control of the applicant, e.g., loss of employment, prolonged strikes, severe illness.

Chapter 13 Bankruptcy

A borrower may qualify if the applicant has made satisfactory payments for at least 12 months and the trustee or bankruptcy judge approves the new mortgage transaction.

Foreclosure

The foreclosure must be over three years old. If a foreclosure or deed-in-lieu of foreclosure exists within the last three years, the VA may approve if a well-documented reason can be provided (the applicant must show that the foreclosure was totally outside his or her control).

Figure 4-4 summarizes the requirements for a VA loan.

The First-Time Home Buyer and Tax-Exempt State and Local Housing Programs

Tax-Exempt Revenue Bond Issues

The Federal Bond Subsidy Act authorizes state and local governments to issue tax-exempt revenue bonds for the purpose of funding loans to low- and middle-income home purchasers. The bonds are attractive to investors because the interest from them is *tax-free* from federal and state income tax. These lower interest rate bonds finance mortgages that also carry interest rates lower than the current market rate.

Characteristics of bond programs are:

- Home prices are generally limited to 90% of average home prices.

- Targeted borrowers have moderate to low incomes. Incomes that are not more than 100% of the median income for the area are considered moderate incomes, and incomes that are less than 80% of the income for the area are considered low incomes.

- Targeted areas are approved as qualified census tracts (in other words, areas of chronic economic distress).

FIGURE 4-4
VA Matrix

LTV Matrix						
Transaction	Owner Occupied		2nd Home	Investor	Property Type	Loan Amount at 100%	Eligible for Agency Sale
	LTV	CLTV	LTV	LTV			
Purchase or Rate and Term Refinance	100%		N/A	N/A	Single Family, Condo, 2-4 Family	$240,000	$322,700
Cash Out	90%		N/A	N/A	Single Family, Condo	$240,000	$322,700
Refinancing	Streamline Refinance – with 12-month mortgage payment history and payment reduction, borrowers do not re-qualify. Loan amount can only be increased for closing costs with new appraisal.						
Programs Offered	Fixed Rate Mortgages and GPM and in some areas, GEM's						
Mortgage Insurance	VA funding fee is in lieu of insurance. See "Risk-Based" Premium charts						
Eligible Properties	SFD, 2–4, Condo, PUD – Condo's and PUD units must be approved						

Eligible Borrowers	ERA	Dates	Time Required
	WW II	9/16/40 – 7/25/47	90 days
	Post WW II	7/26/47 – 6/26/50	181 days
	Korean	6/27/50 – 1/31/55	90 days
	Post Korean	2/1/55 – 8/4/64	181 days
	Vietnam	8/5/64 – 5/7/75 **Note**: The Vietnam Era began 2/28/61 for those individuals who served in the Republic of Vietnam	90 days
	Post Vietnam	5/8/75 – 9/7/80 5/8/75 – 10/16/81 9/8/80 – 8/1/90 10/17/81 – 8/1/90	Enlisted – 181 days Officers – 181 days Enlisted – 2 years** Officers – 2 years**
	Persian Gulf	8/20/90 – Present	2 years **Note: The veteran must have served 2 years or the full period, which called or ordered to active duty (at least 90 days during wartime and 181 during peacetime.)

Secondary Financing	Allowed. Note must be at least 5 years in length. Since VA is no money down formula, 2nd mortgage would be used to exceed the maximum financing of $240,000/$322,700
Automated Approval	FHLMC-Loan Prospector, FNMA-DO/DU, and pmiAURA System for VA
Assumability	$500 Fee and the Borrower must qualify. No release of liability

Income Restrictions	
Qualifying Ratios	41/41
Documentation Types	Full, Alternative Documentation
Non-Occupant Co-Borrowers	Veterans and their spouse only. Eligible veterans have served continuous active duty for at least the time frames listed and have an honorable release or discharge.
Self-Employed	Minimum 2 years

Asset Restrictions	
Cash Reserves	None required
Gift Letters	May come from any source not involved in the transaction. Must verify donor, transfer and receipt of funds.
Seller Contributions	4% of sales price, not including points. Transaction may be structured so that borrower pays no money at closing, but borrowers may not receive cash back at closing.
Borrowed Funds	Funds may be borrowed – must be counted for qualifying

Credit Restrictions	
Multiple Properties	Number of VA loans is limited by entitlement
Credit Scores	Not considered
Major Derogatory	Significant derogatory credit may be acceptable with extenuating circumstances

- The programs provide leniency in qualification standards for targeted areas.

- At least 20% of funds from each bond issue must be available for lending in targeted areas.

While there are significant savings with a below-market interest rate, there is one important aspect to consider. The borrower may be subject to a penalty or *recapture tax* if the home is sold before the incentive period expires. The amount of recapture tax is determined by:

- The date of the sale or transfer.

- The borrower's income in relation to the adjusted qualifying income in the year of sale or transfer.

- The gain from the sale or transfer (if there is no gain, there is no recapture tax). A sale or transfer after nine years does not incur a recapture tax.

These bond issues specifically target first-time home buyers and therefore require no ownership interest in real property for the previous three years. Other first-time home buyer programs are:

- Fannie Mae Community Home Buyer's Program

- Freddie Mac HomeSteps Program

Rural Housing Service

The U.S. Department of Agriculture Rural Housing Service (RHS) provides loans to people in rural areas with low to moderate income. The closing costs are minimal, and no down payment is required. Through Section 502 Guaranteed Rural Housing Loan Program, lenders and mortgage brokers can provide financing to borrowers who have adequate credit history and income, but may lack a down payment. The RHS works with private lenders, providing a guarantee of 90% of the amount of the loan. Loans are made to individuals for up to 100% of the appraised value of the home.

Eligibility

Applicants must be U.S. citizens or permanent resident aliens. The program finances only the purchase of a residential, owner-occupied property, and it does not provide financing for farms. The borrower must have an income of up to 115% of the median income for the area. The program provides 100% financing with no mortgage insurance and no loan limits. In addition, applicants must have reasonable credit histories. The lender determines the eligibility by standard qualifying ratios.

Terms

Loans are for 30 years. The interest rate on the loan must be fixed and is set by the lender. The interest rate cannot exceed the rate specified in the Notice of Funding Availability (NOFA) published yearly in the *Federal Register*.

Standards

Housing must be modest in size, design, and cost. Houses, whether they are constructed, purchased, or rehabilitated, must meet the voluntary national model building code adopted by the state and RHS thermal and site standards. New manufactured homes must be on permanent foundations. Existing manufactured homes can be guaranteed only if they are already financed with an RHS direct or guaranteed loan.

Program Guidelines Quiz

1. Your borrower is a veteran and has full loan entitlement, and the sales price of the home is $359,650. How much would he need for a down payment?
   A. 0
   B. $2,500
   C. $7,500

2. A conventional/conforming loan is a loan that is eligible for purchase through which government-sponsored enterprise?
   A. HUD
   B. FHA
   C. FNMA

3. A jumbo loan will typically carry a little higher rate because the loan amount is over the current conforming loan amount of $359,600.
   A. True
   B. False

4. Each eligible veteran is given a loan guaranty entitlement and is eligible for a no down payment loan of up to:
   A. $200,000
   B. $417,000
   C. $333,700

5. On a conventional/conforming mortgage, what is the least amount of cash that a borrower is required to invest in any purchase transaction?
   A. 5%
   B. 3%
   C. 6%

6. What does a nonconforming mortgage loan mean?
   A. It is a subprime or jumbo loan.
   B. It does not meet FNMA or FHLMC guidelines.
   C. Both A and B.

7. There are advantages to the eligibility process of an FHA loan. Which advantage is incorrect?
   A. FHA allows two or more borrowers to finance a home.
   B. FHA allows an FHA loan to be assumable.
   C. FHA allows the seller to contribute up to 7% without affecting the loan amount.

8. If your borrower were seeking a mortgage loan for a second home, which loan program would you recommend?
   A. An FHA loan

   B. A VA loan

   C. A conforming loan

9. There are several advantages to a VA loan. Which advantage is incorrect?

   A. Zero down payment.

   B. The veteran can receive gift funds for any or all cash requirements.

   C. There are no seller contributions allowed.

10. A borrower is eligible for an FHA loan if he is delinquent or in default of a government student loan.

   A. True

   B. False

11. What is the allowable debt-to-income ratio, most commonly used by FNMA, with a mortgage to 95% loan-to-value?

   A. 29/41

   B. 28/36

   C. 45/41

12. The only reason you would choose a subprime loan for your borrower is if she has bad or poor credit.

   A. True

   B. False

13. On an FHA loan the borrower cannot be charged certain miscellaneous lender fees. Which of the following fees is allowed to be charged?

   A. Processing fee

   B. Underwriting fee

   C. Origination fee

14. The Rural Housing Service guarantees mortgages for rural properties. Which of the properties listed below qualifies for this program?

   A. An owner-occupied single-family residence

   B. A farm

   C. A condo

15. On a conventional conforming mortgage, to satisfy the cash requirement needed for closing costs, your borrower's loan is 95% loan-to-value. Which one of the following options does he have?
   A. 10% seller contribution
   B. 6% seller contribution
   C. A well-documented gift letter from an immediate family member can be used as long as a paper trail can be established.

16. Which type of property is *not* eligible for a conventional conforming mortgage?
   A. A property with partial commercial usage
   B. A PUD
   C. An approved FNMA condo

17. There are three government agencies that insure mortgages. Which agency below is *not* a government agency?
   A. FNMA
   B. VA
   C. RHS

18. What is the greatest disadvantage of an FHA loan?
   A. The 3% a borrower must invest
   B. The up-front mortgage insurance
   C. The monthly homeowner's insurance

19. FHA requires a minimum of how many years from the discharge of a Chapter 7 bankruptcy?
   A. 1
   B. 2
   C. 3

20. Lenders are able to offer lower rates on an FHA loan because an FHA loan is insured by the government. In comparison, what does a VA loan do?
   A. Insures the full amount
   B. Insures only a portion of the mortgage
   C. Guarantees only a portion of the mortgage

Answers to the quiz can be found at the end of Part One.

CHAPTER 5

MORTGAGE FINANCE

The tragedy in life doesn't lie in not reaching your goal.
The tragedy lies in having no goal to reach.

—Benjamin Mays

QUALIFYING RATIOS

In determining a borrower's ability to repay a mortgage loan, lenders rely on a mathematical formula that determines the maximum debt-to-income ratios used for qualification purposes. The program type and loan-to-value determine the maximum ratios allowed.

The Loan-to-Value Ratio

The loan-to-value (LTV) is a ratio that determines the percentage or portion of the loan amount relative to the purchase price or appraised value (whichever is less) of the property. To determine the LTV, the loan amount is divided by the appraised value or purchase price.

The calculation is

$$\frac{\text{Loan amount}}{\text{Appraised value or purchase price}} = \text{LTV}$$

So, for example, let's say the loan amount is $200,000 and the appraised value is $380,000. Then

$$\frac{\$200,000 \text{ (loan amount)}}{\$380,000 \text{ (appraised value)}} = 52.63\% \text{ (LTV)}$$

LTV-DOWN PAYMENT EXAMPLE

5% down payment = 95% LTV
10% down payment = 90% LTV
15% down payment = 85% LTV
20% down payment = 80% LTV

When there are two mortgage liens, there is a *combined loan-to-value* (CLTV). The combined loan-to-value ratio is the sum of *all* mortgages divided by the appraised value or purchase price (whichever is less) of the home.

For example, suppose we have a house with two mortgages:

$100,000	Appraised value or sales price
$80,000	First mortgage lien
$10,000	Second mortgage lien

Then

$$\frac{\$80,000 + \$10,000 \text{ (sum of the mortgages)}}{\$100,000 \text{ (appraised value)}} = 90\% \text{ (CLTV)}$$

(In this case, the LTV is 80%.)

Housing and Debt Ratios

The lender ratio qualification (see Figure 5-1) includes the calculation of both the housing and debt ratios.

How do you qualify your borrower for a mortgage loan?

The first step in qualifying a borrower is to measure the percentage of gross monthly income (GMI). This is the borrower's

FIGURE 5-1
Lender Ratio Qualification

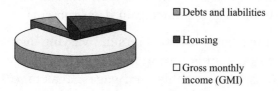

☐ Debts and liabilities

■ Housing

☐ Gross monthly
   income (GMI)

salary *before* any taxes are deducted. To calculate the GMI, divide the annual salary by 12 (months). Say the borrower earns $48,000 yearly. Then

$$\text{GMI} = \frac{\$48,000}{12} = \$4,000$$

The reason you need to know the gross monthly salary is that it serves as the denominator (the lower part) of the calculation of both the housing and debt ratios. These ratios are described in detail in the sections that follow.

What is residual income?

The amount left over after housing, taxes, and debts is what the lender refers to as *residual income*. If there is a high residual income, this can be an excellent compensating factor to justify higher ratios than generally allowed.

GMI	$4,000
Housing	− 900
Monthly debts	− 400
	$2,700 Residual income

The Housing Ratio

The housing ratio, also known as the *front-end* ratio, has the following components:

- Principal and interest payment

- 1/12 of the annual real estate tax

- 1/12 of the annual premium for homeowner's insurance

- Homeowner's association (HOA) dues if the property is a condo or PUD (planned unit development)

Each program that a lender offers has varying qualifying ratios. The maximum front-end ratio for conforming loans is typically 28%. That is, the monthly mortgage payment (PITI) cannot exceed 28% of the gross monthly income. The debt, or back-end, ratio is the total monthly debt obligation, including the monthly mortgage or rent payment, divided by the gross monthly income. The maximum debt ratio for conforming loans is typically 36%. That is, the total monthly debt obligations must not exceed 36% of the gross monthly income. You will see these ratios expressed as 28/36. The list below shows some typical front-end ratios.

Housing (Front-End) Ratios (Generally Accepted)

28% for conforming loans

29% for FHA loans

33% for some jumbo programs

Let's look at an example:

$95,000.00 Conventional mortgage	Housing Expenses (PITI) Would Be:	
$100,000	Sales price	$764.39	PI—principal and interest
9.0%	Interest rate	$104.16	T—monthly taxes
$1,250.00	Annual property taxes	$ 19.79	I—monthly homeowner's insurance
$285.00	Annual homeowner's insurance	$ 0.00	HOA dues
$0.00	Monthly HOA dues	PITI = $888.34	

How do you know how much to calculate for property taxes and insurance? Property taxes and insurance figures vary from region to region. However, as a general rule property taxes are about 1.25% of the purchase price. So, say the purchase price is $100,000. Then

$100,000 × 1.25% = $1,250 annual property taxes

Homeowner's insurance is usually about 0.25% of the loan amount. For a loan of $95,000, then, you would figure

$95,000 × 0.25% = $237.50 annual homeowner's insurance

Now let's calculate the housing ratio:

$$\frac{\$888.34 \text{ (PITI)}}{\$4,000 \text{ (GMI)}} = 22.21, \text{ or } 22\% \text{ (rounded)}$$

The borrower's total housing ratio is 22%. Is this ratio acceptable? Yes, because the maximum allowable housing ratio is 28%.

The Debt-to-Income Ratio

The debt-to-income ratio, sometimes called the *back-end* ratio or simply the debt ratio, adds monthly liabilities to the housing expense to calculate the borrower's monthly debt.

What monthly liabilities are included in the debt ratio?

Generally it is all the debt that appears on a borrower's credit report. Credit card debt is considered *revolving* debt. Car loans and finance company loans are considered *installment* debt. Installment loans that have less than a 10-month period usually can be excluded from this ratio. A car *lease* and credit cards do not apply to the 10-month period. They are always counted. The one debt that can be excluded from the debt column is a cosigned debt. Generally, lenders will not count a cosigned debt if the borrower is capable of providing verification that the other party makes the monthly payments. (Typically canceled checks for the past 12 months are sufficient verification.)

Another debt to consider is rental income. Lenders typically use 75% of actual rental income received and subtract that income from the mortgage payment (PITI) of the rental property.

All the following liabilities are considered when calculating a debt ratio:

- Credit card obligations
- Installment loans

- Car loans

- Student loans

- Any deductions on the borrower's pay stub (e.g., a credit union loan)

- Alimony

- Child support

- Rental property expenses

- Regular business expenses (self-employed borrowers)

- Cosigned loans

Here are some generally accepted debt ratios for different types of loans:

36% for conforming mortgages

38–40% for some jumbo programs

41% for FHA and VA

50–55% for subprime loans

Here is a list of some common housing and debt ratios:

28/36 for conforming

33/38 for prime loans

29/41 for FHA mortgages

41/41 for VA mortgages

50–55 for debt ratio only for subprime products (depends on LTV)

Note that lower loan-to-values allow for more flexibility when it comes to ratio calculations. Also automated underwriting systems allow for higher ratios in some cases.

Let's use the same example we used in the previous section. We can add the borrower debts to determine if his debt ratio qualifies for a conforming loan. The borrower's GMI is $4,000, and his total monthly debts are $400.

$764.39	PI—principal and interest
104.16	T—monthly taxes
19.79	I—monthly homeowner's insurance
0.00	HOA—homeowner's association dues
$888.34	PITI

Now let's calculate the debt ratio (housing plus liabilities divided by GMI):

$$\$888.34 + \$400 = \$1{,}288.34$$

$$\frac{1{,}288.34}{4{,}000} = 32.21$$

Again your borrower is within the conforming guidelines because his debt ratio is 32%, below the required 36%.

Using Ratios to Prequalify

Borrowers frequently want to find out how much of a mortgage they can afford without officially applying for a loan. You can do this by prequalifying your borrowers. *Prequalification* is the process of determining how much money a prospective home buyer will be eligible to borrow prior to the application of a loan.

You know your borrower's income. Now you want to determine the maximum mortgage amount and payment amount for which he qualifies. To accomplish this you will need to work the ratios backward. Instead of GMI divided by housing and debt ratio, your equation will be:

Step 1 Housing ratio

> GMI
> $\times 28\%$
> PITI (maximum allowable mortgage payment)

Step 2 Debt ratio

> GMI
> $\times 36\%$
> PITI + debts (maximum allowable mortgage payment with debts)

Let's use an example. With a monthly income of $4,000 and debts of $400, how much of a mortgage payment can your borrower afford?

Step 1 Housing ratio

$$\begin{array}{r} \$4,000 \\ \underline{\times 28\%} \\ \$1,120 \text{ (max. PITI)} \end{array}$$

Step 2 Debt ratio

$$\begin{array}{r} \$4,000 \\ \underline{\times 36\%} \\ \$1,440 - \$400 = \$1,040 \text{ (max. PITI)} \end{array}$$

Since debts are $400, we deduct that from $1,440 to arrive at the required maximum allowable payment. The maximum mortgage payment is the lower of these two figures, in this case $1,040. If you use $1,120, the ratio would be too high. Take a look:

Step 1

$$\frac{\$1,120 + \$400}{\$4,000} = 38\% \quad \text{D/R } too\ high$$

Step 2

$$\frac{\$1,040 + \$400}{\$4,000} = 36\% \quad \text{D/R } OK$$

After determining the maximum allowable mortgage payment, your next step is to calculate the maximum mortgage amount. At this point you bring in the important factors:

- Interest rate
- Monthly insurance, taxes, and HOA dues
- Term of the mortgage

For our example, let's assume the following:

- The interest rate for a fixed-rate mortgage is 7.50%.
- Taxes and insurance have been rounded to $130.
- The term is 30 years.

To calculate:

Monthly mortgage payment	$1,040
Subtract taxes, insurance, and HOA	− 130
Maximum mortgage payment	$ 910

To determine the loan amount, divide the maximum mortgage payment by the payment factor.

For example, by using the payment factor from Table 5-1 on the following page, the calculation is as follows:

$$\frac{\$910}{6.99 \text{ (payment factor for 30-year term)}} = \$130,186$$

What if your borrower needs a higher loan amount? Let's assume your borrower wants to qualify for a loan amount of $144,000. To calculate, divide the maximum mortgage payment ($910) by the loan amount ($144,000):

$$\frac{\$910}{144} = 6.35$$

If we look at Table 5-1, the nearest payment factor to 6.35 we can find is 6.32—the payment factor on a 30-year mortgage at an interest rate of 6.50%. Therefore, if your borrower has to qualify for a $144,000 loan amount, instead of qualifying the borrower for an 8% 30-year fixed-rate loan, you would need to drop the interest rate by 2%.

How can you lower the rate by 2%? You might suggest an adjustable-rate mortgage or a temporary buydown, both of which can achieve a lower interest rate in the first few years of the loan, enabling your borrower to qualify.

Most loan officers prequalify borrowers with software programs (Quick Qualifier), and we cover prequalification with a financial calculator later in the chapter.

TABLE 5-1
Payment Factor Chart

Interest Rate	Mortgage Term		
	30 Years	20 Years	15 Years
4.00%	4.77	6.06	7.40
4.50%	5.07	6.33	7.65
5.00%	5.37	6.60	7.91
5.25%	5.52	6.74	8.04
5.50%	5.68	6.88	8.17
5.75%	5.84	7.02	8.30
6.00%	6.00	7.16	8.44
6.25%	6.16	7.31	8.57
6.50%	6.32	7.46	8.71
6.75%	6.49	7.60	8.85
7.00%	6.65	7.75	8.99
7.25%	6.82	7.90	9.13
7.50%	6.99	8.06	9.27
7.75%	7.16	8.21	9.41
8.00%	7.34	8.36	9.56
8.25%	7.51	8.52	9.70
8.50%	7.69	8.68	9.85
8.75%	7.87	8.84	9.99
9.00%	8.05	9.00	10.14
9.25%	8.23	9.16	10.29
9.50%	8.41	9.32	10.44
9.75%	8.59	9.49	10.59
10.00%	8.78	9.65	10.75

Note: Monthly P&I payment per $1,000 of loan amount.

MORTGAGE MATH

The interest rate is the effective rate paid on borrowed money and is expressed as a percentage of 100. Interest rates and points

TABLE 5-2
*Converting Common Fractions
to Decimals*

Fraction	Decimal
1/8	0.125
1/4	0.250
3/8	0.375
1/2	0.500
5/8	0.625
3/4	0.750
7/8	0.875

are based on fractions. Basic math has taught us that fractions are expressed as a numerator over a denominator. In mortgage lending, rates and points are written in decimals. Since a loan officer works with fractions and decimals on a daily basis, you must be familiar with these conversions.

So how do you convert a fraction to a decimal? You divide the numerator by the denominator. It is done like this:

$$\frac{\text{Numerator}}{\text{Denominator}} = \text{factor} \qquad \frac{1}{8} = 0.125 \qquad \frac{1}{2} = 0.5$$

The smallest fraction commonly found in the mortgage business is 1/8 (1/8 = 0.125). As an aid to future conversions, see the conversions shown in Table 5-2.

How to Read a Rate Sheet

What is a point?
Simply put, a point is equal to 1% of the loan amount. A point is the price for the loan and is usually paid by the borrower at closing. A discount fee is what the borrower pays up front to discount the rate over time.

A basis point is 1/100 of a point. Normally this figure is used when discussing yields or rates in the secondary market, because this is the smallest possible fraction. For example, a rate change of one-quarter of a percent = 25 basis points.

Identifying the cost and rebate

Understanding the rates of the lender you do business with is key in finding the right program for your borrower. First you want to identify the cost rebate format of the rate sheet. It will look like this:

Interest Rate	Fee/Rebate
5.375%	2.000
5.500%	1.000
6.000%	0.000
6.250%	−1.000
7.000%	−2.000

In this example, the rate sheet shows that there is a fee of 1% (cost) of the loan amount (or 1 point) for a loan with an interest rate of 5.50%. At the same time there is a rebate or overage of 1% of the loan amount (or 1 point) if the rate sold to the borrower is 6.25%. A rate of 6.0% represents par pricing where there is *no* cost or rebate.

Table 5-3 presents an example of a rate sheet. See also Figure 5-2.

What is an add-on or adjustment?

All lenders have a different format for their rate sheets. However, all rate sheets will identify any adjustments, better known in the industry as *add-ons*.

Let's assume you want to price a refinance loan, where your borrower is taking some cash out on a rental property (non-owner-occupied) and his estimated loan-to-value is 71%. By using the example rate sheet shown in Table 5-3, you have two add ons. To price your loan, you start by determining whether you want to include a rebate. For this exercise let's assume you want to receive a 1-point rebate. Therefore your start rate is 6.25%. Now you will need to add 0.50% for the cash-out and an additional 2.00% for a non-owner-occupied (n/o/o) property. For example:

```
   6.25%
 +0.50%  (for cash-out refinance)
 ─────
   6.75%
 +2.0%   (for n/o/o property)
 ─────
   8.75%  (total rate)
```

TABLE 5-3
Sample Rate Sheet

ABC Mortgage Company
123 Main Street
Los Angeles, CA 90001
Tel: (800) 888-8888
Fax: (800) 999-9999

Program Name		Adjustment to Fee	
Rate	30 Yr	Ln amt $50,000–$99,999	0.50
5.000	2.500	Ln amt $30,000–$49,999	1.50
5.375	2.000	Refi cash-out	0.50
5.500	1.000	95% 2-unit purchase	0.50
6.000	0.000	3–4 units	1.00
6.250	−1.000	CLTV > 90%	0.25
6.500	−1.500	CLTV > 95%	0.50
7.000	−2.000	N/O/O* < 80%	2.00
		N/O/O > 80.01–90%	2.50
		Manufactured homes	0.50

*N/O/O means non-owner-occupied.

On conventional loans the rate sheet will include the pricing for 15-day, 30-day, and 45-day rate locks. Notice that the longer the lock-in time, the higher the rate.

What do I have to charge?

Pricing with 0 discount is referred to as *par pricing*. In the above example, 6.00% was the par price. Pricing *below par* means that the rate must be discounted; pricing *above par* means that the lender will pay a premium or rebate money to the loan origina-tor. If, as a loan officer, your company requires that you charge the borrower a 1-point origination fee, then what do you tell your borrower is the interest rate?

Using the above example, the rate would be 6.00% with a 1-point fee to the borrower. If the rate sold was a 5.375% inter-est rate, which requires a 2-point discount, the loan officer would quote 5.375%, 2 discount plus 1-point origination fee. If the rate sold to the borrower is 6.250%, the lender would receive

FIGURE 5-2
Example of a Rate Sheet

| 11:00 AM | CA |

ABC MORTGAGE COMPANY
123 Main Street
Los Angeles, CA 90001
(800) 888-8888
Fax: (800) 999-9999

Conforming Rates

30 Year Fixed (CF30)	Best Effort		
Rate	15 Day	30 Day	45 Day
5.625	97.375	97.000	96.750
5.750	98.500	98.250	98.000
5.875	99.125	98.750	98.500
6.000	99.625	99.375	99.125
6.125	100.125	99.750	99.500
6.250	100.875	100.625	100.375
6.375	101.375	101.250	100.875
6.500	101.875	101.625	101.375
6.625	102.250	102.000	101.750
6.750	102.500	102.250	102.000
6.875	102.750	102.500	102.375
7.000	103.125	102.875	102.750
7.125	103.500	103.125	103.000
7.250	103.625	103.625	103.625

15 Year Fixed (CF15)	Best Effort		
Rate	15 Day	30 Day	45 Day
4.875	97.875	97.500	97.250
5.000	98.250	98.000	97.750
5.125	98.750	98.375	98.125
5.250	99.375	99.000	98.875
5.375	99.875	99.500	99.375
5.500	100.375	100.000	99.750
5.625	100.750	100.375	100.125
5.750	101.250	100.875	100.650
5.875	101.500	101.250	101.000
6.000	102.000	101.625	101.375
6.125	102.250	102.000	101.750
6.250	102.625	102.375	102.125
6.375	102.875	102.625	102.375
6.500	103.250	103.125	103.000

20 Year Fixed (CF20)	Best Effort		
Rate	15 Day	30 Day	45 Day
5.375	97.250	97.000	96.750
5.500	97.750	97.500	97.250
5.625	98.250	98.000	97.625
5.750	99.250	99.000	98.750
5.875	99.750	99.500	99.250
6.000	100.250	100.000	99.750
6.125	100.500	100.250	100.000
6.250	101.000	100.750	100.500
6.375	101.500	101.250	101.000
6.500	101.750	101.500	101.250
6.625	101.750	101.500	101.250
6.750	102.000	101.625	101.500
7.000	102.500	102.250	102.125

10 Year Fixed (CF10)	Best Effort		
Rate	15 Day	30 Day	45 Day
5.125	99.625	99.500	99.125
5.250	100.000	99.875	99.500
5.375	100.500	100.250	100.000
5.500	100.875	100.625	100.250
5.625	101.250	100.875	100.625
5.750	101.375	101.125	100.875
5.875	101.500	101.375	101.000
6.000	101.875	101.625	101.250
6.125	102.000	101.750	101.500
6.250	102.250	102.000	101.750
6.375	102.500	102.250	102.125
6.500	102.875	102.625	102.500
6.625	103.125	102.875	102.625
6.750	103.250	103.250	103.250

1YR ARM (C1YT)	Best Effort		Margin/ Caps 2.75/2/2/6
Rate	15 Day	30 Day	45 Day
2.500	98.500	98.375	98.375
2.625	98.750	98.625	98.625
2.750	99.000	98.875	98.875
2.875	99.250	99.125	99.125
3.000	99.375	99.250	99.250
3.125	99.625	99.500	99.500
3.250	99.750	99.625	99.625
3.375	99.875	99.750	99.750
3.500	99.875	99.750	99.750
3.625	99.875	99.750	99.750
3.750	100.000	99.875	99.875
3.875	100.000	99.875	99.875
4.000	100.000	99.875	99.875
4.125	100.125	100.000	100.000

3/1 ARM (C3YT)	Best Effort		Margin/ Caps 2.75/2/2/6
Rate	15 Day	30 Day	45 Day
2.875	98.000	97.875	97.875
3.000	98.250	98.125	98.125
3.125	98.500	98.375	98.375
3.250	98.750	98.625	98.625
3.375	99.000	98.875	98.875
3.500	99.250	99.125	99.125
3.625	99.500	99.375	99.375
3.750	99.625	99.500	99.500
3.875	99.875	99.750	99.750
4.000	100.125	100.000	100.000
4.125	100.250	100.125	100.125
4.250	100.375	100.250	100.250
4.375	100.500	100.375	100.375
4.500	100.625	100.500	100.500

The Pricing is indication only, actual pricing may vary depending on market condition and loan characteristics. These rates are subject to change without proir notice. This information is prepared for use by Real Estate professionals only. It is not for consumer use and is not an advertisement as defined in Regulation Z section 226.2.

the point origination fee as a rebate, and the borrower would be charged 6.250% interest with 0 discount and 0 origination.

Should I suggest a lower rate with more points or a higher rate with lower points?

When comparing different products with different point options, we can easily adjust for each point by adding 1% to the starting rate for each extra point charged. Each extra point is paid back over a period of time (typically three to five years) through a lower payment.

EXAMPLE

$100,000 mortgage, 30-year fixed rate
Fixed rate of 8.00% with 2 points versus

Option 1:   8.00% with 0 points   Monthly payment $733.76
Option 2:   7.50% with 2 points   Monthly payment $699.21

Monthly savings at 7.50% $34.55   Months to recover cost
                                   of points:

Extra cost of points (2) $2,000.00 $\dfrac{\$2,000}{\$34.55} = 57.88$ months, or

                                     4.82 years

Now to the question, should you advise your borrower to pay the extra points? That will depend on how long your borrower plans to stay in her home. If we use the example above, your borrower would not accrue any savings until she has been in her property for five years. One consideration for your borrower is that the points are prepaid interest and are usually tax deductible. Don't forget to advise your borrower to check with her tax consultant for advice on this matter.

Using a Financial Calculator

There are several Web sites that provide free use of a mortgage calculator. You will also most likely have an origination software program that calculates these figures for you. However, as a mortgage originator, it is necessary for you to know how to

FIGURE 5-3
Texas Instruments Financial Calculator

use a financial calculator. The calculator we use here is a Texas Instruments financial calculator (see Figure 5-3).

The main keystrokes are as follows:

PMT = payment

PV   = loan amount

N   = term or number of payments (e.g., 360 for 30 years)

I/Y   = interest rate

CPT = compute

The financial calculator will enable you to compute basic mortgage equations. We will take a look at the most commonly used equations.

You will encounter the most common equation when you are computing a mortgage payment. To compute the monthly payment, you specify the exact loan amount, interest rate, and duration of the loan (in months).

Example

Enter loan amount (**PV**)	$150,000
Enter interest rate (**I/Y**)	7.50%
Enter the term (**N**)	360 (months)
Press **CPT** (compute)	
Then press **PMT**	$1,050.30

To determine the maximum mortgage amount, you will need to specify gross income, monthly debts, term, and interest rate.

Example

$4,000/mo × 36% (debt ratio)	$1,440 (maximum PITI)
Subtract debt	−$400
Subtract taxes and insurance	−$130
Enter P&I as payment	$ 910 (press 910 and then **PMT**)
Enter rate	7.50% (press 7.50 and then **I/Y**)
Compute loan amount	$130,146 (press **CPT** and then **PV**)

For a conforming loan program your borrower will need a 5% down payment. So to calculate the actual sales price of the home, you will divide the loan amount by the loan-to-value. For example:

$$\$130,146 \div 95\% = \$136,996 \text{ (sales price)}$$

What if your borrower found a home and wants to know how much income he needs to have in order to qualify for this home? In this case you will specify the sales price, interest rate, and loan term.

Example

Sales price $150,000 × 95%	$142,500 (press **PV** button)
Interest rate 7.50%	7.50 (press **I/Y** button)
Loan term 360	360 (press **N** button)
Compute payment	$996.38 (press **CPT** button and then **PV**)
Add taxes and insurance	$200.00
Total	$1,196.38
Divide by qualifying ratio	28%
Monthly income required	$4,272.79

CLOSING COSTS

There are certain standard costs associated with all mortgage transactions. As a loan officer, you must have a clear knowledge of each closing cost in order to help your customer better understand that not all loan charges are *origination* fees; in fact, there are *necessary* costs associated with a mortgage transaction. The breakdown of each fee is carefully itemized in both the good faith estimate given at the time of application and the settlement statement (referred to as HUD-1) given at the closing of the loan. The borrower will be surprised to discover that the loan fee is actually a very small amount of the total closing costs.

There are four categories of closing costs:

- Loan fees or points
- Third-party fees, referred to as *hard costs*—fees charged by service providers in a loan transaction
- Government and municipal charges—taxes and fees required by the jurisdiction in which the property is located
- Prepaid items

Loan Fees or Points

Loan fees or points are units of measure for charges on a loan. The loan origination fee typically covers the lender's administrative costs in preparing and processing the loan. The fee is usually known as a loan origination fee but is sometimes called a *point* or *points*. The fee will vary among lenders but is usually 1 to 1 1/2% of the loan amount for conventional and conforming loans. Each point is equal to 1% of the mortgage amount. For example, 1 point on a $100,000 mortgage loan is $1,000.

Third-Party Fees

Each mortgage transaction involves several individuals and a variety of services and fees. These services are standard, and so the fee on an average is the same for each transaction regardless of the size of the mortgage loan. The fees are payable directly to the service provider and require the service provider to be noted on the settlement statement (HUD-1).

Here is a breakdown:

- *Processing fee.* This fee can be charged by a lender for the processing of a loan by an inside processor or by a contract processor (in the case of some mortgage brokers). Fees range between $400 and $600.

- *Appraisal fee.* Independent appraisers perform these services, and the fee depends on the location of the property. Fees range between $250 and $350.

- *Document preparation fee.* This cost is for the preparation of the closing documents. The fee can be charged by the lender or by the attorney or settlement agent. Fees range from $100 to $250.

- *Attorney fee.* Some states require the closing of a mortgage transaction to be performed by a closing attorney. The closing attorney performs the same tasks as an escrow company. The closing attorney collects all fees, sends deeds to be recorded, pays outstanding taxes and utility bills, pays her own fee and all other closing fees, and gives all remaining money to the seller (in a purchase transaction) or to the borrower (in a refinance). The attorney fees may range from $500 to $1,000 (depending on the amount and type of transaction).

- *Home and pest inspections.* The lender may require that the home be inspected to make sure it is structurally sound and is not being invaded by termites or other destroying insects. Fees range between $175 and $350.

- *Survey.* The survey is a drawing or map showing the legal boundaries of a property and identifies any improvements or encroachments on the property since the last survey. Fees range between $250 and $500.

- *Title fee.* This is the fee for title search and title insurance. It varies depending on the loan amount.

- *Tax service fee*. This fee is charged by the lender and may be payable to the third party directly. The fee usually is $68.

- *Escrow or closing fee*. If the property is located in a state that does not require a closing attorney, an escrow or title company performs the closing of the loan. Fees range between $400 and $600.

- *Flood determination fee*. This fee is for the flood certificate and is usually $20.

Government and Municipal Charges (Taxes)

Depending on the jurisdiction of the city, town, county, or state in which the property is located, different taxes are collected. These charges are referred to as recording tax, transfer tax, tax stamp, etc.

Any time a property changes hands (a transfer of ownership or title of the property), a deed is recorded. Some localities charge a transfer tax; some collect a mortgage tax when a new deed is recorded. In addition, depending on the locality, a tax may be imposed that varies and is based on the loan amount.

Prepaid Expenses

Prepaid items are the fees that are paid at closing for debts that are not yet due. Prepaid expenses are:

- Interim interest
- Homeowner's insurance (and flood insurance if applicable)
- Property taxes
- Mortgage insurance

By law, a mortgage loan *cannot* have more than 30 days of interest outstanding at closing. Still, in the time between the closing date and the first payment, a loan may accrue more than 30 days' worth of interest. For example, if a loan closes on March 15, the first payment will not be due until May 1 (so there is more than

30 days of interest due). The interim interest—the difference in interest between the closing date (in this case March 15–31) and the first day of the next month (April)—must be collected at closing.

It is important to note that no matter what the closing date, FHA requires that at least 15 days of interest be included in the closing cost calculation for qualifying purposes.

Homeowner's, flood, and private insurance premiums must all be paid in advance, regardless of whether they are escrowed or not. If there is an escrow account, the lender will place two months of insurance into escrow in order to make sure there is sufficient money collected by the time the insurance premiums are due the following year.

Property taxes must also be collected by the lender in advance and placed into an escrow account in order to make sure that they are paid when they become due.

It is important to note that nonconforming credit lenders seldom require you to pay mortgage insurance, property taxes, or homeowner's insurance as part of your payment. So those prorated expenses are not collected up front at closing. This can be another advantage of this type of loan; even though the rate may be higher, the monthly payment and closing costs may be competitive because of these features.

HOW TO PREPARE A GOOD FAITH ESTIMATE

Closing Cost Descriptions

It is important that you as the loan officer have a clear knowledge of a good faith estimate. It is a regulatory disclosure, and you must be able to prepare one correctly. The good faith estimate is a disclosure required by the Real Estate Settlement Procedures Act, which ensures all applicants the receipt of this disclosure *no later* than three days from the date of the application.

As noted earlier, there are four categories of closing costs on a good faith estimate. Let's review:

Lender Fees

CATEGORY 1—Section 800 POINTS AND LENDER CHARGES		
800	ITEMS PAYABLE IN CONNECTION WITH LOAN	
801	Origination Fee @ % + $	$ _____
802	Discount Fee @ % + $	$ _____
803	Appraisal Fee	$ _____
804	Credit Report	$ _____
805	Lender's Inspection Fee	$ _____
806	Mortgage Insurance Application Fee	$ _____
807	Assumption Fee	$ _____
808	Mortgage Broker Fee	$ _____
809	Underwriting Fee	$ _____
810	Tax Related Service	$ _____
811	Application Fee	$ _____
812	Commitment Fee	$ _____
813	Lender's Rate Lock-In Fee	$ _____
814	Processing Fee	$ _____
815	Flood Certificate Fee	$ _____
816	Wire Transfer Fee	$ _____

- *801   Loan origination fee.* This fee covers the lender's costs for obtaining financing and administrative costs. It is most often expressed as a percentage of the loan amount (1% = 1 point). It can be a flat fee paid by the borrower, the sellers, or third parties.

- *802   Loan discount fee.* Often called *points*, this is a one-time charge from the lender to lower the interest rate on the loan. Generally, the more points paid, the lower the rate.

- *803   Appraisal fee.* The appraisal fee covers the cost of evaluating the property to estimate the fair market value. The appraised value of the property is used to calculate loan-to-value.

- *804   Credit report fee.* This fee covers the cost of obtaining a credit report, which shows how the borrower has handled other credit transactions. The lender uses this report in conjunction with information you submitted to determine whether your borrower is an acceptable credit risk, and how much the lender can loan and at what interest rate.

- *805   Lender inspection fee.* This covers inspections by the lender or outside inspector of the subject or property. It is most often associated with new construction.

- *806   Mortgage insurance application fee.* A fee may be charged to process an application for mortgage insurance if needed.

- *807   Assumption fee.* The assumption fee is a charge to the borrower if the borrower is taking over an existing mortgage on the house he or she is purchasing.

- *808   Mortgage broker fee.* Any fees charged by the broker are listed here.

- *809   Underwriting fee.* This is a cost to cover the final analysis and approval of the mortgage; it is often the lender's cost to the investor who will subsequently purchase the loan.

- *810   Tax-related service fee.* This fee is paid to set up a service that identifies the payment due date of local taxes for the servicer of the loan.

- *811   Application fee.* This fee reimburses the lender or broker for internal costs associated with initiating the application process.

- *812   Commitment fee.* A lender or broker can charge the borrower a fee to secure the mortgage loan.

- *813   Lender's rate lock-in fee.* This fee is charged by the lender to lock in the rate.

- *814   Processing fee.* This fee is charged by the lender or broker to cover costs associated with the processing and closing of a mortgage loan.

- *815   Flood certificate fee.* This charge is for the search to see if the property is located in a flood zone.

- *816   Wire transfer fee.* The lender can charge a fee to wire the funds into the closing agent's account.

Lender Prepaid Items

CATEGORY 2—Sections 900 and 1000 LENDER PREPAID ITEMS/RESERVES				
900	**ITEMS REQUIRED BY LENDER TO BE PAID IN ADVANCE**			
901	Interest for	days @ $	/day	$ _____
902	Mortgage Insurance Premium			$ _____
903	Hazard Insurance Premium			$ _____
904				$ _____
905	VA Funding fee			$ _____
1000	**RESERVES DEPOSITED WITH LENDER**			
1001	Hazard Insurance	Mo. @ $	Per Mo.	$ _____
1002	Mortgage Insurance	Mo. @ $	Per Mo.	$ _____
1003	School Tax	Mo. @ $	Per Mo.	$ _____
1004	Tax & Assmt.	Mo. @ $	Per Mo.	$ _____
1005	Flood Insurance			$ _____

- *901   Interest.* Lenders require interest due on a mortgage from the close date to the first day of the following full month. The interest due is calculated using the loan's interest rate, the loan amount, and the number of days until the first payment. Mortgage interest is always collected in arrears.

- *902   Mortgage insurance.* Premium lenders usually require private mortgage insurance when the LTV is greater than 80%. The insurance protects the lender in case of loan default.

- *903   Hazard insurance.* At closing, the borrower must pay the first year's premium or prove that he or she already has coverage (if refinancing). Homeowner's insurance covers property against damage from fire, wind, and other natural hazards.

- *905   VA funding fee*. A mandatory fee the VA charges a veteran for a VA loan.

Escrow Account Deposits

An escrow account is an account used when the lender will be paying the homeowner's insurance and property taxes on the behalf of your borrower. The borrower prepays the amounts, and the lender pays the costs as they come due. An initial amount is usually required to start the reserve account.

- *1001   Hazard insurance*. This fee represents the amount the lender withholds to ensure that the homeowner's insurance is paid on time. Typically, the lender will require two months of premiums be paid at closing, and then the remaining payments are included in the monthly payments.

- *1002   Mortgage insurance reserves*. If private mortgage insurance is needed, the borrower may be required to prepay those premiums.

- *1003   School tax*. If the porperty is in a jurisdiction that has in place an additional school tax, the borrower will be required to pay a portion of the tax at closing.

- *1004   Taxes and assessment reserves*. If the property is in a jurisdiction where city taxes apply, the borrower will be required to pay a portion of the taxes and any assessments at closing.

- *1005   Flood insurance reserves*. If the property is in a flood zone and flood insurance is required, a portion of the flood insurance is collected at closing.

Title Charges

- *1101   Closing or escrow fee*. This fee pays for the services of the escrow holder or settlement service that handles all the financial transfers and payments associated with the closing process.

CATEGORY 3—Section 1100 TITLE CHARGES		
1100	**TITLE CHARGES**	
1101	Closing or Escrow Fee	$ _____
1102	Abstract or Title Search	$ _____
1103	Title Examination	$ _____
1105	Document Preparation Fee	$ _____
1106	Notary Fee	$ _____
1107	Attorney's Fee	$ _____
1108	Title Insurance	$ _____
1109	Title Insurance Lender's Coverage	$ _____
1110	Owner's Title Insurance	$ _____
1112	Courier Fee	$ _____

- *1102–1104   Title examination and search fee.* Title fees may include title search, title examination, and title abstract.

- *1105   Document preparation fee.* Lenders or title companies may charge a fee to cover the costs of preparing the final legal documents required for closing.

- *1106   Notary fee.* This fee covers the cost of a person licensed as a notary public to swear to the fact that the individuals named in the documents are the actual persons that signed them.

- *1107   Attorney's fee.* This fee pays for the legal services of a settlement service provider at closing. The lawyer will usually oversee the signing of the documents.

- *1108   Title insurances.* This covers the total cost of the lender's title insurance.

- *1109   Title insurance lender's coverage.* This protects the lender against loss due to problems or defects in connection with the title. The face amount of the coverage is usually written for the amount of the mortgage loan and covers losses due to defects for problems not identified by the title search and examination.

- *1110   Owner's title insurance.* This fee covers the part of the title insurance policy that protects the owner against loss due to disputes over ownership of the property. The owner's policy is not necessary for a refinance transaction, as the existing policy remains in full force and effect, if obtained when the property was purchased, for as long as the owner owns the property.

- *1112   Courier fee.* This is the fee paid to an overnight delivery service for delivery of mortgage documentation.

Government Fees

CATEGORY 4—Sections 1200 and 1300 GOVERNMENT FEES/ADDITIONAL ITEMS		
1200	**GOVERNMENT RECORDING AND TRANSFER CHARGES**	
1201	Recording Fee	$ _____
1202	City/County Tax/Stamp	$ _____
1203	State Tax/Stamp	$ _____
1204	Intangible Tax	$ _____
1300	**ADDITIONAL SETTLEMENT CHARGES**	
1301	Survey Fee	$ _____
1302	Pest Inspection Fee	$ _____
1303	Lead Inspection Fee	$ _____

Government Recording and Transfer Charges

- *1201   Recording fee.* After closing, the mortgage deed is recorded at the county office to make record of the mortgage.

- *1202   City/county tax/stamp.* Only if applicable.

- *1203   State tax/stamp.* Tax may be charged on the mortgage by the state that has jurisdiction over the property.

- *1204   Intangible tax.* Tax may be charged on the mortgage by the state that has jurisdiction over the property.

Additional Settlement Charges

- *1301   Survey fee.* The lender may require a surveyor to conduct a survey of the property. This fee covers the cost of the survey. A survey determines the exact location of the home and the lot line, as well as easements and rights of way. This also protects the borrowers to ensure they have a record of their property boundaries and size.

- *1302 Pest inspection fee.* This fee covers the cost of inspections for termites and other pest infestation.

- *1303 Lead-based paint inspection fee.* Houses built prior to 1978 may be required to have an inspection for lead-based paint hazards.

Other Fees

Some fees may be listed on the HUD-1 settlement statement to the left of the borrower's column and marked *POC*, which stands for *paid outside of closing*. This refers to fees, such as those for credit reports or appraisal, that the borrower usually pays before closing or settlement.

POC can also list the yield spread premium, which is the rebate that is paid to the mortgage broker from the lender after the closing and settlement. This fee is included in the interest rate— it is not an additional cost to the borrower. However, it is a RESPA law to reflect this premium on a good faith estimate in order to disclose to the borrower that the interest obtained is higher than par pricing and therefore provides a rebate to the broker.

REFINANCE

A refinance is the process of paying off an existing mortgage with a new loan secured by the same property. Even if a mortgage was never placed on the property before (if the borrower purchased the home in cash), placing a mortgage on the property for the first time is considered a refinance as long as the owner remains the same. A borrower can benefit from a refinance by saving money (reducing the interest rate) or by cashing out some equity.

There are two basics types of refinance mortgages:

- *A rate reduction refinance.* The transaction is made solely for the purpose of reducing the interest rate. The new mortgage loan generally is increased to include (roll in) the fees or closing costs associated with the new loan. Some loan programs, including Fannie Mae, will allow a small amount of cash to be obtained without considering it a cash-out refinance. Fannie Mae allows up to 2% of the loan balance, or $2,000, whichever is less, as the maximum cash-out.

- *A cash-out refinance.* The transaction is made to obtain cash. The new mortgage balance is increased to pay off the existing mortgage balance, cover the closing costs, and give the borrower the cash-out he or she is requesting. The cash-out can also be used for paying off debt, for paying tax liens, or for any other reason.

The most important objective in refinancing is to correctly evaluate the estimated (new) value of the property against the balance of any existing liens (this includes the balance of the existing mortgage) on the property. This will ensure that there is sufficient equity to satisfy *both* lender maximum loan requirements and your borrower's objectives.

Why Would a Borrower Choose to Refinance?

There are several reasons why a borrower may choose to refinance:

- To reduce the mortgage payment

- To change loan type

- To obtain cash-out for whatever reason

Rate Reduction

The most obvious reason for refinancing is to reduce a higher interest rate to a lower interest rate. This has been the case for

TABLE 5-4
Rate and Payment Reduction Refinance Example

	Current Mortgage	Proposed
Original balance	$100,000	$101,500
Current balance	$98,500	
Closing costs		$3,000
Interest rate	8.50%	6.00%
Term in months	360	360
Monthly payment	$768.91	$608.54
Monthly savings		$160.37
Number of months before closing costs are repaid		18.70
To calculate, divide the actual cost of refinance by monthly savings. For example, $3,000 ÷ $160.37 = 18.70 months (to recoup costs)		

many people during the last two years, with current rates at historical lows. The most common way to refinance is to roll the costs of the refinance into the new mortgage loan.

Let's look at the example in Table 5-4. When does it make sense to refinance? Most experts say refinancing makes sense if the borrower can recoup the costs of refinancing within two to three years.

Term Reduction

Why not consider a reduction in the mortgage term in conjunction with a rate reduction to enhance the savings of a refinance? (See Table 5-5.) Who can benefit from a term reduction?

- Baby boomers planning on retirement at the end of the term

- Investors with plenty of cash flow

- Individuals with second homes

- Those interested in making larger payments in order to accumulate more equity in their homes

Another benefit is that lenders offer slightly lower interest rates for 20-, 15-, and 10-year loans. As you can see from Table 5-5, there is a significant savings when the interest rate is reduced and the term is changed to 15 years. Increasing the loan payment by less than $100 a month saves the borrower over $100,000!

TABLE 5-5
Term Reduction Example

	Current	Proposed 15-Year Term
Original balance	$100,000	
Balance	$98,500	
Closing costs		$3,000
New loan		$101,500
Initial term	360	180
Interest rate	8.50%	6.00%
Payment	$768.91	$856.51
Remaining months	333	180
Payments remaining	$256,047.03	$154,171.80
Life of loan savings		$101,875.23
Present mortgage payment	$768.91 × remaining months of 333 = $256,047.03	
New mortgage payment	$856.51 × remaining months of 180 = $154,171.80	
Savings	$256,047.03 − 154,171.80 $101,875.23	

Change Loan Type

In regard to changing loan types, the most common refinances involve changing from an adjustable-rate mortgage or balloon mortgage to a fixed-rate mortgage. Frequently this occurs when the rates are historically low. However, the reason may simply be that the borrower now qualifies for a fixed-rate loan. In the case of a balloon mortgage, the borrower may be facing a balloon payment and he or she must refinance.

There are also other interesting examples of refinances to change the loan program:

- The homeowner may refinance from one ARM to another ARM. For example, suppose the borrower began with an initial rate of 5%, with a 2% annual cap. He is in year 3 at 9% interest. Instead of risking another 2% increase the following year, he elects to refinance into another 1-year ARM, reducing the payment from 9% to a 5% initial rate.

- The homeowner may want to consolidate her existing first and second mortgage liens. Second liens typically carry higher interest rates. Your borrower may be in her property long enough to have acquired some equity and may benefit from refinancing both first and second liens into one mortgage lien with a lower rate. Keep in mind that a borrower might have purchased her property well below market and she wants to refinance to take advantage of new low rates. Unfortunately, most lenders require the value of the property to be the sales price rather than the new appraised value for at least one year. This is called the *seasoning* period.

- The homeowner may refinance from a high fixed interest rate to a lower ARM rate or balloon mortgage. For example, the borrower has a 9.0% current mortgage fixed rate, and the current market fixed rate is at 8.0% with 1 point. There is not enough savings to refinance into a fixed rate. The savings would be more attractive to a 3/1 ARM (with a maximum cap of 2%) and an initial rate of 6% with 1 point. The borrower now enjoys a 6% interest rate for three years, plus 8% for an additional year. This makes sense for a borrower who plans to be in his home for a short period such as four to five years.

Cash-Out Refinance

When a borrower takes money from some of the equity in his home, the transaction is known as a *cash-out* refinance. Refinancing a home is a great opportunity to borrow money for any reason, because the interest rates on mortgage loans are usually much lower than that for any other line of credit. For many Americans it is generally the first source for cash in a borrowing situation. In addition, there are tax benefits since mortgage interest is tax deductible. This is one reason why so many borrowers refinance their homes and pay off all their credit card debt (which is not tax deductible). Millions of homeowners realize the power they have in their home equity and have taken advantage of this power, as demonstrated in recent years with the record number of refinance transactions.

A borrower may take cash out on a refinance for any of the following reasons:

- To pay off other high-cost loans (the interest on which may not be tax deductible)

- To pay for the cost of education

- To make home improvements

- To make investments

- To finance retirement

The most common reason to cash out is to pay off debts, which can increase the cash flow because you are lowering the monthly payments by extending the payments over a longer term. (See Table 5-6.) In this case, as you can see, the homeowner has reduced his monthly obligations by $1,200 and obtains tax benefits on the mortgage interest.

Another alternative is to take out a second mortgage. When the interest rates are high and the homeowner cannot reduce her existing low mortgage rate, it can be more beneficial for the homeowner to simply obtain a second mortgage.

Cash–Out for Investment Purposes

Many homeowners have used their equity to reinvest in their own companies, invest in stocks, or purchase second homes and investment properties. In fact, home equity has long been a major source of borrowing power for the small business owner, who may not otherwise qualify for a loan.

Most recently we have seen homeowners investing in the stock market and in real estate. Homeowners can use their home equity as a source for the down payment on another home. Why? Because the tax benefits of the mortgage interest generally offset the cash-flow cost.

Refinance Guidelines

There is a large variety of loan products out there for conventional mortgages, with different guidelines and restrictions. To

TABLE 5-6
Debt Consolidation Analysis

Current Loan	
Original mortgage balance	$100,000
Present mortgage balance	$98,500
Present interest rate	8.5%
Present monthly principal and interest	$768.91
Add taxes and insurance	+$130
Present total monthly PITI	$899
Present value of the home	$185,000

Present Debt Analysis			
Loan	*Monthly Payment*	*Balance*	*Present Monthly Payment*
Credit cards	$ 250	$ 5,000	
Auto	500	15,000	Housing/PITI　$ 899
Personal	350	10,000	Monthly debts　$1,350
Personal	250	5,000	Total:　$2,249
Totals:	$1,350	$35,000	

Proposed Loan	
Present balance	$98,500
Closing costs	3,000
Debts to pay off balance	35,000 = new mortgage
Total new mortgage balance	$136,500
New interest rate	7.50%
New mortgage payment	$954.43
New PITI	$1,181.43
Previous debts	$2,349
New PITI	−1,149
Monthly savings	$1,200

find the program best suited to your borrower, you will need to know the basics:

- *Is the property an owner-occupied property?* Remember there is a difference between a second home (vacation home) and an investment property (which is being rented out). This will determine what loan-to-value restrictions you will have.

- *What is the purpose of the refinance?* Does the borrower just want to lower his interest rate (you will then be looking for a rate and term refinance), or does the borrower want to cash out his equity (in this case it will be considered a cash-out refinance). This also will determine what loan-to-value restrictions you may have. Nonconforming loans can go up to 95–100% loan-to-value.

- *Does your borrower qualify for a full income documentation loan?* Is she an employed individual, and does she have two years of income verification? (If not or if she is self-employed and does not have tax returns or does not report sufficient income documentation on her tax returns, then you will need to find a "stated-income" loan program, which will have loan-to-value restrictions.)

Streamline Refinances

Most lenders offer a streamline refinance process in order to retain their existing customers. Both Fannie Mae and Freddie Mac have reduced documentation programs for the refinance of existing mortgages, referred to as an *enhanced streamline refinance*. Reduced documentation means refinancing without the need for appraisal or credit requalification.

Program highlights are:

- The applicant does not have to be requalified if the loan is serviced by the originating mortgage company, if the original income verified has not declined, if there are no mortgage delinquencies for the past 12 months, and if the new payment is within 20% of the old mortgage payment.

- No appraisal is required if the current lender can certify that the value of the property has not declined and if the original appraisal supports the new mortgage amount.

- The applicant can refinance into a shorter term as long as the payment does not increase by more than 20% of the old mortgage payment.

- The applicant can take the lower of 2% of the loan amount or $2,000 in cash after closing.

FHA Refinances

If you are solely reducing a borrower's current mortgage payment, FHA has simplified the refinance process by implementing a program known as the *FHA streamline*. No cash back is allowed, other than $250 at closing. FHA stipulates that:

- The borrower must have an existing FHA mortgage.

- The refinance will lower the borrower's existing monthly principal and interest payments.

- No income, employment, or asset verification is required.

- No cash may be taken out.

- The borrower must have a mortgage payment history reflecting no late payments in the last 12 months.

- If the loan amount is not being increased over the current loan amount, then no appraisal is required.

- If the borrower assumed the FHA mortgage, then he or she must make at least six payments before the refinance.

- If there is a second mortgage, it may remain in place as long as it will be subordinate.

There is also the opportunity to refinance into a full documentation FHA loan. A full documentation FHA loan has the following requirements:

- The present mortgage must be a current FHA-insured mortgage.

- An appraisal, credit report, and income and asset documentation must be obtained as required on an FHA purchase.

- Second mortgages must be seasoned for a minimum of one year.

- When obtaining cash out on an FHA refinance, the borrower is restricted to 85% loan-to-value.

VA Refinancing

Similar to FHA, the VA allows for streamline refinancing. The VA's program is known as the IRRL (interest rate reduction loan). Program highlights include the following:

- The veteran can roll in all closing costs.

- The loan must reduce the interest rate and monthly payments.

- No appraisal requirements are needed in most situations.

- If the property is a rental home, the veteran must be able to certify that he or she once lived in the property.

- There is an option to include up to two months' payments into the loan, allowing the veteran to skip two monthly payments.

- The rate and term funding fee for a VA fast-track refinance is 0.5%, and this fee can be financed.

VA full documentation requirements are:

- The property must be owner-occupied.

- Closing costs can be rolled into the new loan.

- Cash-out refinances have a 90% maximum LTV (80% LTV maximum for Texas).

Note: For FHA and VA refinances, the borrower cannot pay miscellaneous lender charges such as a tax service fee.

Important Facts with Regard to Refinancing

- *Property valuation*. One of the most important factors when considering a refinance is to ensure that the property is appraised for a high enough value to pay off the existing mortgage lien, closing costs, and any cash-out if applicable. Many lenders have access to "property valuation services" that can assist a loan officer in determining an initial price point for the property in order to determine whether a loan is feasible.

- *Up-front costs.* It is likely for a lender to have the home-owner pay for the appraisal and, in some cases, a credit report fee and application fee. Mortgage brokers must abide by state regulations in regard to any up-front fees collected by a borrower prior to the loan closing. In addition, most states require that mortgage brokers disclose in writing the collection of any up-front costs.

- *Intention to sell.* Most lenders will not refinance if the borrower's intention is to sell the property. Lenders will conduct a search on the MLS (Multiple Listing Service, which presents Realtor's listings of houses) to check whether the property has been listed for sale in the previous 12 months. If the property has been listed, a lender may require proof that the home has been removed from the market.

- *Right of rescission.* The federal Truth in Lending Act requires that a lender allow a three-day right of rescission for an owner-occupied refinance transaction. This law gives the borrower a three-business-day (does not include Sundays or holidays) right-to-cancel clause. Within that three-day period, should the borrower decide to cancel, he or she must do so by signing the right-to-cancel document and provide it to the lender within that period in order to recover any costs incurred during the refinance process. The loan may not fund (the funds will not be released) until the right-of-rescission period has expired. The loan is not funded until the day after the rescission date. For example:

  > Closing or signing date (borrower signs loan documents): Friday, October 1
  >
  > Third day of rescission (count Saturday, Monday, and Tuesday): Wednesday, October 6
  >
  > Funding date (funds are released to the settlement agent): Thursday, October 7

- *Subordination.* In many cases a borrower may want to refinance his first mortgage but keep his existing second lien (for example, if the second mortgage is a low-interest-bearing HELOC). But as you have already learned, a second mortgage is recorded into second position behind a first lien, and if the first lien is paid off, the second lien moves into first-lien position. To keep this from happening, a subordination agreement is made between the second-lien holder and the proposed new first-lien holder. The requirements for approval of a subordination agreement vary among lenders. Keep in mind that there may be a fee for the preparation of a subordination agreement, and the process may take two to four weeks.

Key Note: In some cases, the IRS is willing to subordinate an IRS tax lien into a junior encumbrance in order to accommodate a refinance transaction, if the IRS believes such a loan will result in repayment or facilitate the collection of such tax lien.

Mortgage Finance Quiz

1. Ratio qualification plays a major part in the decision-making process of a mortgage loan. There are two ratios that are calculated for most mortgage programs. One ratio is the housing ratio, also known as the front-end ratio. What is the other ratio method?
   A. Residual income ratio
   B. Gross monthly income ratio
   C. Debt, or back-end, ratio

2. There will be many a case in which your borrower will not meet the qualifying standards to qualify for a loan. There must be prevailing circumstances, known as compensating factors, to ask the lender for an exception. Which of the items listed below would be considered a compensating factor?
   A. Large debts
   B. High residual income
   C. A small down payment

3. What is a typical maximum qualifying housing or front-end ratio for a conforming mortgage loan?
   A. 25%
   B. 28%
   C. 36%

4. What is a typical maximum debt, or back-end, ratio on a conforming mortgage?
   A. 28%
   B. 33%
   C. 36%

5. To calculate the decimal equivalent of a fraction, you will need to divide the numerator by the denominator. What is the decimal equivalent of the fraction 5/8?
   A. 0.625
   B. 0.750
   C. 0.875

6. The good faith estimate is a regulatory disclosure. When must the loan originator present a good faith estimate to the borrower?
   A. Before the loan originator takes the application
   B. No later than three days after the application is taken
   C. No later than five days after the application is taken

7. What is 25 basis points equal to?
   A. 1%
   B. 2 1/2%
   C. 1/4%

8. FHA allows cash-out to what loan-to-value?
   A. 75%
   B. 85%
   C. 95%

9. What is the proper definition of a refinance?
   A. The process of paying off your debt with a mortgage
   B. The process of taking out a mortgage and adding it to the existing mortgage

C. The process of paying off an existing mortgage with a new loan secured by the same property

10. What would the monthly P&I payment be on a mortgage loan of $150,000 with an 8.0% fixed interest rate and a 30-year term?
    A. $1,100.65
    B. $1,050.30
    C. $1,153.37

11. What do you have when you subtract the borrower's housing, debts, and other liabilities from the gross monthly income?
    A. Residual income
    B. Debt, or back-end, ratio
    C. Housing, or front-end, ratio

12. Which one of the components listed below can be included in the debt, or back-end, ratio?
    A. Principal and interest
    B. Monthly property taxes
    C. Child-support payments

13. Suppose your borrower's total monthly gross income is $5,700, he has $500 total debt, and his housing payment including taxes, insurance, and HOA is $2,219. What is the total debt-to-income ratio?
    A. 47.70%
    B. 20.96%
    C. 47/70%

14. There is one fee that pertains only to a VA refinance transaction. Which fee is it?
    A. Processing fee
    B. Origination fee
    C. Funding fee

15. What is a discount fee?
    A. What a lender charges for a below-par rate
    B. What a lender pays for an above-par rate
    C. What a borrower pays up front to discount the rate over time

16. If your borrower's monthly gross income is $7,500 and his housing cost is $1,600 plus $500 in debts, what would his debt, or back-end, ratio be?
    A. 25%
    B. 26%
    C. 28%

17. Which one of the components listed below can be included in the housing, or front-end, ratio?
    A. Association dues
    B. Child-support payments
    C. Student loan payments

18. You are trying to qualify your borrower on a conforming mortgage, and therefore, your qualifying ratio is 36%. If your borrower's total gross monthly income is $7,500, how much total debt can your borrower have?
    A. $2,700
    B. $2,650
    C. $2,800

19. If the interest rate on a loan is 5.375% and you need to add 0.75% for a cash-out on a refinance that is over 85% loan-to-value, what would the new interest rate be?
    A. 5.625%
    B. 5.875%
    C. 6.125%

20. A borrower has $5,000 gross monthly income with no debt. The current market interest rate is 7.5%, and the borrower is seeking a conforming mortgage with a 30 year term. Rounding the taxes and insurance to $150 a month, what would be the maximum mortgage amount for the borrower?
    A. $184,000
    B. $189,000
    C. $206,000

Answers to the quiz can be found at the end of Part One.

CHAPTER 6

BORROWER QUALIFICATION

I have learned that success is to be measured not so much by the position that one has reached in life as by the obstacles which he has overcome while trying to succeed.

—**Booker T. Washington**

Several variables factor into the consideration of a borrower's eligibility for a mortgage loan: credit, income, amount of down payment, cash reserves, etc. This chapter addresses all specific aspects of *borrower* eligibility beyond the lender's ratio method of qualification that is covered in the previous chapter.

We begin with a review of credit. As a loan officer, it is important to know how to read a credit report and how to evaluate a borrower's credit history. This is the first step in prequalification of an applicant's eligibility.

CREDIT

Evaluating a credit report is the fundamental part of qualifying your borrower. It is the concept of providing documentation that convinces the lender to extend additional credit based on the borrower's tendencies. A borrower's credit history answers the following:

- *How much does the borrower owe?* As you learned in pre-qualifying with ratios, ineligibility can result when there is too much debt. If the borrower has too much debt at the time of application, he may need to pay off some debt to qualify.

- *Is the existing housing payment current?* The current rent or mortgage history is an important credit factor for the lender. If the borrower is making her housing payments in a timely manner, then she is considered a good credit risk. Lenders will review the housing payment history by taking a look at the last 12 to 24 months of payments. This period is referred to as the *look-back* period.

- *What is the current housing payment?* Is the borrower currently making a housing payment that would reflect his ability to pay the new payment? When there is too much disparity between the current housing payment and the new housing payment, this is known as a *payment shock*. The lender may require compensating factors if there is too much of a payment shock.

- *Are the existing and past liabilities current?* The lender reviews the credit report for all delinquencies specifically in the past 12 to 24 months' credit history. Installment loans are typically viewed as more significant.

- *Are there any major credit troubles in the credit history?* Major credit troubles can pose problems and include bankruptcy, foreclosure, charge-offs, liens, and judgments.

All these factors will affect the credit score of the prospective borrowers.

Here is a general guide to acceptable adverse credit history:

Mortgage payments	*No* late payments in the previous 12 months
Credit card/consumer loans	Two 30-day late payments in the previous 12 months
Legal actions	No open collections, liens, or judgments
Inquiries	Three inquiries in the previous 3- to 6-month period prior to application

All adverse data shown on a borrower's credit history must be explained in writing. The letter of explanation (LOE) should include a logical explanation that convincingly points out the borrower's efforts to properly handle the account. If the adverse credit was a result of someone else's responsibility—for example, divorce, a cosigned loan—then ask the borrower to provide documentation that proves that the incidents indicated were not in the borrower's control. If it was an isolated incident, make sure the borrower indicates the events that led up to the incident.

The lender will focus on three potential problems during the investigation of the credit history, which we discuss in detail.

1. Is the Credit History Acceptable for an Approval?

A pattern of adverse credit history can be a cause for denial of some loan programs. If the borrower has poor credit, here are some suggestions:

- First review the history with your borrower for accuracy. You would be surprised at how many errors are made on credit reports. You may need to provide updated information to the credit bureaus.

- If the negative items are accurate, then you want to make sure your borrower can provide a well-documented letter of explanation.

- At this point you will probably need to offer your borrower a nonconforming loan product, and you can discuss the rate options.

2. Are There Too Many Outstanding Debts?

As we learned earlier, having too much debt can be a problem when it comes to meeting the required debt ratio. Typically, too much debt (just as adverse credit) is reflected by a lower credit score on a credit report.

The easiest way to take care of too much debt is by having your borrower pay off some of the debt. In this case, the borrower would receive the best benefit by paying off the liabilities with the largest monthly cost, effectively lowering the debt-to-income ratio.

Take a look at short-term debts

Don't forget to look out for short-term debts. A lender will eliminate the monthly factor from the debt ratio calculation if your borrower has any installment debt that has fewer than 10 payments remaining. Keep in mind that this does not include auto leases, the reason being that most consumers simply renew their auto lease once it has expired.

Consolidate debt

In some cases a borrower may be able to lower his debt ratio by taking out a personal loan in order to spread out his debt over a longer period of time and thus reduce his total monthly debt.

Should I suggest credit counseling?

Many borrowers find they are overextended with debt and decide to seek assistance with a professional service such as a credit counselor or agency. There are negative factors involved with this course of action:

- There are several companies that charge the borrower up-front fees and never deliver results.

- These companies simply negotiate a repayment plan, which is something your borrowers can do themselves.

- Lenders view consumer credit counseling services (CCCS) as a negative credit rating. This is often the first step before a bankruptcy, and thus most conforming lenders require that a borrower complete a CCCS restructure plan for a minimum of two years (the same as with a bankruptcy rating).

3. Does the Borrower Have Enough Credit to Arrive at a Conclusion for Qualifying?

Having no credit can be as challenging as having adverse credit. If a borrower has *no* credit, how does the lender know your borrower will pay her debts? It is for this reason that most lenders have a minimum *trade-line* (a loan on a credit report) requirement. In addition, lenders want to see a track history on these trade lines, and so *established* history of a minimum of two years is usually required. If your borrower does not have established credit, here are some suggestions:

- Go with a first-time home-buyer program.

- Utilize the FHA low-to-moderate-income programs.

- Build a credit history by gathering 12 months of canceled checks to prove that the person made regular payments for utilities and rent.

Automatic Underwriting

Automatic underwriting service (AUS) systems were developed 10 years ago by the mortgage industry (see Table 6-1). Fannie Mae has Desktop Underwriter (DU), and Freddie Mac has Loan Prospector (LP). These automated systems use statistical models to determine the likelihood of a borrower's defaulting on his loan. An AUS system is basically a computerized loan approval.

AUS systems "score" loans to determine whether to offer an automated approval—what is commonly known as "accept" or "approve"—or to reach a "refer" or "caution" decision. A refer or caution decision means that additional information or documentation will need to be provided and manual underwriting will take place.

AUS is touted to be a simpler and fairer way to approve a mortgage loan. Simpler for obvious reasons: AUS streamlines and speeds up the review and approval process. AUS systems promise to make lending decisions fairly and consistently because the systems are blind to an applicant's race and ethnicity, ensuring fair treatment of minority homeowners.

Automatic underwriting is simply taking the credit score that credit bureaus summarize using the information on an applicant's credit report. AUS has proved that as simple as credit scores are, they are a powerful underwriting tool in

TABLE 6-1
Automated Underwriting Systems

Has its own system:	
FNMA	DU—Desktop Underwriter
FHLMC	LP—Loan Prospector
Allows the following AU systems:	
FHA	LP, DU, and primaAura system
VA	LP, DO/DU, and primaAura system

predicting the loan performance regardless of a borrower's race or income.

The advantage of AUS in many cases is that upon approval only limited documentation is requested. Also as we mentioned before, there is more leniency in debt-to-income ratios in some cases when submitting your loan for approval through automated underwriting. The disadvantage is the disregard for an applicant's income, with the only factor being a credit score. As you may imagine, this is a cause for many discrepancies. As we have discussed, a borrower may have a high income, but if the borrower is carrying a large debt loan, he or she may have a lower credit score that is nonindicative of the person's capability of repaying the loan.

Credit Scores

Fair Isaac & Company, Inc., developed FICO scores for each of the three national credit repositories. The scores are Beacon for Equifax, Fair Isaac Risk Model/FICO for Experian (formerly TRW), and Empirica for TransUnion. Keep in mind, these repositories issue scores that *only* consider the information contained in a person's credit file; they *do not* consider a person's income, savings, or amount of a down payment for a mortgage.

Credit scores became popular in 1995 when Fannie Mae and Freddie Mac approved the use of credit risk scoring by mortgage lenders. Their approval prompted an increase in the use of credit scores in underwriting. These credit scores are objective, consistent, accurate, and fast.

Credit scoring balances and weighs *positive* information along with *negative* information in credit reports. Scoring has transformed credit granting so that it is no longer simply based on whom you know. To develop the models that generate the credit scores, Fair Isaac analyzes anonymous credit report data to statistically determine what factors are most predictive of future credit performance. This process involves the use of a multiple scorecard design. Each repository uses 10 individual scorecards, and the models at each repository are the same.

The actual scoring process is proprietary, and the algorithms are copyrighted. We can share the predictive variables, the portion of the credit file considered, and the weight as provided by Fair Isaac (see Figure 6-1). They are:

1. *Payment history (approximately 35% of the score).* The factor that has the biggest impact on a score is whether payments on past credit accounts have been made on time. However, an overall good credit picture can outweigh a few late payments, and late payments will continue to have less impact over time.

2. *Amounts owed (approximately 30%).* Having credit accounts and owing money doesn't connote a high-risk borrower. But owing a lot of money on numerous accounts can suggest that a person is overextended and more likely to

FIGURE 6-1
Five-Factor Pie Chart

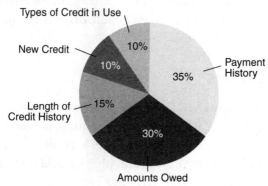

make some payments late or not at all. Part of the science of scoring is determining how much debt is too much for a given credit profile.

3. *Length of credit history (approximately 15%)*. In general, a longer credit history will increase a FICO score. Lenders want to see that borrowers can responsibly manage their available credit over time. However, even people who have not been using credit very long may get high scores, depending on how the rest of their credit report looks.

4. *New credit (approximately 10%)*. People today tend to have more credit and to shop for credit more frequently. But opening several credit accounts in a short period of time can represent greater risk—especially for people with short credit histories. Requests for new credit can also represent greater risk. However, FICO scores are able to distinguish between a search for many new credit accounts and rate shopping. FICO scores generally do not associate shopping for the best rate on a loan with higher risk.

5. *Types of credit in use (approximately 10%)*. The FICO score will reflect a mix of credit cards, retail accounts, installment loans, finance company accounts, and mortgage loans. While a healthy mix will improve a score, it is not necessary to have one of each, and it is not a good idea for borrowers to open credit accounts they do not intend to use. The credit mix usually won't be a key factor in determining a score—but it will be more important if a credit report doesn't have much other information on which to base a score.

Credit Inquiries

One challenge occurs when a borrower shops around for a new car or mortgage loan. Each time a loan request is made, a credit check or inquiry is made on the borrower's credit file. FICO has changed the way it factors these credit checks, and it claims these changes should minimize the "negative" effect or drop in credit score for the borrower. As opposed to counting each inquiry separately, now FICO counts multiple auto or mortgage inquiries in any 14-day period as just one inquiry. In addition, FICO ignores all mortgage and auto inquiries made 30 days prior to scoring, claiming that if a borrower finds a loan within 30 days, the inquiries won't affect the score while the borrower is shopping for credit.

The credit repositories claim that credit inquiries should not change scores significantly, because the variable in the model using inquiries contributes less than 5% of the predictive power of the model. According to Equifax statisticians, an average of 5% of the credit reports in the Equifax consumer credit reporting database (over 200 million consumer files) will see a change in score due to this. Less than 5% of those will see a change significant enough to affect a loan decision.

In order to get a score, a borrower must have information in his or her file that meets the following conditions:

- No "deceased" indicator on the credit file

- At least one undisputed trade line that has been updated in the previous six months

- One trade line open at least six months

A FICO score is a three-digit number. Scores range from 350 (high risk) to 950 (low risk). Even though each credit repository uses the same scoring models, each repository is likely to contain different data and thus carry a different credit score.

Every score is accompanied by a maximum of four reason codes. Reason codes identify the most significant reason that a consumer did not score higher. They are not red flags. Consumers with scores in the 800 range get reason codes just as consumers with scores in the 500 range. The reason codes may be used in describing to the consumer the reason for adverse action. Scores are not part of the credit file and are not covered by the Fair Credit Reporting Act. Scores, if disclosed to the consumer, must be related to the credit file—using the reason codes—since the score has no meaning in itself; the lender and the investor assign the meaning or risk level.

When applicants have erroneous information reported, document the inaccuracies. The easiest way to do that is to have your credit reporting agency upgrade the merged credit file to an edited mid-range report or to a residential mortgage credit report.

The good news is that evaluating a FICO score is no longer as subjective a process as it used to be.

The mortgage industry tends to create its own language, and credit rating is no exception. BC mortgage lending gets its name from the grading of one's credit based on such things as payment history, amount of debt payments, bankruptcies, equity position, and credit scores.

We have compiled a guide to help you estimate your credit grade. This is only a guide, as many companies have exceptions that may result in stricter or more lenient guidelines.

A GENERAL GUIDE TO CREDIT GRADES											
	Credit Score	Debt Ratio	Max LTV	Mortgage			Revolving			Installment		
				30	60	90	30	60	90	30	60	90
A+	670	36	95	0	0	0	2	0	0	1	0	0
A−	660	45	95	1	0	0	3	1	0	2	0	0
B	620	50	85	2	1	0	4	2	1	3	1	0
C	580	55	75	4	2	1	6	5	2	5	4	1
D	550	60	70	5	3	2	8	8	4	7	6	2

A borrower with a FICO score below 620 is considered high risk, and a borrower with a FICO score over 660 is considered a below-average risk.

For a bankruptcy or foreclosure, the grades indicate:

A+   None allowed within 10 years

A−   Minimum 2 years, reestablished credit

B   Minimum 2 years, some lates

C   Minimum 1 year

D   Discharged

The figures shown above are estimates. When trying to figure a credit grade, keep in mind the following principles:

- When the borrower has derogatory credit, all the other aspects of the loan need to be in order. Equity, stability, income, documentation, assets, etc., play a larger role in the approval decision.

- When determining a grade, various combinations are allowed, but the worst case will push the grade to a lower credit guide. Mortgage lates and bankruptcies are the most important.

- Credit patterns are very important. A high number of recent inquiries and more than a few outstanding loans may signal a problem. A "willingness to pay" is important; thus late payments in the same time period are better than random lates, as they signal an effort to pay even after falling behind.

As part of keeping the borrowers informed, share with them the information provided below.

- *Delinquent payments*. There are payments to creditors that are made over 30 days past due. Even if they are paid in full after the incidents, they will remain on a credit report for three to seven years from the date of the first missed payment.

- *Collection accounts*. After three months of payment delinquency, a creditor can turn an account over for collections. The credit report will reflect the collection activity for seven years from the time the first payment was missed. Even if the account is paid after the collection activity has commenced, a credit report will still be marked for seven years, but it can read "paid collection."

- *Inquiries*. Inquiries are notations in a credit report marking a request by an entity to view a credit report. For example, when an applicant fills out an application for a credit card, the credit card company asks the credit bureau for a copy of the individual's credit report, creating an inquiry notation on the credit report. Most inquiries remain for two years.

- *Charge-off*. A charge-off occurs when a creditor decides that, for whatever reason, it would rather write off a debt as a loss than attempt to collect. Such charge-offs remain on a credit report for seven years from the time of the first missed payment that led to the charge-off.

- *Bankruptcy*. Chapters 7, 11, and 12 bankruptcies stay on a credit report for 10 years from the date of filing. Chapter 13 bankruptcy stays on a credit report for 7 years after the discharge, which is usually 3 to 5 years after filing.

  Exception. Note that there is a major exception to the above time frame. If an individual is applying for life insurance for over $50,000 or for a job that pays over $20,000, a credit bureau may provide information that is over 10 years old.

What is the difference between a Chapter 7 and a Chapter 11 bankruptcy?

A filing under any chapter of the Bankruptcy Code creates an estate. The courts act as trustee over the estate. Under Chapter 7, all of a debtor's assets (that are not exempt) and liabilities are liquidated. Unless a creditor objects, all debts included in the bankruptcy are discharged within a few months of filing.

Chapter 13 allows the debtor to pay back creditors in full or in part, based upon income, over a period of up to five years. The payments are made to a trustee, who begins paying creditors as soon as the plan is approved. An individual must have less than $350,000 in secured debt and $100,000 in unsecured debt to file.

Chapter 11 reorganization is a plan available to all individuals and entities, but it is intended to allow an ongoing business to restructure its debt. The filing must be accepted by the court as well as the creditors.

What about credit counseling agencies?

Credit counseling agencies can help borrowers who have overextended themselves by working out repayment plans with creditors, rearranging financial plans, and arranging consolidation loans. The account will typically show up on the credit report as "CCCS account." Credit counseling is perceived as a negative. The perception of a lender can be that the borrowers could not handle their delinquencies on their own. Credit counseling is also considered the first step before a bankruptcy. Check the lender guidelines for credit counseling restrictions.

What is a judgment?

A judgment is a collection action that has been reviewed for merit by a small claim, circuit, or district court—the court depends on the amount or size of the claim. A judgment is a serious problem because the party the ruling inures may seize an individual's property, wages, and assets to satisfy the obligation. When obtaining a mortgage loan, a borrower is not allowed any outstanding judgments.

What about tax liens?

Federal and state tax liens are more serious than judgments because the government is very good at seizing assets and collecting money owed. No matter what the reason for a tax lien, it is viewed primarily as a credit problem.

What is a credit bureau?

A credit bureau, or credit repository, is an entity that collects information about consumers' credit histories. A credit history includes information concerning an individual's identity, payment habits, and public records. Credit bureaus sell credit reports to credit grantors, such as banks, finance companies, and retailers. Credit grantors use credit reports to determine whether or not a potential borrower is creditworthy.

What if your borrowers have questions about the credit industry and how it affects them?

All consumers have specific rights when a credit decision is made.

Federal law carefully regulates how information about credit can be used. The two most important laws for consumers are the Equal Credit Opportunity Act (ECOA) and the Fair Credit Reporting Act (FCRA).

The ECOA mandates that every consumer who applies for credit has an equal opportunity to obtain it. This is not a guarantee that credit will be granted, but rather that the factors used to determine whether an application is accepted or rejected will be consistent and consistently applied to all applicants. The ECOA requires a credit grantor to provide the consumer with a written notice specifically identifying the reason for denial of credit. The consumer must make a request for this notice within 60 days of the application's rejection.

The FCRA ensures that consumers' rights and privacy are protected. There are several informative World Wide Web sites with lots of information about consumer credit issues. These two relate to the FCRA specifically:

www.ftc.gov/bcp/conline/pubs/credit/fcra.htm (summarizes the law)

www.ftc.gov/os/statues/fcra.htm (gives the actual text of the law)

The Three Major Credit Bureaus

There are more than a thousand credit bureaus in the United States. However, most creditors request information from one or all of the three largest. If credit has been denied, or if there is a dispute, or if borrowers want to view their credit file, they need to request a credit report from all three major credit bureaus. In addition, it is recommended that a letter be sent to all three major credit bureaus to ensure that all information being reported is correct. Here is the contact information for the three major credit bureaus.

Equifax

Equifax Credit Information Services, Inc.
P.O. Box 740241
Atlanta, GA 30374
To order a report: (800) 685-1111
To report fraud: (800) 525-6285
www.equifax.com

Experian (formerly TRW)
National Consumer Assistance Center
P.O. Box 2002
Allen, TX 75013
To order a report: (888) 397-3742
To report fraud: (888) 397-3742
www.experian.com

TransUnion, LLC
Consumer Disclosure Center
P.O. Box 1000
Chester, PA 19022
To order a report: (800) 888-4213
To report fraud: (800) 916-8800
www.transunion.com

In general, credit reports are ordered electronically and can be merged in the loan application (1003). Prior to the technology boom, credit had to accompany handwritten explanations for all credit discrepancies, no matter how small or big. With technology advanced as much as it has, automated underwriting can give you the requirements in minutes so the lender knows what is expected.

This does not mean that it is not wise to review the credit report before having it underwritten. It is very important to always go over the credit report in detail with your borrower; invalid information on a credit report can cause an adverse decision and may cause the loan to be declined.

What should you review?

1. *Borrower's identification as ordered.* This section shows the borrower's general identification information, such as first and last name, date of birth, and social security number.

2. *Residence information.* The current resident address, as ordered, appears here. In the case of a purchase, you want to make sure that the previous address listed on the 1003 matches that on the credit report.

3. *AKA*. This section lists any aliases.

4. *Comments*. The comments in this section explain differences in names from what appears to what was ordered.

5. *Credit score information*. The credit scores for each borrower and for each repository ordered are given here.

6. *Public records*. This section reveals any bankruptcy, judgment, or tax lien information.

7. *Summary information*. This is a summary of all the credit information appearing on the credit report.

8. *Employment information*. Employment information is a record of your borrower's employment history. You will want to make sure it matches the information on the 1003.

9. *Credit information*. Credit information lists all the creditors with credit history. It includes the date the trade line was opened, last payment reported, high balance, current balance, and any delinquencies in payment. This section also reflects any collections.

10. *Inquiry information*. Inquiries made by creditors are listed here. Some lenders will look at inquiries for the last 60 to 90 days to reveal any possible new credit debt that has not yet appeared on the credit report.

11. *Credit scan/social security search*. This section presents the results of a search using only the borrower's social security number and will describe why it might differ

12. *Fraud search*. This section is important to pay attention to, as you want to make sure that there is no fraudulent activity being reported.

13. *Information sources*. The credit bureaus that provided the information are named in this section.

See Figure 6-2 for an example of a consumer credit report.

FIGURE 6-2
Example of a Consumer Credit Report

ABC MORTGAGE 111 W. ANYWHERE ST FANTASY ISLAND, TX 78759 (512) 555-1234 (512) 555-1235	Client Tracking **XY246**	Requested by **Joe**	Report ID **12345 BX 0000**
	FD client code **0000-0123**	Date requested **01/25/2001** **09:20:41**	Charges **10.50**

Identification (as requested)

Applicant's last name **SMITH**	First name **ABRAHAM**	Middle	Suffix	DOB	Social Security **000-12-1234**

Residence Information (as requested)

Present	69 Home St.	Bedrock	NC	27601
Former	711 Winner Ln.	Rock Vegas	NC	27609

File Variations

Trans Union	BU1	000-12-1234	SMITH, ABRAHAM	01/25/01 09:03
Equifax	BQ1	000-12-1234	JONES, ABRAHAM ROMERO	01/25/01 09:04
Experian	BX1	000-12-1234	SMITH, ABRAHAM	01/25/01 09:03

AKA

AKA: ABRAHAM
NICKNAME: SMITH
BX1

Database Residence Information			First	Last	
69 HOME ST	BEDROCK	NC 27616	---	---	BU1
4680 CAPTAIN COOK AV	CLEMMONS	NC 27012	---	01/99	BU1
69 HOME ST	BEDROCK	NC 27616	11/00	---	BQ1
468 S. POLE ST APT. B-4	RALEIGH	NC 27603	02/99	---	BQ1
69 HOME ST	BEDROCK	NC 276167754	09/00	11/00	BX1
711 Winner Ln.	RALEIGH	NC 276095032	03/00	03/00	BX1
711 Winner Ln.	RALEIGH	NC 27609	01/00	01/00	BX1

Database Employment Information		First	Last	
BEDROCK QUARRY		---	---	BQ1

Public Records

No Public Records found

Credit Score Information

567	Repository Equifax	Brand Beacon 96	Type FICO	Name JONES, ABRAHAM ROMERO	BQ1
528	Repository TransUnion	Brand Empirica	Type FICO	Name SMITH, ABRAHAM	BU1

FIGURE 6-2 *(Continued)*

| 494 | Repository Experian | Brand New Fair, Isaac | Type FICO | Name SMITH, ABRAHAM | | BX1 |

Credit History						Payment	Balance

| **BEDROCK FURNITURE** C23678 | Opened 12/99 | Reported 09/00 | High balance 473 | Reviewed 9 mos | 30-59 0 / 60-89 1 / 90+ 0 | Past due 78 | Payment Rev x $35 | Balance 329 |
| | Last active 04/00 | *BX1 [Ind] | High credit --- | Revolving (R3) Charge | 09/00 | | | |

RPC 96969	Opened 12/98	Reported 05/00	High balance 111	Reviewed ---	30-59 59 / 60-89 -- / 90+ --	Past due -0-	Payment Collection	Balance -0-
	Last active 05/00	*BU1 BX1 BQ1 [Ind]	High credit 111	Bal Monthly (O9) Unknown				
	Paid collection							

RUBBLE MORTGAGE 78910	Opened 07/00	Reported 12/00	High balance 129,878	Reviewed 3 mos	30-59 3 / 60-89 0 / 90+ 0	Past due -0-	Payment Paid	Balance -0-
	Last active 12/00	*BU1 BX1 BQ1 [Joint undefined]	High credit ---	Installment (I2) Mortgage (FHA)	12/00 11/00 10/00			
	Account transferred or sold							

| **ROCK VEGAS CONSUMER** 56789 | Opened 06/00 | Reported 01/01 | High balance 2,033 | Reviewed 5 mos | 30-59 59 0 / 60-89 89 0 / 90+ 0 | Past due -0- | Payment 30X $67 | Balance 1,754 |
| | Last active 12/00 | BU1 BX1 BQ1 [Joint undefined] | High credit --- | Installment (I1) Refinance | | | | |

TOTALS	High credit	High balance				Past due	Payment	Balance
	111	132,495				78	67	2,083

Inquiry Information

05/20/2001 FACTUAL 603 (BU1)

Summary Information					
General summations	12/98	Oldest tradeline date	**Payment summaries**	35	Open revolving payments
	0	Public records		67	Open installment payments
	21	Number of inquiries 365 days		102	Total open payments
Late payments	3	Payments 30 to 59 days late	**Balance owed**	0	Balance monthly owed
	1	Payments 60 to 89 days late		329	Revolving balance owed
	0	Payments 90 and over days late		1,754	Installment balance owed
				2,083	Total balance owed
Trades numbers	1	Number of open revolving trades	**Amount past due**	78	Revolving amount past due
	1	Number of open installment trades		0	Installment amount past due
	1	Number of balance monthly trades		0	Balance monthly amount past due
	2	Total number of trades			
				78	Total amount past due

FIGURE 6-2 *(Continued)*

Adverse trade lines	1 Number of collection trade lines 0 Number of bankruptcy trade lines 0 Number of foreclosed trade lines 0 Number of profit and loss trade lines 0 Number of repossession trade lines 3 Number of adverse trade lines 4 Total number of trade lines	High credit /balance	0 Revolving credit limit 473 Revolving high balance 131,911 Installment high balance 111 Balance monthly high balance

Information sources

This Bureau Express Report completed by Factual Data is a Merged Credit Report which includes information retrieved from the following repository (ies):

TransUnion Consumer Relations (800) 888-4213 PO BOX 1000 Chester, PA 19022	Equifax Consumer Relations (800) 685-1111 PO Box 740256 Atlanta, GA 30374-0256	Experian Consumer Relations (888) 397-3742 PO Box 2002 Allen, TX 75013

This report is furnished in response to a consumer or business application. The information contained herein meets all guidelines set forth by the Fair Credit Reporting Act; it is to be held in strict confidence and may be revealed only to those whose official duties require the information in relation to which this report was ordered, except that which is required by law. The information has been obtained from sources deemed reliable, the accuracy of which Factual Data does not guarantee.

* Denotes source(s) of adverse information

End of Report	0184EEC34F932.3.20

INCOME

We have already seen how a lender determines a borrower's income eligibility with the ratio method qualification. However, the qualification of a borrower's income goes one step further.

Within the income realm there are two issues that may affect the borrower's approval:

- Stability of income

- Calculation of monthly income

Stability of Income

A lender does not simply use the borrower's current income for qualification purposes. A lender wants to predetermine the borrower's capability for making his or her future mortgage payments. This is accomplished by reviewing the borrower's past wage earnings in order to establish a stable or increasing earning pattern. The lender will require income documentation for the previous two years, and this can be fulfilled with a copy of the borrower's W-2s, 1099s, or full tax returns for the previous two years *or* with written verification from the employer.

If your borrower changed jobs during this time, you will need to provide verification of employment to fulfill the two-year requirement, which typically must be in the same line of work. If the borrower had any interruption in employment, this is referred to as a *gap in employment.* A letter of explanation for that gap will be required. For those who may have been in school or in the military, exceptions may be made with proper documentation.

What if your borrower earns less income now than what he or she earned last year? This is referred to as *declining income.* The lender will require a letter of explanation and a good reason why the income is declining, even if the borrower qualifies for the mortgage at his or her current income.

A stable income is important when considering other sources of income, such as child support, alimony, or income from a note, which tends to carry an *end date.* Generally, the income will need to have a continuance of three to five years (this varies from lender to lender) in order to use that source of income for qualification purposes.

Calculation of Monthly Income

If a borrower has an annual salary, then it is simply divided by 12. For example:

$$\frac{\$75,000 \text{ annual salary}}{12} = \$6,250 \text{ monthly salary}$$

Pay frequency will affect the calculation of monthly salary. For example, a weekly salary of $1,000 is calculated at

$$\$1,000 \times 52 \text{ weeks} = \$52,000 \qquad \frac{\$52,000}{12} = \$4,333.33$$

Income paid biweekly would be

$$\$2,000 \times 26 = \$52,000 \qquad \frac{\$52,000}{12} = \$4,333.33$$

However, if the income were paid twice a month, then it would be

$$\$2,000 \times 2 = \$4,000$$

For the borrower who is paid an hourly wage and for whom work hours fluctuate, the lender will average the last two years of the borrower's income. For example:

2-YEAR AVERAGE CALCULATION	
2002 income	$28,000
2003 income	$38,000
Total	$66,000

$$\frac{\$66,000}{24 \text{ months (2 years)}} = \$2,750 \text{ monthly}$$

If you are far enough into the year when the mortgage application is taken, you may be able to use the previous year's and current year-to-date earnings as an average, as long as your borrower's income is increasing. For example:

CALCULATING INCOME EARNED IN PRESENT YEAR	
Application Date 7/24/2004	
2002 income	$28,000
2003 income	$38,000
2004 income through July 1, 2004 (6 months)	21,000
Total (18 months)	$59,000

$$18\text{-month average} \qquad \frac{\$59,000}{18 \text{ months}} = \$3,277.77 \text{ monthly}$$

For a salaried borrower who needs more income to qualify, you may use overtime, bonus, and commission income. However, in order to use this additional income, you will need to provide verification of both previous history and the probability of continuance of this type of income.

The most efficient way to calculate overtime income is by separating the salary and the overtime income earned. This method of calculation is beneficial because you will be able to take advantage of the current pay rate. The calculation would be

Current pay rate + 2-year average of overtime income = total GMI

You must be prepared to have proper documentation to prove and accurately calculate the overtime earnings. The most effective way is to provide written verification from the employer (and a current pay stub), with the breakdown of the amount of regular pay earned and the amount of overtime earned for the last two years.

CALCULATING OVERTIME INCOME

2001: $28,000 Salary
$~~~~~$3,000 Overtime
$31,000 Total W-2 income

2002: $38,000 Salary
$~~~~~$3,500 Overtime
$41,500 Total W-2 income

If you simply average earnings for the last 2 years, it would be

$$\$31,000 + \$41,500 = \$72,500 \qquad \frac{\$72,500}{24} = \$3,020.83$$

However, if you obtained the verification of overtime earned, then you can use the current salary of

$$\frac{\$38,000}{12} = \$3,166.00$$

plus the overtime income of the last 2 years:

$$\$3,000 + \$3,500 = \$6,500 \qquad \frac{\$6,500}{24} = \$270.83$$

The correct monthly income would be

$3,166.00	Current monthly salary
270.83	Average overtime income per month
$3,436.83	Correct total monthly salary including overtime

Important Factor Regarding Commission Income

When *any* additional income received exceeds *25%* of the base pay, a lender will require tax returns for the past two years and will qualify the borrower as a self-employed individual.

Most borrowers who are paid on commission tend to gain almost 100% of their income from commissions paid, exceeding the 25% requirement, and thus are typically treated as self-employed individuals. The reason is that commissioned applicants can claim nonreimbursed expenses on their federal tax returns, reducing the gross earned income. Most lenders will require the previous two years' tax returns to determine the *average* commission income earned.

Nontaxable Income

If your borrower receives nontaxable income, the lender will allow you to gross up the income. The gross-up amount varies between lenders and is typically 125%.

For example, if your borrower receives $1,200 in monthly social security retirement benefits, the gross-up calculation would be

$$\$1,200 \times 125\% = \$1,500 \text{ (gross monthly income)}$$

Nontaxable income includes:

- Social security benefits (provide the last two years' 1099s and a copy of the current benefits award letter)

- Military housing allowance (provide recent pay stubs along with the last two years' W-2s)

- Trust income (provide copies of the trust agreement or trustee's statement confirming income received)

- Notes receivables (provide copy of the note and two years' tax returns or bank statements)

Alimony and Child-Support Income

In order for alimony and child support to be considered, FNMA requires the borrower to have received the income for the past 12 months and for it to be in continuance for the next 3 years.

If payments have been received for less than 12 months but more than 6 months, the income can still be considered as long as the income is not more than 30% of the total gross qualifying income. To verify income you will need to provide bank statements, tax returns, or canceled checks *and* a copy of the separation agreement or divorce decree.

Rental Income

Rental income (reported on federal tax form Schedule E) generally is used to compensate for an existing mortgage payment for a property that is owned by your borrower but is currently rented or leased out. Lenders have two options on calculating rental income:

1. A lender can require a current one-year lease to determine the income from the property. This income is then lowered by a vacancy factor (typically 25%) before determining the cash flow of the property.

2. The lender can require the previous two years' tax returns in order to calculate the cash flow. In addition to the tax returns, a copy of the current lease agreement will be required.

If the rental property is the property for which the borrower is applying for a mortgage, the lender will generally use the figures presented by the appraiser to calculate the cash flow on the property. The appraiser completes an operating income statement for the rental property, which supplies these figures.

Liquid Asset Income

If you plan to qualify your borrower on income derived from liquid assets, such as dividends and interest (for example, municipals income as reported on federal tax form Schedule B), you will need the following documentation:

- Income tax returns for the last two years

- Verification of assets either by providing two or three months' statements from the investment institution *or* through a direct written verification from the institution (verification of deposit, or VOD, form).

If the income is from the sale of a business or real estate, then your borrower must have an installment agreement. Remember, continuance of income must be at least three to five years (varies according to lender requirements). You will need both of these:

- A copy of the note or installment agreement

- Two years' returns to demonstrate proof of receipt of income

Now onto the most complex and difficult income type: the *self-employed borrower.*

Self-Employed Borrowers

Nearly all of us are aware that most small businesses have a small chance of survival, especially in the first years of conception. It is no wonder that lenders pay such close attention to the application of a self-employed borrower. This is what makes the qualification process so challenging and sensitive. One major challenge is providing sufficient taxable income, the reason being that most small businesses tend to deduct as many expenses as possible in order to reduce tax liability. Lenders are going to qualify a borrower based on the *adjustable gross income* (after all allowable expenses), and this is usually significantly lower than the actual income received. Another challenge is presenting a stable income stream. If there is a significant change in income from one year to the next, then you are not able to present stable income. If the average adjustable gross income is insufficient to qualify your borrower, you may need compensating factors, such as a larger down payment, large reserves, or a mortgage term of 20 years or less.

Below we outline as best possible the types of self-employed borrowers and their provisions with lenders based upon standard requirements.

1. *Sole proprietorship.* An individual who is self-employed with no legal entity. A sole proprietor will need to provide:
   ○ Personal federal tax returns for the last two years
   ○ Year-to-date profit and loss statement

2. *Corporation or partnership.* Any individual who owns 25% or more of the separate legal entities. A corporation or partnership will need to provide:
   - Individual income tax returns for the last two years
   - Business income tax returns for the last two years
   - Year-to-date profit and loss statement
   - Partnership income—reported on Schedule E of the individual tax returns
   - Partnership or Subchapter S K-1, which is equivalent to a W-2 of a salaried employee

A *partnership* is an agreement between two or more individuals for the purpose of conducting a business. A partnership is a legal contract that binds a minimum of two people. It consists of two levels of partner: a general partner and a limited partner. The general partner is the key partner who makes the business decisions on operation and holds the liability of the business debt. A limited partner does not participate in the operations decisions and is only liable to the extent of his or her investment in the partnership. Partnership tax return schedule K-1 will detail ownership interest.

A *C corporation* is a corporation owned by stockholders, although they do not directly manage the corporation. They elect (and can remove) the board of directors. The board of directors is responsible for managing the affairs of the corporation, and the directors normally make the major business decisions and supervise and appoint the officers, who make the day-to-day decisions of the corporation and are responsible for everyday management. In most states, one person can be the sole stockholder, the sole director, and the only officer. The corporation may operate on a fiscal year that is different from a calendar year, which can cause year-to-year analysis to be challenging.

An *S corporation* is a mix between a partnership and a corporation. An S corporation is a standard business corporation that has elected a special tax status with the IRS. This tax treatment allows the corporation not to be a separately taxable entity. Instead, the income of the corporation is treated like the income of a partnership or sole proprietorship; the income is "passed through" to the shareholders. Thus, shareholders' individual tax returns report the income or loss generated by an S corporation.

Business income is required to be claimed within a calendar year and cannot be carried forward. Shares of stock are issued, and owners are limited in their initial investment.

Some things to consider when submitting documentation for a self-employed borrower:

- Tax returns must be completed and signed by the borrowers.

- Supply the lender with a completed and signed 4506, which will allow the lender to request a copy of the taxes directly from the IRS for the verification of income.

- The profit and loss (P&L) statement is required when the application date is more than 120 days (a business quarter) after the end of the prior business tax year. A P&L statement is a bookkeeping record of total gross income (receivables) and total expenses (payables). The P&L statement is usually prepared by an independent accountant. However, exceptions are made with small businesses in which the current income is consistent with the income shown on the tax returns. The P&L must be signed by the borrowers if not prepared by an accountant.

The two-year rule—does it apply? Due to the high rate of failure in start-up businesses, it's easy to understand that a self-employed borrower must be in business for a *minimum* of two years. There are some nonconforming loan products that will be more lenient. You may find a loan program if either of the following applies to your borrower:

- Your borrower was an employee for many years and has now decided to open his or her own business. (The borrower must be in the same line of work.)

- Your borrower was attending school for a new profession, received a degree for that profession, and has now opened his or her own business. (The borrower must have at least one year of filed income tax returns.)

For nonconforming loan programs, the lender may accept one year's filed tax returns and business bank statements for the remaining months.

Calculating Self-Employment Income

Lenders will use only the taxable income or adjusted gross income for qualifying purposes. Basically, the average adjustable gross income for the previous two years is considered. The profit and loss statement is used only to provide documentation that the income remains stable; it is not figured into the calculation of income.

Sole Proprietorship Income

Income is reported on Schedule C of the personal income tax returns. Schedule C contains the profit and loss on the business. The income shown is the bottom line with all expenses taken out.

Income − expenses = taxable line or adjusted gross income

For example:

$80,000 (gross income)
−$50,000 (total expenses claimed)
$30,000 (adjustable gross income)

When reviewing the tax returns of a sole proprietor, if it is a home business, you can add back the portion that would equal rent for an office. In addition, when reviewing income documentation on a self-employed borrower, be sure to look for duplicated expenses. As an example, a car lease appearing on the credit report would be included in the debts and considered in the back-end ratio. However, if the auto lease is also a business debt and is subtracted from the gross income on Schedule C, then you are duplicating that expense. In this case, you can add this income back to the gross income or subtract it from the back-end ratio, but not both.

Partnership and Corporation Income

Partnership income distributed to the borrower is the income used and is reported on a K-1, along with the percentage of ownership. For example, if the corporation earned $75,000 and at that time the borrower owned 60% of the corporation, then $45,000 of that income could be used for qualifying.

What If You Are Not Able to Qualify Your Self-Employed Borrower on His or Her Taxable Income?

The most common option for a self-employed borrower is to consider a "stated-income" loan program, also known as *no-doc loans*. These programs will require a larger down payment or a higher interest rate. In this case, the income is not verified; the borrower's income is simply "stated" on the loan application. Keep in mind that the income stated must be in line with your borrower's profession. You will need to provide verification that your borrower has been self-employed for a minimum of two years, and this can be done with a copy of the business license or a letter from your borrower's certified public account to verify that the borrower has filed income taxes as a self-employed individual for a minimum of two years.

Also available are *low-doc loans* (low or limited documentation). For this kind of loan, you will need to provide 6 to 12 months of income documentation (as opposed to the full 2 years). *NINA loans* (no income, no assets loan program) are still another option.

ASSETS

Liquid assets are an important factor in the loan approval process because they are required for the down payment, closing costs, prepaids, and cash reserves after the loan closes.

The liquid asset requirement is usually the largest obstacle for a first-time home buyer. Cash requirements are referred to as *out-of-pocket* expenses. These out-of-pocket expenses are required from the borrower's own funds.

How Do You Reduce the Amount of Cash Required?

The most obvious choice is to select a mortgage program with the smallest down payment required. VA requires no down payment. FHA requires less than conventional mortgages that require 5%. Most recently there have been many programs that have been introduced that require a zero down payment. FHLMC has introduced a brand-new loan program, Home Possible, offering police officers, firefighters, teachers, and health-care workers a zero down payment and as low as $500 in closing costs.

Mortgage Down Payment Assistance Program

There is a loan program called a 501(C) (3) mortgage, referring to a type of nonprofit corporation offering down payment assistance. Nonprofit agencies work with lenders, buyers, sellers, and real estate agents to put together no-down-payment loan packages.

The buyer must register with one of the nonprofit agencies. Here are three such agencies:

AmeriDream
www.ameridreamcharity.org
Tel: (866) 263-7437

Neighborhood Gold
http://neighborhoodgold.com
Tel: (888) 627-3023

The Nehimiah Program
www.getdownpayment.com
Tel: (877) 634-3642

Above-Par Pricing

To keep the closing costs to a minimum, you can finance the closing costs by qualifying the borrower using a higher interest rate. For example:

Assist in Costs with a Rebate

Sales price	$100,000
Loan amount	$ 95,000
Down payment	$ 5,000
Closing costs	1,500
Total cash required	$ 6,500
Price on loan sale (above par)	103.50%
Cash from rebate	$ 3,325
Less lender cost of loan	1,500
Cash available to borrower	$ 1,825
Net borrower cash required	$ 4,675

As you can see, by qualifying your borrower on a higher interest rate, you reduced the cash requirement from $6,500 to $4,600.

Seller Contributions

If you are working on a purchase loan, you can ask the seller to contribute to the closing costs. If the house appraises for at least the sale price, the seller is allowed to pay certain closing costs. (Check the loan program for restrictions.)

Gifts

All mortgage sources allow gifts to help in the costs of the down payment and closing fees. (Check the loan program for restrictions.)

Borrow the Funds

In all cases the purchaser can borrow the funds necessary for the down payment, closing costs, prepaids, and cash reserves. (Check the loan program for restrictions.)

Assets for Reserves

Lenders require a borrower to have reserves to compensate for any unforeseen cash restrictions the borrower may face after the loan closes. Standard guidelines require a borrower to have two months' PITI (that means two months' total principal, interest, taxes, and insurance) after the down payment, closing costs, and prepaids have been met. FHA requires only 15 days of interest in reserve. VA and some nonconforming loan products do not have any reserve requirements.

RESTRICTIONS

When establishing a borrower's eligibility for a mortgage transaction, many lenders will differentiate between:

- Citizens and permanent resident aliens

- Nonpermanent resident aliens

- Foreign nationals

Outside of the mortgage arena, it is difficult to find anyone who loans money to anyone other than a U.S. citizen or permanent resident alien.

Citizens and Permanent Resident Aliens

In order to obtain a home loan, the borrower must be a person, not a corporation.

In the mortgage lending industry there is no distinct difference between a U.S. citizen and a permanent resident alien. In fact, the only difference between a citizen and a permanent resident alien is the ability to vote. A permanent resident alien will hold an alien registration receipt card (INS Form I-551) or will have his or her foreign passport stamped "processed for I-551 valid employment authorized."

Nonpermanent Resident Aliens

Nonpermanent resident aliens are citizens of another country who reside in the United States under:

- A conditional resident alien card

- A temporary resident card

- A work or student visa

- Other permit for some period of time

FNMA and FHLMC do not require borrowers to possess permanent residency. They can qualify simply with a nonpermanent visa. However, they must provide proof of:

- Two years' employment

- Two years' banking history

- Two years' credit history

FHA and nonconforming loans are additional sources of financing for nonpermanent resident aliens.

Foreign Nationals

Overall, borrowers who have not lived in this country a minimum of two years present a challenge in obtaining financing because of the difficulty in determining income and assets. In addition, some foreign nationals have diplomatic immunity, making them immune to civil prosecution unless their country allows prosecution. This would make it difficult for a lender in case of default of a mortgage. According to the United Nations, there are billions of dollars in outstanding debts incurred by people with diplomatic immunity.

For your reference, listed below are visa classifications.

Visa Class	Description
A1	Head of state, ambassador, public minister, career diplomat, and members of immediate family
A2	Foreign government officials and members of immediate family
A3	Attendant, servant, or personal employee of A1 and A2
B1	Temporary visitor for business—no work authorization
B2	Temporary visitor for pleasure—no work authorization
C1–C3	Alien in transit through the United States
C1/D	Crew member/crew
E1–E2	Treaty trader/investor, spouse and children
F1–F2	Student and dependent of student—work authorized under limited circumstances
G1–G5	Representatives of recognized foreign government to international organization, and immediate family
H1B–H4	Temporary worker in specialized occupation
I	Representative of foreign information media and dependents
J1–J2	Exchange visitor and dependents
L1–L2	Executive or specialized personnel continuing employment with an international firm and dependents
M1–M2	Vocational student and dependents
O1–O3	Aliens with extraordinary abilities in science/art/education/athletics and their staff and dependents
P1–P4	Athletes and entertainers and their staff and dependents
Q	International cultural exchange visitor
R1–R2	Religious worker and dependents
TN–TD	Canadian or Mexican citizen working in a professional capacity under the North American Free Trade Agreement
WB	Waiver for business—no work authorization
WT	Waiver for tourism—no work authorization

Borrower Qualification Quiz

1. Your borrower's front-end, or housing, ratio is 25%, his total gross monthly income is $8,000, and all his other debt totals $720. What would his debt ratio be?

   A. 29%

   B. 34%

   C. 46%

2. A lender reviews a borrower's mortgage and credit card payments and searches for any collections or liens, etc., by "looking back" for a certain period of the borrower's credit history. How long is a typical look-back period for a lender?
   A. 6 months
   B. 12 months
   C. 36 months

3. How long will a Chapter 7 bankruptcy remain on a credit report from the filing date?
   A. 5 years
   B. 7 years
   C. 10 years

4. Which is true of a Chapter 13 bankruptcy?
   A. Allows the debtor to pay back the creditors over a period of up to 5 years
   B. Allows the reorganization of an ongoing business to restructure its debt
   C. Allows all debts included in the bankruptcy to be discharged

5. Generally rental income is used only to offset an existing mortgage payment. The lender will require a current one-year lease agreement and then will lower the amount received for the vacancy factor. What amount is typically deducted for this vacancy factor?
   A. 20%
   B. 25%
   C. 30%

6. When your borrower owns 25% or more of a business partnership, where would you find the partnership income?
   A. Business bank statements
   B. K-1 form
   C. Profit and loss statement

7. What is a credit score designed to do?
   A. Assess the credit risk
   B. Make a credit decision
   C. Assist the borrower in obtaining credit

8. When applying for a full-income documentation loan on a self-employed individual, you will need to provide the last two years' tax returns and what other piece of documentation?
   A. Bank statements
   B. W-2s
   C. Profit and loss statement for the current year

9. A short-term debt can sometimes be eliminated from a borrower's debt ratio calculation when there are fewer than how many payments remaining?
   A. Six
   B. Seven
   C. Ten

10. Why would a borrower who posseses a diplomatic visa—class A—not be eligible for a mortgage loan?
    A. Because the borrower may be immune to civil prosecution
    B. Because the borrower is a nonresident alien
    C. Because the borrower is a resident alien

11. Which of the following adverse credit is the most damaging?
    A. 30-day late payment on an auto loan
    B. 30-day late payment on a mortage
    C. 60-day late payment on a credit card

12. The Equal Credit Opportunity Act (ECOA) is a federal law. This law:
    A. Allows a borrower to be approved for credit
    B. Requires the credit decision to be given verbally
    C. Requires that every consumer who applies for credit have an equal opportunity to obtain it

13. A borrower is generally considered a high risk when the credit score is below:
    A. 680
    B. 660
    C. 620

14. On income that carries an end date, such as child-support income or income from a note, typically the income will need to continue for:
    A. One to two years
    B. Two to three years
    C. Three to five years

15. If a borrower earned a $38,000 salary plus $2,500 in overtime pay for the year 2002 and a salary of $46,000 plus $3,200 in overtime pay for the year 2003, how much is her monthly gross income?
    A. $3,833.33
    B. $4,070.83
    C. $3,716.66

16. Self-employed individuals will need to provide the last two years' tax returns for the calculation of their income. On what income will the lender qualify the self-employed individual?
    A. Average of last two years' gross income
    B. Average of last two years' income
    C. Average of last two years' adjusted gross income

17. If your borrower receives $2,100 from social security income and $2,250 from a trust income, what is your borrower's gross monthly income?
    A. $5,437.50
    B. $4,875.00
    C. $4,350.00

18. Many lenders require the borrower to have reserves for a mortgage transaction. This is to offset an unforeseen cash shortfall after the mortgage transaction. What is the standard guideline for these reserves?
    A. Two months' taxes and insurance
    B. Two months' principal and interest, taxes, and insurance
    C. Two months' principal and interest

19. If your borrower is buying a home for $250,000 with a 20% down payment and obtains a 30-year fixed-rate mortgage at 8.25%, what is her PITI?
    A. $1,502.53
    B. $1,804.57
    C. $1,815.03

20. Your borrower's GMI is $6,000, he is buying a $250,000 home with 20% down, he is obtaining a 30-year fixed-rate mortgage at 8.25%, and his total monthly debt is $150 a month. What is his back-end ratio?
    A. 32%
    B. 34%
    C. 30%

Answers to the quiz can be found at the end of Part One.

CHAPTER 7

PROPERTY QUALIFICATION

The tragedy in life doesn't lie in not reaching your goal.
The tragedy lies in having no goal to reach.

—Benjamin Mays

REVIEW OF PROPERTY TYPES

Owner Occupancy

There is one critical credit risk factor that predicates under-writing guidelines—owner occupancy. Does the borrower intend to live in the property? When people purchase a home in order to reside in that home, they are considered owner occupants. The theory is that when times get hard, borrowers are more willing to repay a loan for a home in which they live; therefore, an owner-occupied property is less of a credit risk.

Can a person live in two properties? In some rare circumstances, borrowers may work a lengthy distance from their primary home, and they will purchase a second home to stay in during a workweek; this would constitute two primary residences.

A borrower can purchase a home as an investment and either lease or rent it out. In this case, the borrower would then be considered a nonowner occupant or an investor. Please note that there is a difference between a second home (which tends to be a vacation home) and a home that is being rented out (an investment property).

For a conforming loan, a borrower is limited to 10 properties (including the primary residence), and all combined, loan balances must not exceed $2 million.

Property Types

Because a mortgage loan is secured against real estate, it is understandable that another major facet of risk is the type of property that is being given as security or collateral. A borrower who buys a single-family residence owns the entire house inside and out, along with the land on which the property sits. The lender considers a single-family residence a limited risk.

However, the risk increases when the property is part of a homeowner's association. Why the higher risk? For one thing, a homeowner's association is responsible for maintaining common areas (known as common elements) such as pools or landscape, and thus the homeowner's association has liability exposure. For example, a construction worker working on the complex could slip and fall and bring suit against the association. The homeowner's association must carry sufficient insurance coverage (requirements vary from state to state) to protect the association's assets. As well, the association also has the responsibility of maintaining the financial condition of the development. In addition, some investors will rent out their units, the problem being that a non-owner occupant will generally have less regard for the upkeep of the unit and common grounds than will an owner resident. For this reason you find guideline restrictions on the amount of non-owner-occupied units per development, and for this reason a PUD and condominium will carry a higher risk.

Underwriting guidelines will always call for a description of property type. Here is a breakdown:

- *Single-family residence (SFR)*. Also referred to as a single-family detached (SFD) house. Located on public streets. Houses have no common areas and no adjoining walls.

- *Planned unit development (PUD)*. A development consisting of single-family detached homes, town homes, or condominiums. These properties pay an association fee to support an association that maintains all common areas.

- *Condominium*. Often called a *condo*. A development consisting of an undivided interest in common areas with a *separate* individual interest in a unit. There is an association and association fees.

- *Cooperative*. Often called a *co-op*. A development in which a corporation holds title to all real property, and the shareholders receive a right of exclusive occupancy in a portion of that real property. The corporation is responsible for paying real estate taxes and maintaining all common areas.

- *Mobile and manufactured homes*. Factory-built homes that are transported and assembled on site.

Type of Ownership

There are two ways an individual can hold ownership to real property:

- *Fee simple*. This is the most common way real estate is owned and is the most complete ownership someone can have in real property.

- *Leasehold*. A leasehold estate is a long-term ground lease. At the end of the lease term, the land is returned to the landlord.

What Restrictions Do Condos Have?

As we have learned, condominiums carry a higher credit risk than do single-family residences; therefore, condos have certain restrictions in regard to financing. FHA and VA have "approved lists" for condominium projects. FNMA and FHLMC have specific guidelines for condominium approval. The lender will warrant (or guarantee) that the condominium meets these guidelines. Most lenders will require a condominium certification as part of their approval process.

What Restrictions Do Mobile and Manufactured Homes Have?

Only certain lenders provide financing for manufactured or mobile homes. In all cases the home must be doublewide, must be set on a permanent foundation, and will carry loan-to-value restrictions. Here is a full description of the various types of manufactured homes:

- *Manufactured home.* A home built entirely in the factory under HUD code, which went into effect June 15, 1976.

- *Modular home.* A factory-built home constructed according to state, local, or regional code.

- *Panelized home.* A factory-built home that is built in panels—each panel is a whole wall with windows, doors, wiring, and outside siding.

- *Precut home.* A kit, log, or dome home; it must meet local, state, or regional building codes.

- *Mobile home.* Term used for a factory-built home produced prior to June 15, 1976, when the HUD code went into effect. By 1970, these homes were built to voluntary industry standards that were eventually enforced by 45 of the 48 contiguous states.

APPRAISAL

When a borrower decides to buy a home, both the property and the borrower must "qualify" for loan approval. Each loan program has certain criteria that the property must meet.

Basically the lender wants to ensure that the property is worth the amount the applicant is borrowing. Should the borrower default on the loan and the lender need to take back the property, the lender wants to make sure it can recover its money.

An appraisal is a written analysis of the estimated value of a property. The appraiser does not create value; the appraiser interprets the market to arrive at a value estimate. An appraisal states the current market value of the subject property in relation to other similar properties in the area. These similar properties are called *comparables*, or *comps*. As the appraiser compiles data pertinent to a report, consideration must be given to the site and amenities as well as the physical condition of the property. An appraiser may spend only a short time inspecting the property; however, this is only the beginning. Considerable research and collection of general and specific data must be done before the appraiser can arrive at a final opinion of value.

An appraisal of value is made using one of three common approaches:

- *The cost approach* to value is what it would cost to replace or reproduce the property as of the date of the appraisal, less the physical deterioration, the functional obsolescence, and the economic obsolescence. The remainder is added to the land value.

- *The comparison approach* to value makes use of other "benchmark" properties of similar size, quality, and location that have been recently sold. A comparison is made to the subject property.

- *The income approach* to value is the approach used for determining the value of income-producing properties (investment properties). This approach provides an objective estimate of what a prudent investor would pay based upon the net income the property produces.

An appraisal is good for (depending on lender guidelines) 120 days or a maximum of 12 months, if the value has been recertified by the original appraiser.

What does an appraisal include?

The appraisal will include:

- Original pictures of the property

- A detailed description of the:
  - Condition
  - Size
  - Age
  - Quality of construction
  - Any other favorable or unfavorable factors that impact the value of the property

Note: A full residential report must be on Fannie Mae Form 1004. An exterior inspection (also known as a *drive-by appraisal*) is on Form 2055.

If the appraisal contains an unfavorable comment on the property, the lender may require any repairs or improvement necessary on the property to be completed prior to loan approval. In this case the owner of the property would have to make any necessary repairs, and then the appraiser is required to return to the property for reinspection. The appraiser provides the lender with a Form 442 (may include photos, if necessary) to certify that the repairs or improvements were completed satisfactorily.

Who conducts an appraisal?

A licensed, bonded professional real estate appraiser conducts the appraisal. Some lenders require the use of someone from their approved appraiser list.

What is the fee for an appraisal?

The fee varies by region. The fee typically is $250 to $450.

The fee for the appraisal is paid in one of two ways:

- The appraiser can bill the lender, and therefore the fees are financed into the loan.

- The fee is paid by the borrower to the appraiser directly. This is the preferred method, as it protects the loan broker or lender against withdrawal of the loan application by the borrower or applicant.

Who arranges the appraisal?

The appraisal is typically ordered by the processor or processing center.

What value will be used to qualify the borrower?

In the case of a purchase, either the *appraised value* or the *sales price* will be used, whichever is less. For example, if the borrower wants to buy a home priced at $100,000 and the property is appraised for $150,000, the loan is based on the sales price.

In the case of refinance, the new appraised value of the property is used. However, in order to use the new appraised value of the property, the borrower must have owned the property for at least one year—a *seasoning* requirement. If the borrower has owned the property for less than a year, the original appraised value or sales price (whichever was less) would have to be used. For example, if the borrower purchased a piece of property for $100,000 in March, even though the property may be appraised for $150,000 three months later, the borrower is bound by the initial appraisal value of $100,000 for one year for refinance purposes. The one-year seasoning requirement is a rule that most lenders impose. However, there are nonconforming loan programs, such as subprime loans, that will make exceptions to this rule on a case-by-case basis. Property qualification also determines whether the loan will be conventional conforming or nonconforming.

There are many reasons a property may *not* be eligible for a conforming loan, including the following:

1. *Excessive acreage or rural property*. A conforming loan will be denied if the acreage exceeds the amount typical for residential homes in the area. The acreage allowed varies per lender or program guidelines. Farms and ranches (rural property) cannot be financed through mortgage lending programs; instead they are covered by the Farmers Home Administration.

2. *Land value that exceeds guidelines*. The appraiser will estimate the land value. This is noted on page 2 of the

Uniform Residential Appraisal Report as "site value" (see Figure 7-1). Most standards limit the value of the land to a maximum of 30 to 35% of total value.

For example, suppose the sales price is $100,000. A land value of $30,000 would fit the guidelines since this would result in a land-to-value ratio of 30%.

An exception to this rule would require the appraiser to state that a higher land-to-value ratio is common to the area, and the appraiser would have to provide information about comparable sales with similar land value.

3. *Subpar conditions of the home.* If the maintenance of the home provides a threat to the health, safety, or marketability of the home, the lender may require the correction of these deficiencies before lending on the home. FHA specifically requires the lender to disclose the possibility of lead paint hazard in homes built before 1978.

4. *Negative marketability factors.* The lender can choose not to mortgage a home if there are factors that negatively inhibit the marketability of the home. The factors may be:
   ○ The market area is declining in value.
   ○ The market area is in transition into commercial use.
   ○ The average marketing time exceeds six to nine months.
   ○ The home is overimproved (the value exceeds the predominant value range of the area).

5. *Commercial zoning.* If the property is zoned as commercial, a residential mortgage will not be approved even if the home is currently in residential use.

6. *Public and private facilities.* There is no rule that the home must be serviced by public water, sewer, or road facilities. The lender will require inspection of a well or septic system, and VA requires hookup to public systems.

Figure 7-1 shows a typical Uniform Residential Appraisal.

FIGURE 7-1
Example of a Uniform Residential Appraisal Report

File No. 75490805   Page #1

UNIFORM RESIDENTIAL APPRAISAL REPORT

File No. 75490805

Property Address **123 Sample Street**	City **Chandler** State **AZ** Zip Code **85224**
Legal Description **Lot 333 Sample Heights**	County **Maricopa**
Assessor's Parcel No. **111-222-333**	Tax Year **2000** R.E. Taxes $ **2061** Special Assessments $ **N/A**

SUBJECT

Borrower **John Smith**   Current Owner **Borrower**   Occupant ☒ Owner ☐ Tenant ☐ Vacant
Property rights appraised ☒ Fee Simple ☐ Leasehold   Project Type ☒ PUD ☐ Condominium (HUD/VA only)   HOA $ **22.00** /Mo.
Neighborhood or Project Name **Sample Heights**   Map Reference **LJ 222**   Census Tract **0000.21**
Sales Price $ **N/A**   Date of Sale **N/A**   Description and $ amount of loan charges/concessions to be paid by seller **None Noted**
Lender/Client **ABC Bank**   Address **222 Water Street, Colorado Springs, CO 80909**
Appraiser **Realink**   Address **617 S. Rockford Dr. Tempe, AZ 85281**

NEIGHBORHOOD

Location	☒ Urban	☐ Suburban	☐ Rural	Predominant occupancy	Single family housing		Present land use %	Land use change

Location ☒ Urban ☐ Suburban ☐ Rural
Built up ☒ Over 75% ☐ 25-75% ☐ Under 25%
Growth rate ☐ Rapid ☒ Stable ☐ Slow
Property values ☐ Increasing ☒ Stable ☐ Declining
Demand/supply ☐ Shortage ☒ In balance ☐ Over supply
Marketing time ☐ Under 3 mos. ☒ 3-6 mos. ☐ Over 6 mos.

Predominant occupancy: ☒ Owner ☐ Tenant ☒ Vacant (0-5%) ☐ Vacant (Over 5%)

Single family housing
PRICE $(000): 150 Low, 500 High, 250 Predominant
AGE (yrs): New Low, 15 High, 5 Predominant

Present land use %: One family 85, 2-4 family 2, Multi-family 3, Commercial 10
Land use change: ☒ Not likely ☐ Likely ☐ In process ☐ To:

Note: Race and the racial composition of the neighborhood are not appraisal factors.

Neighborhood boundaries and characteristics: **Subject is bound by to the north by Ray Rd., to the south by Chandler Blvd., to the east by Dobson Rd. and to the west by Price Rd.**

Factors that affect the marketability of the properties in the neighborhood (proximity to employment and amenities, employment stability, appeal to market, etc.):
The subject is located within a reasonable proximity to municipal services including schools, shopping and employment centers. The improvements conform well to surrounding properties. There are no apparent adverse factors which should affect the subject's marketability. This is a "Summary Appraisal Report".

Market conditions in the subject neighborhood (including support for the above conclusions related to the trend of property values, demand/supply, and marketing time -- such as data on competitive properties for sale in the neighborhood, description of the prevalence of sales and financing concessions, etc.):
Property values in the subject neighborhood appear stable. Financing is conventional, cash and some with assumptions and carrybacks are not uncommon. Typical seller paid points are in the 0-1.5 range. Supply and demand appear in balance with most properties selling within 3-6 months.

PUD

Project Information for PUDs (If applicable) - - Is the developer/builder in control of the Home Owners' Association (HOA)? ☐ Yes ☒ No
Approximate total number of units in the subject project **137**. Approximate total number of units for sale in the subject project _____.
Describe common elements and recreational facilities: **greenbelts**

SITE

Dimensions **60.00 x 8669 x 87 x 40.06 x 3.2886.025**   Topography **Level**
Site area **7345.00 SqFt**   Corner Lot ☒ Yes ☐ No   Size **Typical**
Specific zoning classification and description **PAD - Single Family Residential**   Shape **Irregular**
Zoning compliance ☒ Legal ☐ Legal nonconforming (Grandfathered use) ☐ Illegal ☐ No zoning   Drainage **Adequate**
Highest & best use as improved ☒ Present use ☐ Other use (explain)   View **Typical**

Utilities	Public	Other	Off-site Improvements	Type	Public	Private	
Electricity	☒		Street	Asphalt	☒	☐	Landscaping **Typical for the area**
Gas			Curb/Gutter	Concrete	☒	☐	Driveway Surface **Concrete**
Water	☒		Sidewalk	Concrete	☒	☐	Apparent Easements **Typical**
Sanitary Sewer	☒		Street Lights	Incandescent	☒	☐	FEMA Special Flood Hazard Area ☐ Yes ☒ No
Storm Sewer	☒		Alley	None			FEMA Zone **X** Map Date **12/14/93**

FEMA Map No. **040040 2635F**

Comments (apparent adverse easements, encroachments, special assessments, slide areas, illegal or legal nonconforming zoning use, etc.): **There are no easement encroachments or adverse conditions known or observed.**

DESCRIPTION OF IMPROVEMENTS

GENERAL DESCRIPTION	EXTERIOR DESCRIPTION	FOUNDATION	BASEMENT	INSULATION
No. of Units **One**	Foundation **Slab**	Slab **Concrete**	Area Sq. Ft. **None**	Roof ☐
No. of Stories **Two**	Exterior Walls **Stucco**	Crawl Space **None**	% Finished	Ceiling ☐
Type (Det./Att.) **Detached**	Roof Surface **Tile**	Basement **None**	Ceiling	Walls **Assumd.** ☒
Design (Style) **Contmpry**	Gutters & Dwnspts. **None**	Sump Pump **N/A**	Walls	Floor ☐
Existing/Proposed **Existing**	Window Type **Alum. Slider**	Dampness **N/A**	Floor	None ☐
Age (Yrs.) **6**	Storm/Screens **Screens**	Settlement **None noted**	Outside Entry	Unknown ☐
Effective Age (Yrs.) **2**	Manufactured House **N/A**	Infestation **None noted**		

ROOMS	Foyer	Living	Dining	Kitchen	Den	Family Rm.	Rec. Rm.	Bedrooms	# Baths	Laundry	Other	Area Sq. Ft.
Basement												
Level 1	X	1	1	1	1	1			.25	1		1871
Level 2								4	2.00		Loft	1480

Finished area above grade contains: **9** Rooms; **4** Bedroom(s); **2.25** Bath(s); **3,351** Square Feet of Gross Living Area

INTERIOR	Materials/Condition	HEATING		KITCHEN EQUIP.		ATTIC		AMENITIES		CAR STORAGE:	
Floors	**Vinyl/Tile/Cpt/Avg**	Type	**FWA**	Refrigerator		None	☒	Fireplace(s) #		None	☐
Walls	**Drywall/Avg**	Fuel	**Elec**	Range/Oven	☒	Stairs		Patio **Cov. Patio**	☒	Garage	# of cars
Trim/Finish	**Wood/Avg**	Condition	**Avg**	Disposal	☒☒	Drop Stair		Deck		Attached **3**	
Bath Floor	**Vinyl/Avg**	COOLING		Dishwasher	☒	Scuttle		Porch		Detached	
Bath Wainscot	**Sim Marble/Avg**	Central	**CAC**	Fan/Hood	☒	Floor		Fence **Block**	☒	Built-In	
Doors	**Wood/Avg**	Other		Microwave		Heated		Pool		Carport	
		Condition	**Avg**	Washer/Dryer		Finished				Driveway	

Additional features (special energy efficient items, etc.): **The subject has a covered patio and block fence enclosing rear yard.**

COMMENTS

Condition of the improvements, depreciation (physical, functional, and external), repairs needed, quality of construction, remodeling/additions, etc.: **Subject is in average condition for the age. There was no functional or external obsolescence noted at the time of inspection**

Adverse environmental conditions (such as, but not limited to, hazardous wastes, toxic substances, etc.) present in the improvements, on the site, or in the immediate vicinity of the subject property: **There were no adverse environmental conditions observed or noted at the time of inspection.**

FIGURE 7-1 (*Continued*)

File No. 75490805   Page #2

UNIFORM RESIDENTIAL APPRAISAL REPORT

Valuation Section		File No.	75490805

COST APPROACH

ESTIMATED SITE VALUE . . . . = $	65000.00
ESTIMATED REPRODUCTION COST-NEW OF IMPROVEMENTS:	
Dwelling 3,351 Sq. Ft. @ $ 50.33 = $	168,656.00
Sq. Ft. @ $ =	
Cov. patio	2000.00
Garage/Carport 748.00 Sq. Ft. @ $ 15.00 =	11220.00
Total Estimated Cost-New = $	181,876.00
Less Physical 11 Functional External	
Depreciation 20,006 = $	20,006.00
Depreciated Value of Improvements . . . . = $	161,870.00
"As-is" Value of Site Improvements . . . . = $	10000.00
INDICATED VALUE BY COST APPROACH = $	**236,870.00**

Comments on Cost Approach (such as, source of cost estimate, site value, square foot calculation and, for HUD, VA and FmHA, the estimated remaining economic life of the property): Cost estimates were taken from "Marshall & Swift" Residential Cost Handbook and local builders. Depreciation based on Economic Age/Life Method. Site values based on recent site sales, listings or extractions if sales information is not present.

SALES COMPARISON ANALYSIS

ITEM	SUBJECT	COMPARABLE NO. 1		COMPARABLE NO. 2		COMPARABLE NO. 3	
	123 Sample Street	123 Elm Street		123 Oak		123 Maple	
Address	Chandler, AZ 85224	Chandler, AZ		Chandler, AZ		Chandler, AZ	
Proximity to Subject		1 block east		2 blocks North		2 blocks SE	
Sales Price	$ N/A		$ 224900		$ 242000		$ 237000
Price/Gross Liv. Area	$	$ 67.72		$ 72.87		$ 71.36	
Data and/or		MLS/Pub Records		MLS/Pub Records		MLS/Pub Records	
Verification Sources	MLS/Pub Rec	Doc #		Doc #		Doc #	
VALUE ADJUSTMENTS	DESCRIPTION	DESCRIPTION	+(-) Adjustment	DESCRIPTION	+(-) Adjustment	DESCRIPTION	+(-) Adjustment
Sales or Financing Concessions		Conventional None Noted		Conventional None Noted		Conventional None Noted	
Date of Sale/Time		11/20/00		12/12/2000		02/21/01	
Location	Typical	Average		Average		Average	
Leasehold/Fee Simple	Fee Simple	Fee Simple		Fee Simple		Fee Simple	
Site	7345 Sq Ft	7806		7144		7950	
View	Typical	Typical		Typical		Typical	
Design and Appeal	Contmpry	Contemporary		Contemporary		Contemporary	
Quality of Construction	Stucco/Tile/A	Stucco/Tile/Avg		Stucco/Tile/Avg		Stucco/Tile/Avg	
Age	6 yrs.	4 Yrs.		4 yrs		4 years	
Condition	Average	Average		Average		Average	
Above Grade	Total Bdrms Baths	Total Bdrms Baths		Total Bdrms Baths		Total Bdrms Baths	
Room Count	9 4 2.25	9 5 2.25		9 5 3.00	-1000	8 4 3.00	-1000
Gross Living Area	3,351 Sq. Ft.	3321 Sq. Ft.		3321 Sq. Ft.		3321 Sq. Ft.	
Basement & Finished Rooms Below Grade	None	None		None		None	
Functional Utility	Average	Average		Average		Average	
Heating/Cooling	FWA/CAC	FWA/CAC		FWA/CAC		FWA/CAC	
Energy Efficient Items							
Garage/Carport	3-Garage	3 Garage		3 Garage		2 Garage	5000
Porch, Patio, Deck, etc.	Cov. Patio	Cov. patio		Cov. Patio			
Fireplace(s), etc.	None	None		Fireplace	-1500	Fireplace	-1500
Fence, Pool, etc.	Block Fence	None		Pool	-15000	Pool	-15000
Net. Adj. (total)		☒+ ☐- $	0	☐+ ☒- $	-17,500	☐+ ☒- $	-12,500
Adjusted Sales Price of Comparable		$	224,900	$	224,500	$	224,500

Comments on Sales Comparison (including the subject property's compatibility to the neighborhood, etc.): All comparables are the same model as the subject with similar features. Most weight was placed on comparable #1 which does not have a pool. Additional consideration given to sales 2 and 3.

ITEM	SUBJECT	COMPARABLE NO. 1	COMPARABLE NO. 2	COMPARABLE NO. 3
Date, Price and Data Source for prior sales within year of appraisal	No record of sale within the prior 12 mos.	No record of prior 12 months sales activity other than noted above.	No record of prior 12 months sales activity other than noted above.	No record of prior 12 months sales activity other than noted above.

Analysis of any current agreement of sale, option, or listing of the subject property and analysis of any prior sales of subject and comparables within one year of the date of appraisal: The subject is not currently listed for sale and has not sold within the last 12 months.

RECONCILIATION

INDICATED VALUE BY SALES COMPARISON APPROACH . . . . $	224500
INDICATED VALUE BY INCOME APPROACH (If Applicable) Estimated Market Rent $ N/A /Mo. x Gross Rent Multiplier N/A = $	0

The appraisal is made ☒ "as is" ☐ subject to the repairs, alterations, inspections, or conditions listed below ☐ subject to completion per plans and specifications.
Conditions of Appraisal: This analysis is prepared in accordance with the sale standards issued by the Appraisal Foundation and is consistent with requirements of FNMA. This is a complete summary appraisal report.
Final Reconciliation: Most weight is given the Sales Comparison Approach, with additional support from the Cost Approach. Insufficient and varied data do not support the Income Approach as a reliable indicator in this market segment.

The purpose of this appraisal is to estimate the market value of the real property that is the subject of this report, based on the above conditions and the certification, contingent and limiting conditions, and market value definition that are stated in the attached Freddie Mac Form 439/Fannie Mae Form 1004B (Revised).
I (WE) ESTIMATE THE MARKET VALUE, AS DEFINED, OF THE REAL PROPERTY THAT IS THE SUBJECT OF THIS REPORT, AS OF 04/02/01
(WHICH IS THE DATE OF INSPECTION AND THE EFFECTIVE DATE OF THIS REPORT) TO BE $ 224,500 .

APPRAISER:	SUPERVISORY APPRAISER (ONLY IF REQUIRED):	
Signature *Jane Doe*	Signature	☐ Did ☐ Did Not
Name	Name	Inspect Properly
Date Report Signed 04/03/01	Date Report Signed	
State Certification # 000000 State AZ	State Certification #	State
Or State License # State	Or State License #	State

FIGURE 7-1 (*Continued*)

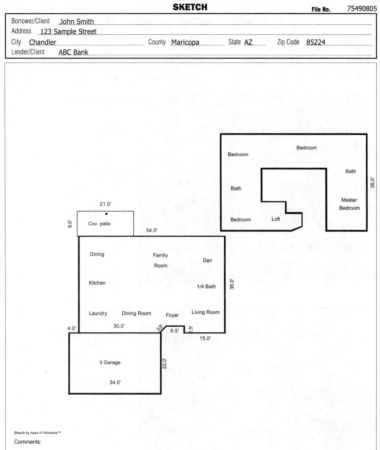

SKETCH

File No.   75490805

Borrower/Client   John Smith
Address   123 Sample Street
City   Chandler   County   Maricopa   State AZ   Zip Code   85224
Lender/Client   ABC Bank

Sketch by Apex IV Windows™
Comments:

AREA CALCULATIONS SUMMARY			
Code	**Description**	**Size**	**Totals**
GLA1	First Floor	1870.62	1870.62
GLA2	Second Floor	1480.50	1480.50
P/P	Patio	189.00	189.00
GAR	Garage	748.00	748.00
	TOTAL LIVABLE (rounded)		3351

LIVING AREA BREAKDOWN		
Breakdown		**Subtotals**
First Floor		
	2.5 x 15.0	37.50
	32.5 x 54.0	1755.00
0.5 x	2.5 x 2.5	3.13
	2.5 x 30.0	75.00
Second Floor		
	15.0 x 33.5	502.50
	9.0 x 9.0	81.00
	12.5 x 39.0	487.50
	5.0 x 6.0	30.00
	15.0 x 22.5	337.50
0.5 x	4.0 x 1.5	3.00
	1.5 x 26.0	39.00
11 Areas Total (rounded)		3351

FIGURE 7-1 *(Continued)*

File No. 75490805   Page #5

COMPARABLE PHOTOGRAPH ADDENDUM

Borrower/Client: John Smith
Address: 123 Sample Street
City: Chandler   County: Maricopa   State: AZ.   Zip Code: 85224
Lender/Client: ABC Bank

Sales Comparable 1

Address:	123 Elm Street
Prox. to Subject:	1 block east
Sales Price: $	224900
Gross Living Area:	3,321.00
Total Rooms:	9
Total Bedrooms:	5
Total Bathrooms:	2.25
Location:	Average

Sales Comparable 2

Address:	123 Oak
Prox. to Subject:	2 blocks North
Sales Price: $	242000
Gross Living Area:	3,321.00
Total Rooms:	9
Total Bedrooms:	5
Total Bathrooms:	3.00
Location:	Average

Sales Comparable 3

Address:	123 Maple
Prox. to Subject:	2 blocks SE
Sales Price: $	237000
Gross Living Area:	3,321.00
Total Rooms:	8
Total Bedrooms:	4
Total Bathrooms:	3.00
Location:	Average

FIGURE 7-1 (*Continued*)

File No. 75490805   Page #6

SUBJECT PHOTOGRAPH ADDENDUM

Borrower/Client: John Smith
Address: 123 Sample Street
City: Chandler   County: Maricopa   State: AZ.   Zip Code: 85224
Lender/Client: ABC Bank

Front View

Subject Rear

Subject Front

FIGURE 7-1 (*Continued*)

File No.   75490805

DEFINITION OF MARKET VALUE: The most probable price which a property should bring in a competitive and open market under all conditions requisite to a fair sale, the buyer and seller, each acting prudently, knowledgeably and assuming the price is not affected by undue stimulus. Implicit in this definition is the consummation of a sale as of a specified date and the passing of title from seller to buyer under conditions whereby: (1) buyer and seller are typically motivated; (2) both parties are well informed or well advised, and each acting in what he considers his own best interest; (3) a reasonable time is allowed for exposure in the open market; (4) payment is made in terms of cash in U.S. dollars or in terms of financial arrangements comparable thereto; and (5) the price represents the normal consideration for the property sold unaffected by special or creative financing or sales concessions* granted by anyone associated with the sale.

*Adjustments to the comparables must be made for special or creative financing or sales concessions. No adjustments are necessary for those costs which are normally paid by sellers as a result of tradition or law in a market area; these costs are readily identifiable since the seller pays these costs in virtually all sales transactions. Special or creative financing adjustments can be made to the comparable property by comparisons to financing terms offered by a third party institutional lender that is not already involved in the property or transaction. Any adjustment should not be calculated on a mechanical dollar for dollar cost of the financing or concession, but the dollar amount of any adjustment should approximate the market's reaction to the financing or concessions based on the appraiser's judgment.

STATEMENT OF LIMITING CONDITIONS AND APPRAISER'S CERTIFICATION

CONTINGENT AND LIMITING CONDITIONS: The appraiser's certification that appears in the appraisal report is subject to the following conditions:

1. The appraiser will not be responsible for matters of a legal nature that affect either the property being appraised or the title to it. The appraiser assumes that the title is good and marketable and, therefore, will not render any opinions about the title. The property is appraised on the basis of it being under responsible ownership.

2. The appraiser has provided a sketch in the appraisal report to show approximate dimensions of the improvements and the sketch is included only to assist the reader of the report in visualizing the property and understanding the appraiser's determination of its size.

3. The appraiser has examined the available flood maps that are provided by the Federal Emergency Management Agency (or other data sources) and has noted in the appraisal report whether the subject site is located in an identified Special Flood Hazard Area. Because the appraiser is not a surveyor, he or she makes no guarantees, expressed or implied, regarding this determination.

4. The appraiser will not give testimony or appear in court because he or she made an appraisal of the property in question, unless specific arrangements to do so have been made beforehand.

5. The appraiser has estimated the value of the land in the cost approach at its highest and best use and the improvements at their contributory value. These separate valuations of the land and improvements must not be used in conjunction with any other appraisal and are invalid if they are so used.

6. The appraiser has noted in the appraisal report any adverse conditions (such as, needed repairs, depreciation, the present of hazardous wastes, toxic substances, etc.) observed during the inspection of the subject property or that he or she became aware of during the normal research involved in performing the appraisal. Unless otherwise stated in the appraisal report, the appraiser has no knowledge of any hidden or unapparent conditions of the property or adverse environmental conditions (including the presence of hazardous wastes, toxic substances, etc.) that would make the property more or less valuable, and has assumed that there are no such conditions and makes no guarantees or warranties, expressed or implied, regarding the condition of the property. The appraiser will not be responsible for any such conditions that do exist or for any engineering or testing that might be required to discover whether such conditions exist. Because the appraiser is not an expert in the field of environmental hazards, the appraisal report must not be considered as an environmental assessment of the property.

7. The appraiser obtained the information, estimates, and opinions that were expressed in the appraisal report from sources that he or she considers to be reliable and believes them to be true and correct. The appraiser does not assume responsibility for the accuracy of such items that were furnished by other parties.

8. The appraiser will not disclose the contents of the appraisal report except as provided for in the Uniform Standards of Professional Appraisal Practice.

9. The appraiser has based his or her appraisal report and valuation conclusion for an appraisal that is subject to satisfactory completion, repairs, or alterations on the assumption that completion of the improvements will be performed in a workmanlike manner.

10. The appraiser must provide his or her prior written consent before the lender/client specified in the appraisal report can distribute the appraisal report (including conclusions about the property value, the appraiser's identity and professional designations, and references to any professional appraisal organizations or the firm with which the appraiser is associated) to anyone other than the borrower; the mortgagee or its successors and assigns; the mortgage insurer; consultants; professional appraisal organizations; any state or federally approved financial institution; or any department, agency, or instrumentality of the United States or any state or the District of Columbia; except that the lender/client may distribute the property description section of the report only to data collection or reporting service(s) without having to obtain the appraiser's prior written consent. The appraiser's written consent and approval must also be obtained before the appraisal can be conveyed by anyone to the public through advertising, public relations, news, sales, or other media.

FIGURE 7-1 (*Continued*)

File No.	75490805

APPRAISER'S CERTIFICATION: The Appraiser certifies and agrees that:

1. I have researched the subject market area and have selected a minimum of three recent sales of properties most similar and proximate to the subject property for consideration in the sales comparison analysis and have made a dollar adjustment when appropriate to reflect the market reaction to those items of significant variation. If a significant item in a comparable property is superior to, or more favorable than, the subject property, I have made a negative adjustment to reduce the adjusted sales price of the comparable and, if a significant item in a comparable property is inferior to, or less favorable than the subject, I have made a positive adjustment to increase the adjusted sales price of the comparable.

2. I have taken into consideration the factors that have an impact on value in my development of the estimate of market value in the appraisal report. I have not knowingly withheld any significant information from the appraisal report and I believe, to the best of my knowledge, that all statements and information in the appraisal report are true and correct.

3. I stated, in the appraisal report, only my own personal, unbiased, and professional analysis, opinions, and conclusions, which are subject only to the contingent and limiting conditions specified in this form.

4. I have no present or prospective interest in the property that is the subject of this report, and I have no present or prospective personal interest or bias with respect to the participants in the transaction. I did not base, either partially or completely, my analysis and/or the estimate of market value in the appraisal report on the race, color, religion, sex, handicap, familial status, or national origin of either the prospective owners or occupants of the subject property or of the present owners or occupants of the properties in the vicinity of the subject property.

5. I have no present or contemplated future interest in the subject property, and neither my current or future employment nor my compensation for performing this appraisal is contingent on the appraised value of the property.

6. I was not required to report a predetermined value or direction in value that favors the cause of the client or any related party, the amount of the value estimate, the attainment of a specific result, or the occurrence of a subsequent event in order to receive my compensation and/or employment for performing the appraisal. I did not base the appraisal report on a requested minimum valuation, a specific valuation, or the need to approve a specific mortgage loan.

7. I performed this appraisal in conformity with the Uniform Standards of Professional Appraisal Practice that were adopted and promulgated by the Appraisal Standards Board of The Appraisal Foundation and that were in place as of the effective date of this appraisal, with the exception of the departure provision of those Standards, which does not apply. I acknowledge that an estimate of a reasonable time for exposure in the open market is a condition in the definition of market value and the estimate I developed is consistent with the marketing time noted in the neighborhood section of this report, unless I have otherwise stated in the reconciliation section.

8. I have personally inspected the interior and exterior areas of the subject property and the exterior of all properties listed as comparables in the appraisal report. I further certify that I have noted any apparent or known adverse conditions in the subject improvements, on the subject site, or on any site within the immediate vicinity of the subject property of which I am aware and have made adjustments for these adverse conditions in my analysis of the property value to the extent that I had market evidence to support them. I have also commented about the effect of the adverse conditions on the marketability of the subject property.

9. I personally prepared all conclusions and opinions about the real estate that were set forth in the appraisal report. If I relied on significant professional assistance from any individual or individuals in the performance of the appraisal or the preparation of the appraisal report, I have named such individual(s) and disclosed the specific tasks performed by them in the reconciliation section of this appraisal report. I certify that any individual so named is qualified to perform the tasks. I have not authorized anyone to make a change to any item in the report; therefore, if an unauthorized change is made to the appraisal report, I will take no responsibility for it.

SUPERVISORY APPRAISER'S CERTIFICATION: If a supervisory appraiser signed the appraisal report, he or she certifies and agrees that: I directly supervise the appraiser who prepared the appraisal report, have reviewed the appraisal report, agree with the statements and conclusions of the appraiser, agree to be bound by the appraiser's certification numbered 4 through 7 above, and am taking full responsibility for the appraisal and the appraisal report.

ADDRESS OF PROPERTY APPRAISED: 123 Sample Street, Chandler, AZ 85224

APPRAISER:

Signature: *Jane Doe*
Name: _____
Date Signed: 04/03/01
State Certification #: 000000
or State License #: _____
State: AZ
Expiration Date of Certification or License: 08/03

SUPERVISORY APPRAISER: (only if required)

Signature: _____
Name: _____
Date Signed: _____
State Certification #: _____
or State License #: _____
State: _____
Expiration Date of Certification or License: _____
☐ Did   ☐ Did Not Inspect Property

Property Qualification Quiz

1. A borrower is purchasing a home for $178,000. During the building of the new home, the value increased in the housing development, and the home is now valued at $225,000. What value will be used to qualify the borrower?
   A. $178,000
   B. $225,000
   C. Neither A nor B

2. Mobile homes have loan-to-value restrictions. What other restrictions do most lenders have on mobile homes?
   A. Must have property taxes
   B. Must be a singlewide unit
   C. Must be on a permanent foundation

3. What is the difference between a co-op and a condominium?
   A. A co-op has common walls.
   B. A co-op has a corporation that maintains all the common areas.
   C. A co-op has an association to maintain all the common areas.

4. Why is an appraisal important?
   A. The mortgage is against a property that will be held as collateral.
   B. The borrower wants to know what the property is worth.
   C. The lender wants a review of the property and its comparables.

5. Why does a lender have increased risk with a PUD or condo versus a single-family residence?
   A. PUDs and condos have common walls.
   B. PUDs and condos have public streets.
   C. PUDs and condos are part of an association.

6. A borrower is seeking a refinance on his home, which he purchased for $200,000 six months ago. The appraised value

came in at $275,000. What value will be used to qualify the borrower?

A. $200,000

B. $275,000

C. Neither A nor B

7. A borrower is seeking a refinance on her home. She has an existing mortgage lien of $224,000, and her home is valued at $320,000. What is the loan-to-value of the home?

A. 70%

B. 75%

C. 80%

8. A borrower wants to refinance. He has good credit, and he is seeking a mortgage loan on an owner-occupied property to obtain cash out to pay off some credit cards. What loan-to-value restrictions will he encounter on a conforming fixed-rate loan program?

A. 85%

B. 90%

C. 95%

9. Why are condos hard to finance?

A. There is no parcel of land.

B. The association can choose who can live in the building.

C. A person can buy a condo and then rent it out, with the renter possibly having less interest in the maintenance of the building.

10. What type of approach is required on an appraisal when an investment property is involved?

A. Cost approach

B. Comparison approach

C. Income approach

Answers to the quiz can be found at the end of Part One.

CHAPTER 8

TAKING THE LOAN APPLICATION TO CLOSING THE LOAN

How many a man has thrown up his hands at a time when a little more effort, a little more patience, would have achieved success?

—Elbert Hubbard

THE INITIAL MEETING WITH YOUR BORROWER

Your initial contact with your borrower is your opportunity to make a great first impression. Convincing your prospective borrowers to choose you for representation in one of their biggest financial decisions is the first step in the loan process. A successful loan originator provides excellent service and professionalism. You should be capable of explaining the entire loan process, including potential problems, up front. Your goal is to become an expert on the loan process and the various loan programs available. This will ensure a satisfying experience for your borrower and should develop into a trusted relationship for future reference and use. This meeting with the prospective borrowers serves as the most important point of contact throughout the loan process. This is when the borrowers are mostly likely to be open-minded and cooperative in providing you with the requirements for getting the loan process started.

First Impression Tips

- Dress like a professional.
- Be on time.
- Be prepared.
- Ask questions related to the borrower's situation.
- Listen well.
- Do as you say.
- Be educated on products and loan programs.

Delivering excellent *follow-up* creates success. It is imperative to keep the borrowers informed throughout the entire loan process. For example, if the interest rate or fees increase from your initial quote, you should immediately call or meet with the borrowers and explain in detail what is changing and why. This should include redisclosure of rate or fees per RESPA regulations (RESPA is discussed in more detail later in the chapter). You should return all phone calls and e-mails promptly. In addition, be a good listener and address potential problems and concerns up front.

Before you meet with your prospective borrowers, you should review with them what documentation you want them to bring along to your meeting. Be sure to explain the reasons why you are asking them to bring these items. Most people will not just bring along their income documentation, tax returns, bank statements, etc., if they don't know why they need them. The more they bring to the meeting, the better chance you have of finding them exactly what they want.

Below is an outline of what documentation your potential borrowers should bring with them to the initial meeting. Additional documents may be required based on the specific situation.

What should the borrower bring to a purchase transaction?

Single-Family Residence

- Photo identification

- Deposit receipt of down payment

- Purchase contract

- Pay stubs for the past 30 days

- Last two years of W-2s

- Last three months' bank statements with *all* pages for checking, savings, credit union, 401(k), IRA, copy of life insurance declaration page, etc., for verification of assets

- Documentation on any other source of income, e.g., pension or social security

- Real estate agent and/or builder's name and phone number to contact about the appraisal

- If renting, a copy of the lease agreement

- If renting, the name, address, and telephone number of the landlord

- If self-employed, personal income tax returns for last two years with all schedules

- If self-employed, corporate returns for the prior two years with all schedules

- If self-employed, profit and loss statement signed by a CPA or the borrower

- If applicable, written explanations for gaps in employment—signed and dated by the borrower

- If applicable, a copy of *all* bankruptcy papers

- If applicable, a copy of the divorce decree

- If applicable, written explanations for any derogatory credit—signed and dated by the borrower

- If a VA loan, certificate of eligibility or DD214

- If a VA loan, nearest living relative information

Condo/PUD (in Addition to Single-Family Residence Requirements)

- Covenants, conditions, and restrictions (CC&R)

- Bylaws

- Name, telephone and fax numbers, and address of HOA management

- Insurance agent's name and telephone number

- HOA financial statement

- HOA certification form completed by management

What should the borrower bring to a refinance transaction?

- Pay stubs for the last 30 days

- Last two year of W-2s

- If applicable, documentation for any other source of income, e.g., pension or social security benefits

- Copy of the current mortgage lender statement (should include telephone number)

- Copy of the declaration page from the current homeowner's insurance policy (to include the name and telephone number of the current insurance agent)

- Paid receipt for the current year's property taxes

- If applicable, a copy of the flood insurance policy

- Cash-out-only letter stating the purpose for the refinance

- If self-employed the last two years' personal income tax returns with all schedules

- If self-employed, the last two years' corporate tax returns with all schedules

- If self-employed, the profit and loss statement signed by a CPA or the borrower

- If applicable, a copy of *all* bankruptcy papers

- If applicable, a copy of the divorce decree

- If applicable, written explanations for any derogatory credit—signed and dated by borrower

These are all very important documents that help in qualifying your potential borrowers for the loans they want. Some loan programs may not require all these documents; however, it is best to gather as much information up front in the event that changes need to be made. This will ensure that there are no delays in the process as a result of having to gather documentation.

Questions in the Initial Meeting

Now that you are meeting your borrowers face-to-face, you should be prepared with questions. There will be general questions and questions specific to their situation. As a guide, here are some questions that you should touch upon in this meeting.

**What questions should you ask
at a purchase transaction?**

- **How much of a down payment do you have to work with?**   This question will help determine the loan amount and the program that best fits the borrower's request.

- **Where or in what form is the down payment being held? Bank, IRA, stocks?**   This money usually has to be seasoned or available for the past 90 or more days.

- **Do you currently own a home? Did you make a contingent or noncontigent offer on the new home?**   When a borrower already owns a home, one of the most common contingencies written into a purchase agreement is a *contingent offer*. This is when a borrower has made an offer on a new home on the condition that he or she sells the current home. This must all be coordinated through escrow.

Many Realtors and builders prohibit these transactions because of the potential for the existing home not selling. A Realtor can write up the sale to include a clause that states the seller will accept backup offers and will require the purchaser (the borrower) the first right of refusal.

If the borrower made a noncontingent offer, then the borrower must be able to qualify for loan financing on the new loan while continuing to bear the obligations of paying the monthly PITI of the current home.

- **How long of an escrow do you have?** Whatever the answer—30, 45, 60, 90 days—it will allow you to gauge how much time you have to preapprove, process, and fund the loan. Extensions to the escrow period are allowed and are usually granted by the seller and buyer.

What questions should you ask at a refinance transaction?

- **What is the purpose of your refinance?** The most important question—you must know what your borrower's goals are in order to select and provide the right loan program.

- **Who is listed on the title of the subject property?** The answer to this question will provide the proper vesting as well as limit those who currently qualify in being included on the refinance.

- **How long have you owned the property?** This is important for seasoning purposes.

- **What was the last date and time you refinanced your property?** This is an important question in case there is a prepayment penalty on the previous loan and the refinance is being done prior to the time allowed by the lender.

- **What interest rate are you currently paying? Is it fixed or adjustable?** This information is essential in selecting a new loan program and rate to ensure there is a benefit to the borrower.

- **Has the property been for sale recently?**   Most lenders will check the MLS listing. If the applicants did have their home up for sale, then you will need a letter from the applicants explaining the events and stating the fact that they decided against selling the property.

- **Is there a current second mortgage on the property?** If so, you need to ask: Are you paying the second lien off with the new proceeds? Or will you need to request a subordination agreement?

What questions are borrowers likely to ask?

The borrowers will also have questions of their own. Here are some questions you may encounter from a potential borrower:

- Do you work for a lender or a broker?

- If a broker, what lenders do you work with?

- Do your programs carry a prepayment penalty?

- What fees do you charge?

- How do you get paid—are you on commission?

- How do you determine which loan program is best for us?

- How do I know you're qualified?

- Are you licensed?

- How long do you take for loan approval?

- How long does the whole process take?

When answering these questions, be sure to be very clear and detailed in your explanations. Just because you found a potential borrower who wants a mortgage loan and an application has been taken, does not mean your job is over. It has just begun; you are the glue that holds the entire process together; you are the point of contact. You will need to:

- Find the best loan program to fit your borrower's needs.

- Review all the information collected from your borrower.

- If applicable, order credit and appraisal.

- Package and submit your loan to the processor.

- Coordinate with the processor throughout the loan process.

- Request any outstanding conditions (if applicable).

- Review any conditions from the lender.

- Follow the loan status with your processor. Every few days you should have an update on the loan status.

- If applicable, coordinate the loan closing.

- *Keep your borrower informed* throughout the loan process, and make sure you let your borrower know of any changes! If any terms change on the loan, make sure you redisclose with proper disclosures!

Figure 8-1 presents a prequalification worksheet, which the loan originator completes during the initial meeting.

UP CLOSE WITH A 1003

This section will be a great reference for anyone completing the residential loan application. The section is intended to guide you through the Uniform Residential Loan Application, also known as the 1003, the initial form in the written application process. Regardless of whether an application is taken online, by mail, or in person, you must complete and sign a 1003.

The *Uniform Residential Loan Application (URLA)* is the official application form for all residential loans and is the central document of the residential loan application process. The loan application, or *1003*, is used to gather all the crucial information about the prospective borrower and is used by the lender to evaluate the applicant's creditworthiness.

FIGURE 8-1
Prequalification Worksheet

Date: _____	
Borrower: _____	
Property Address:	Loan Amount: _____
_____	
_____	Loan-to-Value Ratio: _____
Purchase Price: _____	Interest Rate: _____
OR	
Estimated Value: _____	

RATIO		RESIDUAL	
A) Monthly Gross Income	_____	**A) Monthly Gross Income**	_____
Principal & Interest	_____	Federal Tax (−)	_____
Taxes & Insurance	_____	State Tax (−)	_____
MI	_____	Social Security (−)	_____
Association Fee	_____	Retirement (−)	_____
PI for second trust	_____	Child Care (−)	_____
B) Total Housing Expense	_____	Monthly Debts (−)	_____
Housing Expense (B)	_____	**B)** Rental Negative (−)	_____
Monthly Debt Payments	_____	Nontaxable Income (+)	_____
Rental Negative	_____	**Subtotal**	_____
C) Total Debt Service	_____	Total	_____
		Taxes & Insurance (−)	_____
Housing Ratio:		**C)** Utilities (−)	_____
(B) Divided by (A)	_____%	Maintenance (−)	_____
		Association Fee (−)	_____
Debt Ratio:		Family Support (−)	_____
(C) Divided by (A)	_____%	**Balance Available for principal and interest**	_____

NOTES:
1) **Income:** If income varies (interest, commission, bonus, overtime, part-time) use average of last 2 years (depends on program).
   for self-employed use average "net income" for last 2 years. Do not include expense accounts.
2) **Debt:** remember—if less than 10 months remaining do not include
   a. Child Support and/or alimony payments are monthly debts
   b. For credit cards use 5% of the outstanding balance or minimum of $10. For FHA, alimony can be taken as a reduction in income.
3) **Second Mortgages:** remember—a second lien is calculated in the housing ratio when subject property is being financed
4) **PUDS and Condos:** remember to include homeowner's association fee
5) **Taxes** Estimate purchase price × 1.25 for annual figure
6) **Insurance** Estimate loan amount × .25% for annual figure
7) **Mortgage Insurance** (MI) estimate 1.14% monthly for 95+% LTV, 94% monthly for 90% LTV

The loan application, or 1003, consists of four legal-size pages. The fourth page is an addendum page and is intentionally left blank, while the first three pages contain the following sections:

   I. Type of Mortgage and Terms of Loan

  II. Property Information and Purpose of Loan

III. Borrower Information

IV. Employment Information

V. Monthly Income and Combined Housing Expense Information

VI. Assets and Liabilities

VII. Details of Transaction

VIII. Declarations

IX. Acknowledgment and Agreement

X. Information for Government Monitoring Purposes

A married couple can jointly complete one application form, as the form provides space for two borrowers. The borrower completes the section on the left, and the coborrower completes the section on the right. *If the loan application is being done with a coborrower and the borrowers are not married, a separate loan application must be done.* All borrowers on a loan must complete a 1003. All borrowers bear the same amount of responsibility as the main borrower. The application begins with a paragraph that must be read by the borrower(s), and the appropriate checkbox should be marked. The general concept of this section is to clarify whether there will be one borrower or two. One of the following options should be selected:

❏ The income or assets of a person other than the borrower (including the borrower's spouse) will be used as a basis for loan qualification.

or

❏ The income or assets of the borrower's spouse will not be used as a basis for loan qualification, but his or her liabilities must be considered because the borrower resides in a community property state, the security property is located in a community property state, or the borrower is relying on other property located in a community property state as a basis for repayment of the loan.

A Section-by-Section Look at the 1003

Section I

Section I is used to collect basic information about the loan being requested (see Figure 8-2).

> *Mortgage type (VA, conventional, FHA, RHS, or other).* VA, FHA, and RHS are government-insured or government-guaranteed loan programs. All other mortgage programs are normally considered conventional.

> *Agency and lender case numbers.* Leave these spaces blank. Agency case numbers are assigned by one of the government agencies in a VA, FHA, or RHS loan scenario. The lender assigns lender case numbers.

> *Loan amount.* The loan amount is the dollar figure that the borrower will be requesting from the lender. This can be changed during the loan process; however, a preliminary amount is required to qualify the borrower.

> *Interest rate.* Here you will specify the interest rate for which the borrower is applying, based on the current market rates. You should indicate your borrower's target rate.

> *Number of months.* This is the loan's term shown in months. Common loan terms are 30 years (360 months), 20 years (240 months), 15 years (180 months), and 10 years (120 months).

> *Amortization type.* The borrower may choose a fixed-rate mortgage, a graduated-payment mortgage (GPM), or an

FIGURE 8-2

I. Type of Mortgage and Terms of Loan

I. TYPE OF MORTGAGE AND TERMS OF LOAN		
Mortgage Applied for: ☐VA ☐Conventional ☐Other: ☐FHA ☐USDA/ Rural Housing Service	Agency Case #	Lender Case #
Amount $	Interest Rate %	No. of Months	**Amortization Type:** ☐Fixed Rate ☐GPM	☐Other (explain): ☐ARM (type):

adjustable-rate mortgage (ARM); if another type is chosen, it must be specified. The most common loan types are fixed-rate mortgages and ARMs. Note that balloon loans are considered fixed rate.

Section II

Section II is used to gather information about the property and asks whether the transaction will be a purchase or refinance (see Figure 8-3).

Subject property address. The property's full street address must be provided—especially include the zip code! If the property is a condo, be sure to specify the unit number.

Number of units. A conventional residential mortgage is for one to four units only. Any property with more than four units is categorized as an apartment and will require a commercial loan. A single-family home is one unit. A condo is also considered to be one unit, regardless of the number of units in the entire project.

Legal description of subject property. Here you will insert "see legal description in title." The title insurance policy

FIGURE 8-3

II. Property Information and Purpose of Loan

II. PROPERTY INFORMATION AND PURPOSE OF LOAN

Subject Property Address (street, city, state, ZIP)	No. Of Units

Legal Description of Subject Property (attach description if necessary)	Year Built

Purpose of Loan ☐ Purchase ☐ Construction ☐ Other (explain): ☐ Refinance ☐ Construction-Permanent	Property will be: ☐ Primary Residence ☐ Secondary Residence ☐ Investment

Complete this line if construction or construction-permanent loan.

Year Lot Acquired	Original Cost $	Amount Existing Liens $	(a) Present Value of Lot $	(b) Cost of Improvements $	Total (a+b) $

Complete this line if this is a refinance loan.

Year Acquired	Original Cost $	Amount Existing Liens $	Purpose of Refinance	Describe Improvements ☐ made ☐ to be made Cost $	

Title will be held in what Name(s)		Manner in which Title will be held	Estate will be held in: ☐ Fee Simple
Source of Down Payment, Settlement Charges and/or Subordinate Financing (explain)			☐ Leasehold (show expiration date)

will state this legal survey-language description of the property.

Year built. The borrower or lender should show the year in which the subject property's building was originally constructed.

Purpose of the loan. Select one of the five options listed: purchase, refinance, construction, construction—permanent, or other. Home equity loans, lines of credit, and second mortgages are considered refinances. If other, specify with a description.

Property type. The borrower must choose between one of three property usage options: primary residence, secondary residence, or investment (also considered, non-owner-occupied property).

Information for construction or construction—permanent loan. This line must be completed for construction, rehab, or construction—permanent loans. It requires you to fill in the year the lot was acquired, the original cost of the lot, the amount of any existing liens on the property, the (a) present value of the lot, the (b) costs of the improvements (construction), and then the total of (a) and (b).

Information for a refinance loan. If this application is for a refinance loan, then this line must be completed. It asks for the year the property was originally acquired, the original cost, the amount of any existing liens on the property, the purpose of the refinance, and a description of any recent or upcoming major improvements that may add to the value of the property or that need to be paid off with this loan.

Title will be held in what names. The legal names that will be listed in the property title as owners of the property must be provided here. The borrowers must use the exact full name in all the application and legal documents.

Manner in which the title will be held. If only one owner, indicate "individual"; otherwise, indicate "dual ownership."

Estate will be held in. Title to a property may be held in one of two ways: *fee simple*, which is a permanent ownership, and *leasehold*, which is only temporary ownership. The standard selection is fee simple for full ownership. Leasehold is an option because it's possible that an applicant purchases or constructs a home on land that he or she does not own.

Source of down payment, settlement charges, and subordinate financing. The borrowers must disclose the source of the funds that will cover the down payment, settlement charges, and other subordinate (secondary) financing. Common responses are checking or savings, 401(k), equity, sold home, gift, or seller contribution. Explain in as much detail as possible.

Tips: This is the time to review the sales contract for:

- Loan amount/down payment (Are they correct?)

- Escrow date (Is this amount sufficient for closing?)

- Seller contributions (Check your guidelines to make sure it is OK.)

- Signatures (Is it signed by all parties?)

If a condo or PUD, be sure to:

- Include association dues

- Ask for the HO association contact information

- Obtain the master condo policy

- Request a condo certification

Section III

Section III gathers relevant personal information about the borrowers (see Figure 8-4).

Borrower's name. The applicant must provide his or her legal full name, as it will appear on all title and loan documents. Any discrepancies may delay the loan process.

FIGURE 8-4

III. Borrower Information

Borrower	III. BORROWER INFORMATION	Co-Borrower
Borrower's Name (include Jr. or Sr. if applicable)		Co-Borrower's Name (include Jr. or Sr. if applicable

Social Security Number	Home Phone (incl. area code)	Age	Yrs. School	Social Security #	Home Phone (incl. area code)	Age	Yrs. School

☐ Married ☐ Unmarried (include single, divorced, widowed) ☐ Separated	Dependents (not listed by Co-Borrower) no. ages	☐ Married ☐ Unmarried (include single, divorced, widowed) ☐ Separated	Dependents (not listed by Borrower) no. ages

Present Address (street, city, state, ZIP) ☐ Own ☐ Rent ____ No. Yrs.	Present Address (street, city, state, ZIP) ☐ Own ☐ Rent ____ No. Yrs.

If residing at present address for less than two years, complete the following:

Present Address (street, city, state, ZIP) ☐ Own ☐ Rent ____ No. Yrs.	Present Address (street, city, state, ZIP) ☐ Own ☐ Rent ____ No. Yrs.
Present Address (street, city, state, ZIP) ☐ Own ☐ Rent ____ No. Yrs.	Present Address (street, city, state, ZIP) ☐ Own ☐ Rent ____ No. Yrs.

Social security number. Provide the social security numbers for the borrower in the allotted space. Applicants who do not have a social security number should provide their resident alien identification numbers. All U.S. citizens must provide their social security numbers.

Home phone (including area code). The applicant must have a home phone number.

Age. The borrower must provide either his or her age as of the date of application or his or her date of birth.

Years of schooling. The borrower must indicate how many years of school he or she completed. A high school graduate usually has 12 years of school.

Marital status. The borrower needs to indicate his or her marital status. The categories are married, separated, or unmarried, which includes single, divorced, and widowed.

Dependents (number and ages). In this space the borrower must provide the number and ages of his or her dependents.

The coborrower should not list those dependents listed by the borrower and vice versa.

Present address. Give the borrower's current street address with zip code. A post office box is not acceptable. For each residence, the borrower must indicate whether it is rented or owned and how many years he or she has resided there.

Former address. If the applicant has resided at the current address for less than two years, a former address or addresses must be provided to account for the previous two years of residency.

Section IV

Section IV gathers important information regarding the borrower's employment history (see Figure 8-5).

Name and address of employer. The borrower must provide the full name and address of his or her employer accurately, as an employment verification request will be sent to this address. If self-employed, the applicant needs to check the "self-employed" box.

FIGURE 8-5

IV. Employment Information

Borrower	IV. EMPLOYMENT INFORMATION	Co-Borrower	
☐ Self Employed (check above box) Name and Address of Employer	Yrs. on this job	☐ Self Employed (check above box) Name and Address of Employer	Yrs. on this job
	Yrs. employed in this line of work/profession		Yrs. employed in this line of work/profession
Position/Title/Type of Business	Business Phone (incl. area code)	Position/Title/Type of Business	Business Phone (incl. area code)

If employed in current position for less than two years or if currently employed in more than one position, complete the following:

Borrower		Co-Borrower	
☐ Self Employed (check above box) Name and Address of Employer	Dates (from-to)	☐ Self Employed (check above box) Name and Address of Employer	Dates (from-to)
	Monthly Income $		Monthly Income $
Position/Title/Type of Business	Business Phone (incl. area code)	Position/Title/Type of Business	Business Phone (incl. area code)
☐ Self Employed (check above box) Name and Address of Employer	Dates (from-to)	☐ Self Employed (check above box) Name and Address of Employer	Dates (from-to)
	Monthly Income $		Monthly Income $
Position/Title/Type of Business	Business Phone (incl. Area code)	Position/Title/Type of Business	Business Phone (incl. area code)

Years on this job and years employed in this line of work/ profession. The information required here is the length of time the borrower has worked with his or her current employers, as well as the length of time he or she has worked in this profession.

Position, title, type of business. The borrower must indicate his or her official title or position. If the borrower is self-employed or if the title is vague, then the type of business should be listed.

Business phone. The business's primary phone number, including the area code, must be included.

Former employment. If the borrower has been working with his or her current employer for less than two years, then accurate information must be provided about the past two years of employment. This space can also be used for a second or part-time job; however, the borrower must have been working at the second job for at least two years.

Section V

Section V provides a layout of the borrower's monthly income and projected monthly housing expenses (see Figure 8-6).

FIGURE 8-6

V. Monthly Income and Combined Housing Expense Information

V. MONTHLY INCOME AND COMBINED HOUSING EXPENSE INFORMATION						
Gross Monthly Income	Borrower	Co-Borrower	Total	Combined Monthly Housing Expense	Present	Proposed
Base Empl. Income*	$	$	$	Rent	$	$
Overtime	$	$	$	First Mortgage (P&I)	$	$
Bonuses	$	$	$	Other Financing (P&I)	$	$
Commissions	$	$	$	Hazard Insurance	$	$
Dividends/Interest	$	$	$	Real Estate Taxes	$	$
Net Rental Income	$	$	$	Mortgage Insurance	$	$
Other (see ** below)	$	$	$	Homeowner Assn. Dues	$	$
	$	$	$	Other:	$	$
Total	$	$	$	Total	$	$

*Self Employed Borrower(s) may be required to provide additional documentation such as tax returns and financial statements.
** **Describe Other Income Notice**: Alimony, child support, or separate maintenance income need not be revealed if the Borrower (B) or Co- Borrower(C) does not choose to have it considered for repaying this loan.

B/C		Monthly Amount
.	.	$
.	.	$

Base employment income. This is the borrower's gross income, as documented by pay stubs and W-2s.

Overtime, bonuses, and commissions. Remember—the amount used for the calculation is an average over the past two years.

Dividends and interest. Dividends and interest income may be used but must be supported with statements.

Net rental income. Rental income may be calculated as personal income (using 75% of the gross rental income as personal income).

Other income. Other income, such as alimony, child support, and public assistance, may be listed but must be supported by documentation.

Rent or first mortgage (principal and interest, or P&I). The borrower must indicate how much he or she currently pays each month for rent or on the current mortgage, whichever is applicable.

Other financing. List any other mortgage, such as a second mortgage or line of credit payment, that is due on the *subject property.*

Taxes and hazard and mortgage insurance. On refinance loans, the borrower needs to report how much is paid each month for property taxes and mortgage and hazard insurance premiums.

Homeowner's association dues. This section is only applicable on a condo or a PUD. These association dues usually include hazard insurance payments.

Proposed (last column). Here the loan officer must project the borrower's future mortgage (P&I), property tax, hazard insurance, mortgage insurance, and/or housing association payments per month.

Tips: Make sure to check:

- Do the pay stubs match your borrower's name, address, social security numbers, etc.?

- Do the wage earnings on the pay stubs match your calculations?

- Does the year-to-date on the pay stub reflect a stable or increasing pattern—if higher or lower, make sure to explain?

- Do the pay stubs show any deductions that are not reflected in the credit report (e.g., credit union or 401(k) loans)?

- If there is other income, make sure to get proper documentation.

- Do you have a full 12-month rating on an existing mortgage?

Section VI

Section VI provides information about the borrower's assets and liabilities and calculates a borrower's net worth (see Figure 8-7). The applicant must disclose *all* debts and liabilities; however, the applicant needs to disclose only enough assets to qualify for the loan he or she is trying to obtain.

All information will be compared with what is obtained from banking and credit reporting sources.

> *Completed jointly or not jointly*. At the beginning of this section you will need to indicate whether the assets and liabilities will be completed jointly or not jointly.

> *Assets.* The left column of this section provides space for a list of the borrower's real and personal property (assets). If needed, additional space is available on page 4, the addendum area.

> *Cash deposit toward purchase held by.* If earnest money (the initial down payment) has been received, then the applicant must indicate the deposit amount and which attorney, settlement agent, or Realtor is holding the deposit. These funds will be verified during the loan process.

> *Checking and savings accounts.* Provide the bank name, address, and contact information for the bank. Be sure to include the account number and current balance of at least

one account. This information will also be verified in the processing of the loan.

Stocks and bonds. Fill in if applicable.

Life insurance net cash value. Provide the name and cash value of any life insurance policies owned by the borrower if the policies are required to meet asset requirements for the loan.

Subtotal liquid assets. This section is the sum of the preceding four items: (1) cash deposits, (2) checking and savings accounts, (3) stocks and bonds, and (4) the net cash

FIGURE 8-7

VI. Assets and Liabilities

VI. ASSETS AND LIABILITIES

This statement and any applicable supporting schedules may be completed jointly by both married and unmarried Co- borrowers if their assets and liabilities are sufficiently joined so that the statement can be meaningfully and fairly presented on a combined basis; otherwise separate Statements and Schedules are required. If the Co- Borrower section was completed about a spouse, this Statement and supporting schedules must be completed about that spouse also.

Completed
☐ Jointly
☐ Not Jointly

ASSETS	Cash or Market Value	Liabilities and Pledged Assets. List the creditor's name, address and account number for all outstanding debts, including automobile loans, revolving charge accounts, real estate loans, alimony, child support, stock pledges, etc. Use continuation sheet, if necessary. Indicate by (*) those liabilities, which will be satisfied upon sale of real estate owned or upon refinancing of the subject property.		
Cash deposit toward purchase held by:	$	LIABILITIES	Monthly Pmt. & Mos. Left to Pay	Unpaid Balance
List checking and savings accounts below				
Name & Address of Bank, S&L, or Credit Union		Name & Address of Company	$Payt./Mos.	$
Acct. no.	$	Acct. no.		
Name & Address of Bank, S&L, or Credit Union		Name & Address of Company	$Payt./Mos.	$
Acct. no.	$	Acct. no.		
Name & Address of Bank, S&L, or Credit Union		Name & Address of Company	$Payt./Mos.	$
Acct. no.	$	Acct. no.		
Name & Address of Bank, S&L, or Credit Union		Name & Address of Company	$Payt./Mos.	$

FIGURE 8-7 (*Continued*)

Acct. no.	$	Acct. no.			
Stocks & Bonds (Company name/ number & description)	$	Name & Address of Company		$Payt./Mos.	$
Acct. no.	$	Acct. no.			
Life insurance net cash value	.	Name & Address of Company		$Payt./Mos.	· $
Face amount $	$	Acct. no.			
Subtotal Liquid Assets	$	Name & Address of Company		$Payt./Mos.	$
Real Estate owned enter market value from schedule or real estate owned, (page 3.)	$	Acct. no.			
Vested interest in retirement fund	$	Name & Address of Company		$Payt./Mos.	$
Net worth of business(es) owned (attach financial statement)	$	Acct. no.			
Automobiles owned (make and year)	$	Alimony/Child Support/Separate Maintenance Payments		$	.
Other Assets (itemize)	$	Job Related Expense (child care, union dues, etc.)		$	.
		Total Monthly Payments			.
Total Assets a.	$	**Net Worth (a-b)**	$	**Total Liabilities b.**	$

value of life insurance. The borrower must document enough liquid assets to cover closing costs, the down payment, and any reserve requirements.

Real estate owned (market value). This is an estimate of the total market value of real estate currently held by the borrower. Any market values used here must be detailed in the "Schedule of Real Estate Owned" at the top of page 3 of the application.

Vested interest in retirement fund. If the borrower needs to provide evidence of additional assets in order to qualify for this loan, the borrower may use the vested interest in any retirement fund held.

Net worth of businesses owned. If the borrower owns any businesses and needs to show evidence of other assets, then he or she may include the net worth of any such business in this section.

Automobiles owned. The borrower should specify the vehicle type and value of all automobiles owned, especially if there is a loan outstanding against a vehicle.

Other assets. Other valuables such as jewelry, electronics, valuable furniture, and investment artworks may be included to increase the net worth. This would be necessary only if the borrower's net worth is negative.

Total assets. This combines the total (liquid and nonliquid) assets listed in the preceding asset entries.

Liabilities. The applicant must disclose all liabilities.

Debts owed. Space is provided for seven entries; additional entries may be placed in the addendum area of page 4 of the application. Each entry must include five items: (1) the complete name and address of the creditor, (2) the account number, (3) the monthly payment required on the account, (4) the remaining months left to pay off the account, and (5) the current unpaid balance on the account.

Alimony, child support, or separate maintenance payments owed to. All alimony and child-support payments paid by the borrower must be disclosed and documented.

Job-related expenses. Job-related expenses include child care, transportation, and union dues. If the applicant wishes to list these items, then information about the recipient and payment amount must be indicated.

Total liabilities. This is the sum of all unpaid balances. This is the total amount of liabilities due, not the monthly payment amount.

Net worth. The borrower's net worth is merely the difference between total assets and total liabilities. To arrive at this figure, subtract the total liabilities from the total assets and you have determined the net worth.

Schedule of real estate owned. Continued on the top of page 3 of the application is a table for listing any and all properties owned by the borrower (see Figure 8-8). If there are

FIGURE 8-8

VI. ASSESTS AND LIABILITIES (cont.)							
Schedule of Real Estate Owned (if additional properties are owned, use continuation sheet.)							
Property Address (enter S if sold, PS if pending sale or R if rental being held for income)	Type of Property	Present Market Value	Amount of Mortgage & Liens	Gross Rental Income	Mortgage Payments	Insurance, Maintenance, Taxes & Misc.	Net Rental Income
.	. .	$	$	$	$	$	$
.	. .	$	$	$	$	$	$
.	. .	$	$	$	$	$	$
.	Totals	$	$	$	$	$	$

List any additional names under which credit has previously been received and indicate appropriate creditor name(s) and account number(s):

Alternate Name	Creditor Name	Account Number

any mortgages outstanding, you must account for them on each property owned.

Other name. If the borrower has obtained credit under another name (such as from a previous marriage), provide that other name or any others that have been used.

Tips: Make sure to check:

- Do you have sufficient documentation for assets, down payment, and reserves?

- If any installment debt (with the exception of auto leases) has fewer than 10 payments, have you removed it from your calculation?

- If any debt appears on the credit report but the borrower has paid it off, have you obtained or requested documentation?

- If there is rental property, have you requested tax returns and lease agreements?

- If the borrower owns more than 10 properties, have you checked for lender guidelines and restrictions?

- Have you studied the bank statements to look for large deposits or withdrawals?

- Do you have a 12-month rental or mortgage history?

Section VII

Section VII is a review of the charges that will be incurred during the loan process (see Figure 8-9). This information should match your initial good faith estimate. It is critical that your figures are accurate to ensure that after the fees are calculated, there are sufficient assets to close the loan.

    a. *Purchase price.* If this application is for a purchase loan, then the borrower should indicate the total purchase price for the subject property.

    b. *Alterations, improvements, repairs.* If there have been or will be major improvements to the property and those improvements will be included in the loan, indicate the amount needed or used.

    c. *Land (if acquired separately).* If this application is for a construction loan that will require a separate purchase of the lot, the cost of the land should be listed here.

    d. *Refinance.* If this is an application for a refinance, indicate total liens and other liabilities to be paid by the proceeds

FIGURE 8-9

VII. Details of Transaction

VII. DETAILS OF TRANSACTION	
a. Purchase Price	$
b. Alterations, improvements, repairs	$
c. Land (if acquired separately)	$
d. Refinance (incl. debts to be paid off)	$
e. Estimated prepaid items	$
f. Estimated closing costs	$
g. PMI, MIP, Funding Fee	$
h. Discount (if Borrower wil pay)	$
i. **Total costs (add items a through h)**	$
j. Subordinate financing	$
k. Borrower's closing costs paid by seller	$
l. Other Credits (explain)	$
m. Loan amount (exclude PMI, MIP, Funding Fee financed)	$
n. PMI, MIP, Funding Fee financed	$
o. Loan amount (add m & n)	$
p. Cash from/to Borrower (subtract j, k, l & o from i)	$

From GFE

of the loan. Include the current mortgage being refinanced, as well as any credit card debts or personal loans that are being consolidated with this refinance transaction.

e. *Estimated prepaid items.* This is the total of the escrow and prepaid items calculated in the good faith estimate. To estimate, calculate three monthly housing payments, including mortgage, taxes, and insurance.

f. *Estimated closing costs.* This is the sum of the closing-related costs as found on the good faith estimate.

g. *PMI, MIP, funding fee financed.* Programs such as FHA loans allow the borrower to finance the mortgage insurance premium for a fee. If such a fee is being charged, list it in this entry.

h. *Discount (if paid by borrower).* Leave this blank. The discount points are sometimes listed separately from the closing costs. However, many lenders often include these discount charges in the closing costs estimates.

i. *Total costs.* This is the sum of the above eight entries (lines a–h). This is the total up-front cost.

j. *Subordinate financing.* If the borrower will be using other mortgage loan funds in addition to the first mortgage, such as a second mortgage held by the seller, that amount should be listed here.

k. *Borrower's closing costs paid by seller.* If the seller will be paying any of the borrower's closing costs, the dollar amount of that incentive should be indicated in this space.

l. *Other credits.* If there are other funds or payments, such as closing charges, application fee, appraisal fee, etc., that the borrower has paid, that amount should be indicated in this space.

m. *Loan amount (excluding PMI, MIP, funding fee financed).* This is the loan amount prior to adding additional financing funds to cover the mortgage insurance premium.

n. *PMI, MIP, funding fee financed.* If any portion of the mortgage insurance is being financed, that amount should be shown here. This is an option with government loans.

o. *Loan amount (total).* This is the total of lines m and n and will give you your final loan amount.

p. *Cash from/to borrower.* The borrower must be prepared to pay this amount at the time of the closing. To determine the final amount:
   ○ *Calculate the borrower's credited items.* Add lines j, k, l, and o to determine the total amount that will be credited to the borrower.
   ○ *Determine the remaining debt or surplus.* Subtract the amount of lines j, k, l, and o from line i (total costs) to calculate how much cash the borrower will owe or will receive.

Section VIII

Section VIII contains 13 yes–no declarations that the borrower must answer (see Figure 8-10). If the applicant answers yes to any of the first nine questions (lines a–i), the applicant must provide an explanation on the addendum sheet. *This section of the loan application is one of the most important and must be adhered to without discrepancy.*

a. Are there any outstanding judgments against you?

b. Have you declared bankruptcy within the past seven years?

c. Have you had property foreclosed on or given title or deed in lieu thereof in the last seven years?

d. Are you a party to any lawsuit?

e. Have you directly or indirectly been obligated on any loan that resulted in foreclosure, transfer of title in lieu of foreclosure, or judgment?

f. Are you presently delinquent or in default on any federal debt or any other loan, mortgage, financial obligation, bond, or loan guarantee?

FIGURE 8-10

VIII. Declarations

VIII. DECLARATIONS				
If you answer, "yes" to any questions a through i, please use continuation sheet for explanation.	**Borrower**		**Co-Borrower**	
.	Yes	No	Yes	No
a. Are there any outstanding judgments against you?	☐	☐	☐	☐
b. Have you been declared bankrupt within the past 7 years?	☐	☐	☐	☐
c. Have you had property foreclosed upon or given title or deed in lieu thereof in the last 7 years?	☐	☐	☐	☐
d. Are you a party to a lawsuit?	☐	☐	☐	☐
e. Have you directly or indirectly been obligated on any loan which resulted in foreclosure, transfer of title in lieu of foreclosure, or judgment? (This would include such loans as home mortgage loans, SBA loans, home improvement loans, educational loans, manufactured (mobile) home loans, any mortgage, financial obligation, bond, or loan guarantee. If "Yes," provide details, including date, name and address of Lender, FHA or VA case number, if any, and reasons for the action.)	☐	☐	☐	☐
f. Are you presently delinquent or in default on any federal debt or any other loan, mortgage, financial obligation bond, or loan guarantee? If "Yes," give details as described in the preceding question.	☐	☐	☐	☐
g. Are you obligated to pay alimony, child support, or separate maintenance?	☐	☐	☐	☐
h. Is any part of the down payment borrowed?	☐	☐	☐	☐
i. Are you a co-maker or endorser on a note?	☐	☐	☐	☐
j. Are you a U.S. citizen?	☐	☐	☐	☐
k. Are you a permanent resident alien?	☐	☐	☐	☐
l. Do you intend to occupy the property as your primary residence? If "Yes," complete question m below	☐	☐	☐	☐
m. Have you had an ownership interest in a property in the last 3 years?	☐	☐	☐	☐
(1) What type of property did you own-principal residence (PR), second home (SH), or investment property (IP)?	_____		_____	
(2) How did you hold title to the home? Solely by yourself(S), jointly with your spouse (SP), or jointly with another person (O)?	_____		_____	

g. Are you obligated to pay alimony, child support, or separate maintenance?

h. Is any part of the down payment borrowed?

i. Are you a comaker or endorser on a note?

j. Are you a U.S. citizen?

k. Are you a legal resident alien?

l. Do you intend to occupy the property as your primary residence?

m. Have you owned property during the past three years?

Section IX

Section IX is the acknowledgment and agreement section. Make sure that you and the borrower or borrowers read and understand the text in this section before signing the application. The information in the section is the basic agreement description of the application. The applicant must sign and date this section to certify and authorize the loan application.

Section X

Section X collects information required by the government to monitor lending practices. The borrower may decide not to provide this information, but the loan officer must still provide the data based on visual observation. The government monitors the data for acts of discrimination. The loan officer who gathered the information in this application must also sign and date the application and indicate how the interview was conducted.

The information in this section has no bearing on a loan approval. Sources for these requirements are the Equal Credit Opportunity Act, the Fair Housing Act, and other disclosure laws.

To see what the entire application form looks like, see Figure 8-11.

PREDISCLOSE!

General Information

All lending institutions and origination facilities are required to comply with all regulations governing residential mortgage lending. Each loan file that has been originated or delivered for purchase must be reviewed for compliance with federal regulations as part of the approval process.

FIGURE 8-11

Uniform Residential Loan Application

This application is designed to be completed by the applicant(s) with the Lender's assistance. Applicants should complete this form as "Borrower" or "Co-Borrower," as applicable. Co-Borrower information must also be provided (and the appropriate box checked) when ❑ the income or assets of a person other than the "Borrower" (including the Borrower's spouse) will be used as a basis for loan qualification or ❑ the income or assets of the Borrower's spouse will not be used as a basis for loan qualification, but his or her liabilities must be considered because the Borrower resides in a community property state, the security property is located in a community property state, or the Borrower is relying on other property located in a community property state as a basis for repayment of the loan.

I. TYPE OF MORTGAGE AND TERMS OF LOAN						
Mortgage Applied for: ❑ VA ❑ FHA	❑ Conventional ❑ USDA/Rural Housing Service	❑ Other (explain):		Agency Case Number		Lender Case Number
Amount $	Interest Rate %	No. of Months	Amortization Type: ❑ Fixed Rate ❑ GPM	❑ Other (explain): ❑ ARM (type):		

II. PROPERTY INFORMATION AND PURPOSE OF LOAN	
Subject Property Address (street, city, state, & ZIP)	No. of Units
Legal Description of Subject Property (attach description if necessary)	Year Built

Purpose of Loan ❑ Purchase ❑ Construction ❑ Other (explain): ❑ Refinance ❑ Construction-Permanent	Property will be: ❑ Primary Residence ❑ Secondary Residence ❑ Investment

Complete this line if construction or construction-permanent loan.

Year Lot Acquired	Original Cost $	Amount Existing Liens $	(a) Present Value of Lot $	(b) Cost of Improvements $	Total (a + b) $

Complete this line if this is a refinance loan.

Year Acquired	Original Cost $	Amount Existing Liens $	Purpose of Refinance	Describe Improvements ❑ made ❑ to be made
				Cost: $

Title will be held in what Name(s)	Manner in which Title will be held	Estate will be held in: ❑ Fee Simple ❑ Leasehold (show expiration date)
Source of Down Payment, Settlement Charges and/or Subordinate Financing (explain)		

	Borrower	III. BORROWER INFORMATION	Co-Borrower	
Borrower's Name (include Jr. or Sr. if applicable)			Co-Borrower's Name (include Jr. or Sr. if applicable)	

Social Security Number	Home Phone (incl. area code)	DOB (MM/DD/YYYY)	Yrs. School	Social Security Number	Home Phone (incl. area code)	DOB (MM/DD/YYYY)	Yrs. School

❑ Married ❑ Separated	❑ Unmarried (include single, divorced, widowed)	Dependents (not listed by Co-Borrower) no. ages	❑ Married ❑ Separated	❑ Unmarried (include single, divorced, widowed)	Dependents (not listed by Borrower) no. ages
Present Address (street, city, state, ZIP) ❑ Own ❑ Rent _____ No. Yrs.			Present Address (street, city, state, ZIP) ❑ Own ❑ Rent _____ No. Yrs.		
Mailing Address, if different from Present Address			Mailing Address, if different from Present Address		

If residing at present address for less than two years, complete the following:

Former Address (street, city, state, ZIP) ❑ Own ❑ Rent _____ No. Yrs.	Former Address (street, city, state, ZIP) ❑ Own ❑ Rent _____ No. Yrs.

	Borrower	IV. EMPLOYMENT INFORMATION	Co-Borrower	
Name & Address of Employer	❑ Self Employed	Yrs. on this job	Name & Address of Employer ❑ Self Employed	Yrs. on this job
		Yrs. employed in this line of work/profession		Yrs. employed in this line of work/profession
Position/Title/Type of Business		Business Phone (incl. area code)	Position/Title/Type of Business	Business Phone (incl. area code)

If employed in current position for less than two years or if currently employed in more than one position, complete the following:

Name & Address of Employer	❑ Self Employed	Dates (from – to)	Name & Address of Employer ❑ Self Employed	Dates (from – to)
		Monthly Income $		Monthly Income $
Position/Title/Type of Business		Business Phone (incl. area code)	Position/Title/Type of Business	Business Phone (incl. area code)
Name & Address of Employer	❑ Self Employed	Dates (from – to)	Name & Address of Employer ❑ Self Employed	Dates (from – to)
		Monthly Income $		Monthly Income $
Position/Title/Type of Business		Business Phone (incl. area code)	Position/Title/Type of Business	Business Phone (incl. area code)

Freddie Mac Form 65   01/04   Page 1 of 4   Fannie Mae Form 1003   01/04

FIGURE 8-11 (*Continued*)

V. MONTHLY INCOME AND COMBINED HOUSING EXPENSE INFORMATION

Gross Monthly Income	Borrower	Co-Borrower	Total	Combined Monthly Housing Expense	Present	Proposed
Base Empl. Income*	$	$	$	Rent	$	
Overtime				First Mortgage (P&I)		$
Bonuses				Other Financing (P&I)		
Commissions				Hazard Insurance		
Dividends/Interest				Real Estate Taxes		
Net Rental Income				Mortgage Insurance		
Other (before completing, see the notice in "describe other income," below)				Homeowner Assn. Dues		
				Other:		
Total	$	$	$	Total	$	$

* Self Employed Borrower(s) may be required to provide additional documentation such as tax returns and financial statements.

Describe Other Income *Notice:* Alimony, child support, or separate maintenance income need not be revealed if the Borrower (B) or Co-Borrower (C) does not choose to have it considered for repaying this loan.

B/C		Monthly Amount
		$

VI. ASSETS AND LIABILITIES

This Statement and any applicable supporting schedules may be completed jointly by both married and unmarried Co-Borrowers if their assets and liabilities are sufficiently joined so that the Statement can be meaningfully and fairly presented on a combined basis; otherwise, separate Statements and Schedules are required. If the Co-Borrower section was completed about a spouse, this Statement and supporting schedules must be completed about that spouse also.

Completed ☐ Jointly ☐ Not Jointly

ASSETS Description	Cash or Market Value	Liabilities and Pledged Assets. List the creditor's name, address and account number for all outstanding debts, including automobile loans, revolving charge accounts, real estate loans, alimony, child support, stock pledges, etc. Use continuation sheet, if necessary. Indicate by (*) those liabilities which will be satisfied upon sale of real estate owned or upon refinancing of the subject property.		
Cash deposit toward purchase held by:	$			
		LIABILITIES	Monthly Payment & Months Left to Pay	Unpaid Balance
List checking and savings accounts below		Name and address of Company	$ Payment/Months	$
Name and address of Bank, S&L, or Credit Union				
		Acct. no.		
Acct. no.	$	Name and address of Company	$ Payment/Months	$
Name and address of Bank, S&L, or Credit Union				
		Acct. no.		
Acct. no.	$	Name and address of Company	$ Payment/Months	$
Name and address of Bank, S&L, or Credit Union				
		Acct. no.		
Acct. no.	$	Name and address of Company	$ Payment/Months	$
Name and address of Bank, S&L, or Credit Union				
		Acct. no.		
Acct. no.	$	Name and address of Company	$ Payment/Months	$
Stocks & Bonds (Company name/number & description)	$			
		Acct. no.		
		Name and address of Company	$ Payment/Months	$
Life insurance net cash value	$			
Face amount: $				
Subtotal Liquid Assets	$			
Real estate owned (enter market value from schedule of real estate owned)	$	Acct. no.		
		Name and address of Company	$ Payment/Months	$
Vested interest in retirement fund	$			
Net worth of business(es) owned (attach financial statement)	$			
Automobiles owned (make and year)	$	Acct. no.		
		Alimony/Child Support/Separate Maintenance Payments Owed to:	$	
Other Assets (itemize)	$			
		Job-Related Expense (child care, union dues, etc.)	$	
		Total Monthly Payments	$	
Total Assets a.	$	Net Worth (a minus b) ► $	Total Liabilities b.	$

FIGURE 8-11 (Continued)

VI. ASSETS AND LIABILITIES (cont.)

Schedule of Real Estate Owned (If additional properties are owned, use continuation sheet.)

Property Address (enter S if sold, PS if pending sale or R if rental being held for income)	Type of Property	Present Market Value	Amount of Mortgages & Liens	Gross Rental Income	Mortgage Payments	Insurance, Maintenance, Taxes & Misc.	Net Rental Income
		$	$	$	$	$	$
Totals		$	$	$	$	$	$

List any additional names under which credit has previously been received and indicate appropriate creditor name(s) and account number(s):

Alternate Name	Creditor Name	Account Number

VII. DETAILS OF TRANSACTION

a. Purchase price	$
b. Alterations, improvements, repairs	
c. Land (if acquired separately)	
d. Refinance (incl. debts to be paid off)	
e. Estimated prepaid items	
f. Estimated closing costs	
g. PMI, MIP, Funding Fee	
h. Discount (if Borrower will pay)	
i. Total costs (add items a through h)	
j. Subordinate financing	
k. Borrower's closing costs paid by Seller	
l. Other Credits (explain)	
m. Loan amount (exclude PMI, MIP, Funding Fee financed)	
n. PMI, MIP, Funding Fee financed	
o. Loan amount (add m & n)	
p. Cash from/to Borrower (subtract j, k, l & o from i)	

VIII. DECLARATIONS

If you answer "Yes" to any questions a through i, please use continuation sheet for explanation.

	Borrower		Co-Borrower	
	Yes	No	Yes	No
a. Are there any outstanding judgments against you?	☐	☐	☐	☐
b. Have you been declared bankrupt within the past 7 years?	☐	☐	☐	☐
c. Have you had property foreclosed upon or given title or deed in lieu thereof in the last 7 years?	☐	☐	☐	☐
d. Are you a party to a lawsuit?	☐	☐	☐	☐
e. Have you directly or indirectly been obligated on any loan which resulted in foreclosure, transfer of title in lieu of foreclosure, or judgment? (This would include such loans as home mortgage loans, SBA loans, home improvement loans, educational loans, manufactured (mobile) home loans, any mortgage, financial obligation, bond, or loan guarantee. If "Yes," provide details, including date, name and address of Lender, FHA or VA case number, if any, and reasons for the action.)	☐	☐	☐	☐
f. Are you presently delinquent or in default on any Federal debt or any other loan, mortgage, financial obligation, bond, or loan guarantee? If "Yes," give details as described in the preceding question.	☐	☐	☐	☐
g. Are you obligated to pay alimony, child support, or separate maintenance?	☐	☐	☐	☐
h. Is any part of the down payment borrowed?	☐	☐	☐	☐
i. Are you a co-maker or endorser on a note?	☐	☐	☐	☐
j. Are you a U.S. citizen?	☐	☐	☐	☐
k. Are you a permanent resident alien?	☐	☐	☐	☐
l. **Do you intend to occupy the property as your primary residence?** If "Yes," complete question m below.	☐	☐	☐	☐
m. Have you had an ownership interest in a property in the last three years?	☐	☐	☐	☐
(1) What type of property did you own—principal residence (PR), second home (SH), or investment property (IP)?				
(2) How did you hold title to the home—solely by yourself (S), jointly with your spouse (SP), or jointly with another person (O)?				

IX. ACKNOWLEDGMENT AND AGREEMENT

Each of the undersigned specifically represents to Lender and to Lender's actual or potential agents, brokers, processors, attorneys, insurers, servicers, successors and assigns and agrees and acknowledges that: (1) the information provided in this application is true and correct as of the date set forth opposite my signature and that any intentional or negligent misrepresentation of this information contained in this application may result in civil liability, including monetary damages, to any person who may suffer any loss due to reliance upon any misrepresentation that I have made on this application, and/or in criminal penalties including, but not limited to, fine or imprisonment or both under the provisions of Title 18, United States Code, Sec. 1001, et seq.; (2) the loan requested pursuant to this application (the "Loan") will be secured by a mortgage or deed of trust on the property described herein; (3) the property will not be used for any illegal or prohibited purpose or use; (4) all statements made in this application are made for the purpose of obtaining a residential mortgage loan; (5) the property will be occupied as indicated herein; (6) any owner or servicer of the Loan may verify or reverify any information contained in the application from any source named in this application, and Lender, its successors or assigns may retain the original and/or an electronic record of this application, even if the Loan is not approved; (7) the Lender and its agents, brokers, insurers, servicers, successors and assigns may continuously rely on the information contained in the application, and I am obligated to amend and/or supplement the information provided in this application if any of the material facts that I have represented herein should change prior to closing of the Loan; (8) in the event that my payments on the Loan become delinquent, the owner or servicer of the Loan may, in addition to any other rights and remedies that it may have relating to such delinquency, report my name and account information to one or more consumer credit reporting agencies; (9) ownership of the Loan and/or administration of the Loan account may be transferred with such notice as may be required by law; (10) neither Lender nor its agents, brokers, insurers, servicers, successors or assigns has made any representation or warranty, express or implied, to me regarding the property or the condition or value of the property; and (11) my transmission of this application as an "electronic record" containing my "electronic signature," as those terms are defined in applicable federal and/or state laws (excluding audio and video recordings), or my facsimile transmission of this application containing a facsimile of my signature, shall be as effective, enforceable and valid as if a paper version of this application were delivered containing my original written signature.

Borrower's Signature	Date	Co-Borrower's Signature	Date
X		X	

X. INFORMATION FOR GOVERNMENT MONITORING PURPOSES

The following information is requested by the Federal Government for certain types of loans related to a dwelling in order to monitor the lender's compliance with equal credit opportunity, fair housing and home mortgage disclosure laws. You are not required to furnish this information, but are encouraged to do so. The law provides that a lender may discriminate neither on the basis of this information, nor on whether you choose to furnish it. If you furnish the information, please provide both ethnicity and race. For race, you may check more than one designation. If you do not furnish ethnicity, race, or sex, under Federal regulations, this lender is required to note the information on the basis of visual observation or surname. If you do not wish to furnish the information, please check the box below. (Lender must review the above material to assure that the disclosures satisfy all requirements to which the lender is subject under applicable state law for the particular type of loan applied for.)

BORROWER	☐ I do not wish to furnish this information.	CO-BORROWER	☐ I do not wish to furnish this information.
Ethnicity:	☐ Hispanic or Latino ☐ Not Hispanic or Latino	**Ethnicity:**	☐ Hispanic or Latino ☐ Not Hispanic or Latino
Race:	☐ American Indian or Alaska Native ☐ Asian ☐ Black or African American ☐ Native Hawaiian or Other Pacific Islander ☐ White	**Race:**	☐ American Indian or Alaska Native ☐ Asian ☐ Black or African American ☐ Native Hawaiian or Other Pacific Islander ☐ White
Sex:	☐ Female ☐ Male	**Sex:**	☐ Female ☐ Male

To be Completed by Interviewer This application was taken by: ☐ Face-to-face interview ☐ Mail ☐ Telephone ☐ Internet	Interviewer's Name (print or type)	Name and Address of Interviewer's Employer
	Interviewer's Signature Date	
	Interviewer's Phone Number (incl. area code)	

FIGURE 8-11 *(Continued)*

Continuation Sheet/Residential Loan Application		
Use this continuation sheet if you need more space to complete the Residential Loan Application. Mark **B** for Borrower or **C** for Co-Borrower.	Borrower:	Agency Case Number:
	Co-Borrower:	Lender Case Number:

I/We fully understand that it is a Federal crime punishable by fine or imprisonment, or both, to knowingly make any false statements concerning any of the above facts as applicable under the provisions of Title 18, United States Code, Section 1001, et seq.

Borrower's Signature	Date	Co-Borrower's Signature	Date
X		X	

Freddie Mac Form 65 01/04	Page 4 of 4	Fannie Mae Form 1003 01/04

The models reflect federal disclosure requirements under the Truth in Lending Act, Real Estate Settlement Procedures Act, National Flood Insurance Program, and Equal Opportunity Act. Please refer to Chapter 9 for a detailed explanation of each of these.

There are certain disclosures that need to be provided to the borrower *no later* than three days after the application or credit report date, whichever comes first. The lender will require these disclosures to be signed by the borrower, as acknowledgment of receipt. Therefore, we suggest you have your borrower sign these disclosures at the time of application. They are the following:

- *Certification and authorization form.* Allows the broker or lender to investigate credit history and verify income and mortgage history.

- *Truth in lending disclosure.* Must be provided to your borrower *no later* than three days from application or credit report date. The disclosure reflects the amount financed and the annual percentage rate (APR).

- *Good faith estimate (GFE).* Must also be provided to your borrower *no later* than three days from application or credit report date. The GFE disclosure, as explained earlier, details all costs associated with the loan.

- *Transfer of service disclosure.* Describes the mortgage lender's policies and track record concerning selling the servicing rights of the mortgages the lender originates.

- *Equal Credit Opportunity Act disclosure.* Known as ECOA, constitutes unlawful discrimination.

- *Notice of right to appraisal report.* Discloses the borrower's right to request a copy of the appraisal.

- *ARM program disclosure and CHARM booklet.* Applicable to adjustable-rate mortgages.

When working for a lender, there are several other disclosures that are mailed out to the borrower by the processor. If you are working for a mortgage broker, then the lender will mail out all disclosures. Keep in mind that there are state-specific disclosures, which we may not have covered above.

Truth in Lending Act

The Truth in Lending Act (TILA) ensures that the consumer has been provided with all the appropriate disclosures in both a timely and accurate manner as required by TILA. The time limit required for the documentation to be sent to the consumer is no more than three days from the time of the signed initial application or the date the credit report is requested. The following is a list of required disclosures by TILA and its implementing regulation (Regulation Z), as applicable:

- Estimated truth in lending statement

- Itemization of amount financed (may be replaced by the good faith estimate in RESPA-related transactions)

- Notice of right to cancel (if a refinance)

- Section 32 (high-cost loan) disclosure (typically Section 32 loans are no longer allowed)

- ARM program disclosure and CHARM booklet

- Final truth in lending statement (usually mailed out by the processor or lender)

Real Estate Settlement Procedures Act

The Real Estate Settlement Procedures Act (RESPA) ensures that the consumer has been provided with all the appropriate disclosures in both a timely and accurate manner as required by RESPA. The time limit that is required for the documentation to be sent to the consumer is no more than three days from the time of the signed initial application or the date the credit report is requested. The following is a list of required disclosures by RESPA and its implementing regulation (Regulation X), as applicable:

- Good faith estimate of closing costs

- *Settlement Cost Booklet* (usually mailed out by the processor or lender)

- Notice of possible transfer of servicing

- Initial escrow statement (usually mailed out by the processor or lender)

- HUD-1/settlement statement (usually mailed out by the processor or lender)

Home Mortgage Disclosure Act

Certain information is required by the Home Mortgage Disclosure Act (HMDA, Regulation C) in order to be in compliance. This information is found on the Uniform Residential Loan Application (1003) and a separate government monitoring form.

Note: There are no disclosures associated with Regulation C.

Equal Credit Opportunity Act

All credit applications will be reviewed without regard to *race, color, religion, national origin, sex, marital status, age, handicap,* or *familial status*.

The Equal Credit Opportunity Act (ECOA, Regulation B) identifies certain practices that automatically constitute *unlawful discrimination and are strictly prohibited*. They are as follows:

- Discounting part-time income if the consumer *only* has a part-time job. However, it is permissible to discount part-time income from a second job or from a secondary source of income if it is irregular or short term.

- Discriminating against an applicant because the applicant's income is derived from a public assistance program.

- Inquiring about child-bearing plans, birth control methods, or child-rearing plans.

- Requiring a spouse's signature.

Note: ECOA strictly prohibits any evidence of any statement that would discourage a borrower from applying for or proceeding with an application.

The following disclosures are required by ECOA:

- Notice of counteroffer and notice of adverse action

- Notice of right to receive appraisal report

- Notices of action taken, including notice of incomplete application

There are also several disclosures unique to FHA and VA applications.

Required Disclosures for FHA Mortgages

- *Addendum to the uniform residential loan application.* Includes a variety of certifications by the lender and applicant.

- *Important notice to home buyer.* Informs the applicant that FHA does not warrant the condition or value of the property; states that FHA does not set the rates or discount points—these are negotiable with the lender; warns of the penalties of loan fraud; and discusses discrimination. Also includes a disclosure regarding prepay (prepayment must be received on the installment due date).

- *Lead paint disclosure.* Self-explanatory.

- *Assumption notice—release of liability.* Provides a release of personal liability from FHA, ensuring that the borrower is not responsible for making payments after an assumption takes place.

- *Informed consumer choice disclosure notice.* Compares the cost of an FHA mortgage with a conventional finance, including the cost of mortgage insurance.

- *Real estate certification.* Certifies the terms of the real estate purchase contract. Both the buyer and the seller are required to sign the form.

- *Social security number certification.* Self-explanatory.

- *FHA identity of interest certification.* Requires the borrower to disclose whether he or she has any relationship to the seller of the property.

- *Notice to the home buyer (home buyer summary).* Provided by the FHA appraiser to disclose whether the home meets minimum FHA property standards.

- *For your protection.* Explains that an appraisal is not an inspection, and advises the borrower to get an inspection.

VA Required Disclosures

- *Addendum to uniform residential loan application.* Same as for FHA, this addendum includes a variety of certifications.

- *VA debt questionnaire (Form 26-0551).* Asks the veteran about previous foreclosures, judgments, defaults, or present delinquencies on any federal regulators.

- *Interest rate and discount statement.* States that the rate and points are not set by VA and are negotiable by the lender.

- *Federal collection policy notice.* Informs the veteran of actions the government can take if scheduled payments are not made.

- *Assumption of VA-guaranteed mortgages.* Provides a release of personal liability from VA, ensuring that the veteran is not responsible for making payments after an assumption of the loan.

- *Borrower's acknowledgments of disclosures.* Acknowledges receipt of the good faith estimate.

- *For homes built prior to 1978—notice of possible lead-based paint.* Self-explanatory.

- *Counseling checklist for military homeowners.* Active-duty applicants must sign to certify that they have received homeownership and loan obligation counseling.

TRUTH IN LENDING

Truth in Lending Act

The Truth in Lending Act is implemented by Federal Reserve Board Regulation Z. The intent of the law was to standardize the method of calculating the cost of credit by disclosing the APR—the annual percentage rate. The APR is the cost of consumer credit as a percentage spread (it is expressed as an annual percentage rate). We are all familiar with an APR tied to a credit card or auto loan; the APR is the same as the interest rate. The difference with mortgages is that the APR *includes* all the costs associated with the loan transaction. Consequently, you have an APR that is higher than the interest rate on the loan.

The APR includes all fees incurred with *obtaining the loan*. In other words the APR excludes the fees that a borrower would incur had he or she purchased the property in cash. The APR *excludes*:

- Title fees

- Recording fees

- County, city, or state taxes

- Appraisal fee

- Termite report

- Any other inspection fees (such as a well or septic inspection)

The fees incurred in obtaining a mortgage are the same as most of the fees disclosed on the good faith estimate. The APR includes:

- Origination fees

- Discount fees

- Private mortgage insurance

- Tax service fee

- Underwriting or processing fees

- Document preparation fee

- All prepaid items

- One-time MIP for FHA loans

- VA funding fee

All loans require a truth in lending (TIL) disclosure. Mortgage lending is unique in that mortgages covered under RESPA, the Real Estate Settlement Procedures Act, require an initial TIL to be given to the applicant within three days of the initial loan application, along with the good faith estimate of closing charges. The idea was to provide early disclosure of the APR, allowing the consumer plenty of time to comparison-shop and to help avoid any hidden finance charges by the lender.

Also TILA, as we previously read, gives borrowers the right to cancel a refinance transaction that results in a lien against their primary residence; this is known as a *right of rescission*.

Calculating the APR

Now let's look at how the APR is calculated:

Example 1

Loan amount	$100,000
Interest rate	7.0%
Term	30 years
Monthly payment	$665.30
1-point origination fee	$1,000
Processing fee	$350
Other closing fees	$1,150
Total fees	$2,500

Subtract the total fees from the loan amount to get the new loan amount:

$$\$100,000 - \$2,500 = \$97,500$$

Now that we have the new loan amount—$97,500—we can figure the true cost of the loan. To find the APR, we need to determine the interest rate that would equate to a monthly payment of $665.30 for a loan of $97,500. In this case, that is 7.25%.

Example 2

Loan amount	$100,000
Monthly payment	$665.30
Interest rate	7.0%
Term	30 years
Origination fee of 3%	$3,000
Other fees	$1,000
Total fees	$4,000

We can calculate the new loan amout:

$$\$100,000 - \$4,000 = \$96,000$$

To find the APR, we need to determine the interest rate that would equate to $665.30 for a loan amount of $96,000, which in this case is 7.40%.

Here are some other things to consider when you look at the APR:

- The more money being financed, the less impact all those fees will have on the APR, simply because the APR is calculated based on the total loan amount.

- The length of time the borrower is in the home before he or she sells or refinances has a direct influence on the effective interest rate the borrower ultimately gets. For example, if the borrower moves or refinances after 3 years instead of 30, and after having paid 2 points at the loan closing, the effective interest rate for the loan is much higher than if the buyer stays for the full loan term.

Below is a close-up of the portion of the Truth in Lending Disclosure Statement that is most reviewed. Let's use the previous example of a loan amount of $100,000 with an origination cost of 3% or $3,000 and other closing costs of $1,000, for a total closing cost fee of $4,000 and at an interest rate of 7.0% on a 30-year term.

APR (annual percentage rate)	Finance Charge	Amount Financed	Total of Payments
The cost of your credit as a yearly rate.	The dollar amount the credit will cost you.	The amount of credit provided to you on your behalf.	The amount you will have paid after you have made all payments as scheduled.
1	2	3	4
7.409%	$143,510.98	$96,000.00	$239,510.98

Item 1 is where you will find the APR. Item 2 is the finance charge—the total *finance* cost for the loan should the borrower keep the loan for its full term. Item 3 is the amount financed. This is the actual loan amount minus the cost for the loan (loan fees). Item 4 is the total of payments. This amount—the total finance cost (item 2) plus the actual loan amount (item 3)—is what the borrower will pay on this loan should he keep the loan for its full term.

What the Truth in Lending Disclosure Discloses

1. *The total of payments.* Compute the *total of payments* by multiplying the payment schedule, including the PMI, by the amount of payments.

2. *The amount financed.* The amount financed is the loan amount less points, prepaid interest, PMI, and lender fees.

3. *The finance charge.* The finance charge is the *total of payments* less the *amount financed.*

4. *The APR.* Compute the *APR* by dividing the *total of payments* by the number of payments and apply that against the *amount financed*, as if it were the loan amount.

Important

If during the loan approval process, there are any changes to the interest rate or to any fees that are not beneficial to your borrower, you are required to redisclose with a revised truth in lending disclosure and a good faith estimate.

LOAN SETUP

After the Application Is Finished, What Do I Do?

After you have taken an initial application, you will need to review the information provided by your borrower, set up your loan package, and submit it for approval.

After the Application Is Finished

- Review the documentation you received from your borrower.

- Lock in the rate!

- Set up your loan package for the processor or underwriter.

- Hand in your loan package within 24 hours. Time is $$$.

Review the Documentation Received

Here are several tips for preparing your loan prior to the loan setup.

Pay Stubs and W-2s

- Does the year-to-date income amount show the monthly salary? If you notice there is a discrepancy, then you will need a letter of explanation. Your borrower might have been out on sick leave. In this case you can also request a verification of employment from the employer, which would then complete section 20 of the VOE form.

- On the pay stub—are there any regular deductions? The borrower might have a credit union loan. If this loan also appears on the credit report, you are OK; but if it is not on the credit report, you must count it in the borrower's debts.

- On the pay stub—is there overtime or bonus pay? If so, make sure that you have properly calculated the borrower's income.

- Does all the personal information match? This is important; make sure the borrower's address and social security match what is on your application.

Tax Returns

- If you are providing tax returns, make sure all schedules are included and signed by the borrower. Again, make sure all personal information matches.

Bank Statements

- If you are using bank statements, make sure all pages are complete.

- Is there an amount that is regularly withdrawn from the account each month? This might indicate a debt that is not disclosed (this could affect your ratios).

- Are there any large deposits or withdrawals? If so, you will need an explanation.

It is important to obtain answers to any questions up front in the loan process. With a proper review of the information, you are better prepared for a loan approval.

Give your borrower a professional follow-up list of additional items needed and include a deadline date. This will give your borrower a sense of urgency to keep the loan a priority. On a purchase you can also give the outstanding list to the Realtor; then the Realtor is less likely to blame you if the loan gets delayed waiting for outstanding conditions.

Lock in the Loan Rate

The most important thing to do after taking and reviewing a loan application is to lock in the rate. If you have quoted your borrower a rate and have supplied your borrower with proper disclosures, you have a responsibility to advise your borrower to lock in the rate. What if your borrower is qualifying with a tight debt ratio and on the current market interest rate—and the rate increases tomorrow? Your borrower would no longer qualify. It is ultimately the borrower's decision whether to lock in the rate or float the rate; however, we suggest that you lock in the rate. If your borrower decides to float the rate, then it would be prudent to have your borrower sign a statement acknowledging the fact that he or she has decided to float the rate.

Set Up the Loan

After you have reviewed the documents received by your borrower for accuracy, you are ready to package your loan application for the processor. The first step is to put all the items in a stacking order for either your processor or underwriter. It is standard practice to use a legal-size manila folder and punch a hole in both sides. Most stacking orders require right- and left-side use. Here is a sample of a standard stacking order for a processor:

SAMPLE OF STANDARD LOAN FILE SETUP ORDER TWO-HOLE FASTENED

Left Side from Top to Bottom	Right Side from Top to Bottom
– Conversation log	– Original application
– Loan registration	– Application supplements—
– Appraisal request	e.g., green cards, reason for
– Prequal worksheet	refinance, etc.
– Copy of application fee	– Credit report
or appraisal fee	– Credit-related info—e.g.,
– Purchase agreement	explanations of payment
– Your contact information	history
– Nonpertinent information	– Income and employment info
(face down)	– Asset documentation
	– Miscellaneous

What will the processor do?

The processor is responsible for getting the loan ready for submission to the underwriter or lender for final approval. Please note that the processor's duties will vary and will depend on whether you are working for a mortgage company or you are using an independent contract processor. Either way, you should set up a system with your processor and discuss up front what his or her duties will be. There are certain standard steps that the processor will need to take:

- Register the loan in the system. Regardless of whether you work for a lender or broker or work independently, the mortgage application will need to be entered into an origination software program and tracked for RESPA compliance.

- Check for disclosures. If any disclosures are missing, the processor will mail them out to your borrower. However, the truth in lending disclosure and good faith estimate must be provided *no later* than three days after the application date or credit report date, whichever comes first.

Therefore, most loan officers have these forms signed at the application date.

- If there is not a credit report on file, order the credit report.

- If there is not an appraisal on file, order the appraisal.

- Open title and escrow.

- Order verifications:
  Verification of employment (VOE)
  Verification of deposits (VOD) (sent to banks to verify liquid assets)
  Verification of mortgage (VOM) or verification of rent (VOR) (the request will be sent to the present landlord or mortgage lien holder if for some reason the mortgage history is not reported on the credit report)

The processor will review the loan package for all other items. For example, the processor will:

- Check for property types. If the property is a condo, will need to make sure it is an approved complex. Request master condo insurance policy and "condo cert." If property is an investment property, will check for lease agreements and operating income statement from appraiser.

- Review the credit report for any late payments, judgments, or bankruptcies.

After all the information has been reviewed for any discrepancies, the loan is packaged for the underwriter and/or lender to review for final approval.

Who is the underwriter?

If you are working for a mortgage lender or banker, most likely there are in-house underwriters who underwrite and approve in-house loan products. If you are working independently or for a mortgage broker, the processor is probably sending the loan package to the underwriter at the lender you have agreed upon.

Underwriting is basically checking to make sure the loan meets the specified lender guidelines; if it does, it's approved.

However, it is very important to package the loan properly and to address any discrepancies up front! This saves the underwriter time, and your loan package is reviewed and an answer is given in a timely manner. If the underwriter does not have a clear picture, your loan can be suspended or denied. This is not only a waste of time but also a big delay for all involved. In most cases an approval is made with conditions. The lender, on a form referred to as a Conditional Loan Approval, issues the loan approval with listed conditions. These conditions (also known as *stipulations*) must be met in order to close the loan. As the conditions are met, the underwriter signs off on each. Only when all conditions are met will the loan be ready to close.

If the loan is declined, the loan processor will advise the loan officer. When this happens, determine the reason for denial and see if there are any compensating factors to justify a re-review. It is the loan officer's job to act as the borrower's advocate.

What the Underwriter May Ask For

- More recent bank statements because the bank statements that were provided to verify assets are over three months old.

- An explanation of the source of funds for the down payment, because a large sum of money was deposited in the borrower's account last month.

- Further information about the comparables, because the comparables that were used by the appraiser are a year old and are for properties that are 3 miles away. The appraiser will need to explain why the comparables used are over six months old and will need to use comparables from within 0.5 to 1 mile, for most cities and towns.

These are issues that should have been addressed with the loan package, which would have saved you time.

If your loan package is approved with no conditions, then the closing conditions would read as follows:

- Pest inspection report
- Survey

- Final truth in lending disclosure

- Homeowner's insurance policy

- Escrow instructions

- Rate lock-in

- Seller contribution to match that in the contract

Your loan could be approved through *automatic underwriting,* which we have previously discussed. Today, almost all lenders provide automatic approval through their Web sites. Keep in mind that only a quarter of the percentage of loans submitted through these systems are approved. But if your loan is approved through automatic underwriting, it is a much smoother process.

Congratulations, your loan has been approved! What's next?

CLOSING THE LOAN

Settlement Agent

A settlement agent is also known as the closing attorney, escrow, or title company. The settlement agent handles the following duties:

- Coordinates signing of the loan documents. The settlement agent does not usually draw the legal documents; the lender supplies the documents, and the settlement agent brings the parties together to sign as required by the lender. The lender provides lender instructions for the settlement agent.

- Receives and holds all monies, instructions, and documents pertaining to the purchase transaction.

- Requests a payoff demand from the existing mortgage lien holder.

- Orders the loss payee clause from the homeowner's insurance; see the details below.

- Provides the title commitment or binder; see the detailed description below.

- Orders home inspection, survey, and termite and pest reports.

- Calculates the funds needed. The settlement agent does the official calculation of the cash the borrower needs to bring in and the cash to be received by the seller. The lender or mortgage broker or loan officer supplies most of the information; however, the closing agent compiles the information and prorates any expenses.

- Disburses the funds to all parties. The settlement agent receives and disburses all funds. The settlement agent pays the real estate commissions, pays off the current loan on the property, and pays fees to the lender, title company, etc. For purchases, when all other expenses are paid, the remaining funds (net proceeds) are sent to the seller.

- Prepares the deed and is responsible for the recording of the deed with the county courthouse.

In a refinance, some settlement agents have traveling notaries, in which case the notary will bring the loan documents to your borrower, eliminating the need for the borrower to make a trip to the settlement company.

Title Commitment, Binder, Insurance

A lender requires a title commitment or binder, which includes a title search to prove who the legal owner is. The title search includes researching a chain of title and examining public records; records of deaths, divorces, court judgments, liens, and contests over wills (all of which can affect ownership rights) are examined. In addition to a formal title search, the lender will require a title insurance policy. The policy guards the lender against an error by whoever searched the title.

The cost of the policy (a one-time premium) is usually based on the loan amount and is often paid by the purchaser. However, the seller can be asked during negotiations to pay part of or the entire premium. The title insurance required by the lender protects only the lender. To protect the borrower against unforeseen title problems, he or she is offered an owner's title insurance policy. The additional premium varies from region to region.

Homeowner's Insurance Policy

All mortgage transactions require that the property be insured against fire or other hazards (fire and hazard insurance). The policy must:

- Have dwelling coverage in the amount of the loan

- Be in force and up to date

- On refinances, if the policy is expiring within 60 days, be replaced with a new policy

- Reflect the borrower's name and correct property address

- Be paid for the first year's premium

- Include a loss payee clause (which shows the lender as the lien holder)

Condominiums will have a master policy, which is provided by the management company. You will need an individual certificate showing the unit number with the loss payee clause.

Home Inspection and Termite Report

The inspection is needed to ensure the house is structurally sound and to show there is no damage or pest infestation. The original report form must be dated within 45 days of the closing date. Condominiums may be exempt from this requirement if the association shows a line item in the budget for pest control. New construction requires a soil treatment certificate. Refinances are typically exempt from this requirement.

Survey

This is a map or sketch of the property that shows the boundary lines of the lot and details any encroachments or improvements since the last survey.

Well or Septic Certification

If the property is serviced by a well or septic system, a certification from the local health authority is required.

Taking Title to the Property

Early in the escrow process, your borrower will be asked how he or she would like to *take title* to the property. Your escrow officer may also refer to this as your *vesting*. The vesting will be indicated on the *deed*, which the seller will sign in order to convey title to the property to the new owner. The deed is the original loan document that will be recorded at the local land records office in the jurisdiction where the property is located. The type of deed may affect the owner's interest. A *general warranty deed* conveys the property with the seller's guarantee that the title is good. A *special warranty deed* is basically a statement from the seller of the property saying that as far as he or she knows, the title is good. A *quitclaim deed* releases a seller from any liability of ownership.

There are four common forms of ownership:

- *Joint tenants with the right of survivorship*. Means that when one owner dies, the property automatically becomes the property of the survivor.

- *Tenants by entirety*. Is a form of ownership reserved for married couples. The property reverts to the survivor but shields the owner from claims of individual creditors.

- *Tenants in common.* Allows the owners to assign a percentage of ownership to each owner. When one owner dies, an estate is created, which will be distributed under the terms of the owner's will.

- *Sole and separate.* Means there is no other title holder.

Figure 8-12 is provided for informational purposes only. There may be significant legal and tax consequences associated with

FIGURE 8-12
The Four Common Forms of Ownership

	Tenancy in Common	Joint Tenancy	Community Property	Tenancy in Partnership
Parties	Any number of persons (can be husband and wife).	Any number of persons (can be husband and wife).	Only husband and wife.	Only partners (any number).
Division	Ownership can be divided into any number of interests equal or unequal.	Ownership interests must be equal.	Ownership interests are equal.	Ownership interest is in relation to interest in partnership.
Title	Each co-owner has a separate legal title to his undivided interest.	There is only one title to the whole property.	Title is in the "community" (similar to title being in partnership).	Title is in the "partnership."
Possession	Equal right of possession.	Equal right of possession.	Equal right of possession.	Equal right of possession but only for partnership purposes.
Conveyance	Each co-owner's interest may be conveyed separately by its owner.	Conveyance by one co-owner without the others breaks the joint tenancy.	Both co-owners must join in conveyance of real property. Separate interests cannot be conveyed.	Any authorized partner may convey whole partnership property. No partner may sell his interest in the partnership without the consent of his co-partners.
Purchaser's Status	Purchaser becomes a tenant in common with the other co-owners.	Purchaser becomes a tenant in common with the other co-owners.	Purchaser can only acquire whole title of community. Cannot acquire a part of it.	Purchaser can only acquire the whole title.
Death	On co-owner's death his interest passes by will to his devisees or heirs. No survivorship right.	On co-owner's death his interest ends and cannot be willed. Survivor owns the property by survivorship.	On co-owner's death, half goes to survivor in severalty. Up to one-half goes by will to decedent's devisees or by succession to survivor.	On partner's death, his partnership interest passes to surviving partner pending liquidation of partnership. Share of deceased partner then goes to his estate.
Successor's Status	Devisees or heirs become tenants in common.	Last survivor owns property in severalty.	If passing by will, tenancy in common between devisee and survivor results.	Heirs or devisees have right in partnership interest but not in specific property.
Creditor's Rights	Co-owner's interest may be sold on execution sale to satisfy creditor. Creditor becomes a tenant in common.	Co-owner's interest may be sold on execution sale to satisfy creditor. Joint tenancy is broken. Creditor becomes a tenant in common.	Co-owner's interest can't be seized and sold separately. Whole property may be sold to satisfy debts of either husband or wife, depending on the debt.	Partner's interest cannot be seized or sold separately by his personal creditor, but his share of profits may be obtained by a personal creditor. Whole property may be sold on execution sale to satisfy partnership creditor.
Presumption	Favored in doubtful cases except husband and wife case.	Must be expressly stated and properly formed. Not favored.	Strong presumption that property acquired by husband and wife is community.	Arises only by virtue of partnership status in property placed in partnership.

the manner in which title is held. You should always suggest that your borrower consult an attorney, estate planner, or CPA to obtain specific advice on how to take title.

Wet and Dry Settlements

The "wet settlement" act requires that actual cash be at the closing table. This will ensure that all accounting be based on actual receipts and disbursements so that the settlement agent may accurately disburse all funds at the closing. In the 38 non-escrow states (called "wet-funding" states because the funds are passed out while the ink is still wet on the documents), the borrower will sign the documents and receive title to his or her new home the same day. When all parties meet at the closing table, this is referred to as a *round-table closing*.

In escrow states (called "dry" states, e.g., California), the borrower will sign the loan documents and bring in any money necessary a couple of days before the loan is closed. The lender then reviews the documents and wires the funds to the escrow company for disbursement to the other parties. You must then wait for escrow to do its job (get the deed recorded at the county courthouse) before any money is distributed. You can figure in a couple of days for this process.

Note: There is a federal legal requirement, applicable in all states, for a three-day waiting period after signing for a refinance of an owner-occupied property. The purpose of this rescission period is to give borrowers time to reconsider what they have signed.

The Settlement Statement, or HUD-1 Form

The Uniform Settlement Statement (known as the HUD-1) is required as part of RESPA. The form is completed and issued by the settlement agent and is given to both the buyer and seller in virtually all one- to four-unit residential transactions. See Figure 8-13 for a sample of the HUD-1 form.

FIGURE 8-13
Example of a HUD-1 Form

A. U.S. DEPARTMENT OF HOUSING AND URBAN DEVELOPMENT SETTLEMENT STATEMENT

B. TYPE OF LOAN			6. File Number	7. Loan Number
	1. FHA	2. FmHA		
3. CONV. UNINS.	4. VA	5. CONV. INS.	8. Mortgage Insurance Case Number	

C. NOTE: *This form is furnished to give you a statement of actual settlement costs. Amounts paid to and by the settlement agent are shown. Items marked "(p.o.c.)" were paid outside the closing; they are shown here for informational purposes and are not included in the totals.*

D. NAME AND ADDRESS OF BORROWER:	E. NAME AND ADDRESS OF SELLER:	F. NAME AND ADDRESS OF LENDER:
G. PROPERTY LOCATION:	H. SETTLEMENT AGENT: NAME, AND ADDRESS	
	PLACE OF SETTLEMENT:	I. SETTLEMENT DATE:

J. SUMMARY OF BORROWER'S TRANSACTION		K. SUMMARY OF SELLER'S TRANSACTION	
100. **GROSS AMOUNT DUE FROM BORROWER:**		400. **GROSS AMOUNT DUE TO SELLER:**	
101. Contract sales price		401. Contract sales price	
102. Personal property		402. Personal property	
103. Settlement charges to borrower (line 1400)		403.	
104.		404.	
105.		405.	
Adjustments for items paid by seller in advance		*Adjustments for items paid by seller in advance*	
106. City/town taxes to		406. City/town taxes to	
107. County taxes to		407. County taxes to	
108. Assessments to		408. Assessments to	
109.		409.	
110.		410.	
111.		411.	
112.		412.	
120. **GROSS AMOUNT DUE FROM BORROWER**		420. **GROSS AMOUNT DUE TO SELLER**	

FIGURE 8-13 (*Continued*)

200. AMOUNTS PAID BY OR IN BEHALF OF BORROWER:		500. REDUCTIONS IN AMOUNT DUE TO SELLER:	
201. Deposit of earnest money		501. Excess deposit (see instructions)	
202. Principal amount of new loan(s)		502. Settlement charges to seller (line 1400)	
203. Existing loan(s) taken subject to		503. Existing loan(s) taken subject to	
204.		504. Payoff of first mortgage loan	
205.		505. Payoff of second mortgage loan	
206.		506.	
207.		507.	
208.		508.	
209.		509.	
Adjustments for items unpaid by seller		*Adjustments for items unpaid by seller*	
210. City/town taxes to		510. City/town taxes to	
211. County taxes to		511. County taxes to	
212. Assessments to		512. Assessments to	
213.		513.	
214.		514.	
215.		515.	
216.		516.	
217.		517.	
218.		518.	
219.		519.	
220. TOTAL PAID BY/FOR BORROWER		520. TOTAL REDUCTION AMOUNT DUE SELLER	

FIGURE 8-13 *(Continued)*

300. **CASH AT SETTLEMENT FROM/TO BORROWER**		600. **CASH AT SETTLEMENT TO/FROM SELLER**	
301. Gross amount due from borrower (line 120)		601. Gross amount due to seller (line 420)	
302. Less amounts paid by/for borrower (line 220)		602. Less reductions in amount due seller (line 520)	
303. **CASH (☐ FROM) (☐ TO) BORROWER**		603. **CASH (☐ TO) (☐ FROM) SELLER**	

L. SETTLEMENT CHARGES		
700. **TOTAL SALES/BROKER'S COMMISSION based on price $ @ %=**	PAID FROM BORROWER'S FUNDS AT SETTLEMENT	PAID FROM SELLER'S FUNDS AT SETTLEMENT
Division of Commission (line 700) as follows:		
701. $ To		
702. $ To		
703. Commission paid at Settlement		
704.		
800. **ITEMS PAYABLE IN CONNECTION WITH LOAN**		
801. Loan Origination Fee %		
802. Loan Discount %		
803. Appraisal Fee to		
804. Credit Report to		
805. Lender's Inspection Fee		
806. Mortgage Insurance Application Fee to		
807. Assumption Fee		
808.		
809.		
810.		
811.		
900. **ITEMS REQUIRED BY LENDER TO BE PAID IN ADVANCE**		
901. Interest from to @$ /day		
902. Mortgage Insurance Premium for months to		

FIGURE 8-13 (*Continued*)

903. Hazard Insurance Premium for years to		
904.		
905.		
1000. **RESERVES DEPOSITED WITH LENDER**		
1001. Hazard Insurance months @ $ per month		
1002. Mortgage insurance months @ $ per month		
1003. City property taxes months @ $ per month		
1004. County property taxes months @ $ per month		
1005. Annual assessments months @ $ per month		
1006. months @ $ per month		
1007. months @ $ per month		
1008. Aggregate Adjustment months @ $ per month		
1100. **TITLE CHARGES**		
1101. Settlement or closing fee to		
1102. Abstract or title search to		
1103. Title examination to		
1104. Title insurance binder to		
1105. Document preparation to		
1106. Notary fees to		
1107. Attorney's fees to		
(*includes above items numbers;*)		
1108. Title Insurance to		
(*includes above items numbers;*)		
1109. Lender's coverage $		
1110. Owner's coverage $		
1111.		

FIGURE 8-13 (*Continued*)

1112.		
1113.		
1200. **GOVERNMENT RECORDING AND TRANSFER CHARGES**		
1201. Recording fees: Deed $; Mortgage $; Releases $		
1202. City/county tax/stamps: Deed $; Mortgage $		
1203. State tax/stamps: Deed $; Mortgage $		
1204.		
1205.		
1300. **ADDITIONAL SETTLEMENT CHARGES**		
1301. Survey to		
1302. Pest inspection to		
1303.		
1304.		
1305.		
1400. **TOTAL SETTLEMENT CHARGES** (*enter on lines 103, Section J and 502, Section K*)		

- Page 1 is a summary that shows where the money for closing came from and how it was spent.

- Page 2 contains the details of the charges to the buyer and seller.

- Page 3 is a statement signed by the buyer and seller concerning the accuracy of the information.

The HUD-1 form is available for the buyer and seller to review at least 24 hours prior to the closing. This "estimated" HUD-1 should be given to you in advance so you can ensure that sufficient cash is available to close.

It is at the closing that questions may arise from your borrower regarding any disparities between the good faith estimate the borrower has already received and the settlement statement you are now providing. This is another reason why we recommend that prior to the closing you always obtain the estimated settlement statement from escrow in order to ensure accuracy.

From the Loan Application to the Closing Quiz

1. On a refinance, why is it important to know how long the borrower has owned his property?
   A. To know how much you can charge on the loan.
   B. To know when to order a pest control report.
   C. To determine what loan program to choose.

2. When is a survey report required?
   A. In a purchase of a single-family residence
   B. In a refinance of a single-family residence
   C. In a purchase of a condo

3. There are certain disclosures that must be provided to your borrower either at application or no later than three days after the application date. Which disclosure below is *not* one of the required disclosures?
   A. Flood insurance disclosure
   B. Truth in lending disclosure
   C. Certificate and authorization form

4. Which federal law requires the good faith estimate to be provided to the borrower no later than three days after the application date?
   A. Real Estate Settlement Procedures Act
   B. Equal Credit Opportunity Act
   C. Truth in Lending Act

5. Which federal law does not require any disclosures?
   A. Real Estate Settlement Procedures Act
   B. Home Mortgage Disclosure Act
   C. Equal Credit Opportunity Act

6. When more that one person takes title to a property and the parties have unequal ownership interests, how should they take title?
   A. Joint tenancy
   B. Community property
   C. Tenancy in common

7. A married couple want to take title, and they want to have the right of survivorship and the ability to shield the surviving owner from claims of individual creditors. How should they take title?
   A. Joint tenancy
   B. Tenancy by entirety
   C. Tenants in common

8. It is important that your borrower provide you with proper documentation. This will enable the loan officer to find the proper loan program. That being said, which item listed below would *not* be a requested piece of documentation necessary for a purchase money loan?
   A. Purchase contract
   B. Last two years' W-2s
   C. Copy of the declaration page from the current homeowner's insurance policy

9. Specific documentation will be required if your borrower is purchasing a condo. What item is required?
   A. Copy of the mortgage statement
   B. HOA certification form completed by management
   C. Copy of the lease agreement

10. If a borrower has a tax lien or mechanics lien, where will you find that information?
    A. The 1003
    B. The title commitment
    C. The settlement statement

11. Why is it important for the loan officer to review the estimated HUD prior to the loan signing?
    A. To make sure the loan will close as scheduled
    B. To make sure the loan program is correct
    C. To make sure the fees match the good faith estimate

12. What is the most important thing a loan officer will do after taking the loan application?
    A. Lock the rate
    B. Submit the loan to the lender for preapproval
    C. Set up the loan in a proper stacking order

13. A borrower had her home up for sale the prior month, decided against selling, and is now seeking a refinance. Because she had her home listed for sale, the lender will not approve her for a refinance at this time.
    A. True
    B. False

14. What does the Truth in Lending Act allow the consumer?
    A. The right to receive the good faith estimate in order to review all the fees involved with the mortgage transaction
    B. The right to receive a settlement statement
    C. The right to cancel a transaction that results in a lien on a primary residence

15. Any fee that would not be necessary if a borrower paid cash for a home is included in the APR calculation. Therefore, the appraisal fee is not included in the APR.
    A. True
    B. False

Answers to the quiz can be found at the end of Part One.

CHAPTER 9

LAWS AND ETHICS

*Our goals can only be reached through a vehicle of a plan,
in which we must fervently believe, and upon which we
must vigorously act. There is no other route to success.*
                                        —Stephen A. Brennen

ETHICS AND LAWS IN THE
MORTGAGE INDUSTRY

Ethics in the Mortgage Industry

The real estate and mortgage profession is a highly competitive
industry. A successful loan originator is a professional and
abides by all the laws and guidelines that the federal, local, and
state governments have put into place. As a real estate agent or
mortgage originator, you have a fiduciary responsibility to your
applicants. You are expected to provide *trust*, the confidence
which is placed upon you to prove your ability; *honesty*, fair
and genuine character; and *integrity*, the adherence to ethical
behavior.

The two biggest complaints I hear from mortgage applicants
are that (1) their loan originator failed to follow up and (2) the

applicants had been given false promises. There are certain loan originators who promise they can get a loan funded in a shorter period of time than possible, quote a lower rate than achievable, or promise an approval, just to get the loan. All this does is result in a very unhappy customer, one who is unlikely to return or refer any business. Repeat business and referrals should be one of your main objectives. What else *should you not* do?

- Do not state that an applicant is going to occupy a property when you are aware that the applicant will be using it as a rental. Some people will give a false statement about occupancy in order to get a lower interest rate and a smaller down payment, but the practice is dishonest.

- Do not lock the rates with more than one lender when interest rates go down to get a better rate. This is the same as delaying the closing to make a profit.

- Do not publish or use rate sheets with false information, such as rates that do not exist or that only a small portion of applicants could qualify for, just to lure applicants in. This kind of false advertising practice, known as "bait and switch," is not only unethical; it is also a violation of the truth in lending regulations.

- Do not pay a referral fee to a real estate agent. It is against the law.

- From time to time the lender will request an explanation letter for employment gaps or late payments that may show up on an applicant's credit report. Do not write this letter for the applicant or instruct the applicant on what to write. However, you can explain how the underwriter will use the information that is given.

- "Gift" monies used for a down payment are to be tracked and are not to be repaid. Do not assist in the falsifying of this information.

- Never falsify leases on the applicant's rental properties to show a steady income.

- Do not allow the use of fraudulent tax returns, and do not falsify any information on the application (1003). Doing either of these is illegal.

- Even if the rates go down, don't solicit borrowers for whom you originated a loan just a few months before—a process known as "churning." Lenders tend to suspend broker relationships if they see that the loan officer or broker is engaged in churning.

What else *should you do?*

- Give a lock-in agreement to the applicant even if the loan is not locked. This is to protect you in the event that rates go up and the applicant claims that you promised a lower rate or the applicant believes the rate was previously locked.

- Always make sure that all of your predisclosures are sent to the borrower within three days of application.

Lending Laws

Fair Credit Reporting Act

The purpose of the Fair Credit Reporting Act is to ensure that the reporting agencies are reporting accurate information and that no one can view a person's credit report without authorization. The loan originator will have the applicant sign an authorization form at the time of loan application. This authorization form gives the loan originator permission to run a credit report for the purpose of obtaining the loan approval. The lender cannot share this information with other agencies or use it for marketing purposes. If the lender does share the information on the credit report with affiliates, the consumer must be given the opportunity to "opt out." It is permissible to share this information with agencies or investors that are part of the lending approval process.

Fair Housing Act

The Fair Housing Act is a part of the Civil Rights Act that was enacted in 1968. The purpose of this act was to forbid any kind of discrimination in any form of residential real estate transaction, with regard to race, color, religion, national origin, sex, handicap, or familial status. The Department of Housing and Urban Development (HUD) enforces this act. If an applicant wants to file a complaint for a violation, he or she has up to one year to contact HUD.

In regard to *penalties* for violating this act,

- Civil penalties of $10,000 to $50,000 can be imposed.

- Criminal penalties can be added for those who do not adhere to the action recommended by HUD or who hinder an investigation.

Flood Disaster Protection Act

Lenders are required to have the applicant purchase flood insurance if the subject property lies in an area deemed by the National Flood Insurance Program to be in a flood zone. Typically lenders will contract with a flood certification service that has maps published by the government. Lenders cannot lend on any property that is in a flood zone without flood insurance in place upon funding the loan.

Right to Financial Privacy Act

The Right to Financial Privacy Act was Congress's response to a U.S. Supreme Court decision finding that bank customers had no legal right to privacy in financial information of theirs held by financial institutions.

The law specifies when, and under what conditions, a financial institution may release customer financial records to a federal government authority: pursuant to customer authorization; in response to a search warrant, judicial subpoena, or administrative subpoena or summons.

Real Estate Settlement Procedures Act

The Real Estate Settlement Procedures Act (RESPA) was passed in 1974 to regulate residential real estate transactions by protecting consumers in various ways. RESPA guidelines include:

- Both final and predisclosures must be provided to applicants to ensure that they have an estimate and true account of any and all settlement (closing) costs for their loan.

- Certain disclosures must be sent to applicants within three days of application for credit approval. The disclosures are the good faith estimate, TILA, *Settlement Cost Booklet* (lender), notice of possible transfer of servicing, itemization of costs, and affiliated business arrangement disclosure (if applicable).

- The handling and disclosure of escrow accounts must be regulated to ensure that any settlement service provider is not conducting business illegally. In the event a provider either received or paid any kickbacks, referral fees, or gifts (i.e., anything of value) in connection with the transaction, the provider can be fined up to $10,000 or three times the amount of the amount charged for the service (Section 8 of the act).

- Real estate records must be regulated with regard to the recording and safekeeping of land title records by public officials.

- Sellers cannot force a buyer to use a certain title company as a condition of sale of the property. If made to use a certain title company, the buyer can sue the seller for three times the amount charged for the title work (Section 9).

- Taxing authorities, lenders, and insurance companies must be regulated to ensure they do not require the applicant to deposit more funds than needed to set up impound accounts for taxes, insurance, and other lender-required accounts. Once servicing starts for the mortgage loan, the lender cannot require a borrower to pay more than one-twelfth of the premium into the impound account per month. The only time the servicer is allowed to charge over the one-twelfth premium is when there is a shortage in the impound account and there are insufficient monies to pay the yearly premium once it becomes due.

- The lender may require a cushion in the event that the taxes, insurance, etc., are not an accurate amount, but the cushion is not to exceed one-sixth of the total disbursements for the year. Lenders are also required to perform an audit on all impound accounts each year. If there is an excess of $50 or more, a refund is due to the borrower (Section 10).

Mortgage loans are exempt from RESPA rules under certain conditions:

- 25 acres or more—regardless of the purpose of the loan or whether or not there is a structure on the property

- Agricultural, business, or commercial use

- Temporary financing—construction loans with a term of two years or less

- Loan transfers in the secondary market (excluding table funding)

- Nonlender-approved assumptions

- ARM conversion to a fixed-rate loan (e.g., 5/28)

- Vacant land with the stipulation that no mobile home or structure will be built within the first two years

RESPA Enforcement

If a borrower believes that his or her rights have been violated, the borrower has up to one year to start a private civil lawsuit for violations covered by Section 8 or 9. The lawsuit would be entered into a federal district court in the district of the subject property. Section 6 allows the borrower to submit a complaint on loan servicing to the lender's servicing department, which in turn has 20 days to acknowledge the complaint in writing to the borrower. The servicing department then has 60 days in which to satisfy the complaint, or the borrower may bring a private civil lawsuit against the servicer for failure to comply.

Truth in Lending Act

In order to allow consumers the ability to comparison-shop with various lenders for the best loan offer, the Truth in Lending Act (Regulation Z, or Reg Z) was enacted. Transactions that fall under the coverage of Reg Z are defined as any transaction (1) where credit is either offered or extended to a consumer, (2) when credit is subject to a finance charge, (3) when there is a written agreement with a term of five or more installments, and (4) when the loan is used first and foremost for household, personal, or family purposes.

A truth in lending disclosure, or TIL, must be sent within three days of the application and again at closing if a credit approval (mortgage) is given to the applicant of a closed-end transaction. In the case of an open-end transaction (credit cards), a disclosure must be provided to the consumer before the transaction and along with the periodic billing statement.

Any lender that does not adhere to the disclosure requirements is subject to penalties that can include all costs, attorney fees, and twice the amount of the finance charge.

Financial Institutions Reform, Recovery, and Enforcement Act

FIRREA was enacted to protect federally related real estate transactions by requiring real estate appraisers to be properly licensed or certified. An appointed subcommittee conducts the monitoring or regulation of appraisers.

Alternative Mortgage Transaction Parity Act

Also known as the Parity Act, this law was put into action to enable non-federally chartered housing creditors (lenders) to bypass state laws (on any alternative mortgage) as long as the transactions conform to certain federal lending regulations. The Office of Thrift Supervision regulates this act.

Alternative mortgage transactions are:

- Adjustable-rate mortgages—the rate and finance charge may be changed or renegotiated.

- Fixed-rate mortgages—allowable rate adjustments having the debt mature before the term of amortization, also known as a *growing equity mortgage.*

- Other programs not like the normal fixed-rate or term loans.

The Office of Thrift Supervision regulates:

- Late charges

- Adjustments

- Prepayments

A rule enacted July 2003 removes the prepayment and late fee rules from the list of OTS regulations as applicable to state housing creditors. What this means is that state housing creditors, such as mortgage bankers, will once again be subject to state law and regulations concerning prepayment penalties and late fees, rather than OTS rules. Federally chartered thrifts supervised by OTS will continue to follow OTS rules.

Home Mortgage Disclosure Act

The Home Mortgage Disclosure Act (HMDA) was enacted by Congress in 1975 and is implemented by the Federal Reserve Board's Regulation C. HMDA is designed to prevent any and all discrimination by the lender and to determine whether financial institutions are serving the housing needs of their communities.

HMDA requires lenders to gather certain information from the loan application. The loan data is submitted to the Federal Financial Institutions Examination Council (FFIEC), which in turn provides a disclosure statement. The disclosure statement is available to the public by both the lender and the FFIEC.

The information the lender is required to gather from a loan application is:

- Loan type

- Property type

- Purpose of the loan or application

- Owner-occupancy

- Loan amount

- Indication of whether the application is a request for preapproval

- Type of action taken

- Date of action

- Property location

The information the lender is required to gather from the applicant is:

- How did the applicant apply (mail, Internet, telephone, or in person)?

- Ethnicity of the borrower or applicant

- Race of the borrower or applicant

- Sex of the borrower or applicant

- Income (from the application)

- Type of loan purchaser (FNMA, FHLMC, GNMA, etc.)

- If denied, reason for denial

The government-monitoring information, found toward the bottom of page 3 of the application (1003), is voluntary and does not have to be provided by the applicant. However, the lender is required to fill in the information based on visual observation.

In addition the lender must report:

- If the loan is subject to Regulation Z, the spread between the APR and the applicable Treasury yield

- Home Ownership and Equity Protection Act (HOEPA) status

- Lien status (first or second)

Home Ownership and Equity Protection Act

HOEPA was enacted in 1994 due to ever-increasing evidence about abusive practices involving high-cost loans, also known as

Section 32 loans. These loans can be tracked through rates and fees charged to the borrower that are above a specified percentage or amount.

HOEPA requirements for lenders include:

- Disclosure statement provided at least three business days before the loan is closed

- Truth in lending disclosure

- A *six*-day right of rescission

The purpose of the disclosure statement is to inform the applicants that they are not under any obligation to complete the transaction and to also let them know that they could potentially lose their home if they fail to make their mortgage payments. The disclosure also states that a lender cannot refinance a high-cost loan into another high-cost loan within the first 12 months of the existing loan.

HOEPA does *not* allow:

- Short-term balloon notes

- Prepayment penalties

- Nonamortizing payment schedules

- Higher interest rates upon default of loan payments

Here are some calculation changes for Section 32 loans:

- The first mortgage cannot exceed 8% of the Treasury securities, or else it is considered a high-cost loan.

- The second mortgage cannot exceed 10% of the Treasury securities, or else it is considered a high-cost loan.

- Optional credit insurance is also now calculated in the APR to determine if the loan is a high-cost loan.

Equal Credit Opportunity Act

The Equal Credit Opportunity Act became law in 1974. ECOA prohibits discrimination on the basis of certain factors in any aspect of a credit transaction. ECOA and Regulation B prohibit discrimination against a credit applicant or coapplicant on the basis of race, color, religion, national origin, sex, marital status, age, or receipt of income from a public assistance program. Regulation B also imposes certain affirmative obligations designed to assist in the efforts to monitor compliance with ECOA and Regulation B. ECOA and Regulation B, which also apply to commercial loans and consumer credit, prohibit discrimination in loan servicing and collection activities as well as in the application and credit granting process.

ECOA and Regulation B define an adverse action as a refusal to grant credit in the terms or amount requested in an application. An adverse action must be sent out within 30 days of taking such action. This notification must include a statement of the action taken, the lender's name and address, the name and address of the federal agency that administers compliance concerning notification, and a statement of the specific reasons for the action taken. The notification must include a contact person's name, address, and telephone number.

The Federal Deposit Insurance Corporation (FDIC) Improvement Act added a provision to ECOA that requires a lender to provide promptly a mortgage loan applicant with a copy of the appraisal if the applicant requests the appraisal in writing within a reasonable period of time of the application. If the applicant has not paid for the appraisal, the lender can request payment as a condition for providing a copy of the appraisal. In 1992, lenders were required to inform applicants, by way of a form, of their right to receive a copy of the appraisal. The applicant must request this within 90 days after notice of a credit approval or denial or withdrawal of the loan request.

Permissible under the Act

Lenders are permitted to make inquiries about marital status and age if the information is necessary to determine the amount and probability of income, credit history, or other pertinent element of creditworthiness. It is also not a violation to refuse to extend credit pursuant to programs authorized by law for economically disadvantaged classes of people or for programs administered by nonprofit organizations for their members.

Penalties

Creditors can be liable for actual damages, punitive damages to $10,000 (for individual actions, and the lesser of $500,000 or 1% of the creditor's net worth for class actions), and the recovery of costs and legal fees.

Community Reinvestment Act

The Community Reinvestment Act was created to encourage FDIC banks and thrifts to meet the credit needs of their communities. This act requires financial institutions to give back to their communities by providing programs specifically targeting low- to moderate-income neighborhoods and to abide by the Fair Housing Act.

Telemarketing and Consumer Fraud and Abuse Prevention Act

The Federal Trade Commission (FTC) has put the Telemarketing Act in place to prevent deceptive and abusive telemarketing practices and acts relating to the consumer. The Telemarketing Act authorizes state attorneys general, other appropriate state officials, and private persons to bring civil actions in federal district court to enforce compliance with the FTC's rule.

The Telemarketing Sales Rule requires telemarketers to disclose specific information to consumers, prohibits misrepresentation of the cost of services, and places time limitations on telemarketing calls to consumers.

In 2003, the FTC announced the creation of a "do not call" registry in which consumers have access to a toll-free number to remove their names from telemarketing lists.

Financial Services Modernization Act of 1999

This act (also known as the Gramm-Leach Bliley Act) places certain restrictions on banks affiliating with insurance companies and securities firms. The act includes provisions to protect the applicant's personal financial information. Any financial institution that offers financial products is required to provide to the applicant a privacy disclosure that describes the sharing of nonpublic personal information to third parties and any affiliates and explains how the information will be used (e.g., marketing). The applicant will have the opportunity to opt out if he or she does not want this information shared. Since lenders and mortgage companies do not use this information for marketing, they are allowed to use a simplified private policy notice in order to satisfy this requirement.

Homeowners Protection Act

The Homeowners Protection Act was enacted in 1998 for the purpose of defining the guidelines for the mandatory cancellation of mortgage insurance on home loans. There are certain criteria that a borrower must meet before the cancellation of this insurance can be completed through the lender.

Laws and Ethics Quiz

1. It is permissible for your best friend, a real estate agent, to send you all her business for a small referral fee.
   A. True
   B. False

2. Your borrower has several late payments on his credit that require a letter of explanation. Your borrower says he is not good at writing letters and asks you to write it for him. Is this allowed?
   A. Yes
   B. No

3. Is a borrower required to have flood insurance?
   A. Yes in all cases
   B. Only if the property is in a flood zone
   C. Depends on the loan program

4. Your borrower is purchasing a home. His Realtor has told him that the seller wants his choice of title company and he

will not sell if his choice of title company is not used. The Realtor tells your borrower that this is permissible.

A. True—this is allowed.

B. False—it is not allowed.

5. A lender is not required to abide by RESPA rules when a mortgage transaction is on a home with 30 acres.

A. True

B. False

6. The Truth in Lending Act was basically enacted to allow the consumer to shop around for the best offer with the use of the APR.

A. True

B. False

7. A borrower is working with a lender on a refinance. An appraisal has been done, and the lender, who ordered it, has the responsibility to pay for it. The borrower has decided to use another lender for her refinance and has, in writing, requested a copy of her appraisal from the lender. Can she receive a copy?

A. Yes, if she requested the appraisal within 90 days of the application date.

B. Yes, if she agrees to pay for the appraisal.

C. No, she is not allowed to receive a copy of the appraisal.

8. A female borrower is applying for a mortgage loan on her own. A lender is allowed to ask about her marital status and age in order to extend her credit.

A. True

B. False

9. Under the Homeownership Protection Act, applicant's are allowed to cancel their mortgage insurance when certain conditions are met.

A. True

B. False

10. You are a loan originator, and you are going to place an ad in your neighborhood paper. You want to attract as many people as possible, and so you are going advertise the lowest rate available, even though you know that only a few people will qualify. Is this permissible?
    A. Yes, as long as you include the APR.
    B. Yes, as long as you include all necessary regulations as described by law.
    C. No, it is not allowed. This is considered bait and switch.

Answers to the quiz can be found at the end of Part One.

CHAPTER 10

CUSTOMER SERVICE

The one thing that contributes to anyone's reaching the goal he wants is simply wanting that goal badly enough.
>   —Charles E. Wilson

CUSTOMER SERVICE

There are a number of characteristics that are necessary to be successful as a loan officer. Here are a few:

- Professionalism

- Hard work and determination

- Goal-oriented

- A positive attitude

- Excellent communication skills

- Knowledgeable

- Honesty and integrity

- Flexibility

- A good listener

- Providing the best customer service!

At one time or another, we all have been on the receiving end of lousy customer service. You walk into a store to find the clerk at the register on his cell phone, with no concern for his customers. Or you are on hold with a company only to finally be answered by a bored customer service representative who is not very helpful. Now you are that clerk or representative. You want your customers to be happy, to come back again, and to refer you some customers. What do you do? Simple. Treat your customers the same way you expect to be treated.

In this chapter you will learn some of the steps to take to provide responsive, caring service. As you read about how customer service works, you'll transform what you learn into your own special style.

The foundation you need is one of courtesy, caring, a willingness to serve, and an attitude that lets your customers know that they matter—and that you care. These are characteristics that can help you put it all into practice. Don't be swayed with all the sales hype and other tools that are out there. Great customer service has its basis in good manners. To retain your customers it's simple; just serve them—and do it well.

Customer service involves living up to your word, and this means *following up*. In fact, the most important thing you can do for your borrower is to follow up. Follow-up is a basic business principle. Keep in mind that your borrowers have chosen you to handle one of the most important matters in their lives and that purchasing or refinancing a home is a very delicate and stressful issue. There are several things that can go wrong and do go wrong. Sometimes preventing dissatisfaction can be as simple as returning your borrower's call. Make sure you keep your borrowers abreast of all your actions, and make sure you get their permission before taking any action.

You may be surprised to learn that your customer service skills will really shine when something goes *wrong*. Here is why mistakes are opportunities. Studies show that satisfied customers will tell two to three people about their experience with you.

Dissatisfied consumers will share their grief with eight to ten people. If you fix the problem or complaint and do it quickly, you have turned a potentially dissatisfied customer into a loyal client who is more likely to tell other people good things about you.

When you first land a new client, make sure you let that client know from the beginning what he or she can expect with the loan process. Give the client an estimated and *realistic* timeline. Don't make the mistake of overpromising, as it will surely be a problem if you are not able to deliver what you promise. Make sure that when you call your borrower, you are familiar with the loan, that you have checked with your processor and you know what stage the loan process is in and what—if anything—is needed.

Admitting any mistakes is not only honest, but admirable. Your borrower will be much less irritated and upset if you simply acknowledge the error. Let your borrower know if you are able to correct the problem and how quickly and promptly you can do so.

Be a good listener. Listening to your borrower's needs not only will help develop a good relationship, but will help you discover what your borrower's true needs really are. Make sure you know all the right questions to ask *before* you meet or call your customer. The best salesperson will tell you that the key to a good sale is to listen to your customer and be prepared! Here are a few suggestions:

1. If you are meeting with a borrower, start by creating a relaxed and friendly atmosphere so your borrower will be comfortable.

2. Have a list of questions ready to make the application process easy.

3. Allow plenty of time for the applicant to fully answer the questions.

4. Begin your interview with open questions that will encourage your applicant to talk (these questions will begin with *who, what, when, where, why, how*).

5. If you need more detailed information, make sure you ask. If the borrower is going to refinance and wants cash out, make sure you ask what the funds are going to be used for.

The more detailed and prepared you are to present this loan package, the better. It is also better to get all the information you need up front.

6. Don't monopolize the conversation.

7. Don't paint an unrealistic picture of the loan process.

8. Don't allow any interruptions—put phones on hold, close your door, etc.

9. Make sure that you have allowed yourself enough time to take a proper application and that you are not rushed for your next client.

SALES TECHNIQUES

As a loan originator, your major skill will involve selling. You will be selling your loan product to your borrower, and you must be capable of selling yourself to Realtors, builders, tax consultants—anyone and everyone who can refer you new business.

A good salesperson in a conversation understands how important it is to put the client at ease while developing a relationship. Making your client comfortable will enable you to determine what your client's wants and needs are. To do so you must *listen* very carefully to what your client says. Do not monopolize the conversation. Now that you know what your borrower truly wants, you can properly present your outcome correlating your client's needs. Your borrower will feel like you have truly met his or her needs, allowing you to win your borrower's commitment.

As simple as this sounds, you would be surprised to hear that most loan originators do not practice these techniques. They tend to talk about themselves—how great they are, how great their products are—talk, talk, talk. They end up talking themselves right out of a loan or a referral. The best salesperson will tell you that the key to a good sale is to listen to your customer and be prepared.

Here are a few tips and suggestions on how to be a better salesperson:

- *Be adaptable.* You should be able to deal with any type of personality, from the stern to the jovial. You should be able to adjust to the mood and tone of the person to whom you are speaking.

- *Be articulate.* A well-spoken salesperson can sometimes make or break a deal. Proper grammar, vocabulary, and usage are important for anyone who acts as a representative of a company.

- *Be energetic.* The energy level and the alertness you present are directly related to your success. You must possess both an energy level that will keep you on the trail of leads and a level of keen alertness that will enable you to notice details that may lead to future business.

- *Be confident.* Giving the impression of knowing what you're talking about can go a long way. You should possess this quality if nothing else! Confidence when selling your product or service can be built through training and practice.

- *Be enthusiastic.* Enthusiasm is contagious. It is also a very necessary attribute for a successful salesperson. Being enthusiastic rubs off—it helps your borrowers be enthusiastic about their decision to purchase or refinance their home.

- *Be self-reliant.* One of the more independent positions within any company is that of the salesperson. Many loan officers will work alone (out in the field) or work out of a home office. For this reason, you will need to be self-motivated and self-reliant.

- *Show integrity.* Make sure you present yourself as a loyal, trustworthy, and ethical person.

- *Show patience and perseverance.* These are two very important traits for a salesperson. Some potential home buyers may not actually buy their home for months; you have to have patience and drive to keep on working the deal. These qualities also come into play when dealing with various customer personality types. Listen patiently as clients talk.

- *Be sincere.* Without the sincerity and desire to help customers, many loan officers will fail. It is all too often very obvious that a loan officer simply wants to make the commission and does not care about the borrower's needs. Your borrowers will know if you are looking out after their interests or yours.

- *Be pleasant.* A warm smile and a handshake can go a long way. The initial impression you make is as important as you've always been told it is. Simply smiling and having a cheerful demeanor can help you reach and retain clients.

- *Be goal-oriented.* Every successful loan officer must be goal-oriented, and the entire mortgage industry revolves around monthly quotas. Almost everyone in the industry is paid with production incentives. Set a goal that is challenging but not impossible to reach.

TELEPHONE SKILLS

Developing your telephone skills is an important aspect of becoming a good loan originator. I developed my best telephone sales skills as an outbound salesperson. The biggest obstacle to overcome is the fear of rejection. But as Wayne Gretzky said, "You miss 100% of the shots you never take." In other words, not every customer you call will say yes and accept your loan proposal, but you are guaranteed a no if you don't call at all.

Nobody likes rejection, and you experience a lot of it in this business. I can tell you from experience, though, that the more consumers you call, the less fear you will have. So take a shot and pick up the phone.

Here is a list of tips for your outbound telemarketing:

- You have just a few seconds to make a good initial impression on the phone. Your careful preparation for the call can increase your chances of having a conversation with a prospect rather than hearing that familiar dial tone.

- Always be courteous and professional. Remember, you are a sales professional who just happens to use the phone to sell.

- Be sincere at all times. People will sense insincerity on the phone even though they can't see your facial expressions or other nonverbal communication clues such as hand gestures, head nods, and body posture.

- Keep your work area neat—it will keep you focused and organized.

- Dress like a sales professional even if your prospects will never see you.

- Keep a mirror handy so you can check to see if you're smiling during calls.

- Don't practice on *prospects* with a few warm-up calls at the beginning of the day or week. Role-play with a friend, colleague, or family member if you need to, or just talk out loud in an imaginary conversation to warm up.

- Meeting annual goals requires setting and meeting daily goals. Record your progress on a daily basis.

- Keep records of the contacts you make for future reference. Note dates for follow-up.

- Use your prime selling time—the hours your prospects are most easily reached by phone and are the most receptive—for selling activities only. (Experience will quickly let you know when your prospects are most receptive!)

- Develop a script for the call to keep you on track, but *never* read directly from it. Write the script as *you* talk. That way, when you vary from the script, your words and phrases will be consistent.

- Consider using introductory or follow-up letters, product fliers, or other marketing materials.

- Use other communication tools as necessary to support your telephone sales, including fax and e-mail. For example, part of your selling process may be to offer a new homeowner prospect a rental equivalency flier by fax or e-mail.

- End calls quickly, but politely, when it becomes evident that a prospect is either not qualified for your product or simply not interested. Your time on the phone is precious. Always end the conversation with a thank you.

A telephone sales presentation moves through stages, just like an in-person sale does.

- At the beginning of a call, you should *qualify* prospects to determine if they are interested in talking and are, indeed, viable prospects.

- Next, you should *gather information* from prospects to uncover problems or unmet needs and determine how a loan will benefit the prospect (is the person a new home buyer or an existing homeowner who may be interested in refinancing?).

- After gathering information, you will be able to introduce prospects to the *benefits, features, and proof* of a mortgage loan, specifying how the loan will benefit them.

- Finally, when you feel your prospect's questions and concerns about a mortgage loan have been addressed, then you *close the sale*.

There is no quiz at the end of this chapter. Instead here is suggested reading material: *Overcoming the Fear of Cold Calling*, a book written by Jeffrey Mayer.

CHAPTER 11

LEGAL DOCUMENTS AND FORMS

Luck often means simply taking advantage of a situation at the right moment. It is possible to make your "luck" by always being prepared.

—Michael Korda

LEGAL LOAN DOCUMENTS

Many forms are included in a set of loan documents—too many to include here. Instead, we present the most important legal loan documents with a brief description of their purpose.

Deed of Trust

A deed of trust (see Figure 11-1) involves a third party, called a *trustee*, usually a title insurance company, which acts on behalf of the lender. When a borrower signs a deed of trust, the borrower is in effect giving a trustee the title (ownership) of the property, but holding the rights and privileges to the property. The trustee holds the original deed for the property until the loan is repaid, and the trustee has the right to foreclose if payments are not made. The deed of trust must be notarized.

FIGURE 11-1
Sample Deed of Trust

[Space Above This Line For Recording Data]

DEED OF TRUST

THIS DEED OF TRUST ("Security Instrument') is made on. The trustor is

('Borrower'). The trustee is

("Trustee").

The beneficiary is
which is organized and existing under the laws of
, and whose

address is

(Lender). Borrower owes Lender the principal sum of
Dollars (U.S. $).
This debt is evidenced by Borrower's note dated the same date as this Security Instrument (Note), which provides
for monthly payments, with the full debt, if not paid earlier, due and payable on This Security Instrument secures to
Lender: (a) the repayment of the debt evidenced by the Note, with interest, and all renewals, extensions and
modifications of the Note; (b) the payment of all other sums, with interest, advanced under paragraph 7 to protect
the security of this Security Instrument; and (c) the performance of Borrower's covenants and agreements under
this Security Instrument and the Note. For this purpose, Borrower irrevocably grants and conveys to Trustee, in
trust, with power of sale, the following described property located in

County, California:

Which has the address of
(Street, City), California   (Zip Code)

FIGURE 11-1 (*Continued*)

TOGETHER WITH all the improvements now or hereafter erected on the property, and all easements, appurtenances and fixtures now or hereafter a part of the property. All replacements and additions shall also be covered by this Security Instrument. All of the foregoing is referred to in this Security Instrument as the "Property."

BORROWER COVENANTS that Borrower is lawfully seized of the estate hereby conveyed and has the right to grant and convey the Property and that the Property is unencumbered, except for encumbrances of record. Borrower warrants and will defend generally the title to the Property against all claims and demands, subject to any encumbrances of record.

THIS SECURITY INSTRUMENT combines uniform covenants for national use and non-uniform covenants with limited variations by jurisdiction to constitute a uniform security instrument covering real property.

UNIFORM COVENANTS. Borrower and Lender covenant and agree as follows:

1. Payment of Principal and Interest; Prepayment and Late charges. Borrower shall promptly pay when due the principal of and interest on the debt evidenced by the Note and any prepayment and late charges due under the Note.

2. Funds for Taxes and Insurance. Subject to applicable law or to a written waiver by Lender, Borrower shall pay to Lender on the day monthly payments are due under the Note, until the Note is paid in full, a sum ('Funds') for: (a) yearly taxes and assessments which may attain priority over this Security Instrument as a lien on the Property; (b) yearly leasehold payments or ground rents on the Property, if any; (c) yearly hazard or property insurance premiums; (d) yearly flood Insurance premiums, if any; (e) yearly mortgage Insurance premiums, it any; and (f) any sums payable by Borrower to Lender, in accordance with the provisions of paragraph 8, in lieu of the payment of mortgage insurance premiums. These items are called 'Escrow Items.' Lender may, at anytime, collect and hold Funds in an amount not to exceed the maximum amount a lender for a federally related mortgage loan may require for Borrower's escrow account under the federal Real Estate Settlement Procedures Act of 1974 as amended from time to time, 12 U.S.C. Section 2601 et seq. ('RESPA'), unless another law that applies to the Funds sets a lesser amount. If so, Lender may, at any time, collect and hold Funds in an amount not to exceed the lesser amount. Lender may estimate the amount of Funds due on the basis of current data and reasonable estimates of expenditures of future Escrow Items or otherwise in accordance with applicable law.

The Funds shall be held in an institution whose deposits are insured by a federal agency, instrumentality, or entity (including Lender, if Lender is such an institution) or in any Federal Home Loan Bank. Lender shall apply the Funds to pay the Escrow Items. Lender may not charge Borrower for holding and applying the Funds, annually analyzing the escrow account, or verifying the Escrow Items, unless Lender pays Borrower interest on the Funds and applicable law permits Lender to make such a charge. However, Lender may require Borrower to pay a one-time charge for an independent real estate tax reporting service used by Lender in connection with this loan, unless applicable law provides otherwise. Unless an agreement is made or applicable law requires Interest to be paid, Lender shall not be required to pay Borrower any interest or earnings on the Funds. Borrower and Lender may agree in writing, however, that interest shall be paid on the Funds. Lender shall give to Borrower, without charge, an annual accounting of the Funds, showing credits and debits to the Funds and the purpose for which each debit to the Funds was made. The Funds are pledged as additional security for all sums secured by this Security Instrument.

If the Funds held by Lender exceed the amounts permitted to be held by applicable law, Lender shall account to Borrower for the excess Funds in accordance with the requirements of applicable law. If the amount of the Funds held by Lender at any time is not sufficient to pay the Escrow Items when due, Lender may so notify Borrower in writing, and, in such case Borrower shall pay to Lender the amount necessary to make up the deficiency. Borrower shall make up the deficiency in no more than twelve monthly payments, at Lenders sole discretion.

Upon payment in full of all sums secured by this Security Instrument, Lender shall promptly refund to Borrower any Funds held by Lender. If, under paragraph 21, Lender shall acquire or sell the Property, Lender, prior to the acquisition or sale of the Property, shall apply any Funds held by Lender at the time of acquisition or sale as a credit against the sums secured by this Security Instrument.

3. Application of Payments. Unless applicable law provides otherwise, all payments received by Lender under paragraphs 1 and 2 shall be applied: first, to any prepayment charges due under the Note; second, to amounts payable under paragraph 2; third, to Interest due; fourth, to principal due; and last, to any late charges due under the Note.

4. Charges; Liens. Borrower shall pay all taxes, assessments, charges, fines and Impositions attributable to the property which maintain priority over this Security Instrument, and leasehold payments or ground rents, if any. Borrower shall pay these obligations in the manner provided in paragraph 2, or if not paid in that manner.

Borrower shall pay them on time directly to the person owed payment. Borrower shall promptly furnish to Lender all notices of amounts to be paid under this paragraph. If Borrower makes these payments directly, Borrower shall promptly furnish to Lender receipts evidencing the payments.

Borrower shall promptly discharge any lien which has priority over this Security Instrument unless Borrower: (a) agrees in writing to the payment of the obligation secured by the lien in a manner acceptable to Lender; (b) contests in poor faith the lien by, or defends against enforcement of the lien in, legal proceedings which in the Lender's opinion operate to prevent the enforcement of the lien; or (c) secures from the holder of the lien an agreement satisfactory to Lender subordinating the lien to this Security Instrument. If Lender determines that any part of the Property is subject to a lien, which may attain priority over this Security Instrument, Lender may give borrower a notice identifying the lien. Borrower shall satisfy the lien or take one or more of the actions set forth above within 10 days of the giving of notice.

CALIFORNIA-Single Family-Fannie Mae/Freddie Mac UNIFORM INSTRUMENT   **Page 2 of 6**
Form 3005 9/90 GENESIS 2000,INC. *V9.3/WI1.0*(818) 223-3260 Amended 5/91
                    Initials:_____ _____ _____ _____

FIGURE 11-1 (*Continued*)

5. Hazard or Property Insurance. Borrower shall keep the improvements now existing or hereafter erected on the Property insured against loss by fire, hazards included within the term 'extended coverage' and any other hazards, including floods or flooding, for which Lender requires insurance, This insurance shall be maintained in the amounts and for the periods that Lender requires. The insurance carrier providing the insurance shall be chosen by Borrower subject to Lender's approval, which shall not be unreasonably withheld. If Borrower fails to maintain coverage described above, Lender may, at Lender's option, obtain coverage to protect Lenders rights in the Property in accordance with paragraph 7.

All insurance policies and renewals shall be acceptable to Lender and shall include a standard mortgage clause. Lender shall have the right to hold the policies and renewals, If Lender requires, Borrower shall promptly give to Lender all receipts of paid premiums and renewal notices. In the event of loss, Borrower shall give prompt notice to the insurance carrier and Lender. Lender may make proof of loss if not made promptly by Borrower.

Unless Lender and Borrower otherwise agree in writing, insurance proceeds shall be applied to restoration or repair of the Property damaged, if the restoration or repair is economically feasible and Lender's security is not lessened. If the restoration or repair Is not economically feasible or Lender's security would be lessened, the insurance proceeds shall be applied to the sums secured by this security Instrument, whether or not then due, with any excess paid to Borrower. If Borrower abandons the Property, or does not answer within 30 days a notice from Lender that the insurance carrier has offered to settle a claim, then Lender may collect the insurance proceeds.
Lender may use the proceeds to repair or restore the Property or to pay sums secured by this Security Instrument, whether or not then due. The 30-clay period will begin when the notice is given.

Unless Lender and Borrower otherwise agree in writing, any application of proceeds to principal shall not extend or postpone the due date of the monthly payments referred to in paragraphs 1 and 2 or change the amount of the payments. If under paragraph 21 the Property is acquired by Lender, Borrower's right to any insurance policies and proceeds resulting from damage to the Property prior to the acquisition shall pass to Lender to the extent of the sums secured by this Security Instrument immediately prior to the acquisition.

6. Occupancy, Preservation, Maintenance and Protection of the Property; Borrower's Loan Application; leaseholds. Borrower shall occupy establish, and use the Property as Borrowers principal residence within sixty days after the execution of this security Instrument and shall continue to occupy the Property as Borrower's principal residence for at least one year after the date of occupancy, unless Lender otherwise agrees in writing, which consent shall not be unreasonably withheld, or unless extenuating circumstances exist which are beyond Borrowers control. Borrower shall not destroy, damage or impair the Property, allow the Property to deteriorate, or commit waste on the Property. Borrower shall be in default if any forfeiture action or proceeding, whether civil or criminal, is begun that in Lender's good faith judgment could result in forfeiture of the Property or otherwise materially impair the lien created by this Security Instrument or Lender's security interest. Borrower may cure such a default and reinstate, as provided in paragraph 18, by causing the action or proceeding to be dismissed with a ruling that, in Lenders good faith determination, precludes forfeiture of the Borrower's interest in the Property or other material impairment of the lien created by this Security Instrument or Lenders security interest. Borrower shall also be in default If Borrower, during the loan application process, gave materially false or inaccurate Information or statements to Lender (or failed to provide Lender with any material information) in connection with the loan evidenced by the Note, including, but not limited to, representations concerning Borrower's occupancy of the Property as a principal residence, If this Security Instrument is on a leasehold, Borrower shall comply with all the provisions of the lease. If Borrower acquires fee title to the Property, the leasehold and the fee title shall not merge unless Lender agrees to the merger in writing.

7. Protection of Lender's Rights in the Property. If Borrower fails to perform the covenants and agreements contained in this Security Instrument, or there is a legal proceeding that may significantly affect Lender's rights in the Property (such as a proceeding in bankruptcy, probate, for condemnation or forfeiture or to enforce laws or regulations), then Lender may do and pay for whatever is necessary to protect the value of the Property and~ Lender's rights in the Property. Lender's actions may include paying any sums secured by a lien, which has priority over this Security Instrument, appearing in court, paying reasonable attorneys' fees and entering on the Property to make repairs. Although Lender may take action under this paragraph 7, Lender does not have to do so.

Any amounts disbursed by Lender under this paragraph 7 shall become additional debt of Borrower secured by this security Instrument. Unless Borrower and Lender agree to other terms of payment, these amounts shall bear interest from the date of disbursement at the Note rate and shall be payable, with interest, upon notice from Lender to Borrower requesting payment.

8. Mortgage Insurance. If Lender required mortgage insurance as a condition of making the loan secured by this Security Instrument, Borrower shall pay the premiums required to maintain the mortgage insurance in effect. If, for any reason, the mortgage insurance coverage required by Lender lapses or ceases to be in effect,
Borrower shall pay the premiums required to obtain coverage substantially equivalent to the mortgage insurance previously in effect, at a cost substantially equivalent to the cost to Borrower of the mortgage insurance previously in effect, from an alternate mortgage insurer approved by Lender. If substantially equivalent mortgage insurance coverage is not available, Borrower shall pay to Lender each month a sum equal to one-twelfth of the yearly mortgage insurance premium being paid by Borrower when the insurance coverage lapsed or ceased to be in effect. Lender will accept, use and retain these payments as a loss reserve in lieu of mortgage insurance. Loss reserve payments may no longer be required, at the option of Lender, if mortgage Insurance coverage (in the amount and for the, period that Lender requires) provided by an insurer approved by Lender again becomes available and is obtained. Borrower shall pay the premiums required to maintain mortgage insurance in effect, or to provide a loss reserve, until the requirement for mortgage insurance ends in accordance with any written agreement between Borrower and Lender or applicable law.

CALIFORNIA-Single Family-Fannie Mae/Freddie Mac UNIFORM INSTRUMENT **Page 3 of 6**
Form 3005 9/90 GENESIS 2000, INC. *V9.3/W11.0 * (818) 223-3280   Amended 5/91
                                      Initials: _____ _____ _____ _____

FIGURE 11-1 (*Continued*)

9. Inspection. Lender or its agent may make reasonable entries upon and inspections of the Property. Lender shall give Borrower notice at the time of or prior to an Inspection specifying reasonable cause for the inspection.

10. Condemnation. The proceeds of any award or claim for damages, direct or consequential, in connection with any condemnation or other taking of any part of the Property, or for conveyance in lieu of condemnation, are hereby assigned and shall be paid to Lender. In the event of a total taking of the Property, the proceeds shall be applied to the sums secured by this Security Instrument, whether or not then due, with any excess paid to Borrower. In the event of a partial taking of the Property in which the fair market value of the Property Immediately before the taking is equal to or greater than the amount of the sums secured by this Security Instrument immediately before the taking, unless Borrower and Lender otherwise agree in writing, the sums secured by this Security Instrument shall be reduced by the amount of the proceeds multiplied by the following fraction: (a) the total amount of the sums secured immediately before the taking, divided by (b) the fair market value of the Property immediately before the taking. Any balance shall be paid to Borrower. In the event of a partial taking of the Property in which the fair market value of the Property immediately before the taking is less than the amount of the sums secured immediately before the taking, unless Borrower and Lender otherwise agree in writing or unless applicable law otherwise provides, the proceeds shall be applied to the sums secured by this Security Instrument whether or not the sums are then due.

If the Property is abandoned by Borrower, or if, after notice by Lender to Borrower that the condemnor offers to make an award or settle a claim for damages, Borrower fails to respond to lender within 30 days after the date the notice is given, Lender is authorized to collect and apply the proceeds, at its option, either to restoration or repair of the Property or to the sums secured by this Security Instrument, whether or not then due.

Unless Lender and Borrower otherwise agree in writing, any application of proceeds to principal shall not extend or postpone the due date of the monthly payments referred to in paragraphs 1 and 2 or change the amount of such payments.

11. Borrower Not Released; Forbearance By Lender Not a Waiver. Extension of the time for payment or modification of amortization of the sums secured by this Security Instrument granted by Lender to any successor in interest of Borrower shall not operate to release the liability of the original Borrower or Borrower's successors in interest. Lender shall not be required to commence proceedings against any successor in interest or refuse to extend time for payment or otherwise modify amortization of the sums secured by this Security Instrument by reason of any demand made by the original Borrower or Borrower's successors in interest. Any forbearance by Lender in exercising any right or remedy shall not be a waiver of or preclude the exercise of any right or remedy.

12. Successors and Assigns Bound; Joint and Several Liability; Co-Signers. The covenants and agreements of this Security Instrument shall bind and benefit the successors and assigns of Lender and Borrower, subject to the provisions of paragraph 17. Borrower's covenants and agreements shall be joint and several. Any Borrower who co-signs this Security Instrument but does not execute the Note: (a) is co-signing this Security Instrument only to mortgage, grant and convey that Borrower's interest in the Property under the terms of this Security instrument;(b) is not personally obligated to pay the sums secured by this Security Instrument; and (c) agrees that Lender and any other Borrower may agree to extend, modify, forbear or make any accommodations with regard to the terms of this Security Instrument or the Note without that borrower's consent.

13. Loan Charges. If the loan secured by this Security instrument is subject to a law which sets maximum loan charges, and that law is finally interpreted so that the interest or other loan charges collected or to be collected in connection with the loan exceed the permitted limits, then: (a) any such loan charge shall be reduced by the amount necessary to reduce the charge to the permitted limit; and (b) any sums already collected from Borrower which exceeded permitted limits will be refunded to Borrower. Lender may choose to make this refund by reducing the principal owed under the Note or by making a direct payment to Borrower. If a refund reduces principal, the reduction will be treated as a partial prepayment without any prepayment charge under the Note.

14. Notices. Any notice to Borrower provided for in this Security Instrument shall be given by delivering it or by mailing it by first class mail unless applicable law requires use of another method. The notice shall be directed to the Property Address or any other address Borrower designates by notice to Lender. Any notice to Lender shall be given by first class mail to Lenders address stated herein or any other address Lender designates by notice to Borrower. Any notice provided for in this Security Instrument shall be deemed to have been given to Borrower or Lender when given as provided in this paragraph.

15. Governing Law; Severability. This Security Instrument shall be governed by federal law and the law of the jurisdiction in which the Property is located. In the event that any provision or clause of this Security Instrument or the Note conflicts with applicable law, such conflict shall not affect other provisions of this Security Instrument or the Note, which can be given effect without the conflicting provision. To this end the provisions of this Security Instrument and the Note are declared to be severable.

16. Borrower's Copy. Borrower shall be given one conformed copy of the Note and of this Security instrument.

17. Transfer of the Property or a Beneficial Interest in Borrower. If all or any part of the Property or any interest in it is sold or transferred (or if a beneficial interest in Borrower is sold or transferred and Borrower is not a natural person) without Lenders prior written consent, Lender may, at its option, require immediate payment in full of all sums secured by this Security Instrument. However, this option shall not be exercised by Lender if exercise is prohibited by federal law as of the date of this Security Instrument.

If Lender exercises this option, Lender shall give Borrower notice of acceleration. The notice shall provide a period of not less than 30 days from the date the notice is delivered or mailed within which Borrower must pay all sums secured by this Security Instrument, If Borrower fails to pay these sums prior to the expiration of this period,

CALIFORNIA-Single Family-Fannie Mae/Freddie Mac UNIFORM INSTRUMENT　**Page 4 of 6**
Form 3005 9/90 GENESIS 2000, INC. (818) 222-3260　　　　　　　　　　　　Amended 5/91
　　　　　　　　　　Initials: _____ _____ _____ _____

FIGURE 11-1 (*Continued*)

Lender may invoke any remedies permitted by this Security Instrument without further notice or demand on Borrower.

18. Borrower's Right to Reinstate. If Borrower meets certain conditions, Borrower shall have the right to have enforcement of this Security instrument discontinued at any time prior to the earlier of: (a) 5 days (or such other period as applicable law may specify for reinstatement) before sale of Property pursuant to any power of sale contained in this Security instrument; or (b) entry of a judgment enforcing this Security Instrument. Those conditions are that Borrower: (a) pays Lender all sums which then would be due under this Security Instrument and the Note as If no acceleration had occurred; (b) cures any default of any other covenants or agreements; (c) pays all expenses incurred in enforcing this Security Instrument, including, but not limited to, reasonable attorneys fees; and (d) takes such action as Lender may reasonably require to assure that the lien of this Security Instrument, Lender's rights in the Property and Borrower's obligation to pay the sums secured by this Security Instrument shall continue unchanged. Upon reinstatement by Borrower, this Security Instrument and the obligations secured hereby shall remain fully effective as if no acceleration had occurred. However, this right to reinstate shall not apply In the case of acceleration under paragraph 17.

19. Sale of Note; Change of Loan Servicer. The Note or a partial Interest in the Note (together with this Security instrument) may be sold one or more times without prior notice to Borrower. A sale may result in a change in the entity (known as the 'Loan Servicer') that collects monthly payments due under the Note and this Security Instrument. There also may be one or more changes of the Loan Servicer unrelated to a sale of the Note. If there is a change of the Loan Servicer, Borrower will be given written notice of the change In accordance with paragraph 14 above and applicable law. The notice will state the name and address of the new Loan Servicer and the address to which payments should be made. The notice will also contain any other information required by applicable law.

20. Hazardous Substances. Borrower shall not cause or permit the presence, use, disposal, storage, or release of any Hazardous Substances on or in the Property. Borrower shall not do, nor allow anyone else to do, anything affecting the Property that is in violation of any Environmental Law. The preceding two sentences shall not apply to the presence, use, or storage on the Property of small quantities of Hazardous Substances that are generally recognized to be appropriate to normal residential uses and to maintenance of the Property.

Borrower shall promptly give Lender written notice of any investigation, claim, demand, lawsuit or other action by any governmental or regulatory agency or private party involving the Property and any Hazardous Substances or Environmental Law of which Borrower has actual knowledge. If Borrower deems, or is notified by any governmental or regulatory authority, that any removal or other remediation of any Hazardous Substances affecting the Property is necessary, Borrower shall promptly take all necessary remedial actions in accordance with Environmental Law.

As used in this paragraph 20, 'Hazardous Substances" are those substances defined as toxic or hazardous substances by Environmental Law and the following substances: gasoline, kerosene, other flammable or toxic petroleum products, toxic pesticides and herbicides, volatile solvents, materials containing asbestos or formaldehyde, and radioactive materials. As used in this paragraph 20, 'Environmental Law' means federal laws and laws of the jurisdiction where the Property Is located that relate to health, safety or environmental protection.

NON-UNIFORM COVENANTS. Borrower and Lender further covenant and agree as follows:

21. Acceleration; Remedies. LENDER SHALL GIVE NOTICE TO BORROWER PRIOR TO ACCELERATION FOLLOWING BORROWER'S BREACH OF ANY COVENANT OR AGREEMENT IN THIS SECURITY INSTRUMENT (BUT NOT PRIOR TO ACCELERATION UNDER PARAGRAPH 11 UNLESS APPLICABLE LAW PROVIDES OTHERWISE). THE NOTICE SHALL SPECIFY: (A) THE DEFAULT; (5) THE ACTION REQUIRED 10 CURE THE DEFAULT; (C) A DATE, NOT LESS THAN 30 DAYS FROM THE DATE THE NOTICE IS GIVEN TO BORROWER, BY WHICH THE DEFAULT MUST BE CURED; AND (D) THAT FAILURE TO CURE THE DEFAULT ON OR BEFORE THE DATE SPECIFIED IN THE NOTICE MAY RESULT IN ACCELERATION OF THE SUMS SECURED BY THE SECURITY INSTRUMENT AND SALE OF THE PROPERTY. THE NOTICE SHALL FURTHER INFORM BORROWER OF THE RIGHT TO REINSTATE AFTER ACCELERATION AND THE RIGHT TO BRING A COURT ACTION TO ASSERT THE NONEXISTENCE OF A DEFAULT OR ANY OTHER DEFENSE OF BORROWER TO ACCELERATION AND SALE. IF THE DEFAULT IS NOT CURED ON OR BEFORE THE DATE SPECIFIED IN THE NOTICE, LENDER, AT ITS OPTION, MAY REQUIRE IMMEDIATE PAYMENT IN FULL OF ALL SUMS SECURED BY THIS SECURITY INSTRUMENT WITHOUT FURTHER DEMAND AND MAY INVOKE THE POWER OF SALE AND ANY OTHER REMEDIES PERMITTED BY APPLICABLE LAW. LENDER SHALL BE ENTITLED TO COLLECT ALL EXPENSES INCURRED IN PURSUING THE REMEDIES PROVIDED IN This PARAGRAPH 21, INCLUDING, BUT NOT LIMITED TO, REASONABLE ATTORNEYS' FEES AND COSTS OF TITLE EVIDENCE.

IF LENDER INVOKES THE POWER OF SALE, LENDER SHALL EXECUTE OR CAUSE TRUSTEE TO EXECUTE A WRITTEN NOTICE OF THE OCCURRENCE OF AN EVENT OF DEFAULT AND OF LENDERS ELECTION TO CAUSE THE PROPERTY TO BE SOLD. TRUSTEE SHALL CAUSE THIS NOTICE TO BE RECORDED IN EACH COUNTY IN, WHICH ANY PART OF THE PROPERTY IS LOCATED. LENDER OR TRUSTEE SHALL MAIL COPIES OF THE NOTICE AS PRESCRIBED BY APPLICABLE LAW TO BORROWER AND TO THE OTHER PERSONS PRESCRIBED BY APPLICABLE LAW. TRUSTEE SHALL GIVE PUBLIC NOTICE OF SALE TO THE PERSONS AND IN THE MANNER PRESCRIBED BY APPLICABLE LAW. AFTER THE TIME REQUIRED BY APPLICABLE LAW, TRUSTEE, WITHOUT DEMAND ON BORROWER, SHALL SELL THE PROPERTY AT PUBLIC AUCTION TO THE HIGHEST BIDDER AT THE TIME AND PLACE AND UNDER THE TERMS DESIGNATED IN THE NOTICE OF SALE IN ONE OR MORE PARCELS AND IN ANY ORDER TRUSTEE DETERMINES. TRUSTEE MAY POSTPONE SALE OF ALL OR ANY PARCEL OF THE PROPERTY BY PUBLIC ANNOUNCEMENT AT THE TIME AND PLACE OF ANY PREVIOUSLY SCHEDULED SALE. LENDER OR ITS DESIGNATE MAY PURCHASE THE PROPERTY AT ANY SALE.

TRUSTEE SHALL DELIVER TO THE PURCHASER TRUSTEE'S DEED CONVEYING THE PROPERTY WITHOUT ANY COVENANT OR WARRANTY, EXPRESSED OR IMPLIED. THE RECITALS IN THE TRUSTEE'S DEED SHALL BE PRIMA FACIE EVIDENCE OF THE TRUTH OF THE STATEMENTS MADE THEREIN. TRUSTEE SHALL APPLY THE PROCEEDS OF THE SALE IN THE FOLLOWING ORDER: (A) TO ALL EXPENSES OF THE SALE, INCLUDING, BUT NOT LIMITED TO, REASONABLE TRUSTEE'S AND ATTORNEYS' FEES;

CALIFORNIA. Single Family-Fannie Mae/Freddie Mae UNIFORM INSTRUMENT   **Page 5 of 6**
Form 3005 9/90 GENESIS 2000, INC. * V9.3/W11.0 *(818) 223-2260 Amended

Initials: _____ _____ _____ _____

FIGURE 11-1 (*Continued*)

(B)TO ALL SUMS SECURED BY THIS SECURITY INSTRUMENT; AND (C) ANY EXCESS TO THE PERSON OR PERSONS LEGALLY ENTITLED TO IT.

22. Reconveyance. Upon payment of all sums secured by this Security Instrument, Lender shall request Trustee to reconvey the Property and shall surrender this Security Instrument and all notes evidencing debt secured by this Security Instrument to Trustee. Trustee shall reconvey the Property without warranty to the person or persons legally entitled to it. Such person or persons shall pay any reconveyance fees or recordation costs.

23. Substitute Trustee. Lender, at its option, may from time to time appoint a successor trustee to any Trustee appointed hereunder by an instrument executed and acknowledged by Lender and recorded in the office of the Recorder of the county in which the Property is located, The instrument shall contain the name of the original Lender, Trustee and Borrower, the book and page where this Security Instrument is recorded and the name and address of the successor trustee, Without conveyance of the Property, the successor trustee shall succeed to call the title, powers and duties conferred upon the Trustee herein and by applicable law. This procedure for substitution of trustee shall govern to the exclusion of all other provisions for substitution.

24. Request for Notices. Borrower requests that copies of the notices of default and sale be sent to Borrower's address, which is the Property Address.

25. Statement of Obligation Fee. Lender may collect a fee not to exceed the maximum amount permitted by law for furnishing the statement of obligation as provided by Section 2943 of the Civil Code of California.

26. Riders to this Security Instrument. If one or more riders are executed by Borrower and recorded together with this Security Instrument, the covenants and agreements of each such rider shall be incorporated into and shall amend and supplement the covenants and agreements of this Security Instrument as if the rider(s) were a part of this Security Instrument.

[Check applicable box(es)]

☐ Adjustable Rate	☐ Condominium	☐ 1-4 Family
☐ Graduated Payment	☐ Planned Unit Development	☐ Biweekly Payment
☐ Balloon	☐ Rate Improvement	☐ Second Home
☐ V.A.	☐ Other Rider(s) [specify]	

BY SIGNING BELOW, Borrower accepts and agrees to the terms and covenants contained in this Security Instrument and in any rider(s) executed by Borrower and recorded with it.

Witnesses:

_____ (Seal)
                                    -Borrower

_____ (Seal)
                                    -Borrower

_____ (Seal)
                                    -Borrower

_____ (Seal)
                                    -Borrower

_____ (Seal)
                                    -Borrower

State of California   } **ss.**
County of
On   before me,

                                    Personally appeared

personally known to me (or proved to me on the basis of satisfactory evidence) to be the person(s) whose name(s) is/are

subscribed to within instrument and acknowledged to me that he/she/they executed the same in his/her/their authorized

capacity(ies), and that by his/her/their signature(s) on the instrument the person(s) or the entity upon behalf of which

the person(s) acted, executed the Instrument.

WITNESS my hand and official seal.

_____

(This area for official notarial seal)
CALIFORNIA Single Family-Fannie Mae/Freddie Mac UNIFORM INSTRUMENT   **Page 6 of 6**
Penn 30059/90 GENESIS 2000, Inc. * V9.3/WII.O *(818) 223-3260   Amended 5/91

Warranty Deed

If a deed is intended to be a general warranty deed (see Figure 11-2), it should contain a phrase specified by state law such as "conveys and warrants." These words, called *operative words of conveyance*, carry with them several warranties that the grantor is making to the grantee. Examples of the warranties are:

- The grantor warrants that the grantor is the lawful owner of the property at the time the deed is made and delivered and that the grantor has the right to convey the property.

- The grantor warrants that the property is free from all encumbrances or liens.

- The grantor warrants that he or she will defend title to the estate so that the grantee and the grantee's heirs and assigns may enjoy quiet and peaceable possession of the premises with the power to convey the property.

Quitclaim Deed

A quitclaim deed (see Figure 11-3) is sometimes called a *quick claim deed*; however, *quitclaim*—all one word—is the correct term. The quitclaim deed is an instrument that conveys all ownership rights to another co-owner of a property without guarantees. Quitclaim deeds are commonly used by married people seeking a divorce. Usually one spouse signs all his or her rights to the real estate over to the other. Please understand that this device conveys ownership rights only and will *not* end an obligation to repay a loan.

Promissory Note

A promissory note is a written promise to pay a debt. The note represents an unconditional promise to pay on demand or at a fixed or determined future time a particular sum of money to or to the order of a specified person or to the bearer. (See Figure 11-4.)

FIGURE 11-2
Sample Warranty Deed

WARRANTY DEED

[*list name of person conveying the property*], an individual with an address of [*list address of grantor*], being married, ("Grantor"), in consideration of $ [*e.g. 100,000.00*] and other good and valuable consideration to Grantor paid, the receipt of which is acknowledged, does hereby grant, bargain, sell, convey and warrant to [*list name of person receiving property*], an individual with an address of [*list address of grantee*], ("Grantee"), all the following real estate:

[*enter the exact legal description*].

Subject to: [*list encumbrances the property will be subject to, e.g. mortgages, easements, etc.*].

Subject to real estate taxes and assessments for the current year and subsequent years.

Subject to all valid easements, rights of way, covenants, conditions, reservations and restrictions of record, if any, and also to applicable zoning, land use and other laws and regulations.

To have and to hold the same, together with all the buildings, improvements and appurtenances belonging thereto, if any, to the Grantee and Grantee's heirs, successors and assigns forever.

Grantor, for Grantor and Grantor's heirs and successors, covenants with Grantee and Grantee's heirs, successors and assigns, that:

1. Grantor is lawfully seized in fee simple of the above property, and has good right to convey the same;

2. The above property is free from all encumbrances, except as set forth above;

3. Grantee shall quietly enjoy the above property; and

4. Grantor will forever warrant and defend the title to the above property against the lawful claims and demands of all persons.

This property was acquired by the Grantor by: [*statement explaining how grantor acquired the property*].

I, [*list name of grantor's spouse*], of [*list address of grantor's spouse*], spouse of [*list name of person conveying the property*], in consideration of the above sum and other good and valuable consideration received, do hereby waive and release to Grantee all rights of dower, courtesy, homestead, community property, and all other right, title and interest, if any, in and to the above property.

IN WITNESS WHEREOF, this Warranty Deed is executed under seal on

the_____day of_____, 20_____.

Signed, sealed and delivered
in the presence of:

_____   _____(Seal)
(Signature of witness)   [*list name of person conveying the property*]

STATE OF _____

FIGURE 11-3
Sample Quitclaim Deed

QUITCLAIM DEED

THIS INDENTURE, Made on the _____day of _____, 200 , by and between _____, a single person (sample could be spouse), of _____ County, _____ (state), party of the first part, Grantor's mailing address _____% _____, _____(address) _____(city), _____(state) ____(zip code) and _____ (co-owner), a single person (sample could be spouse), of _____ County, California, party of the second part, Grantee's mailing address _____.

WITNESSETH, that the said party of the first part, in consideration of the sum of _____Dollar amount and Other Good and Valuable Consideration, to him/her paid by the said party of the second part (the receipt of which is hereby acknowledged) does by these presents **REMISE, RELEASE and FOREVER QUIT CLAIM** unto the said party of the second part, the following described lots, tracts or parcels of land, lying, being and situated in the County of _____, State of _____, to-wit:

LEGAL DESCRIPTION

TO HAVE AND TO HOLD THE SAME, with all the rights, immunities, privileges and appurtenances thereto belonging, unto the said party of the second part and unto his heirs and assigns forever; so that neither the said party of the first part nor her heirs nor any other person or persons, for her or in her name or behalf, shall or will hereinafter claim or demand any right or title to the aforesaid premises or any part thereof, but they and each of them shall, by these presents, be excluded and forever barred.

IN WITNESS WHEREOF, the said party of the first part has hereunto set her hand and seal the day and year above written.

_____
Signature

In the State of _____, County of _____, on this _____ day of _____, 200 , before me, the undersigned, a Notary Public in and for said County and State, personally appeared _____**(recipient's name)** to me known to be the person described in and who executed the foregoing instrument, and acknowledged that she executed the same as her free act and deed.

Witness my hand and Notarial Seal and affixed in said County and State, the day and year in this certificate above written.

_____
Notary Public

FIGURE 11-4
Sample Mortgage Note

Mortgage Note

_____(date)

_____
(property address)

1. Borrower's Promise to Pay
In return for a loan that I have received, I promise to pay U.S. $_____
(this **amount** is called "principal"), plus interest, to the order of the Lender. The Lender is

I understand that the Lender may transfer this Note. The Lender or anyone who takes this Note by transfer and who is entitled to receive payment under this Note is called the "Note Holder."

2. Interest
Interest will be charged on unpaid principal until the full amount of principal has been paid. I will pay interest at a yearly rate of _____ %. This interest rate required by this Section 2 is the rate I will pay both before and after any default described in Section 6W of this Note.

3. Payments
(A) Time and Place of Payments
I will pay principal and interest by making payments every month.
I will make my monthly payments on the _____ day of each month beginning on _____ 20__. I will make these payments every month until I have paid all of the principal and interest and any other charges described below that I may owe under this Note. My monthly payments will be applied to interest before principal. If, on _____ , _____ , I still owe amounts under this Note, I will pay those amounts in full on that date, which is called the "maturity date."
I will make my monthly payments at:

_____
__ or at a different place if required by the Note Holder.
(B) Amount of Monthly Payments
My monthly payment will be in the amount of U.S. $_____

4. Borrower's right to prepay
I have the right to make payments of principal at any time before they are due. A payment of principal only is known as a "prepayment." When I make a prepayment, I will tell the Note Holder in writing that I am doing so. I may make a full prepayment or partial prepayments without paying any prepayment charges. The Note Holder will use all of my prepayments to reduce the amount of the principal that I owe under this Note. If I make a partial prepayment, there will be no changes in the due date or in the amount of my monthly payment unless the Note Holder agrees in writing to those changes.

FIGURE 11-4 (*Continued*)

5. Loan charges

If a law, which applies to this loan and which sets maximum loan charges, is finally interpreted so that the interest or other loan charges collected or to be collected with this loan exceed the permitted limits, then: (i) any such loan charge shall be reduced by the amount necessary to reduce the charge to the permitted limit; and (ii) any sums already collected from me which exceed permitted limits will be refunded to me. The Note Holder may choose to make this refund by reducing the principal I owe under this Note or by sending a direct payment to me. If a refund reduces principal, the reduction will be treated as a partial payment.

6. Borrower's failure to pay as required

(*A*) *Late charge for overdue payments*
If the Note Holder has not received the full amount of any monthly payment by the end of_____ calendar days after the date it is due, I will pay a late charge to the Note Holder. The amount of the charge will be _____ % of my overdue payment of principal and interest. I will pay this late charge but only once on each late payment.
(*B*) *Default*
If I do not pay the full amount of each monthly payment on the date it is due, I will be in default.
(*C*) *Notice of Default*
If I am in default, the Note Holder may send me a written notice telling me that if I do not pay the overdue amount by a certain date, the Note Holder may require me to pay immediately the full amount of principal which has not been paid and all the interest that I owe on that amount. That date must be at least 30 days after the date on which the notice is delivered or mailed to me.
(*D*) *No waiver by Note Holder*
Even if, at a time when I am in default, the Note Holder does not require me to pay immediately in full as described above, the Note Holder will still have the right to do so if I am in default at a later time.
(*E*) *Payment of Note Holder's costs and expenses*
If the Note Holder has required me to pay immediately in full as described above, the Note Holder will have the right to be paid back by me for all of its costs and expenses in enforcing this Note to the extent not prohibited by applicable law. Those expenses include, for example, reasonable attorney's fees.

7. Giving of notices

Unless applicable law requires a different method, any notice that must be given to me under this Note will be given by delivering it or by mailing it by first class mail to me at the Property Address above or at a different address if I give the Note Holder a notice of my different address. Any notice that must be given to the Note Holder under this Note will be given by mailing it by first class mail to the Note Holder at the address stated in Section 3(A) above or at a different address if I am given a notice of that different address.

8. Obligations of persons under this note

If more than one person signs this Note, each person is fully and personally obligated to keep all of the promises made in this Note, including the promise to pay the full amount owed. Any person who is a guarantor, surety or endorser of this Note is also obligated to do these things. Any person who takes over these obligations, including the obligations of a guarantor, surety or endorser of this Note, is also obligated to keep all of the promises made in this Note. The Note Holder may enforce its rights under this Note against each person individually or against all of us together. This means that any one of us may be required to pay all of the amounts owed under this Note.

FIGURE 11-4 (*Continued*)

9. Waivers

I and any other person who has obligations under this Note waive the rights of presentment and notice of dishonor. "Presentment" means the right to require the Note Holder to demand payment of amounts due. "Notice of dishonor" means the right to require the Note Holder to give notice to other persons that amounts due have not been paid.

10. **Uniform secured Note**

This Note is a uniform instrument with limited variations in some jurisdictions. In addition to the protections given to the Note Holder under this Note, a Mortgage, Deed of Trust or Security Deed (the "Security Instrument"), dated the same date as this Note, protects the Note Holder from possible losses which might result if I do not keep the promises which I make in this Note. That Security Instrument described how and under what conditions I may be required to make immediate payment in full of all amounts I owe under this Note. Some of those conditions are described as follows:

Transfer of the Property or a Beneficial Interest in Borrower. If all or any part of the Property or any interest in it is sold or transferred (or if a beneficial interest in Borrower is sold or transferred and Borrower is not a natural person) without Lender's prior written consent, Lender may, at its option, require immediate payment in full of all sums secured by this Security Instrument. However, this option shall not be exercised by Lender if exercise is prohibited by federal law as of the date of this Security Instrument.

If Lender exercises this option, Lender shall give Borrower notice of acceleration. The notice shall provide a period of not less than 30 days from the date the notice is delivered or mailed within which Borrower must pay all sums secured by this Security Instrument. If Borrower fails to pay these sums prior to the expiration of this period, Lender may invoke any remedies permitted by this Security Instrument without further notice or demand on Borrower.

_____   _____
Borrower   Co-Borrower

APPLICATION AND DISCLOSURE FORMS

We have described in detail the use and preparation of the loan application, good faith estimate, and truth in lending forms. Figures 11-5 to 11-21 are copies of the most commonly used disclosures.

FIGURE 11-5

Uniform Residential Loan Application

This application is designed to be completed by the applicant(s) with the Lender's assistance. Applicants should complete this form as "Borrower" or "Co-Borrower," as applicable. Co-Borrower information must also be provided (and the appropriate box checked) when ☐ the income or assets of a person other than the "Borrower" (including the Borrower's spouse) will be used as a basis for loan qualification or ☐ the income or assets of the Borrower's spouse will not be used as a basis for loan qualification, but his or her liabilities must be considered because the Borrower resides in a community property state, the security property is located in a community property state, or the Borrower is relying on other property located in a community property state as a basis for repayment of the loan.

I. TYPE OF MORTGAGE AND TERMS OF LOAN

Mortgage Applied for:	☐ VA ☐ FHA	☐ Conventional ☐ USDA/Rural Housing Service	☐ Other (explain):	Agency Case Number	Lender Case Number

Amount $	Interest Rate %	No. of Months	Amortization Type:	☐ Fixed Rate ☐ GPM	☐ Other (explain): ☐ ARM (type):

II. PROPERTY INFORMATION AND PURPOSE OF LOAN

Subject Property Address (street, city, state, & ZIP)	No. of Units

Legal Description of Subject Property (attach description if necessary)	Year Built

Purpose of Loan ☐ Purchase ☐ Construction ☐ Other (explain): ☐ Refinance ☐ Construction-Permanent	Property will be: ☐ Primary Residence ☐ Secondary Residence ☐ Investment

Complete this line if construction or construction-permanent loan.

Year Lot Acquired	Original Cost $	Amount Existing Liens $	(a) Present Value of Lot $	(b) Cost of Improvements $	Total (a + b) $

Complete this line if this is a refinance loan.

Year Acquired	Original Cost $	Amount Existing Liens $	Purpose of Refinance	Describe Improvements ☐ made ☐ to be made Cost: $

Title will be held in what Name(s)	Manner in which Title will be held	Estate will be held in: ☐ Fee Simple ☐ Leasehold (show expiration date)

Source of Down Payment, Settlement Charges and/or Subordinate Financing (explain)

III. BORROWER INFORMATION

Borrower / Co-Borrower

Borrower's Name (include Jr. or Sr. if applicable)	Co-Borrower's Name (include Jr. or Sr. if applicable)

Social Security Number	Home Phone (incl. area code)	DOB (MM/DD/YYYY)	Yrs. School	Social Security Number	Home Phone (incl. area code)	DOB (MM/DD/YYYY)	Yrs. School

☐ Married ☐ Unmarried (include single, ☐ Separated divorced, widowed)	Dependents (not listed by Co-Borrower) no. ages	☐ Married ☐ Unmarried (include single, ☐ Separated divorced, widowed)	Dependents (not listed by Borrower) no. ages

Present Address (street, city, state, ZIP) ☐ Own ☐ Rent ____No. Yrs.	Present Address (street, city, state, ZIP) ☐ Own ☐ Rent ____No. Yrs.

Mailing Address, if different from Present Address	Mailing Address, if different from Present Address

If residing at present address for less than two years, complete the following:

Former Address (street, city, state, ZIP) ☐ Own ☐ Rent ____No. Yrs.	Former Address (street, city, state, ZIP) ☐ Own ☐ Rent ____No. Yrs.

IV. EMPLOYMENT INFORMATION

Borrower / Co-Borrower

Name & Address of Employer ☐ Self Employed	Yrs. on this job	Name & Address of Employer ☐ Self Employed	Yrs. on this job
	Yrs. employed in this line of work/profession		Yrs. employed in this line of work/profession
Position/Title/Type of Business	Business Phone (incl. area code)	Position/Title/Type of Business	Business Phone (incl. area code)

If employed in current position for less than two years or if currently employed in more than one position, complete the following:

Name & Address of Employer ☐ Self Employed	Dates (from – to)	Name & Address of Employer ☐ Self Employed	Dates (from – to)
	Monthly Income $		Monthly Income $
Position/Title/Type of Business	Business Phone (incl. area code)	Position/Title/Type of Business	Business Phone (incl. area code)

Name & Address of Employer ☐ Self Employed	Dates (from – to)	Name & Address of Employer ☐ Self Employed	Dates (from – to)
	Monthly Income $		Monthly Income $
Position/Title/Type of Business	Business Phone (incl. area code)	Position/Title/Type of Business	Business Phone (incl. area code)

FIGURE 11-5 (Continued)

V. MONTHLY INCOME AND COMBINED HOUSING EXPENSE INFORMATION

Gross Monthly Income	Borrower	Co-Borrower	Total	Combined Monthly Housing Expense	Present	Proposed
Base Empl. Income*	$	$	$	Rent	$	
Overtime				First Mortgage (P&I)		$
Bonuses				Other Financing (P&I)		
Commissions				Hazard Insurance		
Dividends/Interest				Real Estate Taxes		
Net Rental Income				Mortgage Insurance		
Other (before completing, see the notice in "describe other income," below)				Homeowner Assn. Dues		
				Other:		
Total	$	$	$	Total	$	$

* Self Employed Borrower(s) may be required to provide additional documentation such as tax returns and financial statements.

Describe Other Income *Notice:* Alimony, child support, or separate maintenance income need not be revealed if the Borrower (B) or Co-Borrower (C) does not choose to have it considered for repaying this loan.

B/C		Monthly Amount
		$

VI. ASSETS AND LIABILITIES

This Statement and any applicable supporting schedules may be completed jointly by both married and unmarried Co-Borrowers if their assets and liabilities are sufficiently joined so that the Statement can be meaningfully and fairly presented on a combined basis; otherwise, separate Statements and Schedules are required. If the Co-Borrower section was completed about a spouse, this Statement and supporting schedules must be completed about that spouse also.

Completed ☐ Jointly ☐ Not Jointly

ASSETS Description	Cash or Market Value	Liabilities and Pledged Assets. List the creditor's name, address and account number for all outstanding debts, including automobile loans, revolving charge accounts, real estate loans, alimony, child support, stock pledges, etc. Use continuation sheet, if necessary. Indicate by (*) those liabilities which will be satisfied upon sale of real estate owned or upon refinancing of the subject property.		
Cash deposit toward purchase held by:	$			
		LIABILITIES	Monthly Payment & Months Left to Pay	Unpaid Balance
List checking and savings accounts below		Name and address of Company	$ Payment/Months	$
Name and address of Bank, S&L, or Credit Union				
		Acct. no.		
Acct. no.	$	Name and address of Company	$ Payment/Months	$
Name and address of Bank, S&L, or Credit Union				
		Acct. no.		
Acct. no.	$	Name and address of Company	$ Payment/Months	$
Name and address of Bank, S&L, or Credit Union				
		Acct. no.		
Acct. no.	$	Name and address of Company	$ Payment/Months	$
Name and address of Bank, S&L, or Credit Union				
		Acct. no.		
Acct. no.	$	Name and address of Company	$ Payment/Months	$
Stocks & Bonds (Company name/number & description)	$			
		Acct. no.		
		Name and address of Company	$ Payment/Months	$
Life insurance net cash value	$			
Face amount: $				
Subtotal Liquid Assets	$			
Real estate owned (enter market value from schedule of real estate owned)	$	Acct. no.		
Vested interest in retirement fund	$	Name and address of Company	$ Payment/Months	$
Net worth of business(es) owned (attach financial statement)	$			
Automobiles owned (make and year)	$	Acct. no.		
		Alimony/Child Support/Separate Maintenance Payments Owed to:	$	
Other Assets (itemize)	$			
		Job-Related Expense (child care, union dues, etc.)	$	
		Total Monthly Payments	$	
Total Assets a.	$	Net Worth (a minus b) ➤ $	Total Liabilities b.	$

FIGURE 11-5 (*Continued*)

VI. ASSETS AND LIABILITIES (cont.)

Schedule of Real Estate Owned (If additional properties are owned, use continuation sheet.)

Property Address (enter S if sold, PS if pending sale or R if rental being held for income) ➤	Type of Property	Present Market Value	Amount of Mortgages & Liens	Gross Rental Income	Mortgage Payments	Insurance, Maintenance, Taxes & Misc.	Net Rental Income
		$	$	$	$	$	$
Totals		$	$	$	$	$	$

List any additional names under which credit has previously been received and indicate appropriate creditor name(s) and account number(s):

Alternate Name	Creditor Name	Account Number

VII. DETAILS OF TRANSACTION | VIII. DECLARATIONS

VII. DETAILS OF TRANSACTION		VIII. DECLARATIONS	Borrower		Co-Borrower	
		If you answer "Yes" to any questions a through i, please use continuation sheet for explanation.	Yes	No	Yes	No
a. Purchase price	$					
b. Alterations, improvements, repairs		a. Are there any outstanding judgments against you?	☐	☐	☐	☐
c. Land (if acquired separately)		b. Have you been declared bankrupt within the past 7 years?	☐	☐	☐	☐
d. Refinance (incl. debts to be paid off)		c. Have you had property foreclosed upon or given title or deed in lieu thereof in the last 7 years?	☐	☐	☐	☐
e. Estimated prepaid items		d. Are you a party to a lawsuit?	☐	☐	☐	☐
f. Estimated closing costs		e. Have you directly or indirectly been obligated on any loan which resulted in foreclosure, transfer of title in lieu of foreclosure, or judgment?	☐	☐	☐	☐
g. PMI, MIP, Funding Fee		(This would include such loans as home mortgage loans, SBA loans, home improvement loans, educational loans, manufactured (mobile) home loans, any mortgage, financial obligation, bond, or loan guarantee. If "Yes," provide details, including date, name and address of Lender, FHA or VA case number, if any, and reasons for the action.)				
h. Discount (if Borrower will pay)						
i. Total costs (add items a through h)		f. Are you presently delinquent or in default on any Federal debt or any other loan, mortgage, financial obligation, bond, or loan guarantee? If "Yes," give details as described in the preceding question.	☐	☐	☐	☐
j. Subordinate financing		g. Are you obligated to pay alimony, child support, or separate maintenance?	☐	☐	☐	☐
k. Borrower's closing costs paid by Seller		h. Is any part of the down payment borrowed?	☐	☐	☐	☐
l. Other Credits (explain)		i. Are you a co-maker or endorser on a note?	☐	☐	☐	☐
		j. Are you a U.S. citizen?	☐	☐	☐	☐
		k. Are you a permanent resident alien?	☐	☐	☐	☐
m. Loan amount (exclude PMI, MIP, Funding Fee financed)		l. **Do you intend to occupy the property as your primary residence?** If "Yes," complete question m below.	☐	☐	☐	☐
		m. Have you had an ownership interest in a property in the last three years?	☐	☐	☐	☐
n. PMI, MIP, Funding Fee financed		(1) What type of property did you own—principal residence (PR), second home (SH), or investment property (IP)?				
o. Loan amount (add m & n)		(2) How did you hold title to the home—solely by yourself (S), jointly with your spouse (SP), or jointly with another person (O)?				
p. Cash from/to Borrower (subtract j, k, l & o from i)						

IX. ACKNOWLEDGMENT AND AGREEMENT

Each of the undersigned specifically represents to Lender and to Lender's actual or potential agents, brokers, processors, attorneys, insurers, servicers, successors and assigns and agrees and acknowledges that: (1) the information provided in this application is true and correct as of the date set forth opposite my signature and that any intentional or negligent misrepresentation of this information contained in this application may result in civil liability, including monetary damages, to any person who may suffer any loss due to reliance upon any misrepresentation that I have made on this application, and/or in criminal penalties including, but not limited to, fine or imprisonment or both under the provisions of Title 18, United States Code, Sec. 1001, et seq.; (2) the loan requested pursuant to this application (the "Loan") will be secured by a mortgage or deed of trust on the property described herein; (3) the property will not be used for any illegal or prohibited purpose or use; (4) all statements made in this application are made for the purpose of obtaining a residential mortgage loan; (5) the property will be occupied as indicated herein; (6) any owner or servicer of the Loan may verify or reverify any information contained in the application from any source named in this application, and Lender, its successors or assigns may retain the original and/or an electronic record of this application, even if the Loan is not approved; (7) the Lender and its agents, brokers, insurers, servicers, successors and assigns may continuously rely on the information contained in the application, and I am obligated to amend and/or supplement the information provided in this application if any of the material facts that I have represented herein should change prior to closing of the Loan; (8) in the event that my payments on the Loan become delinquent, the owner or servicer of the Loan may, in addition to any other rights and remedies that it may have relating to such delinquency, report my name and account information to one or more consumer credit reporting agencies; (9) ownership of the Loan and/or administration of the Loan account may be transferred with such notice as may be required by law; (10) neither Lender nor its agents, brokers, insurers, servicers, successors or assigns has made any representation or warranty, express or implied, to me regarding the property or the condition or value of the property; and (11) my transmission of this application as an "electronic record" containing my "electronic signature," as those terms are defined in applicable federal and/or state laws (excluding audio and video recordings), or my facsimile transmission of this application containing a facsimile of my signature, shall be as effective, enforceable and valid as if a paper version of this application were delivered containing my original written signature.

Borrower's Signature	Date	Co-Borrower's Signature	Date
X		X	

X. INFORMATION FOR GOVERNMENT MONITORING PURPOSES

The following information is requested by the Federal Government for certain types of loans related to a dwelling in order to monitor the lender's compliance with equal credit opportunity, fair housing and home mortgage disclosure laws. You are not required to furnish this information, but are encouraged to do so. The law provides that a lender may discriminate neither on the basis of this information, nor on whether you choose to furnish it. If you furnish the information, please provide both ethnicity and race. For race, you may check more than one designation. If you do not furnish ethnicity, race, or sex, under Federal regulations, this lender is required to note the information on the basis of visual observation or surname. If you do not wish to furnish the information, please check the box below. (Lender must review the above material to assure that the disclosures satisfy all requirements to which the lender is subject under applicable state law for the particular type of loan applied for.)

BORROWER ☐ I do not wish to furnish this information.		CO-BORROWER ☐ I do not wish to furnish this information.	
Ethnicity: ☐ Hispanic or Latino ☐ Not Hispanic or Latino		**Ethnicity:** ☐ Hispanic or Latino ☐ Not Hispanic or Latino	
Race: ☐ American Indian or Alaska Native ☐ Asian ☐ Black or African American ☐ Native Hawaiian or Other Pacific Islander ☐ White		**Race:** ☐ American Indian or Alaska Native ☐ Asian ☐ Black or African American ☐ Native Hawaiian or Other Pacific Islander ☐ White	
Sex: ☐ Female ☐ Male		**Sex:** ☐ Female ☐ Male	

To be Completed by Interviewer This application was taken by: ☐ Face-to-face interview ☐ Mail ☐ Telephone ☐ Internet	Interviewer's Name (print or type)	Name and Address of Interviewer's Employer
	Interviewer's Signature Date	
	Interviewer's Phone Number (incl. area code)	

FIGURE 11-5 (*Continued*)

Continuation Sheet/Residential Loan Application		
Use this continuation sheet if you need more space to complete the Residential Loan Application. Mark **B** for Borrower or **C** for Co-Borrower.	Borrower:	Agency Case Number:
	Co-Borrower:	Lender Case Number:

I/We fully understand that it is a Federal crime punishable by fine or imprisonment, or both, to knowingly make any false statements concerning any of the above facts as applicable under the provisions of Title 18, United States Code, Section 1001, et seq.

Borrower's Signature	Date	Co-Borrower's Signature	Date
X		X	

FIGURE 11-6

GOOD FAITH ESTIMATE

Applicants: Application No:
Property Address: Date Prepared:
Prepared By: Loan Program:

The information provided below reflects an estimate of the charges which you are likely to incur at the settlement of your loan. The fees listed are estimates— actual charges may be more or less. Your transaction may not involve a fee for every item listed. The numbers listed beside the estimates generally correspond to the numbered lines contained in the HUD-1 settlement statement which you will be receiving at settlement. The HUD-1 settlement statement will show you the actual cost for items paid at settlement.

Total Loan Amount $ Interest Rate: %   Term: mths

800	ITEMS PAYABLE IN CONNECTION WITH LOAN:	
801	Loan Origination Fee	$
802	Loan Discount	
803	Appraisal Fee	
804	Credit Report	
805	Lender's Inspection Fee	
808	Mortgage Broker Fee	
809	Tax Related Fee	
810	Processing Fee	
811	Underwriting Fee	
812	Wire Transfer Fee	
1100	TITLE CHARGES:	
1101	Closing or Escrow Fee:	$
1105	Document Prep Fee:	
1106	Notary Fee	
1107	Attorney Fee	
1108	Title Insurance:	
1200	GOVERNMENT RECORDING & TRANSFER CHARGES:	
1201	Recording Fees:	$
1202	City/County Tax/ Stamps:	
1203	State Tax/Stamps:	
1300	ADDITIONAL SETTLEMENT CHARGES:	
1302	Pest Inspection	$

		Estimated Closing Costs	
900	ITEMS REQUIRED BY LENDER TO BE PAID IN ADVANCE:		
901	Interest for day @ $ per day		$
902	Mortgage Insurance Premium		
903	Hazard Insurance Premium		
904			
905	VA Funding Fee		

1000	RESERVES DEPOSITED WITH LENDER:			
1001	Hazard Insurance Premium	months @ $	per month	$
1002	Mortgage Insurance Premium	months @ $	per month	$
1003	School Tax	months @ $	per month	$
1004	Tax and Assessment Reserves	months @ $	per month	$
1005	Flood Insurance Reserves	months @ $	per month	$
		months @ $	per month	$

Estimated Prepaid Items/Reserves

TOTAL ESTIMATED SETTLEMENT CHARGES
COMPENSATION TO BROKER (Not Paid Out of Loan Proceeds)

TOTAL ESTIMATED FUNDS NEEDED TO CLOSE:		**TOTAL ESTIMATED MONTHLY PAYMENT:**
Purchase Price/Payoff (+)	New First Mortgage (−)	Principal & Interest
Loan Amount (−)	Sub Financing (−)	Other Financing (P&I)
Est. Closing Costs (+)	New 2nd Mtg Closing Costs (+)	Hazard Insurance
Est. Prepaid Items/Reserves (+)		Real Estate Taxes
Amount Paid by Seller (−)		Mortgage Insurance
		Homeowners Assn. Dues
		Other
Total Est. Funds needed to close		**Total Monthly Payment**

☐   This Good Faith Estimate is being provided by   , a mortgage broker, and no lender has been obtained. These estimates are provided pursuant to the Real Estate Settlement Procedures Act of 1974, as amended (RESPA).   Additional information can be found in the HUD Special Information Booklet, which is to be provided to you by your mortgage broker or lender, if your application is to purchase residential property and the lender will take a first lien on the property. The undersigned acknowledges receipt of the booklet "Settlement Costs," and if applicable the Consumer Handbook on ARM Mortgages.

_____   _____   _____   _____
Applicant   Date   Applicant   Date

FIGURE 11-7
Mortgage Loan Disclosure Statement
This is a combination form that can be used, in some cases, in lieu of a good faith estimate.

STATE OF CALIFORNIA

DEPARTMENT OF REAL ESTATE
MORTGAGE LENDING

MORTGAGE LOAN DISCLOSURE STATEMENT/GOOD FAITH ESTIMATE

RE 883 (New 12/93)

Borrower's Name(s): _____

Real Property Collateral: The intended security for this proposed loan will be a Deed of Trust on (street address or legal description) _____

This joint Mortgage Loan Disclosure Statement/Good Faith Estimate is being provided by _____ , a real estate broker acting as a mortgage broker, pursuant to the Federal Real Estate Settlement Procedures Act (RESPA) and similar California law. In a transaction subject to RESPA, a lender will provide you with an additional Good Faith Estimate within three business days of the receipt of your loan application. You will also be informed of material changes before settlement/close of escrow. The name of the intended lender to whom your loan application will be delivered is:

☐ Unknown   ☐ _____ (Name of lender, if known)

GOOD FAITH ESTIMATE OF CLOSING COSTS

The information provided below reflects estimates of the charges you are likely to incur at the settlement of your loan. The fees, commissions, costs and expenses listed are estimates; the actual charges may be more or less. Your transaction may not involve a charge for every item listed and any additional items charged will be listed. The numbers listed beside the estimate generally correspond to the numbered lines contained in the HUD-1 Settlement Statement which you will receive at settlement if this transaction is subject to RESPA. The HUD-1 Settlement Statement contains the actual costs for the items paid at settlement. When this transaction is subject to RESPA, by signing page two of this form you are also acknowledging receipt of the HUD Guide to Settlement Costs.

HUD-1	Item	Paid to Others	Paid to Broker
800	*Items Payable in Connection with Loan*		
801	Lender's Loan Origination Fee	$ _____	$ _____
802	Lender's Loan Discount Fee	$ _____	$ _____
803	Appraisal Fee	$ _____	$ _____
804	Credit Report	$ _____	$ _____
805	Lender's Inspection Fee	$ _____	$ _____
808	Mortgage Broker Commission/Fee	$ _____	$ _____
809	Tax Service Fee	$ _____	$ _____
810	Processing Fee	$ _____	$ _____
811	Underwriting Fee	$ _____	$ _____
812	Wire Transfer Fee	$ _____	$ _____
		$ _____	$ _____
900	*Items Required by Lender to be Paid in Advance*		
901	Interest for ____ days at $_____ per day	$ _____	$ _____
902	Mortgage Insurance Premiums	$ _____	$ _____
903	Hazard Insurance Premiums	$ _____	$ _____
904	County Property Taxes	$ _____	$ _____
905	VA Funding Fee	$ _____	$ _____
		$ _____	$ _____
1000	*Reserves Deposited with Lender*		
1001	Hazard Insurance: ____ months at $_____ /mo.	$ _____	$ _____
1002	Mortgage Insurance: ____ months at $_____ /mo.	$ _____	$ _____
1004	Co. Property Taxes: ____ months at $_____ /mo.	$ _____	$ _____
		$ _____	$ _____
1100	*Title Charges*		
1101	Settlement or Closing/Escrow Fee	$ _____	$ _____
1105	Document Preparation Fee	$ _____	$ _____
1106	Notary Fee	$ _____	$ _____
1108	Title Insurance	$ _____	$ _____
		$ _____	$ _____
1200	*Government Recording and Transfer Charges*		
1201	Recording Fees	$ _____	$ _____
1202	City/County Tax/Stamps	$ _____	$ _____
		$ _____	$ _____
1300	*Additional Settlement Charges*		
1302	Pest Inspection	$ _____	$ _____
		$ _____	$ _____

Subtotals of Initial Fees, Commissions, Costs and Expenses $ _____ $ _____

Total of Initial Fees, Commissions, Costs and Expenses $ _____

Compensation to Broker (Not Paid Out of Loan Proceeds):
Mortgage Broker Commission/Fee $ _____
Any Additional Compensation from Lender   ☐ No   ☐ Yes $ _____ (if known)

FIGURE 11-7 (*Continued*)

ADDITIONAL REQUIRED CALIFORNIA DISCLOSURES

I. Proposed Loan Amount: $_____

Initial Commissions, Fees, Costs and
Expenses Summarized on Page 1: $_____

Payment of Other Obligations (List):
Credit Life and/or Disability Insurance (see VI below) $_____

_____ $_____

_____ $_____

Subtotal of All Deductions: $_____

Estimated Cash at Closing ☐ **To You** ☐ **That you must pay** $_____

II. Proposed Interest Rate: _____%   ☐ Fixed Rate   ☐ Initial Variable Rate

III. Proposed Loan Term: _____   ☐ Years   ☐ Months

IV. Proposed Loan Payments: Payments of $_____ will be made ☐ Monthly ☐ Quarterly ☐ Annually for _____ (number of months, quarters or years). If proposed loan is a variable interest rate loan, this payment will vary (see loan documents for details).

The loan is subject to a balloon payment: ☐ No ☐ Yes. If Yes, the following paragraph applies and a final balloon payment of $_____ will be due on ___/___/___ *[estimated date (day/month/year)]*.

NOTICE TO BORROWER: IF YOU DO NOT HAVE THE FUNDS TO PAY THE BALLOON PAYMENT WHEN IT COMES DUE, YOU MAY HAVE TO OBTAIN A NEW LOAN AGAINST YOUR PROPERTY TO MAKE THE BALLOON PAYMENT. IN THAT CASE, YOU MAY AGAIN HAVE TO PAY COMMISSIONS, FEES, AND EXPENSES FOR THE ARRANGING OF THE NEW LOAN. IN ADDITION, IF YOU ARE UNABLE TO MAKE THE MONTHLY PAYMENTS OR THE BALLOON PAYMENT, YOU MAY LOSE THE PROPERTY AND ALL OF YOUR EQUITY THROUGH FORECLOSURE. KEEP THIS IN MIND IN DECIDING UPON THE AMOUNT AND TERMS OF THIS LOAN.

V. Prepayments: The proposed loan has the following prepayment provisions.

☐ No prepayment penalty.
☐ Other (see loan documents for details).
☐ Any payment of principal in any calendar year in excess of 20% of the ☐ original balance ☐ unpaid balance will include a penalty not to exceed _____ months advance interest at the note rate, but not more than the interest that would be charged if the loan were paid to maturity (see loan documents for details).

VI. Credit Life and/or Disability Insurance: The purchase of credit life and/or disability insurance by a borrower is NOT required as a condition of making this proposed loan.

VII. Other Liens: Are there liens currently on this property for which the borrower is obligated?   ☐ No ☐ Yes
If Yes, describe below:

Lienholder's Name	*Amount Owing*	*Priority*

Liens that will remain or are anticipated on this property after the proposed loan for which you are applying is made or arranged (including the proposed loan for which you are applying):

Lienholder's Name	*Amount Owing*	*Priority*

NOTICE TO BORROWER: Be sure that you state the amount of all liens as accurately as possible. If you contract with the broker to arrange this loan, but it cannot be arranged because you did not state these liens correctly, you may be liable to pay commissions, costs, fees, and expenses even though you do not obtain the loan.

VIII. Article 7 Compliance: If this proposed loan is secured by a first deed of trust in a principal amount of less than $30,000 or secured by a junior lien in a principal amount of less than $20,000, the undersigned licensee certifies that the loan will be made in compliance with Article 7 of Chapter 3 of the Real Estate Law.

A. This loan ☐ may ☐ will ☐ will not be made wholly or in part from broker controlled funds as defined in Section 10241(j) of the Business and Professions Code.

B. If the broker indicates in the above statement that the loan "may" be made out of broker-controlled funds, the broker must inform the borrower prior to the close of escrow if the funds to be received by the borrower are in fact broker-controlled funds.

_____	_____	_____	_____
Name of Broker	*License #*	*Broker's Representative*	*License #*

_____
Broker's Address

_____			_____	
Signature of Broker	*Date*	OR	*Signature of Representative*	*Date*

IX. NOTICE TO BORROWER: THIS IS NOT A LOAN COMMITMENT. Do not sign this statement until you have read and understood all of the information in it. All parts of this form must be completed before you sign. Borrower hereby acknowledges the receipt of a copy of this statement.

_____	_____	_____	_____
Borrower	*Date*	*Borrower*	*Date*

Review completed on _____ by _____

Date	*Broker or Designated Representative*	*Dept. of Real Estate License #*

FIGURE 11-8

TRUTH IN LENDING DISCLOSURE STATEMENT
(THIS IS NEITHER A CONTRACT NOR A COMMITMENT TO LEND)

Applicants   Prepared By:

Property Address:

Application No: Date Prepared:

ANNUAL PERCENTAGE RATE	FINANCE CHARGE	AMOUNT FINANCED	TOTAL OF PAYMENTS
The cost of your credit as a yearly rate	The dollar amount the credit will cost you	The amount of credit provided to you on your behalf	The amount you will have paid after making all payments as scheduled
%	$	$	$

☐ REQUIRED DEPOSIT: The annual percentage rate does not take into account your required deposit
PAYMENTS: Your payment schedule will be:

Number of Payments	Amount of Payments**	When Payments Are Due	Number of Payments	Amount of Payments**	When Payments Are Due	Number of Payments	Amount of Payments**	When Payments Are Due
		Monthly Beginning			Monthly Beginning			

☐ DEMAND FEATURE: This obligation has a demand feature.
☐ VARIABLE RATE FEATURE: This loan contains a variable rate feature. A variable rate disclosure has been provided earlier.

CREDIT LIFE/CREDIT DISABILITY: Credit life insurance and credit disability insurance are not required to obtain credit, and will not be provided unless you sign and agree to pay the additional cost.

Type	Premium	Signature	
Credit Life		I want credit life insurance.	Signature:
Credit Disability		I want credit disability insurance.	Signature:
Credit Life and Disability		I want credit life and disability insurance.	Signature:

INSURANCE: The following insurance is required to obtain credit:
☐ Credit life insurance ☐ Credit Disability ☐ Property Insurance ☐ Food Insurance
You may obtain the insurance from anyone you want that is acceptable to creditor
☐ If you purchase ☐ property   ☐ flood insurance from creditor you will pay $ for a one year term.
SECURITY: You are giving a security interest in:
☐ The goods or property being purchased   ☐ Real property you already own.
FILING FEES: $
LATE CHARGE: If a payment is more than   days late, you will be charged   %
PREPAYMENT: If you pay off early, you
☐ may   ☐ will not have to pay a penalty.
☐ may   ☐ will not be entitled to a refund of part of the finance charge.
ASSUMPTION: Someone buying your property
☐ may   ☐ may, subject to conditions   ☐ may not assume the remainder of your loan on the original terms.
See your contract documents for any additional information about nonpayment, default, any required repayment in full before the scheduled date and prepayment refunds and penalties
☐ * means an estimate   ☐ all dated and numerical

** NOTE: The Payments shown above include reserve deposits for Mortgage Insurance (if applicable), but exclude Property Taxes and Insurance.

THE UNDERSIGNED ACKNOWELDGES RECEIVING A COMPLETED COPY OF THIS DISCLOSURE.

_____   _____   _____   _____
(Applicant)   (Date)   (Applicant)   (Date)

_____   _____   _____   _____
(Applicant)   (Date)   (Applicant)   (Date)

_____   _____
(Lender)   (Date)

306 • THE MORTGAGE ORIGINATOR SUCCESS KIT

FIGURE 11-9
Itemization of Amount Financed

Applicants: Lender:

Property Address:

Application No: Date Prepared:

Total Loan Amount $	Prepaid Finance Charge $	Amount Financed $

Applicant   Date   Applicant   Date

FIGURE 11-10
Borrowers' Certification and Authorization

A release of information form that allows the lender to verify any information necessary in order to make a decision on the loan.

Borrowers' Certification and Authorization

CERTIFICATION

The Undersigned certify the following:

1. I/We have applied for a mortgage loan from_____. In applying for the loan, I/We completed a loan application containing various information on the purpose of the loan, the amount and source of the downpayment, employment and income information, and the assets and liabilities. I/We certify that all of the information is true and complete. I/We made no misrepresentations in the loan application or other documents, nor did I/We omit any pertinent information.

2. I/We understand and agree that _____reserves the right to change the mortgage loan review processes to a full documentation program. This may include verifying the information provided on the application with the employer and/or the financial institution.

3. I/We fully understand that it is a Federal crime punishable by fine or imprisonment, or both, to knowingly make any false statements when applying for this mortgage, as applicable under the provisions of Title 18, United States Code, Section 1014.

AUTHORIZATION TO RELEASE INFORMATION

To Whom It May Concern:

1. I/We have applied for a mortgage loan from _____. As part of the application process, _____ and the mortgage guaranty insurer (if any), may verify information contained in my/our loan application and in other documents required in connection with the loan, either before the loan is closed or as part of its quality control program.

2. I/We authorize you to provide to _____ and to any investor to whom _____ may sell my mortgage, any and all information and documentation that they request. Such information includes, but is not limited to, employment history and income; bank, money market and similar account balances; credit history; and copies of income tax returns.

3. _____ or any investor that purchases the mortgage may address this authorization to any party named in the loan application.

4. A copy of this authorization may be accepted as an original.

Borrower Signature_____   Co-Borrower Signature_____

SSN: _____Date: _____   SSN: _____ Date: _____

FIGURE 11-11
Privacy Policy Disclosure
Advises the borrower of the lender's privacy policies regarding confidentiality of information provided by the borrower.

PRIVACY POLICY DISCLOSURE
(Protection of the Privacy of Personal Nonpublic Information)

Respecting and protecting customer privacy is vital to our business. By explaining our Privacy Policy to you, we trust that you will understand how we keep our customer information private and secure while using it to serve you better. Keeping customer information secure is a top priority, and we are disclosing our policies to help you understand how we handle the personal information about you that we collect and disclose. This notice explains how you can limit our disclosing of personal information about you. The provisions of this notice will apply to former customers as well as current customers unless we state otherwise.

The Privacy Policy Explains the Following:
- Protecting the confidentiality of our customer information.
- Who is covered by the Privacy Policy.
- How we gather information.
- The types of information we share, why, and with whom.
- Opting Out—how to instruct us not to share certain information about you or not to contact you.

Protecting the Confidentiality of Customer Information:

We take our responsibility to protect the privacy and confidentiality of customer information very seriously. We maintain physical, electronic, and procedural safeguards that comply with federal standards to store and secure information about you from unauthorized access, alteration, and destruction. Our control policies, for example, authorize access to customer information only by individuals who need access to do their work.

From time to time, we enter into agreements with other companies to provide services to us or make products and services available to you. Under these agreements, the companies may receive information about you but they must safeguard this information, and they may not use it for any other purposes.

Who Is Covered by the Privacy Policy:

We provide our Privacy Policy to customers when they conduct business with our company. If we change our privacy policies to permit us to share additional information we have about you, as described below, or to permit disclosures to additional types of parties, you will be notified in advance. This Privacy Policy applies to consumers who are current customers or former customers.

How We Gather Information:

As part of providing you with financial products or services, we may obtain information about you from the following sources:
- Applications, forms, and other information that you provide to us, whether in writing, in person, by telephone, electronically, or by any other means. This information may include your name, address, employment information, income, and credit references;
- Your transaction with us, our affiliates, or others. This information may include your account balances, payment history, and account usage;
- Consumer reporting agencies. This information may include account information and information about your credit worthiness;
- Public sources. This information may include real estate records, employment records, telephone numbers, etc.

Information We Share:

We may disclose information we have about you as permitted by law. We are required to or we may provide information about you to third parties without your consent, as permitted by law, such as:

- To regulatory authorities and law enforcement officials.
- To protect against or prevent actual or potential fraud, unauthorized transactions, claims, or other liability.
- To report account activity to credit bureaus.
- To consumer reporting agencies.

FIGURE 11-11 (*Continued*)

- To respond to a subpoena or court order, judicial process or regulatory authorities.
- In connection with a proposed or actual sale, merger, or transfer of all or a portion of a business or an operating unit, etc.

In addition, we may provide information about you to our service providers to help us process your applications or service your accounts. Our service providers may include billing service providers, mail and telephone service companies, lenders, investors, title and escrow companies, appraisal companies, etc.

We may also provide information about you to our service providers to help us perform marketing services. This information provided to these service providers may include the categories of information described above under "How We Gather Information" limited to only that which we deem appropriate for these service providers to carry out their functions.

We do not provide non-public information about you to any company whose products and services are being marketed unless you authorize us to do so. These companies are not allowed to use this information for purposes beyond your specific authorization.

Opting Out

We also may share information about you within our corporate family of office(s). We may share all of the categories of information we gather about you, including identification information (such as your name and address), credit reports (such as your credit history), application information (such as your income or credit references), your account transactions and experiences with us (such as your payment history), and information from other third parties (such as your employment history).

By sharing this information we can better understand your financial needs. We can then send you notification of new products and special promotional offers that you may not otherwise know about. For example, if you originally obtained a mortgage loan with us, we would know that you are a homeowner and may be interested in hearing how a home equity loan may be a better option than an auto loan to finance the purchase of a new car.

You may prohibit the sharing of application and third-party credit-related information within our company or any third-party company at anytime. If you would like to limit disclosures of personal information about you as described in this notice, just check the appropriate box or boxes to indicate your privacy choices.

- ☐ Please do not share personal information about me with non-affiliated third parties.
- ☐ Please do not share personal information about me with any of your affiliates except as necessary to effect, administer, process, service or enforce a transaction requested or authorized by myself.
- ☐ Please do not contact me with offers of products or services by mail.
- ☐ Please do not contact me with offers of products or services by telephone.

Note for Joint Accounts: Your Opt Out choices will also apply to other individuals who are joint account holders. If those individuals have separate accounts, your Opt Out will not apply to those separate accounts.

Name_____	Company Name_____
Address_____	Address_____
City, State, Zip_____	City, State, Zip_____
Phone #_____	Phone #_____
Loan # _____	
Signature_____	Date _____

FIGURE 11-12
Notice of Applicant's Right to Receive a Copy of Appraisal Report
A borrower has the right to request a copy of the appraisal as long as the borrower paid for it. Typically the request is required in writing and within 30 days of the closing date.

**· NOTICE TO APPLICANT OF RIGHT
TO RECEIVE COPY OF APPRAISAL REPORT**

APPLICATION NO:

PROPERTY ADDRESS:

You have the right to receive a copy of the appraisal report to be obtained in connection with the loan for which you are applying, provided that you have paid for the appraisal. We must receive your written request no later than _____ days after we notify you about the action taken on your application or you withdraw your application. If you would like a copy of the appraisal report, contact: _____.

_____ _____ _____ _____
(Applicant)　　　　　　　　　　　　　(Date)　　　　　　(Applicant)　　　　　　　　　　　　　(Date)

FIGURE 11-13
Servicing Disclosure Statement
This form advises the borrower of the lender's right to sell or transfer the servicing rights of the loan.

SERVICING DISCLOSURE STATEMENT

Lender:　　　　　　　　　　　　　　　　　　　　　　　　Date:

NOTICE TO　　　　　MORTGAGE LOAN APPLICANTS: THE RIGHT TO COLLECT YOUR MORTGAGE LOAN PAYMENTS MAY BE TRANSFERRED. FEDERAL LAW GIVES YOU CERTAIN RELATED RIGHTS. IF YOUR LOAN IS MADE, SAVE THIS STATEMENT WITH YOUR LOAN DOCUMENTS. SIGN THE ACKNOWLEDGMENT AT THE END OF THIS STATEMENT ONLY IF YOU UNDERSTAND ITS CONTENTS.

Because you are applying for a mortgage loan covered by the Real Estate Settlement Procedures Act (RESPA) (12 U.S.C. Section 2601 et seq.) you have certain rights under that Federal law.

This statement tells you about those rights. It also tells you what the chances are that the servicing for this loan may be transferred to a different loan servicer. "Servicing" refers to collecting your principal, interest and escrow account payments, if any. If your loan servicer changes, there are certain procedures that must be followed. This statement generally explains those procedures,

Transfer practices and requirements
If the servicing of your loan is assigned, sold, or transferred to a new servicer, you must be given written notice of that transfer. The present loan servicer must send you notice in writing of the assignment, sale or transfer of the servicing not less than 15 days before the effective date of the transfer. The new loan servicer must also send you notice within 15 days after the effective date of the transfer. The present servicer and the new servicer may combine this information in one notice, so long as the notice is sent to you 15 days before the effective date of transfer. The 15 day period is not applicable if a notice of prospective transfer is provided to you at settlement. The law allows a delay in the time (not more than 30 days after a transfer) for servicers to notify you, upon the occurrence of certain business emergencies.

Notices must contain certain information. They must contain the effective date of the transfer of the servicing of your loan to the new servicer, and the name, address, and toll-free or collect call telephone number of the new servicer, and toll-free or collect call telephone numbers of a person or department for both your present servicer and your new servicer to answer your questions. During the 60 day period following the effective date of the transfer of the loan servicing, a loan payment received by your old servicer before its due date may not be treated by the new loan servicer as late, and a late fee may not be imposed on you.

Complaint Resolution
Section 6 of RESPA (12 U.S.C. Section 2605) gives you certain consumer rights, whether or not your loan servicing is transferred. If you send a "qualified written request" to your servicer, then your servicer must provide you with a written acknowledgment within 20 Business Days of receipt of your request. A "qualified written request" is a written correspondence, other than notice on a payment coupon or other payment medium supplied by the servicer, which includes your name and account number, and the information regarding your request. Not later than 60 Business Days after receiving your request, your servicer must make any appropriate corrections to your account, or must provide you with a written clarification regarding any dispute. During this 60 Business Day period, your servicer may not provide information to a consumer reporting agency concerning any overdue payment related to such period or qualified written request.

A Business Day is any day in which the offices of the business entity are open to the public for carrying on substantially all of its business functions.

Damages and Costs
Section 6 of RESPA also provides for damages and costs for individuals or classes of individuals in circumstances where servicers are shown to have violated the requirements of that Section.

Page 1 of 2

FIGURE 11-13 (*Continued*)

Servicing Transfer Estimates

1.   The following is the best estimate of what will happen to the servicing of your mortgage loan:
          ☐   We may assign, sell or transfer the servicing of your loan while the loan is outstanding.
We are able to service your loan, and we
          ☐   will service your loan.
          ☐   will not service your loan.
          ☐   haven't decided whether to service your loan.
_____We do not service mortgage loans_____ and we have not serviced mortgage loans in the past three years.
We presently intend to assign, sell or transfer the servicing of your mortgage loan. You will be informed about your servicer.

2.   For all mortgage loans that we make in the 12 month period after your mortgage loan is funded, we estimate that the percentage of such loans for which we will transfer servicing is between:
                _____ 0 to 25%   _____ 26 to 50% _____ 51 to 75% _____ 76 to 100%

This estimate _____ does _____ does not include assignments, sales or transfers to affiliates or subsidiaries.

This is only our best estimate and it is not binding. Business conditions or other circumstances may affect our future transferring decisions.

3.   A. __ We have previously assigned, sold, or transferred the servicing of mortgage loans.

      B. ____This is our record of transferring the servicing of mortgage loans we have made in:
                Year   Percentage of Loans Transferred
                              %
                              %
                              %
This information ___does ___ does not include assignments, sales or transfers to affiliates or subsidiaries.

Acknowledgment of Mortgage Loan Applicant(s)

I/We have read and understood the disclosure; and understand that the disclosure is a required part of the mortgage application as evidenced by my/our signature(s) below;

_____		_____	
Applicant	Date	Applicant	Date
_____		_____	
Applicant	Date	Applicant	Date

FIGURE 11-14
Credit Score Information Disclosure
This is a state-specific requirement—mostly noted in California and not required in all states.

NOTICE TO HOME LOAN APPLICANT
CREDIT SCORE INFORMATION DISCLOSURE

APPLICANT(S) NAME AND ADDRESS	LENDER NAME AND ADDRESS

In connection with your application for a home loan, the lender must disclose to you the score that a consumer reporting agency distributed to users and the lender used in connection with your home loan, and the key factors affecting your credit score.

The credit score is a computer-generated summary calculated at the time of the request based on information a consumer reporting agency or lender has on file. The scores are based on data about your credit history and payment patterns. Credit scores are important because they are used to assist the lender in determining whether you will obtain a loan. They may also be used to determine what interest rate you may be offered on the mortgage. Credit scores can change over time, depending on your conduct, how your credit history and payment patterns change, and how credit-scoring technologies change.

Because the score is based on information in your credit history, it is very important that you review the credit related information that is being furnished to make sure it is accurate. Credit records may vary from one company to another.

If you have questions about your credit score or the credit information that is furnished to you, contact the consumer reporting agency at the address and telephone number provided with this notice, or contact the lender, if the lender developed or generated the credit score. The consumer reporting agency plays no part in the decision to take any action on the loan application and is unable to provide you with specific reasons for the decision on a loan application.

If you have questions concerning the terms of the loan, contact the lender.

The credit bureau(s) listed below provided a credit score that was used in connection with your home loan application.

CREDIT BUREAU #1	CREDIT BUREAU #2	CREDIT BUREAU #3
Model Used: _____ Range of Possible Scores _____ to _____	Model Used: _____ Range of Possible Scores _____ to _____	Model Used: _____ Range of Possible Scores _____ to _____
BORROWER Name: _____ Score: _____ Created: _____ Factors:	**BORROWER** Name: _____ Score: _____ Created: _____ Factors:	**BORROWER** Name: _____ Score: _____ Created: _____ Factors:
CO-BORROWER Name: _____ Score: _____ Created: _____ Factors:	**CO-BORROWER** Name: _____ Score: _____ Created: _____ Factors:	**CO-BORROWER** Name: _____ Score: _____ Created: _____ Factors:

I/We have received a copy of this disclosure.

_____   _____   _____   _____
Applicant   Date   Applicant   Date

FIGURE 11-15
Disclosure Notices

This is a combination disclosure that includes an affidavit of occupancy, an anticoercion statement, and a Fair Credit Reporting Act statement.

DISCLOSURE NOTICES

Date:

Applicant(s):	Property Address:

AFFIDAVIT OF OCCUPANCY

Applicant(s) hereby certify and acknowledge that, upon taking title to the real property described above, their occupancy status will be as follows:

☐   Primary Residence – Occupied by Applicant(s) within 30 days of closing.

☐   Secondary Residence – To be occupied by Applicant(s) at least 15 days yearly, as second home (vacation, etc.) while maintaining principal residence elsewhere. [Please check this box if you plan to establish it as your primary residence at a future date (e.g., retirement].

☐   Investment Property – Not owner occupied. Purchased as an investment to be held or rented.

The Applicant(s) acknowledge it is a federal crime punishable by fine or imprisonment, or both, to knowingly make any false statement concerning this loan application as applicable under the provisions of Title 18, United Stated Code, Section 1014.

_____   _____
APPLICANT SIGNATURE   CO-APPLICANT SIGNATURE

ANTI-COERCION STATEMENT

The insurance laws of this state provide that the lender may not require the applicant to take insurance through any particular insurance agent or company to protect the mortgaged property. The applicant, subjected to the rules adopted by the insurance Commissioner, has the right to have the insurance placed with an insurance agent or company of his choice, provided the company meets the requirements of the lender. The lender has the right to designate reasonable financial requirements as to the company and the adequacy of the coverage.
I have read the foregoing statement, or the rules of the Insurance Commissioner relative hereto, and understand my rights and privileges and those of the lender relative to the placing of such insurance.
I have selected the following agencies to write the insurance covering the property described above:

_____   _____
Insurance Company Name   Agent

_____   _____
Agent's Address   Agent's Telephone Number

_____   _____
APPLICANT SIGNATURE   CO-APPLICANT SIGNATURE

FAIR CREDIT REPORTING ACT

An investigation will be made as to the credit standing of all individuals seeking credit in this application. The nature and scope of any investigation will be furnished to you upon written request made within a reasonable period of time. In the event of credit denial due to an unfavorable consumer report, you will be advised of the identify of the Consumer Reporting Agency making such report and of your right to request within sixty (60) days the reason for the adverse action, pursuant to provisions of section 615(b) of the Fair Credit Reporting Act.

_____   _____
APPLICANT SIGNATURE   CO-APPLICANT SIGNATURE

FHA LOANS ONLY

IF YOU PREPAY YOUR LOAN ON OTHER THAN THE REGULAR INSTALLMENT DATE, YOU MAY BE ASSESSED INTEREST CHARGED UNTIL THE END OF THAT MONTH.

GOVERNMENT LOANS ONLY

RIGHT TO FINANCIAL PRIVACY ACT OF 1978 – This is a notice to you as required by the Right to Financial Privacy Act of 1978 that the Department of Housing and Urban Development or Department of Veterans Affairs has a right of access to financial records held by a financial institution in connection with the consideration of administration of assistance to you.

_____   _____
APPLICANT SIGNATURE   CO-APPLICANT SIGNATURE

FIGURE 11-16

EQUAL CREDIT OPPORTUNITY ACT

APPLICATION NO:

PROPERTY ADDRESS:

The Federal Equal Credit Opportunity Act prohibits creditors from discriminating against credit applicants on the basis of race, color, religion, national origin, sex, marital status, age (provided the applicant has the capacity to enter into a binding contract); because all or part of the applicant's income derives from any public assistance program; or because the applicant has in good faith exercised any right under the Consumer Credit Protection Act. The Federal Agency that administers compliance with this law concerning this company is

We are required to disclose to you that you need not disclose income from alimony, child support or separate maintenance payment if you choose not to do so.

Having made this disclosure to you, we are permitted to inquire if any of the income shown on your application is derived from such a source and to consider the likelihood of consistent payment as we do with any income on which you are relying to qualify for the loan for which you are applying.

(Applicant)	(Date)	(Applicant)	(Date)

FIGURE 11-17
Fair Lending Notice

THE HOUSING FINANCIAL DISCRIMINATION ACT OF 1977

FAIR LENDING NOTICE

DATE: COMPANY:

APPLICATION NO:

PROPERTY ADDRESS:

It is illegal to discriminate in the provisions of or in the availability of financial assistance because of the consideration of:

1. Trends, characteristics or conditions in the neighborhood or geographic area surrounding a housing accommodation, unless the financial institution can demonstrate in the particular case that such consideration is required to avoid an unsafe and unsound business practice; or

2. Race, color, religion, sex, marital status, national origin or ancestry.

It is illegal to consider the racial, ethnic, religious or national origin composition of a neighborhood or geographic area surrounding a housing accommodation or whether or not such composition is undergoing change, or is expected to undergo change, in appraising a housing accommodation or in determining whether or not, or under what terms and conditions, to provide financial assistance.

These provisions govern financial assistance for the purpose of the purchase, construction, rehabilitation or refinancing of a one-to-four unit family residence occupied by the owner and for the purpose of the home improvement of any one-to-four unit family residence.

If you have any questions about your rights, or if you wish to file a complaint, contact the management of this financial institution or the agency noted below:

I/we received a copy of this notice.

_____   _____
Date   Date

FIGURE 11-18
Standard Flood Hazard Determination Letter

Advises the borrower of the requirement of flood insurance if the property is located in a flood zone.

Federal Emergency Management Agency **STANDARD FLOOD HAZARD DETERMINATION**	See the Attached Instructions	O.M.B. No. 3067-0264 Expires October 31,2005

SECTION I – LOAN INFORMATION

1. LENDER NAME AND ADDRESS	2. COLLATERAL (Building/Mobile Home/Personal Property) PROPERTY ADDRESS (Legal Description may be attached)	
3. LENDER ID. NO.	4. LOAN IDENTIFIER	5. AMOUNT OF FLOOD INSURANCE REQUIRED $

SECTION II

A. NATIONAL FLOOD INSURANCE PROGRAM (NFIP) COMMUNITY JURISDICTION

1. **NFIP Community** Name	2. **County (ies)**	3. **State**	4.	**NFIP Community** **Number**

B. NATIONAL FLOOD INSURANCE PROGRAM (NFIP) DATA AFFECTING BUILDING/MOBILE HOME

1. NFIP Map Number or Community-Panel Number (Community name, if not the same as "A")	2. **County (ies)**	3. **LOMA/LOMR**	4. **Flood Zone**	5. **No NFIP** **Map**
		☐ Yes ——— **Date**		

C. FEDERAL FLOOD INSURANCE AVAILABILITY   (Check all that apply)

1. ☐   Federal Flood Insurance is available   (community participates in NFIP).   ☐   Regular Program   ☐   Emergency Program of NFIP
2. ☐   Federal Flood Insurance is not available because community is not participating in the NFIP

3. ☐   Building/Mobile Home is in a Coast Barrier Resource Area (CBRA) or Otherwise Protected Area (OPA), Federal Flood Insurance may not be available.
   CBRA/OPA designation date: _____

D. DETERMINATION

IS BUILDING/MOBILE HOME IN SPECIAL FLOOD HAZARD AREA
(ZONES CONTAINING THE LETTERS "A" OR "V")?   ☐   YES   ☐   NO

If yes, flood insurance is required by the Flood Disaster Protection Act of 1973.
If no, flood insurance is not required by the Flood Disaster Protection Act of 1973.

E. COMMENTS (Optional):

This determination is based on examining the NFIP map, any Federal Emergency Management Agency revisions to it, and any other information needed to locate the building/mobile home on the NFIP map.

F. PREPARER'S INFORMATION

NAME, ADDRESS, TELEPHONE NUMBER (If other than Lender)	DATE OF DETERMINATION

FIGURE 11-19
Flood Hazard Notice and Flood Disaster Protection Act

**FLOOD DISASTER
PROTECTION ACT OF 1973**

DATE:

APPLICATION NO:

PROPERTY ADDRESS:

I/We hereby acknowledge that we have been advised of the Flood Disaster Protection Act of 1973 and the requirements that I/We provide such insurance coverage on any property located within an area designated as a Flood Hazard Area. Should the subject property fall within a flood hazard area as defined in the Act, then I/We authorize its successors and/or assigns to purchase such insurance and I/We further agree to pay promptly the cost thereof.

_____   _____   _____   _____
(Applicant)   (Date)   (Applicant)   (Date)

FIGURE 11-20
Mortgage Broker Business Contract

This is a state-specific disclosure and requires the broker to disclose any fees charged to the borrower.

MORTGAGE BROKERAGE BUSINESS CONTRACT

_____
(hereinafter called Borrower) , employs _____ (hereinafter
called Business) to obtain a mortgage loan commitment (hereinafter called Commitment) within days from the date hereof and
acknowledges that Business cannot make loans or commitments or guarantee acceptance into specific programs, terms or conditions
of any loan. However, Business may issue a rate lock-in or commitment on behalf of a lender to the Borrower.

I. PROPERTY:

Address:

Borrower's estimates of fair market value: $

Borrower's estimates of the balances on any existing mortgage loan: $

II. TERMS OF LOAN APPLICATION:

Loan Amount: $ Interest Rate: %   Loan Term/Due In: months   months

Monthly Payment: $

Loan Type: _____First Mortgage_____ Second/Junior Mortgage

III. MORTGAGE BROKERAGE FEE

Business, in consideration of the Borrower's agreement to pay a mortgage brokerage fee along with actual costs incurred in
connection with this loan, agrees to exert its best efforts to obtain a bona fide mortgage loan commitment in accordance with the terms
(or better terms) and conditions set forth herein. The Business and its associates or employees shall be held harmless from any liability
resulting from failure to obtain said loan commitment. Borrower hereby agrees to pay the actual costs as estimated herein and
Borrower agrees to pay Business a mortgage broker age fee of **$**_____ for obtaining the commitment. Additionally, Borrower
acknowledges that Business may receive additional compensation from Lender based on the mortgage program and terms Borrower
has engaged Business to obtain in securing the commitment and that Business will receive a sum in range of   **%** to   **%** of the
total loan amount. This additional compensation, the exact amount of which will be disclosed at the time of closing, is part of the total
brokerage fee due Business. In no event will the brokerage fee, additional compensation included, exceed the maximum fee permitted
by the applicable state law.

IV. APPLICATION FEE

An application fee is charged for the initial cost of processing, verifying and preparing your loan package to submit to a lender for
commitment, and will be credited against the amount the Borrower owes if closing occurs. This fee is ____Refundable _____Non-
refundable ____ applicable to your closing costs at the time of the settlement of your loan. Business acknowledges the receipt of
$ as an Application Fee.

V. DEPOSIT

Business acknowledges the deposit of $ will be used toward the costs incurred by the Business, or by third party, on behalf
of Borrower, to pay expenses necessary to secure the mortgage loan commitment. Actual costs incurred by the Business for items
listed on Good Faith Estimate are non-refundable, even if the mortgage loan commitment is not received. In the event of default by the
Borrower, Business is authorized to immediately disburse from the deposit all sums then due Business or any third party. The
disbursement is not a waiver of any other sums due Business by Borrower, as more fully enumerated herein. Money retained by
Business as the deposit shall be returned to the Borrower, within 60 days of disposition of the loan, in accordance with the following:

    (a) the services for which the money is expended are not performed,

    (b) the services for which the money is expended are performed, but there is an excess amount that would be paid as
        brokerage fee but this commitment is not obtained.

VI. SERVICES TO BE PROVIDED BY MORTGAGE BROKERAGE BUSINESS

In consideration for Business earning its fee, the services to be provided by Business are: assembling information, compiling files and
completing credit application for borrower(s), processing the application file including verifying of information received and ordering
vendor reports, preparing and submitting the completed file for conditional loan commitment between borrower(s) and lender, and any
incidental services necessary to obtain commitment including courier, express mail, photographs, and telephone toll charges.

_____   _____
Applicant   Date   Mortgage Broker Business   License #

_____   _____
Applicant   Date   By   Date

Page 1 of 2

FIGURE 11-20 (*Continued*)

STANDARDS AND DISCLOSURES

COMMITMENT: Brokerage Business hereby agrees to act on behalf of Borrower to secure a mortgage loan commitment. Brokerage Business cannot guarantee acceptance into any particular loan program or promise that any specific loan terms or conditions will be obtained. Receipt of a mortgage loan commitment by Brokerage Business satisfies Brokerage Business's obligation under the Mortgage Brokerage Business Contract and Good Faith Estimate of Borrower's Costs and the terms of this contract are deemed fulfilled upon receipt of the mortgage loan commitment. Brokerage Business cannot make a mortgage loan or a Mortgage Loan Commitment. A Commitment may, however, be passed through to the Borrower if received from a lender. The term "Commitment' shall mean a written or oral Commitment received by the Brokerage Business, unless otherwise agreed in writing between Brokerage Business and Borrower. Upon demand by the Borrower, the Brokerage Business shall produce for the Borrower's inspection evidence of the mortgage loan commitment.

AGENCY; NON-LIABILITY FOR LENDER'S ACTS: Borrower acknowledges that Brokerage Business is acting as an 'agent' on behalf of the Borrower in securing a mortgage commitment pursuant to this Agreement. Borrower acknowledges that Brokerage Business shall not be responsible for any errors of the Lender or Investor nor for any term or condition of the loan documentation that may be contrary to any or federal law. Brokerage Business shall not be responsible for any non-performance of a commitment or mortgage by any Lender or Investor.

LITIGATION: In the event of any litigation arising out of this Agreement, Brokerage Business shall be entitled to all costs incurred, including attorney's fees, whether before trial, at trial, on appeal, or in any other administrative or quasi-judicial proceedings.

ADDITIONAL CLAUSES: If not precluded by the provisions of this Agreement, any loan commitment and loan obtained by Brokerage Business may contain such additional clauses or provisions as the Lender may request including, but not limited to, non-assumable clauses, late fee clauses and prepayment penalties.

TIME FOR PAYMENT: Unless otherwise agreed between Brokerage Business and Borrower, the mortgage brokerage fee shall be due and payable in full upon delivery to the Borrower of mortgage loan commitment from the Lender or Investor, or may be paid at closing, if agreed to by Brokerage Business.

DECISION: In applying for this loan, Borrower acknowledges that Borrower has reviewed his personal and financial situation and that it is in Borrower's best interest to proceed with the loan. Borrower further acknowledges that Borrower has not relied on the advice of the Mortgage Brokerage Business or its colleagues as to wisdom of doing so.

GOOD FAITH ESTIMATE OF COSTS: The estimated costs stated may be expressed as a range of possible costs and can be charged only when such costs have actually been incurred in connection with securing the loan or loan commitment. Actual costs incurred for items which include, but are not limited to, express mail fees, long distance calls and photographs will be paid by Borrower unless otherwise stated herein.

TITLE: Borrower represents and warrants that he is the fee simple title-holder to the property described in this Agreement and there are no liens, judgements, unpaid taxes or mortgages, which will affect title to the property except Borrower agrees to pay all costs necessary to clear any defect if status of the title differs from the representation made herein

DEFAULT: If commitment is secured and title is not found to be good, marketable and insurable by the attorney or title company acting for the lender, or the Borrower refuses to execute and deliver the documents required by the lender, or in any other way fails to comply with this Agreement, or if for any reason the loan referenced to herein cannot be closed through no fault of the Brokerage Business, Borrower acknowledges that the full brokerage fee has been earned by Brokerage Business and agrees to immediately pay same plus any and all costs incurred on Borrower's behalf

DISCLOSURE: Borrower acknowledges that Brokerage Business has advised him of any existing business relationship Brokerage Business has with any vendor. Borrower also acknowledges that Lender may require certain pre-approved vendors be used exclusively for services required by this agreement. Brokerage Business has no business relationship with any vendor except as may be listed on attached Provider Relationship form.

SEVERABILITY OF CLAUSES CONTAINED HEREIN: In the event that any part or portion of this Agreement is held invalid or unlawful through any administrative, quasi-judicial, or judicial proceeding, the invalidity or illegality thereof shall not affect the validity of this Agreement as a whole and the other provisions and terms contained herein shall remain in full force and effect as if the illegal or invalid provision had been eliminated.

_____	_____	_____	_____
Applicant	Date	Applicant	Date

FIGURE 11-21
Mortgage Loan Origination Agreement
Another state-specific disclosure; not required in all states.

MORTGAGE LOAN ORIGINATION AGREEMENT
(Warning to Broker: The content of this form may vary depending upon the state in which it is used.)

You   agree to enter into this Mortgage Loan Origination
Agreement with   as an independent contractor to apply for a
residential mortgage loan from a participating lender with which we from time to time contract upon such terms and
conditions as you may request or a lender may require. You inquired into mortgage financing with
                                         on
We are licensed as a "Mortgage Broker" under

SECTION 1. NATURE OF RELATIONSHIP. In connection with this mortgage loan:

•   We are acting as an independent contractor and not as your agent.

•   We will enter into separate independent contractor agreements with various lenders.

•   While we seek to assist you in meeting your financial needs, we do not distribute the products of all lenders
    or investors in the market and cannot guarantee the lowest price or best terms available in the market.

SECTION 2. OUR COMPENSATION. The lenders whose loan products we distribute generally provide their
loan products to us at a wholesale rate.

•   The retail price we offer you—your interest rate, total points and fees—will include our compensation.

•   In some cases, we may be paid all of our compensation by either you or the lender.

•   Alternatively, we may be paid a portion of our compensation by both you and the lender. For example, in
    some cases, if you would rather pay a lower interest rate, you may pay higher up-front points and fees.

•   Also, in some cases, if you would rather pay less up front, you may be able to pay some or all of our
    compensation indirectly through a higher interest rate in which case we will be paid directly by the lender.

We also may be paid by the lender based on (i) the value of the Mortgage Loan or related servicing rights in the
market place or (ii) other services, goods or facilities performed or provided by us to the lender.

By signing below, the mortgage loan originator and mortgage loan applicant(s) acknowledge receipt of a copy of
this signed Agreement.

MORTGAGE LOAN ORIGINATOR	APPLICANT(S)
Company Name	Applicant Name(s)
Address	Address
City, State, Zip	City, State, Zip
Phone/Fax	Borrower Signature Date
Broker or Authorized Agent Signature Date	Co-Borrower Signature Date

---

PROCESSING FORMS

We have also discussed different verification processing forms. Figures 11-22 to 11-24 present three of them.

FIGURE 11-22
Verification of Employment Form

Request for Verification of Employment

FIGURE 11-23
Verification of Rent or Mortgage Form

REQUEST FOR VERIFICATION OF RENT OR MORTGAGE

We have received an application for a loan from the applicant listed below, to whom we understand you rent or have extended a loan.

INSTRUCTIONS: Broker – Complete Items 1 through 8. Have applicant(s) complete Item 9. Forward directly to broker named in Item 1.
LANDLORD/CREDITOR – Please complete Part II as applicable. Sign and return directly to the broker name in Item 2.

PART I—REQUEST

1. TO (Name and address of Landlord/Creditor)		2. FROM (Name and address of broker)	
3. SIGNATURE OF BROKER	4. TITLE	5. DATE	6. BROKER'S NUMBER

7. INFORMATION TO BE VERIFIED.

☐ MORTGAGE ☐ LAND CONTRACT ☐ RENTAL ☐	PROPERTY ADDRESS	ACCOUNT IN THE NAME OF:	ACCOUNT NO.
8. NAME AND ADDRESS OF APPLICANT(S)		9. SIGNATURE OF APPLICANT(S)	

PART II—TO BE COMPLETED BY LANDLORD/CREDITOR

☐ RENTAL ACCOUNT	☐ MORTGAGE ACCOUNT ☐ LAND CONTRACT
Tenant has rented since _____ to _____ Amount of rent $ _____ per _____ Is rent in arrears? Yes ____ No ___ Amount $ _____ Period _____ Number of times 30 days past due* _____ Is account satisfactory? Yes ____ No ___ _____	Date mortgage originated _____ Interest rate _____ Original mortgage amount $_____ Fixed _____ ARM _____ Current mortgage balance $_____ FHA _____ VA _____ Monthly payment P & I only $_____ FNAM _____ CONV _____ Payment with taxes & ins _____ Next pay date _____ Is mortgage current? Yes ____ No ____ No. of late payments* _____ Is mortgage assumable? Yes ____ No ____ Insurance agent: _____ Satisfactory account? Yes ____ No ____ _____ *Number of times account has been 30 days overdue in the last 12 months

ADDITIONAL INFORMATION WHICH MAY BE OF ASSISTANCE IN DETERMINING APPLICANT(S)' CREDIT WORTHINESS

SIGNATURE OF CREDITOR	TITLE	DATE

The confidentiality of the information you furnished will be preserved except where disclosure of this information is required by applicable law. The form is to be transmitted directly to the broker and is not to be transmitted through the applicant or any other party.

FIGURE 11-24
Verification of Deposit Form

Request for Verification of Deposit

Privacy Act Notice: This information is to be used by the agency collecting it or its assignees in determining whether you qualify as a prospective mortgagor under its program. It will not be disclosed outside the agency as required and permitted by law. You do not have to provide this information, but if you do not your application for approval as a prospective mortgagor or borrower may be delayed or rejected. The information requested in this form is authorized by Title 38, USC, Chapter 37 (If VA); by 12 USC, Section 1701 et Seq. (If HUD/FHA); by 42 USC, Section 1452b (If HUD/CPD); and Title 42 USC, 1471 et Seq., or 7 USC, 19 21 et Seq. (If USDA/FmHA).

Instructions: **Broker** – Complete items 1 through 8. Have applicant complete item 9. Forward directly to depository named in item 1. **Depository** – Please complete Items 10 through 18 and return to broker named in Item 2. **The form is to be transmitted directly to the broker and is not to be transmitted through the applicant(s) or any other party.**	Broker 's phone No.

Part I—Request

1. To (Name and address of employer)	2. From (Name and address of broker)

I certify that this verification has been sent directly to the bank or depository and has not passed through the hands of the applicant or any other interested party.

3. Signature of Broker	4. Title	5. Date	6. Broker's No. (Optional)

7. Information to Be Verified

Type of Account	Account in Name of	Account Number	Balance
			$
			$
			$
			$

To Depository: I/We have applied for a mortgage loan and stated in my/our financial statement that the balance on deposit with you is as shown above. You are authorized to verify this information and to supply the broker identified above with the information requested in items 10 through 13. Your response is soley a matter of courtesy for which no responsibility is attached to your institution or any of your officers.

8. Name and Address of Applicant(s)	9. Signature of Applicant(s)
	X
	X

To Be Completed by Depository

Part II—Verification of Depository

10. Deposit Accounts of Applicant(s)

Type of Account	Account Number	Current Balance	Average Balance for Previous Two Months	Date Opened
		$	$	
		$	$	
		$	$	
		$	$	
		$	$	

11. Loans Outstanding to Applicant(s)

Loan Number	Date of Loan	Original Amount	Current Balance	Installments (Monthly/Quarterly)	Secured By	No. of Late Payments
		$	$	$ per		
		$	$	$ per		
		$	$	$ per		

12. Please include any additional information which may be of assistance in determination of credit worthiness (Please include information on loans paid-in full in Item 11 above.)

13. If the name(s) on the account(s) differ from those listed in Item 7, please supply the name(s) on the accounts(s) as reflected by your records.

Part II—Authorized Signature

Federal statutes provide severe penalties for any fraud, intentional misrepresentation or criminal connivance or conspiracy purposed to influence the issuance of any guaranty or insurance by the VA Secretary, the U.S.D.A., FmHA/FHA Commissioner, or the HID/CPD Assistance Secretary.

14. Signature of Depository Representative	15. Title (Please print or type)	16. Date
17. Print or type name signed in Item 14	18. Phone No.	

Quiz Answers

Chapter 1: Mortgage Terms Quiz

1.	C
2.	B
3.	A
4.	C
5.	B
6.	C
7.	A
8.	A
9.	A
10.	B

Chapter 2: Mortgage Basics Quiz

1.	C
2.	B
3.	C
4.	B
5.	B
6.	A
7.	B
8.	C
9.	A
10.	C

Chapter 3: Mortgage Loan Types Quiz

1.	C	11.	A
2.	B	12.	A
3.	B	13.	B
4.	B	14.	B
5.	C	15.	C
6.	A	16.	C
7.	A	17.	B
8.	B	18.	C
9.	B	19.	B
10.	A	20.	A

Chapter 4: Program Guidelines Quiz

1.	A	11.	B
2.	C	12.	B
3.	A	13.	C
4.	B	14.	A
5.	A	15.	C
6.	C	16.	A
7.	C	17.	A
8.	C	18.	B
9.	C	19.	B
10.	B	20.	C

Chapter 5: Mortgage Finance Quiz

1.	C	11.	A
2.	B	12.	C
3.	B	13.	A
4.	C	14.	C
5.	A	15.	C
6.	B	16.	C
7.	C	17.	A
8.	B	18.	A
9.	C	19.	C
10.	A	20.	A

Chapter 6: Borrower Qualification Quiz

1.	B	11.	B
2.	B	12.	C
3.	C	13.	C
4.	A	14.	C
5.	B	15.	B
6.	B	16.	C
7.	A	17.	A
8.	C	18.	B
9.	C	19.	B
10.	A	20.	B

Chapter 7: Property Qualification Quiz

1.	A
2.	C
3.	B
4.	A
5.	C
6.	A
7.	A
8.	B
9.	C
10.	C

Chapter 9: Laws and Ethics Quiz

1.	B
2.	B
3.	B
4.	B
5.	A
6.	A
7.	B
8.	A
9.	A
10.	C

Chapter 8: From the Loan Application to the Closing Quiz

1.	C
2.	A
3.	A
4.	A
5.	B
6.	C
7.	B
8.	C
9.	B
10.	B

11.	C
12.	A
13.	B
14.	C
15.	A

EDUCATIONAL AND LICENSING REQUIREMENTS FOR THE LOAN ORIGINATOR

It is common sense to take a method and try it.
If it fails, admit it frankly and try another.
But above all, try something.
                                    —Franklin D. Roosevelt, 1882

INTRODUCTION

In order to start your career as a mortgage loan originator, you must meet certain *state-specific* educational or licensing requirements. The following section outlines state-specific requirements for when one is employed by a *mortgage broker* company. Be aware that in some states there are *no* educational or licensing requirements to become a mortgage loan originator. Another important factor to note is that certain mortgage lenders, banks, and savings and loans may be exempt from these requirements. Therefore, if a mortgage lender, bank, or savings and loan employs you, it may not be necessary for you to fulfill the requirements.

Recently a number of states have begun to include a criminal background check as part of the requirement of registration for loan originators. A loan originator handles very sensitive financial information, and therefore it is no wonder that to become a licensed loan originator you must have good moral character and no felony or misdemeanor charges involving morale turpitude. What does *morale turpitude* mean? Crimes of moral turpitude are acts that violate accepted moral standards of the community. Some examples of such crimes include, but are not limited to, fraud, forgery, theft, sex crimes, violent crimes against a person, and murder.

In the following section you will find that we have appropriately noted whether a state has any of the following requirements:

- Education

- Testing or exams

- Experience

- Licensing

- Registration

- Background or criminal check

In addition, if a state *does* have educational requirements, we have included a list of *approved* educational providers and their contact information. The same applies for testing and exam requirements. States requiring an exam typically have a designated vendor to provide testing; for those states, we have included appropriate contact information and fees.

We have identified and provided contact information for the appropriate regulating agencies. Due to possible state and local agency changes, you should contact the appropriate regulating agency as provided to verify any specific information.

At the time of printing, all information contained herein was reviewed for accuracy by my staff at Mortgage-Smarts, LLC (www.mortgage-smarts.com). We regularly review and maintain all state and local content for any changes to laws, fees, forms, etc. However, it is inevitable that changes in state and local agency regulations and laws will continue, and so we do not and cannot guarantee that the fees quoted or the laws or requirements provided have not changed.

Definitions for the Loan Originator

A *loan originator* is an individual who, on behalf of a mortgage banker or mortgage broker, finds a loan or negotiates a land contract, loan, or commitment for a loan. A loan originator is any individual, including an officer, W-9 subcontractor employee, or W-2 hourly or salaried employee, who performs these activities:

Finds a loan. Assists a loan applicant both in locating a lender to obtain a loan for the applicant and in making arrangements for the loan applicant to obtain the loan.

Negotiates. Discusses with, explains to, or presents to a loan applicant the terms and conditions of a loan or land contract.

Originates. Makes an underwriting decision on a loan and closes a loan.

EDUCATIONAL AND LICENSING REQUIREMENTS FOR THE LOAN ORIGINATOR, ALABAMA TO WYOMING

The information that follows was last updated July 2005. For changes in laws and updated information, please contact the appropriate regulatory agency; the contact information is provided.

How to Become...

A Loan Originator in Alabama

Regulatory agency: Alabama Banking Department

Contact info: www.bank.state.al.us or call (334) 242-3452

Type of license: Loan originator

Requirements
Education
None required for loan originators.

Licensing
None required for loan originators.

A Loan Originator in Alaska

Regulatory agency: Alaska Banking, Securities, & Corporations Department

Contact info: www.dced.state.ak.us or call (907) 465-2530

Type of license: Loan originator

Requirements

Education
None required for loan originators.

Licensing
None required for loan originators.

A Loan Originator in Arizona

Regulatory agency: Arizona State Banking Department

Contact info: www.azbank.gov or call (602) 255-4421

Type of license: Loan originator

Requirements

Education
None required for loan originators.

Licensing
None required for loan originators.

A Loan Officer in Arkansas

Regulatory agency: Arkansas Securities Department

Contact info: www.arkansas.gov/arsec/ or call (501) 324-9260

Type of license: Loan officer

Requirements

Education
None required for loan officers.

Licensing
$50 annual fee

As of July 2004, licensing is required for all loan officers. To obtain a license, you must:

- Be at least 18 years old

- File an application form (FMLA Form LO-001)

All information must be kept current with the regulating department. If any changes take place, then the loan officer is responsible for filing a Loan Officer Notice of Change FMLA Form LO-002 within 30 days from the date in which the change takes place.

A Real Estate Salesperson in California

In California it is important to note that a loan officer working for a company that is licensed under the California Department of Corporations with a California Residential Mortgage Lender (CRML) license or a California Finance Lenders (CFL) license does *not* need any educational or licensing requirements.

> *Regulatory agency:* California Department of Real Estate (DRE)
>
> *Contact info:* www.dre.ca.gov or call (916) 227-0904
>
> *Type of license:* Real estate salesperson

Requirements

To obtain a real estate salesperson license you must:

- Qualify for and pass a real estate salesperson written exam

- Be 18 years of age or older

- Provide proof of legal presence in the United States and a completed State Public Benefits Statement (Form RE205)

- Be honest and truthful—conviction of a crime may be cause for denial

- Fulfill the necessary educational requirements as listed below

Exam
> $25 fee

In order to take the exam, the applicant must currently be enrolled in a real estate principles course or submit evidence of completion of a real estate principles course. The real estate principles course must be completed prior to the issuance of a real estate salesperson license.

Education

After completion of the exam and real estate principles course a conditional salesperson license is issued. Within 18 months of the conditional license issuance date, the salesperson must submit evidence of completion of a course in real estate practice and one additional course selected from among the following:

- Real estate appraisal

- Property management

- Real estate finance

- Real estate economics

- Legal aspects of real estate

- Real estate office administration

- General accounting

- Business law

- Escrows

- Mortgage loan brokering and lending

- Computer applications in real estate

Note: Each college-level course must be a minimum of three semester units or four quarter units. Copies of official transcripts are generally acceptable evidence of completed courses. Transcripts of equivalent courses, submitted in lieu of the statutory college-level courses, must be supported by an official course or catalog description in order to be evaluated for equivalency. Courses must be completed at an institution of higher learning accredited by the Western Association of Schools and Colleges or by a private real estate school that has had its courses approved by the California Real Estate Commissioner. Courses that are completed through foreign institutions of higher learning must be evaluated by a foreign credentials evaluation service approved by the DRE.

Exemption

If you are a member of the bar of any state in the United States or a graduate of a law school recognized by the California State Bar, you will generally qualify on the basis of your education, and as such you are exempt from the college-level course requirements.

Evidence of admission to practice law, such as a photocopy of both sides of a current state bar membership card or of an LL.B. or J.D. degree, should accompany your application.

In Addition

Applicants who submit evidence of having completed the eight statutory college-level courses required for the broker examination are eligible to take the salesperson examination without providing further evidence of education or experience.

Licensing

$120 fee if applicant is qualified for exam with all three required courses or submits evidence of completing the remaining two courses with license application.

$145 fee if applicant is qualified for exam with real estate principles course only and does not include evidence of completing the remaining two courses with the license application. (In this case, the license obtained is a conditional license.)

Each license is valid for four years.

You will need to allow at least six weeks from the date your transcripts are mailed to the Department of Real Estate to receive the nonconditional license certificate that is issued if the transcripts for the two additional courses are accepted.

Failure to submit transcripts of the two additional required courses within the initial 18-month license period will result in an automatic suspension of the conditional license. The suspension will be in effect for 18 months after issuance, and it will not be lifted until evidence of course completion has been submitted and the Department of Real Estate has mailed notification that the suspension has been removed. If the transcripts for the two additional courses are not submitted within four years of the license issuance date, the license will not be renewed, and it will be necessary to requalify through the examination process if you wish to be licensed as a salesperson again.

Background Check and Fingerprints
There is a $56 fingerprint processing fee and also a live scan service fee that should be paid directly to the live scan provider (not to the DRE).

For any real estate license, the applicant must submit one set of classifiable fingerprints, acceptable to the State Department of Justice (DOJ), unless the applicant is currently licensed by the DRE or has held a real estate license that expired less than two years ago. All fingerprints must be submitted through the DOJ's Live Scan Program, which takes and transmits fingerprints to the DOJ electronically.

A Live Scan Service Request form (RE 237) will be sent to all applicants who successfully complete the real estate examination. An original license will not be issued until a report from the DOJ is received either stating that there is no criminal history or disclosing criminal history information, which then must be reviewed and evaluated.

When you are ready to be fingerprinted, take the RE 237 to a participating live scan service provider. After the live scan service provider takes the fingerprints, the applicant must submit to the DRE a copy of the RE 237 with Part 3 completed, along with the applicant's completed original license application and the appropriate fee.

A list of live scan service providers is available at http://caag. state.ca.us/fingerprints/publications/contact.pdf.

Schools for California

A+ INSTITUTE
14525 N. Newport Highway
Mead, WA 99021
(509) 465-4343

Correspondence Course:
Real Estate Principles

ACCREDITED REAL ESTATE SCHOOLS
4120 Manzanita Avenue
Carmichael, CA 95608
(661) 484-4866

Correspondence Courses:
Escrows
Legal Aspects of Real
    Estate
Mortgage Loan Brokering
    and Lending
Property Management
Real Estate Appraisal
Real Estate Economics
Real Estate Finance
Real Estate Practice
Real Estate Principles
Resident Course:
Real Estate Principles

AFFORDABLE INVESTMENT ACADEMY
1566 Alum Rock Avenue
San Jose, CA 95116
(408) 347-0710

Resident Course:
Real Estate Principles

ALLIED REAL ESTATE SCHOOL
22952 Alcalde Drive
Laguna Hills, CA 92653
(949) 598-0875

Correspondence Courses:
Escrows
Legal Aspects of Real
    Estate
Property Management
Real Estate Appraisal
Real Estate Economics
Real Estate Finance
Real Estate Office
    Administration
Real Estate Practice
Real Estate Principles

AMERICA REAL ESTATE SCHOOL
3333 Wilshire Boulevard, #504
Los Angeles, CA 90010
(213) 385-8808

Resident Course:
Real Estate Principles

**AMERICA WEST SCHOOL
OF REAL ESTATE**
1820 Westwind Drive
Bakersfield, CA 93301
(805) 327-2121

Correspondence Course:
Real Estate Principles
Resident Course:
Real Estate Principles

AMERICAN BUSINESS COLLEGE
142 N. 9th Street, Suite 14
Modesto, CA 95350
(209) 523-1333

Resident Courses:
Property Management
Real Estate Principles

**AMERICAN MASTERS
REAL ESTATE SCHOOL**
2801 S. Vermont Avenue, #3
Los Angeles, CA 90007
(909) 437-2904

Resident Course:
Real Estate Principles

AMERICAN SCHOOLS
PO Box 5161
Torrance, CA 90510
(310) 544-2090

Correspondence Courses:
Legal Aspects of Real Estate
Mortgage Loan Brokering
and Lending
Property Management
Real Estate Appraisal
Real Estate Economics
Real Estate Finance
Real Estate Office
Administration
Real Estate Practice
Real Estate Principles

**AMERISTAR REAL ESTATE
SCHOOL**
PO Box 1143
San Gabriel, CA 91778
(415) 681-6188

Correspondence Courses:
Legal Aspects of Real Estate
Property Management
Real Estate Appraisal
Real Estate Economics

Real Estate Finance
Real Estate Office
  Administration
Real Estate Practice
Real Estate Principles

ANTHONY SCHOOLS, A KAPLAN PROFESSIONAL COMPANY

2646 Dupont Drive, Suite 230
Irvine, CA 92612
(800) 726-7767

Correspondence Courses:
Escrows
Legal Aspects of Real
  Estate
Mortgage Loan Brokering
  and Lending
Property Management
Real Estate Appraisal
Real Estate Economics
Real Estate Finance
Real Estate Office
  Administration
Real Estate Practice
Real Estate Principles

Resident Courses:
Escrows
Legal Aspects of
  Real Estate
Mortgage Loan Brokering
  and Lending
Property Management
Real Estate Appraisal
Real Estate Economics
Real Estate Finance
Real Estate Office
  Administration
Real Estate Practice
Real Estate Principles

BAYTECH COLLEGE

1580 Oakland Road, #C210
San Jose, CA 95131
(408) 452-1700

Resident Course:
Real Estate Principles

**BEST FINANCIAL REAL ESTATE
SCHOOL**
2211 Hacienda Boulevard, #100M
Hacienda Heights, CA 91745
(626) 369-3877

Correspondence Courses:
Real Estate Finance
Real Estate Practice
Real Estate Principles

**CALIFORNIA ACADEMY
OF REAL ESTATE**
18817 Napa Street
Northridge, CA 91324
(818) 885-7828

Correspondence Courses:
Escrows
Legal Aspects of Real Estate
Property Management
Real Estate Appraisal
Real Estate Economics
Real Estate Finance
Real Estate Practice
Real Estate Principles

**CALIFORNIA ASSOCIATION
OF REALTORS**
525 S. Virgil Avenue
Los Angeles, CA 90020
(213) 739-8200

Resident Courses:
Legal Aspects of Real Estate
Real Estate Practice

CALIFORNIA BROKERS INSTITUTE
21133 Victory Boulevard, #216
Canoga Park, CA 91303
(818) 715-0088

Correspondence Courses:
Escrows
Legal Aspects of Real Estate
Mortgage Loan Brokering
  and Lending
Property Management
Real Estate Appraisal
Real Estate Economics
Real Estate Finance
Real Estate Office
  Administration
Real Estate Practice
Real Estate Principles

CALIFORNIA CAREER COLLEGE
977 W. Center Street, Suite 3
Manteca, CA 95337
(209) 239-1700

Correspondence Courses:
Property Management
Real Estate Finance
Real Estate Practice
Real Estate Principles

Resident Courses:
Property Management
Real Estate Finance
Real Estate Principles

**CALIFORNIA SCHOOL OF
REAL ESTATE**
7700 Edgewater Drive, Suite 745
Oakland, CA 94621
(510) 568-6460

Correspondence Courses:
Escrows
Legal Aspects of Real Estate
Mortgage Loan Brokering
　and Lending
Property Management
Real Estate Appraisal
Real Estate Economics
Real Estate Finance
Real Estate Practice
Real Estate Principles

CALIFORNIALICENSE.COM
400 S. Beverly Drive, #210
Beverly Hills, CA 90212
(310) 553-7686

Correspondence Courses:
Property Management
Real Estate Appraisal
Real Estate Finance
Real Estate Practice
Real Estate Principles

CAREER WEBSCHOOL
1395 S. Marietta Parkway
Building 400, Suite 107
Marietta, GA 30067
(404) 919-9191

Correspondence Course:
Real Estate Principles

**CENTURY 21 REAL ESTATE
SCHOOLS**
2428 N. Grand Avenue, Suite K
Santa Ana, CA 92705
(800) 300-7375

Resident Course:
Real Estate Principles

CENTURY 21 REGION V
2428 N. Grand Avenue, Suite K
Santa Ana, CA 92705
(800) 872-4679

Correspondence Course:
Real Estate Principles

**CHAMBERLIN REAL ESTATE
SCHOOL, INC.**
1825 Winchester Boulevard
Campbell, CA 95008
(408) 378-4400

Correspondence Courses:
Business Law
Legal Aspects of Real Estate
Mortgage Loan Brokering
   and Lending
Property Management
Real Estate Appraisal
Real Estate Economics
Real Estate Finance
Real Estate Office
   Administration
Real Estate Practice
Real Estate Principles

CLARE INSTITUTE
8360 Clairemont Mesa Boulevard, #106
San Diego, CA 92111
(858) 467-9280

Correspondence Courses:
Legal Aspects of Real Estate
Mortgage Loan Brokering
   and Lending
Property Management
Real Estate Appraisal
Real Estate Economics
Real Estate Finance
Real Estate Practice
Real Estate Principles
Resident Courses:
Legal Aspects of Real Estate
Property Management
Real Estate Appraisal
Real Estate Finance
Real Estate Practice
Real Estate Principles

COLLEGE OF THE REDWOODS
7351 Tompkins Hill Road
Eureka, CA 95501-9300
(707) 476-4136

Correspondence Courses:
Legal Aspects of Real Estate
Real Estate Appraisal
Real Estate Finance
Real Estate Practice
Real Estate Principles

COOK SCHOOL OF REAL ESTATE
4305 Freeport Boulevard
Sacramento, CA 95822
(916) 451-6702

Correspondence Course:
Real Estate Principles

COSMOS REALTY SCHOOL
4282 Wilshire Boulevard, #200
Los Angeles, CA 90010
(323) 937-1212

Correspondence Course:
Real Estate Principles
Resident Course:
Real Estate Principles

DENNIS REAL ESTATE COLLEGE
3030 W. Ball Road
Anaheim, CA 92804
(714) 530-2080

Correspondence Courses:
Escrows
Legal Aspects of Real Estate
Real Estate Appraisal
Real Estate Economics
Real Estate Finance
Real Estate Office
   Administration
Real Estate Practice
Real Estate Principles
Resident Course:
Real Estate Principles

DESERT CITIES REAL ESTATE SCHOOL, INC.
34-400 Date Palm Drive, Suite J
Cathedral City, CA 92234
(760) 328-8955

Correspondence Courses:
Business Law
Escrows
Legal Aspects of Real Estate
Mortgage Loan Brokering
   and Lending
Property Management
Real Estate Appraisal
Real Estate Economics
Real Estate Finance
Real Estate Office
   Administration
Real Estate Practice
Real Estate Principles
Resident Course:
Real Estate Principles

DUANE GOMER SEMINARS
23312 Madero Street, Suite J
Mission Viejo, CA 92691
(949) 457-8930

Correspondence Courses:
Business Law
Escrows
Legal Aspects of
   Real Estate
Mortgage Loan Brokering
   and Lending
Property Management
Real Estate Appraisal
Real Estate Economics
Real Estate Finance
Real Estate Practice
Real Estate Principles

DYNASTY SCHOOL
2373 S. Hacienda Boulevard
Hacienda Heights, CA 91745
(800) 888-8827

Correspondence Courses:
Advanced Real Estate
   Appraisal
Escrows
Legal Aspects of
   Real Estate
Property Management
Real Estate Appraisal
Real Estate Economics
Real Estate Finance
Real Estate Office
   Administration
Real Estate Practice
Real Estate Principles

ELITE LICENSING SERVICE
8335 Winnetka Avenue, Suite #235
Canoga Park, CA 91306
(818) 709-0725

Correspondence Courses:
Escrows
Legal Aspects of
   Real Estate
Property Management
Real Estate Appraisal
Real Estate Economics
Real Estate Finance
Real Estate Practice
Real Estate Principles

EXECUTIVE PROGRAMS
210 St. Mary's Drive, #I
PO Box 5407
Oxnard, CA 93030
(800) 416-1996

Correspondence Courses:
Business Law
Escrows
Legal Aspects of Real Estate
Mortgage Loan Brokering
    and Lending
Property Management
Real Estate Appraisal
Real Estate Economics
Real Estate Finance
Real Estate Office
    Administration
Real Estate Practice
Real Estate Principles

FELDE PUBLICATIONS AND PROGRAMS
PO Box 175
San Clemente, CA 92674
(949) 481-2937

Correspondence Courses:
Advanced Real Estate
    Appraisal
Legal Aspects of Real Estate
Mortgage Loan Brokering
    and Lending
Property Management
Real Estate Appraisal
Real Estate Economics
Real Estate Finance
Real Estate Practice
Real Estate Principles
Resident Course:
Real Estate Principles

NOBLE FIELDS
870 Market Street, Suite 623
San Francisco, CA 94102
(415) 956-6169

Correspondence Courses:
Escrows
Legal Aspects of Real Estate
Property Management
Real Estate Appraisal
Real Estate Economics
Real Estate Finance
Real Estate Practice
Real Estate Principles

Resident Courses:
Escrows
Legal Aspects of Real Estate
Mortgage Loan Brokering
  and Lending
Property Management
Real Estate Appraisal
Real Estate Finance
Real Estate Practice
Real Estate Principles

FIRST TUESDAY
PO Box 20069
Riverside, CA 92516-0069
(909) 781-7300

Correspondence Courses:
Legal Aspects of Real Estate
Mortgage Loan Brokering
  and Lending
Property Management
Real Estate Appraisal
Real Estate Economics
Real Estate Finance
Real Estate Practice
Real Estate Principles

GLENN COUNTY OFFICE
OF EDUCATION
525 W. Sycamore
Willows, CA 95988
(530) 934-6575

Resident Courses:
Legal Aspects of Real Estate
Property Management
Real Estate Appraisal
Real Estate Economics
Real Estate Finance
Real Estate Practice
Real Estate Principles

GOLD COAST SCHOOLS
2192 Martin Street, Suite 120
Irvine, CA 92612
(949) 477-2070

Correspondence Courses:
Escrows
Legal Aspects of Real Estate
Property Management
Real Estate Appraisal
Real Estate Economics
Real Estate Finance
Real Estate Practice
Real Estate Principles

GOLDEN CITY PROFESSIONAL STUDIES
2550 W. Main Street, Suite 105
PO Box 7125
Alhambra, CA 91801
(626) 457-8836

Resident Course:
Real Estate Principles

Correspondence Courses:
Escrows
Legal Aspects of Real Estate
Mortgage Loan Brokering
  and Lending
Property Management
Real Estate Appraisal
Real Estate Economics
Real Estate Finance
Real Estate Practice
Real Estate Principles

GOLDEN HYDE REAL ESTATE CENTER
1168 San Gabriel Boulevard, Suite J
Rosemead, CA 91770
(626) 571-0751

Correspondence Courses:
Escrows
Legal Aspects of Real Estate
Property Management
Real Estate Appraisal
Real Estate Economics
Real Estate Finance
Real Estate Practice
Real Estate Principles

GREATER EAST BAY TRAINING CENTER
10749 San Pablo Avenue
El Cerrito, CA 94530
(510) 526-5202

Correspondence Course:
Real Estate Principles

GROSSMONT ADULT SCHOOL
1550 Melody Lane
El Cajon, CA 92019
(619) 579-4770

Resident Course:
Real Estate Principles

HACIENDA LA PUENTE ADULT EDUCATION
1600 Pontenova
Hacienda Heights, CA 91745
(818) 855-3510

Resident Courses:
Escrows
Property Management
Real Estate Appraisal
Real Estate Finance

Real Estate Practice
Real Estate Principles

**HOWARD HANS REAL ESTATE
INSTITUTE**
695 S. Vermont Avenue, #1201
Los Angeles, CA 90005
(213) 385-8889

Correspondence Course:
Real Estate Principles

JOY REAL ESTATE COLLEGE
3699 Wilshire Boulevard, #200
Los Angeles, CA 90010
(213) 365-7700

Correspondence Courses:
Legal Aspects of Real Estate
Property Management
Real Estate Appraisal
Real Estate Economics
Real Estate Finance
Real Estate Office
  Administration
Real Estate Practice
Real Estate Principles
Resident Course:
Real Estate Principles

KOTAI REAL ESTATE SCHOOL
820 E. Mission Drive
San Gabriel, CA 91776
(626) 237-2170

Correspondence Course:
Real Estate Principles

THE LEARNING SOURCE
270 E. Douglas Avenue
El Cajon, CA 92020
(619) 401-4011

Resident Course:
Real Estate Principles

LICENSE EXAM TRAINERS, INC.
2428-K N. Grand Avenue
Santa Ana, CA 92701
(714) 972-2211

Resident Course:
Real Estate Principles

LONDON PROPERTIES, LTD.
6442 N. Maroa Avenue
Fresno, CA 93704
(559) 436-4080

Correspondence Course:
Real Estate Principles

LONG DRAGON REAL ESTATE SCHOOL
2633 S. Baldwin Avenue
Arcadia, CA 91007
(626) 309-7999

Resident Course:
Real Estate Principles

**LOS ANGELES UNIFIED SCHOOL
DISTRICT DIVISION OF ADULT
& CAREER EDUCATION**
333 S. Beaudry Avenue, 18th Floor
Los Angeles, CA 90017
(213) 241-3150

Resident Courses:
Escrows
Real Estate Appraisal
Real Estate Finance
Real Estate Practice
Real Estate Principles

**THE LUMBLEAU REAL ESTATE
SCHOOL, INC., A TEXAS CORPORATION**
14208 Hughes Lane
Dallas, TX 75254
(972) 503-5050

Correspondence Courses:
Escrows
Legal Aspects of Real Estate
Mortgage Loan Brokering
   and Lending
Property Management
Real Estate Appraisal
Real Estate Economics
Real Estate Finance
Real Estate Practice
Real Estate Principles

MERCURY REAL ESTATE SCHOOLS
3500 Buchanan Street, #104
Riverside, CA 92503
(909) 924-0545

Correspondence Courses:
Escrows
Legal Aspects of Real Estate
Property Management
Real Estate Appraisal
Real Estate Economics
Real Estate Finance
Real Estate Office
   Administration
Real Estate Practice
Real Estate Principles

**MIKE RUSS FINANCIAL
TRAINING CENTERS**
8322 Clairemont Mesa Boulevard, #103
San Diego, CA 92111-1317
(858) 571-5827

Correspondence Courses:
Escrows
Legal Aspects of Real Estate
Mortgage Loan Brokering
   and Lending

Property Management
Real Estate Appraisal
Real Estate Economics
Real Estate Finance
Real Estate Office
    Administration
Real Estate Practice
Real Estate Principles

MT. SAN ANTONIO COLLEGE
1100 N. Grand Avenue
Attn: Gary Kay
Walnut, CA 91789
(909) 468-3933

Correspondence Course:
Real Estate Principles

NATIONAL LICENSE SERVICES
1701 Corinthian Way, Suite H
Newport Beach, CA 92660
(949) 975-1605

Correspondence Courses:
Escrows
Legal Aspects of Real Estate
Mortgage Loan Brokering
    and Lending
Property Management
Real Estate Appraisal
Real Estate Economics
Real Estate Finance
Real Estate Office
    Administration
Real Estate Practice
Real Estate Principles

NEW STAR REAL ESTATE SCHOOL
9625 Garden Grove Boulevard
Garden Grove, CA 92844
(714) 636-6900

Correspondence Courses:
Escrows
Legal Aspects of Real Estate
Property Management
Real Estate Appraisal
Real Estate Economics
Real Estate Finance
Real Estate Practice
Real Estate Principles
Resident Course:
Real Estate Principles

**NORTH ORANGE COUNTY REGIONAL
OCCUPATIONAL PROGRAM**
385 N. Muller Street
Attn: Lynn Porter
Anaheim, CA 92801-5445
(714) 502-5808

Resident Course:
Escrows

NORWALK-LA MIRADA ADULT SCHOOL
15711 S. Pioneer Boulevard
Norwalk, CA 90650
(562) 868-9858

Resident Course:
Real Estate Principles

**PACIFIC SOUTHWEST ASSOCIATION
OF REALTORS**
880 Canarios Court
Chula Vista, CA 91910
(619) 421-7811

Resident Course:
Real Estate Principles

PACIFIC STATES UNIVERSITY
1516 S. Western Avenue
Los Angeles, CA 90006
(323) 731-2383

Resident Course:
Real Estate Principles

**PARAMOUNT PROPERTIES SCHOOL
OF REAL ESTATE**
9338 Reseda Boulevard, #102
Northridge, CA 91324-2986
(818) 349-9997

Resident Course:
Real Estate Principles

PREMIER SCHOOLS, INC.
11600 W. Olympic Boulevard
Los Angeles, CA 90064
(310) 312-8867

Correspondence Courses:
Escrows
Legal Aspects of Real Estate
Mortgage Loan Brokering
    and Lending
Property Management
Real Estate Appraisal
Real Estate Economics
Real Estate Finance
Real Estate Practice
Real Estate Principles

PREP REAL ESTATE PROGRAMS, INC.
24007 Ventura Boulevard, #110
Calabasas, CA 91302
(800) 662-7737

Correspondence Courses:
Legal Aspects of Real Estate
Real Estate Appraisal
Real Estate Principles

**PROPERTY MANAGEMENT
TRAINING INSTITUTE**
111 Jackson Street, Suite A
Hayward, CA 94544
(510) 881-4390

Resident Courses:
Property Management
Real Estate Principles

**PRUDENTIAL CALIFORNIA SCHOOL
OF REAL ESTATE**
5724 W. Las Positas Boulevard, #100
Pleasanton, CA 94588
(925) 924-4780

Correspondence Courses:
Escrows
Legal Aspects of Real Estate
Property Management
Real Estate Appraisal
Real Estate Finance
Real Estate Practice
Real Estate Principles

**QUICK LEARNING SCHOOL
OF SAN JOSE**
123 E. Gish Road
San Jose, CA 95112
(408) 453-8133

Correspondence Courses:
Legal Aspects of Real Estate
Mortgage Loan Brokering
   and Lending
Property Management
Real Estate Appraisal
Real Estate Economics
Real Estate Finance
Real Estate Office
   Administration
Real Estate Practice
Real Estate Principles

REAL ESTATE INSTITUTE USA
15751 Brookhurst Street, #230
Westminster, CA 92683
(323) 775-1909

Correspondence Courses:
Escrows
Legal Aspects of Real Estate
Property Management
Real Estate Appraisal
Real Estate Economics
Real Estate Finance

Real Estate Office
   Administration
Real Estate Practice
Real Estate Principles
Resident Course:
Real Estate Principles

Correspondence Courses:
Escrows
Legal Aspects of Real Estate
Mortgage Loan Brokering
   and Lending
Property Management
Real Estate Appraisal
Real Estate Economics
Real Estate Finance
Real Estate Office
   Administration
Real Estate Practice
Real Estate Principles

**REAL ESTATE LEARNING
CENTER, INC.**
1001 Hermosa Avenue
Building #203
Hermosa Beach, CA 90254
(888) 281-2302

REAL ESTATE LICENSE SERVICES
5059 Newport Avenue, Suite 209
San Diego, CA 92107
(619) 222-2425

Correspondence Courses:
Business Law
Escrows
Legal Aspects of Real Estate
Property Management
Real Estate Appraisal
Real Estate Economics
Real Estate Finance
Real Estate Practice
Real Estate Principles

THE REAL ESTATE SCHOOL
413 Court Street
Woodland, CA 95695
(530) 666-6121

Correspondence Courses:
Escrows
Legal Aspects of Real Estate
Property Management
Real Estate Appraisal
Real Estate Economics
Real Estate Finance

REAL ESTATE TRAINERS
2428 N. Grand Avenue, Suite K
Santa Ana, CA 92705-8708
(714) 972-2211

Real Estate Office
    Administration
Real Estate Practice
Real Estate Principles

Correspondence Courses:
Legal Aspects of Real Estate
Mortgage Loan Brokering
    and Lending
Property Management
Real Estate Appraisal
Real Estate Economics
Real Estate Finance
Real Estate Office
    Administration
Real Estate Practice
Real Estate Principles
Resident Courses:
Real Estate Appraisal
Real Estate Principles

REALTY COLLEGE
2708 W. Alhambra Road
Alhambra, CA 91801
(800) 295-5336

Correspondence Courses:
Escrows
Legal Aspects of Real Estate
Mortgage Loan Brokering
    and Lending
Property Management
Real Estate Appraisal
Real Estate Economics
Real Estate Finance
Real Estate Practice/
    Principles

THE REALTY INSTITUTE
PO Box 10309
San Bernardino, CA 92423
(909) 872-1933

Correspondence Courses:
Business Law
Legal Aspects of Real Estate
Property Management
Real Estate Appraisal
Real Estate Economics

Real Estate Finance
Real Estate Office
   Administration
Real Estate Practice
Real Estate Principles

**REALTY WORLD REAL ESTATE
SCHOOL**
2428 N. Grand Avenue, Suite K
Santa Ana, CA 92705
(800) 532-7673

Correspondence Course:
Real Estate Principles
Resident Course:
Real Estate Principles

RE'KULF REALTORS INC
1100 N. Hollywood Way, Suite A
Burbank, CA 91505
(818) 238-0300

Correspondence Course:
Real Estate Principles

ROCKWELL INSTITUTE
13218 NE 20th Street
Bellevue, WA 98005
(800) 221-9347

Correspondence Course:
Real Estate Principles

**ROWLAND ADULT AND COMMUNITY
EDUCATION**
19100 E. Killian Avenue
Rowland Heights, CA 91748
(213) 965-5975

Resident Course:
Real Estate Principles

ROYAL REAL ESTATE SCHOOL
230 S. Garfield Avenue, #200
Monterey Park, CA 91755
(626) 571-8118

Correspondence Courses:
Legal Aspects of
   Real Estate
Property Management
Real Estate Appraisal
Real Estate Economics
Real Estate Finance
Real Estate Office
   Administration
Real Estate Practice
Real Estate Principles

SAMUEL TONG SCHOOL
1016 Johnson Avenue
San Jose, CA 95129
(408) 799-9588

Correspondence Courses:
Escrows
Legal Aspects of Real Estate
Property Management
Real Estate Appraisal
Real Estate Economics
Real Estate Finance
Real Estate Practice
Real Estate Principles
Resident Course:
Real Estate Principles

SANTA MONICA COLLEGE (EXTENSION)
1900 Pico Boulevard
Santa Monica, CA 90405
(310) 450-5150

Resident Courses:
Legal Aspects of Real Estate
Real Estate Finance
Real Estate Practice
Real Estate Principles

SELECT SCHOOL OF REAL ESTATE
7919 Pebble Beach Drive, Suite 206
Citrus Heights, CA 95610-5700
(916) 536-4131

Correspondence Course:
Real Estate Principles

SIERRA SEMINARS
8037 Fair Oaks Boulevard, Suite 110
Carmichael, CA 95608
(916) 965-1020

Correspondence Courses:
Legal Aspects of Real Estate
Real Estate Appraisal
Real Estate Finance
Real Estate Practice
Real Estate Principles

SIMI VALLEY ADULT SCHOOL & CAREER INSTITUTE
3192 Los Angeles Avenue
Simi Valley, CA 93065
(805) 579-6200

Correspondence Courses:
Real Estate Finance
Real Estate Practice
Real Estate Principles
Resident Courses:
Legal Aspects of Real Estate
Real Estate Appraisal
Real Estate Finance
Real Estate Practice
Real Estate Principles

SONOMA/MARIN SCHOOL OF REAL ESTATE
5430 Commerce Boulevard, Suite J
Rohnert Park, CA 94928
(707) 586-9448

Correspondence Courses:
Business Law
Escrows
Legal Aspects of Real Estate
Property Management
Real Estate Appraisal
Real Estate Economics
Real Estate Finance
Real Estate Office
　Administration
Real Estate Practice
Real Estate Principles

SOUTHEAST ROP
20122 Cabrillo Lane
Cerritos, CA 90703
(562) 860-1927

Resident Course:
Real Estate Principles

SOUTHERN NEVADA SCHOOL OF REAL ESTATE
3441 W. Sahara, Suite C6
Las Vegas, NV 89102
(702) 364-2525

Resident Course:
Real Estate Principles

SWEETWATER UNION HIGH SCHOOL DISTRICT
1355 Second Avenue
Chula Vista, CA 91911
(619) 691-5611

Resident Course:
Real Estate Principles

TELEVISION EDUCATION, INC.
PO Box 929
Davis, CA 95617
(530) 756-4991

Correspondence Courses:
Business Law
Escrows
Legal Aspects of Real Estate
Mortgage Loan Brokering
　and Lending
Property Management
Real Estate Appraisal
Real Estate Economics
Real Estate Finance

Real Estate Practice
Real Estate Principles

TEMPLE CITY ADULT SCHOOL
9229 Pentland Street
Temple City, CA 91780
(626) 548-5113

Resident Courses:
Property Management
Real Estate Practice
Real Estate Principles

THIRTIETH CENTURY COLLEGE
OF CALIFORNIA, (T.C.C.)
605 S. Wilton Place
Los Angeles, CA 90005
(213) 383-0030

Correspondence Courses:
Escrows
Legal Aspects of Real Estate
Property Management
Real Estate Appraisal
Real Estate Economics
Real Estate Finance
Real Estate Practice
Real Estate Principles
Resident Course:
Real Estate Principles

TRI-COMMUNITY ADULT EDUCATION/
COVINA-VALLEY UNIFIED
SCHOOL DISTRICT
16209 E. San Bernardino Road
Covina, CA 91722
(626) 472-7681

Resident Course:
Real Estate Principles

UNITED EDUCATIONAL SERVICES
1320 Yuba Street, Suite 102
Redding, CA 96001
(800) 655-2703

Correspondence Courses:
Business Law
Escrows
Legal Aspects of Real Estate
Mortgage Loan Brokering
  and Lending
Property Management
Real Estate Appraisal
Real Estate Economics
Real Estate Finance
Real Estate Practice
Real Estate Principles

USA SCHOOLS
PO Box 2253
Carmichael, CA 95609
(800) 987-7402

Correspondence Courses:
Legal Aspects of Real Estate
Property Management
Real Estate Appraisal
Real Estate Economics
Real Estate Finance
Real Estate Office
  Administration
Real Estate Practice
Real Estate Principles

WASHINGTON INTERNATIONAL EDUCATIONAL CENTER
16530 Ventura Boulevard, Suite 204
Encino, CA 91436
(818) 285-1978

Correspondence Courses:
Escrows
Legal Aspects of Real Estate
Property Management
Real Estate Appraisal
Real Estate Economics
Real Estate Finance
Real Estate Practice
Real Estate Principles

WEST COAST SCHOOLS
9146 Santa Margarita Road
Atascadero, CA 93422
(805) 438-3455

Correspondence Courses:
Business Law
Escrows
Legal Aspects of Real Estate
Mortgage Loan Brokering
  and Lending
Property Management
Real Estate Appraisal
Real Estate Economics
Real Estate Finance
Real Estate Practice
Real Estate Principles

GERALD N. WHITEMAN
2285 Via Munera
La Jolla, CA 92037
(858) 456-7578

Resident Course:
Real Estate Finance

A Mortgage Solicitor in Colorado

Regulatory agency: Colorado Division of Securities

Contact info: www.dora.state.co.us/securities/index.htm or call (303) 866-4500

Type of license: Mortgage solicitor

Requirements
Education
None required for mortgage solicitors.

Licensing
None required for mortgage solicitors.

A Loan Originator in Connecticut

Regulatory agency: Connecticut Department of Banking, Consumer Credit Division

Contact info: www.state.ct.us/dob/ or call (860) 240-8209

Type of license: Loan originator

Requirements
Education
None required for loan originators.

Registration and Licensing
$50 application fee

$100 renewal fee

License is valid for two years and expires September 30 of the even-numbered year following its issuance. All loan originators must be registered with the regulatory agency listed above.

A Loan Originator in Delaware

Regulatory agency: Delaware Office of State Bank Commissioner

Contact info: www.state.de.us/bank or call (302) 739-4235

Type of license: Loan originator

Requirements
Education
None required for loan originators.

Licensing
None required for loan originators.

A Loan Originator in the District of Columbia

Regulatory agency: District of Columbia Department of Banking and Financial Institutions

Contact info: http://app.dbfi.dc.gov/contact.shtm or call (202) 727-1563

Type of license: Loan originator

Requirements
Education
None required for loan originators.

Licensing
None required for loan originators.

A Loan Originator or Mortgage Broker in Florida

In Florida a loan originator is exempt from licensing *if* the loan originator is employed through a mortgage *lender*. In this case, a loan originator is required to have 14 hours of *continuing* education. The continuing education is required every year its lender renews his or her licensing with the state of Florida.

A loan originator working for a mortgage broker must be licensed as a mortgage broker and is reported as an "associate."

Regulatory agency: Florida Department of Financial Services, Office of Financial Regulation (OFR), Division of Securities and Finance

Contact info: www.fldfs.com/ofr/licensing, or call (850) 410-9805

Type of license: Loan originator if an employee (W-2) for a mortgage lender. Mortgage broker (associate) if an independent contractor (1099).

Requirements
Education and Exam

- Complete 24 hours of classroom education

- Must pass state exam

The requirement can be met only by your attending the required 24-hour mortgage broker training course offered by an approved mortgage business school.

During the time your background check is being completed, you will receive a deficiency letter notifying you of what is required before your license can be issued. The letter will provide you with your test date and time and should give you at least a seven-day advance notice of the testing date. Testing days are usually the fourth Tuesday and Wednesday of each month.

There are six testing sites for the exam, spread out within the state. You may be assigned to a site that is not necessarily nearest to your home. The exam consists of 100 multiple-choice questions. You must achieve a score of 75 or higher to pass. You are given three hours to complete the exam.

Registration and Licensing
$200 initial license fee

$150 renewal fee

License expires August 31 of each odd-numbered year.

All requirements for licensure (including a passing score on the exam) must be completed within 90 days from the date of request. In order to ensure that you have an opportunity to take the exam the following month after application, you must submit your application on or before the fifteenth of the month. Use the Friday before the fifteenth if the fifteenth falls on a weekend.

Fingerprints
$23 fee

The fingerprint card must be completed and returned with the application for licensure.

Schools for Florida

A BETTER CHOICE EDUCATION CENTER CORP.
Miami/Dade and Broward County
(305) 430-0770
E-mail: mypoints4@aol.com

A BRIGHT FUTURE MORTGAGE INST.
Miami Area
(305) 559-4242
E-mail: JCC_mortgage@yahoo.com
(Course available in Spanish)

THE ACADEMY
Celebration, Orlando, and Central
   Florida
(866) 254-6763
E-mail: info@theacademy1.com

ACADEMY OF MORTGAGE EDUCATION
West Palm Beach and
   South Florida
(561) 721-3439

ALL FLORIDA REAL ESTATE SCHOOLS, INC.
Port St. Lucie and
   Southeast Florida
(773) 337-2390
E-mail: reschool@
   allfloridarealty.com

ALLIANCE MORTGAGE BUSINESS SCHOOLS, INC.
Jacksonville and North Florida
(904) 880-8070
E-mail: repaeditor@aol.com

BANCASA REAL ESTATE SCHOOL, INC.
Weston, Miami, and
   South Florida
(954) 660-0333
E-mail: realestateschool@
   bancasa.com

BERMINGHAM/FITZPATRICK SCHOOL OF REAL ESTATE (A DBA)
Palm Beach County and
   South Florida
(561) 622-4300
E-mail: gobsr@msn.com

BOB HOGUE SCHOOL OF REAL ESTATE, INC.
Tampa Bay and St. Petersburg
   (West Coast Area)
(800) 330-9411
E-mail: mortgagebrokers@
   bobhogue-school.com

CENTRAL FLORIDA REAL ESTATE & MORTGAGE BROKER SCHOOL (A DBA)
Orlando and Central Florida
(407) 999-9824
E-mail: cflreschool@aol.com

CENTURY 21 UNIVERSITY OF LEARNING
Miami, Sunrise, and
   West Palm Beach
(800) 432-3226
E-mail: C21ulearn@aol.com

C.F.C. SCHOOL OF REAL ESTATE, INC.
Miami and South Florida
(786) 621-5994
E-mail: vinlu23@aol.com

CNID SCHOOLS (A DBA)
Plantation (South Florida)
(954) 327-1766
E-mail: Academicom@hotmail.com

ED KLOPFER SCHOOLS OF REAL ESTATE
Tampa, Sarasota, Ft. Myers, and Naples
(800) 370-1750
E-mail: trish@edklopfer.com

FLORIDA INSTITUTE OF PROFESSIONAL STUDIES
Orlando and Central Florida
(407) 481-8015

FLORIDA MORTGAGE BROKER SCHOOL
Tampa, Miami, Ft. Lauderdale, Jacksonville, Ft. Myers, Orlando, West Palm Beach, Sarasota, and Pensacola
(800) 735-8565
E-mail: jlmontrym@hotmail.com

FLORIDA MORTGAGE ORIGINATION SCHOOL
Port Richey and Tampa Bay Area
(727) 845-9092
E-mail: j@fmos.net

FLORIDA REAL ESTATE INSTITUTE, INC.
Jacksonville and Orange Park

(Northeast Florida)
(904) 269-2555
E-mail: ronfrei@fair.net

FLORIDA SCHOOL OF REAL ESTATE, INC.
Hialeah, Dade County, and South Florida
(305) 231-9600
E-mail: danny@usamoney.com

FRED SEGESMAN MORTGAGE BUSINESS SCHOOL
Tampa Bay Area
(800) 320-2863
E-mail: freds@realty-finance.com

FUTURES IN FINANCE
Panama City and Northwest Florida
(850) 769-6483
E-mail: leslie4432@yahoo.com

GOLD COAST PROFESSIONAL SCHOOLS, INC.
Miami, Ft. Lauderdale, Boca Raton, and West Palm Beach
(800) 940-7277
E-mail: jim@goldcoastschools.com

GRAYSTONE MORTGAGE BUSINESS SCHOOL, INC.
Ft. Lauderdale, Miami, and South Florida
(954) 525-2935
E-mail: crobinson@ graystoneschool.com

HOMEBANC UNIVERSITY (A DBA)
Atlanta, GA
(404) 303-4146
E-mail: nmantia@homebanc.com

THE INSTITUTE OF MORTGAGE EDUCATION, LLC

Davie and Broward County
 (South Florida)
(954) 255-3090
E-mail: loanpro@teamlending.net

KAMBUCK RESOURCES, LLC

Orlando and Central Florida
(407) 571-2449
E-mail: kambuck@kambuck.com

MIAMI SCHOOL OF BROKERS, INC.

Miami and South Florida
(305) 491-1656
E-mail: miamischoolbrokers
 @hotmail.com
(Course available in Spanish)

THE MORTGAGE BROKER SCHOOL

Lynn Haven, Panama City, and
 West Florida
(850) 265-3504
E-mail: johnbobbytolbert@aol.com

PINES SCHOOL OF REAL ESTATE

Pembroke Pines and South Florida
(954) 967-0277
E-mail: amesamosa@aol.com

REAL ESTATE SCHOOL MADE EASY, LLC

Ft. Myers, Naples, and
 Southwest Florida
(239) 274-2000
E-mail: pbrandoperkins@yahoo.com

REGENCY MORTGAGE INSTITUTE

Davie, Ft. Lauderdale, and
 Hollywood
(954) 434-5782
E-mail: regencyorg@aol.com

SALES INSTITUTE OF ORLANDO, INC.

Orlando and Central Florida
(407) 294-6877
E-mail: institutestaff@yahoo.com
(Course available in Spanish)

SOUTH FLORIDA SCHOOL OF REAL ESTATE, INC.

Miami (305) 273-7215
Hollywood (305) 412-0700
E-mail: danoquinn@msn.com

TEACH YOUR REAL ESTATE SCHOOL

Miami and South Florida
(305) 275-0515

VICTORY MORTGAGE ACADEMY, INC.

Pembroke Pines, Miami, and
 South Florida
(305) 652-8282
E-mail: info@victorymortgage
 academy.net

A Loan Originator in Georgia

Regulatory agency: Georgia Department of Banking and Finance

Contact info: www.gadbf.org or call (770) 986-1633

Type of license: Loan originator

Requirements

Education
None required for loan originators.

Licensing
None required for loan originators.

A Mortgage Solicitor in Hawaii

In Hawaii a mortgage solicitor working for a mortgage lender has *no* educational or licensing requirements to fulfill. However, a mortgage solicitor working for a mortgage broker will need to fulfill the requirements listed below.

> *Regulatory agency:* Hawaii Department of Commerce and Consumer Affairs
>
> *Contact info:* www.hawaii.gov/dcca/pvl or call (808) 586-3000 for mortgage brokers and (808) 586-2821 for mortgage bankers and lenders
>
> *Type of license:* Mortgage solicitor

Requirements

Education
None required for mortgage solicitors.

Registration and Licensing
> $145 fee if applying for licensure from January 1, odd-numbered year, to December 31, odd-numbered year (for example, if applying for licensure in the year of 2007)

The fee breaks down this way:

> $25 application fee

> $25 license fee

$70 CRF and for the second year of two-year license period, the fee is $25

or:

$85 fee if applying for licensure from January 1, even-numbered year, to December 31, even-numbered year (for example, if applying for licensure in the year of 2006)

In this case, the fee breaks down as:

$25 application fee

$25 license fee

$35 CRF

A Loan Originator in Idaho

Regulatory agency: Idaho Department of Finance

Contact info: http://finance.idaho.gov/mortgagesection.aspx or call (208) 332-8002

Type of license: Loan originator

Requirements

Education
None required for loan originators.

Licensing
Effective January 2006, loan originators will require licensing. No details are currently available.

A Loan Originator in Illinois

Regulatory agency: Illinois Division of Banks and Real Estate/Department of Financial and Professional Regulation

Contact info: www.obre.state.il.us/resfin/NEWS/Loan Originators.htm or call (312) 793-1409 for the licensing division

Type of license: Loan originator

Requirements

Education

Complete three hours of education every year for Illinois residents only.

Registration and Licensing

Effective July 1, 2004, state law mandates the registration and licensing of all loan originators.

As of January 1, 2005, loan originators are required to pass a written test and are subject to a criminal background check.

Loan originators are required to carry a pocket card issued by OBRE (Office of Banks and Real Estate) to provide proper identification to consumers and law enforcement officials. A list of all registered loan originators can be accessed via a Web site roster (www.idfpr.com).

Effective January 1, 2005:

$125 license fee

$115 background check

Exam

$74 fee

Testing is performed by AMP, Inc. You may schedule an appointment for testing online at www.goAMP.com or call (800) 345-6559. AMP Assessment Centers are typically located in H & R Block offices. To find a full list of locations, go to www.goAMP.com.

The test is composed of 100 questions, and you will have two hours to complete the exam.

Candidates who hold a professional certification approved by the Department of Financial and Professional Regulation, which requires at least 18 hours of continuing education every three years, are exempt from taking the full Loan Originator Exam and are required to take only the Legal, Regulatory, and Ethical portion of the exam. Those who qualify for this partial exemption include a certified residential mortgage specialist (CRMS), certified mortgage consultant (CMC), and certified mortgage banker (CMB).

Fingerprints

For a list of approved fingerprint companies, go to www.obre. state.il.us/resfin/LO/FingerPrint.htm.

A Loan Originator in Indiana

Regulatory agency: Indiana Secretary of State Securities Division

Contact info: www.in.gov/sos/ (press "securities") or call (317) 232-6681

Type of license: Loan originator

Requirements

Education

Complete 24-hour Indiana approved mortgage broker course. Continuing education requirement is 12 hours every two years.

Registration and Licensing

No licensing requirements for loan originators; however, all loan originators must be registered by their employer with the Office of the Secretary of State, Securities Division.

24-Hour Indiana Mortgage Broker Course Providers

FINANCIAL STRATEGIES
3500 DePauw Boulevard, #3070
Indianapolis, IN 46268
(317) 871-2380
www.mymortgagetrainer.com

Course:
Indiana Mortgage Education
   Course (24 hours)

INDIANA ASSOCIATION OF MORTGAGE BROKERS
212 West 10th Street, #A-390
Indianapolis, IN 46202
(317) 964-1225
www.inamb.com

Courses:
Residential Mortgage Lending
   (24 hours)
Sub-prime Loan Origination
   (8 hours)

INDIANA MORTGAGE ACADEMY
3352 N. Shore Acres Loop
Monticello, IN 47960
(574) 583-2431

Courses:
Residential Mortgage Training for
   Originators (24 hours)
Conventional Loan Processing (12 hours)

THE MORTGAGE INSTITUTE
823 Russell Street
Covington, KY 41011
(859) 578-8181
E-mail: mtginst@aol.com

Course:
The Complete Loan Originator
   (24 hours)

**NATIONAL ASSOCIATION OF
MORTGAGE BROKERS**
Educational Foundation (NAMBEF)
8201 Greensboro Drive, #300
McLean, VA 22102
(703) 610-9007
www.namb.org

Course:
Residential Mortgage Lending
   School (24 hours)

A Loan Originator in Iowa

Regulatory agency: Iowa Division of Banking

Contact info: www.idob.state.ia.us or call (515) 281-4014

Type of license: Loan originator

Requirements
Education
None required for loan originators.

Licensing
None required for loan originators.

A Loan Originator in Kansas

In Kansas a loan originator working for a supervised lender has *no* educational or licensing requirements to fulfill. However, if working for a mortgage broker, you must meet the following requirements.

Regulatory agency: Kansas Office of the State Bank Commissioner

Contact info: www.osbckansas.org or call (785) 296-2266

Type of license: Loan originator

Requirements
Education

No initial educational requirements are necessary. However, eight hours of *continuing* education are required.

Registration and Licensing
> $75 annual fee

> $54 fingerprint processing fee

The Kansas Office of the State Bank Commissioner requires all loan originators to be registered. Loan Originator Form G must be signed and notarized.

A loan originator working for a mortgage broker is required to have eight hours of continuing education by September 30 of *each* year. Each registrant issued a certificate of registration on or after the first day of July of any year will have until the thirtieth day of September the following year to comply with annual continuing professional education (CPE) requirements.

A Loan Officer or Mortgage Broker in Kentucky

> *Regulatory agency:* Kentucky Office of Financial Institutions

> *Contact info:* www.dfi.ky.gov or call (502) 573-3390 or (800) 223-2579

> *Type of license:* Loan officer is an employee of a loan company. Mortgage broker is an employee of a loan broker.

Requirements
Education

As of 2004, 12 hours of approved mortgage educational courses are required before registering.

Registration and Licensing
> $50 annual fee

All loan officers and mortgage brokers must be registered with the Office of Financial Institutions.

Background Check and Fingerprints
> $18 fee

All persons applying for registration as a mortgage loan broker or loan officer shall submit proof of an FBI criminal background check, to include fingerprints, as part of the application. In addition, the applicant will need to submit an educational certificate to verify the completion of the 12 hours of education along with the application fee.

Fingerprint cards can be obtained at any local law enforcement agency. Send a completed fingerprint card, $18 certified check or money order, and a short letter requesting a personal review to:

Federal Bureau of Investigation
Criminal Justice Information Services Division
SCU Custer Hollow Road
Clarksburg, WV 26306

Schools for Kentucky

CAREER DEVELOPMENT CENTER
PO Box 23356
Lexington, KY
(859) 273-3340
E-mail: Tlambuth@
　careerdevelopmentcenter.net

FINANCIAL STRATEGIES
3500 DePauw Boulevard, #3070
Indianapolis, IN 46268
(317) 871-2380
www.mymortgagetrainer.com

KENTUCKY MORTGAGE BROKERS ASSOCIATION
PO Box 4584
Frankfort, KY 40604
(502) 223-4840
www.kmba.net

MORTGAGE RESEARCH
2959 Cherokee Street, #202
Kennesaw, GA 30144
(888) 557-6770
www.mortgage-education.com

A Loan Originator in Louisiana

Regulatory agency: Louisiana Office of Financial Institutions

Contact info: www.ofi.state.la.us or call (225) 925-0634

Type of license: Loan originator

Requirements
Education
All licensees must complete 10 hours of professional education courses approved by the commissioner annually to renew their licenses.

Exam
$100 fee

All originator applicants must pass a written exam prior to applying for a license. The exam is conducted by PSI. Applicants should contact PSI at (800) 733-9267 in order to schedule a test.

An applicant can be exempt from the exam if the applicant can provide the following:

- Certified transcripts evidencing a bachelor's or master's degree from an accredited college or university

- **AND** during the immediate three years preceding the date of license application, the applicant can provide W-2 forms and a copy of the applicant's job description signed by his or her previous employer verifying *12 months* of full-time employment as a mortgage broker or lender, underwriter, processor, or originator

- **OR** the applicant can provide W-2 forms and a copy of the applicant's job description signed by his or her previous employer(s) verifying *24 months* of full-time employment as a mortgage broker or lender, underwriter, processor, or originator.

Applicant's qualifying for exemption from the written examination *must* complete 10 hours of professional education from an approved provider. See the list of approved providers below.

Licensing
$100 fee for new loan originators

$50 fee for licensed originators transferring to another company

License is valid for one year. Renewals must be received by December 1 to avoid any late penalties.

New originators and those originators transferring from one company to another *cannot* engage in residential mortgage lending activities for the company until a license has been received. Originators may originate loans only for the company whose name appears on their license.

These forms and stipulations must be submitted with your licensing fee:

- Employer Certification Form (must be notarized)

- Proof of professional education requirement

- Authority to Obtain Information from Outside Sources (must be notarized)

- Employment/Residential History Form

Approved List of Continuing Education Providers

ADVANCED EDUCATION SYSTEMS
11350 McCormick Road
Executive Plaza 3, Suite 1001
Hunt Valley, Maryland 21031
Toll-free (877) 878-3600
Contact: Christopher D. Nickerson
www.TrainingPro.com
(Online course provider)

BEDFORD GROUP, LLC
713 Heavens Drive, #4
Mandeville, LA 70471
(985) 845-3782 or
   toll-free (800) 701-0390
Contact: Rod Russell
E-mail: rodrussel@
   bedfordgroup.info
www.bedfordgroup.info/

BOB BROOKS SCHOOL OF REAL ESTATE & INSURANCE, INC.
6721 Pecue Lane
Baton Rouge, LA 70817
(225) 752-2920 or
   toll-free (800) 448-5693
Fax: (225) 752-6815
Contact: Bob Brooks
www.bobbrooksschool.com
(Online course and live
   class provider)

DIRECT MORTGAGE CONSULTING
5136 Belle Drive
Metairie, LA 70006
(504) 231-8936
Fax: (504) 780-1518

DONALDSON EDUCATION SERVICES
(504) 456-1785 or
 toll-free (800) 257-2741
Fax: (504) 456-1789
Contact: Keith Donaldson
www.donaldsoneducational.com

FINANCIAL STRATEGIES
690 Pro Med Lane
Carmel, IN 46032
(317) 566-0425 or
 toll-free (866) 411-9752
Fax: (317) 566-0601
Contact: Don Huntzinger
www.mymortgagetrainer.co

FIRST PROFESSIONAL REAL ESTATE SCHOOL, INC.
Metairie, LA
(504) 454-9866 or
 toll-free (800) 966-9866
Fax: (504) 888-0346
Contact: Roy L. Ponthier, Jr., Ph.D.
www.proeducate.com
(Online course and live
 class provider)

LOUISIANA MORTGAGE LENDERS ASSOCIATION
8550 United Plaza Boulevard
Suite 1001
Baton Rouge, LA 70809
(225) 922-4642
Contact: Sarah Phillips
www.lmla.com

MORTGAGE BANKERS ASSOCIATION
1919 Pennsylvania Avenue, NW
Washington, DC 20006
(202) 557-2763
Fax: (202) 721-0166
Contact: Jennifer Ridings, BCA
www.campusmba.org
(Online class provider)

MORTGAGE RESEARCH, INC.
2959 Cherokee Street, Suite 202
Kennesaw, GA 30144
Toll-free 1-888-557-6770
Contact: Dan G. Johnson or
 Jerry Lee Kelly
www.mortgage-education.com
(Online course provider)

MORTGAGE TRAINING INSTITUTE, INC.
Denver, CO
(303) 758-9037 or
 toll-free (877) 684-3549
Fax: (303) 759-3925
Contact: Jon Exley
E-mail: jexley@
mortgageknowledge.com
www.mortgageknowledge.com

WEB TAUGHT
4640 South Carrolton, Suite 2B-204
New Orleans, LA 70119
(504) 482-0109 or
 toll-free (866) 482-0109
Contact: Rudy Schmidt
www.executaught.com
(Online and live class provider)

A Loan Officer in Maine

Regulatory agency: Maine Office of Consumer Credit Regulation

Contact info: www.state.me.us/pfr/cep/ccp.index.htm or call (207) 624-8527

Type of license: Loan officer

Requirements

Education
None required for loan officers.

Registration and Licensing
No license required for loan officers. Effective January 2006, registration of loan officers employed by mortgage brokers and non-bank mortgage lenders will be required. Registration fee will be $20 for each loan originator up to a maximum of $200.

A Loan Originator or "Branch Office" in Maryland

Regulatory agency: Maryland Commissioner of Financial Regulation

Contact info: www.dllr.state.md.us or call (410) 230-6086 or (888) 784-0136

Type of license: A loan originator is considered a "covered employee" (W-2). An independent contractor (1099) would need to be licensed as a "branch office" through the employing broker or lender.

Requirements

Education
Must complete 20 hours of continuing education if less than 10 years' experience in loan origination.

Required Courses

Ethics (2 hours)

Federal Real Estate Settlement Procedures Act (RESPA) compliance (2 hours)

Federal Truth in Lending Act compliance (2 hours)

Federal Equal Credit Opportunity Act and fair lending compliance (2 hours)

Maryland law update (2 hours)

Federal law update (2 hours)

Electives (8 hours)

An employee who has been a covered employee with any licensee for the immediately preceding 10 years will be considered to have satisfied the continuing education requirements by completing only 6 hours of education with the courses listed below:

Ethics (2 hours)

Maryland law update (2 hours)

Federal law update (2 hours)

Licensing

None is required for a covered employee (W-2). An independent contractor must be licensed as a "branch office" through the employing broker or lender.

Schools for Maryland

ADVANCED EDUCATION SYSTEMS
73 Timonium Road
Timonium, MD 21093
(877) 878-3600
Contact: Chris Nickerson
www.trainingpro.com
(Online courses available)

CAPSTONE INSTITUTE
2000 Powers Ferry Road
Marietta, GA 30067
(800) 229-8556
Contact: James Morris
www.capinst.com
(Online courses available)

MARYLAND ASSOCIATION OF MORTGAGE BROKERS
720 Light Street
Baltimore, MD 21230
(410) 752-6262
www.mamb.com

A Loan Originator in Massachusetts

Regulatory agency: Massachusetts Division of Banks

Contact info: www.state.ma.us/dob or call (617) 956-1500

Type of license: Loan originator

Requirements

Education
None required for loan originators.

Licensing
None required for loan originators.

A Loan Originator in Michigan

Regulatory agency: Michigan Department of Labor and Economic Growth, Office of Financial & Insurance Services

Contact info: www.michigan.gov or call (517) 373-0220

Type of license: Loan originator

Requirements

Education
None required for loan originators.

Licensing
None required for loan originators.

A Loan Officer in Minnesota

Regulatory agency: Minnesota Department of Commerce

Contact info: www.commerce.state.mn.us or call (651) 296-2135

Type of license: Loan officers are considered employees (W-2)

Requirements

Education
None required for loan officers.

Licensing

None required for loan officers; they are employees paid with a W-2. An independent contractor (1099) working for a mortgage broker (licensed residential mortgage originator) must be licensed as a mortgage broker.

A Loan Originator in Mississippi

> *Regulatory agency:* Mississippi Department of Banking and Consumer Finance
>
> *Contact info:* www.dbcf.state.ms.us/ or call (601) 359-1031
>
> *Type of license:* Loan originator

Requirements

Education

There are no initial educational requirements to become a registered loan originator. However, for renewal there is a requirement of 12 hours of education.

As a loan originator in the state of Mississippi, you must be registered. You are allowed to work for only one mortgage broker at a time, and you are not allowed to work out of your home. You must work out of a licensed location.

Registration and Licensing

> $100 new originator license fee
>
> $50 annual renewal

To accompany the Loan Originator Registration Application, you must submit a state-issued fingerprint card. Both are obtainable through the Mississippi Department of Banking and Consumer Finance.

An applicant will be denied a license if he or she has been convicted of a felony in any jurisdiction and a misdemeanor in any jurisdiction if the misdemeanor involves fraud within the last 10 years of the application date.

Schools for Mississippi

MISSISSIPPI ASSOCIATION OF MORTGAGE BROKERS
201 Belmont Street
Clinton, MS 39060
(601) 924-4006
Contact: Rebecca Ainsworth
www.msamb.org

MORTGAGE BANKERS ASSOCIATION OF MISSISSIPPI
PO Box 22865
Jackson, MS 39225
(601) 605-6687
Contact: Joe McNeese at
  jmcneese@msmba.org
www.msmba.org

MORTGAGE-EDUCATION.COM
2959 Cherokee Street, Suite 202
Kennesaw, GA 30144
(888) 557-6770
Contact: Dan Johnson or
  any staff member
www.mortgage-education.com
(Online course facility)

UNITED GUARANTY/ PARTNERSHIPS FOR TRAINING DEVELOPMENT
230 N. Elm Street
Greensboro, NC 27401
(800) 334-8966
Contact: Stephanie Scott
www.ugcorp.com

A Loan Originator in Missouri

Regulatory agency: Missouri Division of Finance

Contact info: www.missouri-finance.org or call (573) 751-3242

Type of license: Loan originator

Requirements
Education
None required for loan originators.

Licensing
None required for loan originators.

A Loan Originator in Montana

Regulatory agency: Montana Division of Banking and Financial Institutions

Contact info: www.discoveringmontana.com/doa/banking/ mortgage.asp or call (406) 841-2920

Type of license: Loan originator

Requirements

Experience

A loan originator must have a minimum of six months' experience working in a related field.

Education

Effective September 1, 2004, all mortgage loan originators are required to be licensed and pass an examination. At the time of application you are required to take and pass an exam. You will be tested on the following:

- Loan origination

- Proper disclosures

- State and federal laws

- The ability to read appraisals and title commitments

- The ability to evaluate credit and calculate ratios

In addition, loan originators are required to have 12 hours of continuing education. There are no initial educational requirements for licensing.

Exam

Currently there are only two approved examination and education providers:

- Mortgage-education.com

- Montana Association of Mortgage Brokers

Registration and Licensing

 $400 fee

License is valid for one year and expires on June 30. An applicant shall pay one-half of the $400 initial fee for any license period of less than six months.

Each original license issued to a loan originator must be provided to and maintained by the employing broker at the broker's main office. A copy of the license must be displayed at the office where the loan originator principally conducts business.

At termination of employment the loan originator license is returned by the employing broker to the regulating department as listed above.

Background Check and Fingerprints
$34 processing fee

A Loan Originator in Nebraska

Regulatory agency: Nebraska Department of Banking and Finance

Contact info: www.ndbf.org or call (402) 471-2171

Type of license: Loan originator

Requirements
Education
None required for loan originators.

Licensing
None required for loan originators.

A Mortgage Agent in Nevada

Regulatory agency: Nevada Business & Industry, Mortgage Lending Division

Contact info: www.mld.nv.gov or call (702) 684-7060

Type of license: Mortgage agent

Requirements
Licensing
$185 annual fee

Effective July 1, 2004, the licensing of mortgage agents completely replaces loan agent registration. A Mortgage Agent License Application must be submitted along with the license fee.

An applicant is eligible to receive a license if the applicant:

- Has not been convicted of a felony involving fraud

- Has not had a financial services license suspended or revoked in the immediate 10 years prior to application

- Has not made any false statement of material fact on his or her application

- Has a good reputation for honesty, trustworthiness, and integrity

With the agent license application, each person must submit:

- Employer's mortgage broker information

- Child-support statement

- Personal history record

- Fingerprint cards issued by a local law enforcement agency

The second part of the application is an acknowledgment that must be completed by the employer responsible for you as a loan agent. A complete and notarized Loan Agent Registration and a License Application Form must be submitted prior to any loan originations.

For renewal purposes a mortgage agent is required to provide proof of 10 hours of certified courses of continuing education. However, no education or testing is required at the initial application stage.

A Loan Originator in New Hampshire

Regulatory agency: New Hampshire Banking Department

Contact info: www.state.nh.us/banking (click on consumer credit division) or call (603) 271-3561

Type of license: Loan originator

Requirements
Education
None required for loan originators.

Licensing
None required for loan originators.

A Mortgage Solicitor in New Jersey

Regulatory agency: New Jersey Department of Banking and Insurance

Contact info: www.state.nj.us/dobi/index.shtml or call (609) 282-5360

Type of license: Mortgage solicitor

Requirements
Registration
$100 annual fee

The fee should accompany the Mortgage Solicitor Registration Form. No mortgage solicitor may be employed by more than one of the following at a time: mortgage banker, correspondent mortgage banker, or mortgage broker.

A Loan Originator in New Mexico

Regulatory agency: New Mexico Financial Institutions Division

Contact info: www.rld.state.nm.us/fid or call (505) 476-4885

Type of license: Loan originator

Requirements
Education
None required for loan originators.

Licensing
None required for loan originators.

A Loan Originator in New York

Regulatory agency: New York Banking Department

Contact info: www.banking.state.ny.us or call (212) 618-6642

Type of license: Loan originator

Requirements

Education

None required for loan originators.

Licensing

None required for loan originators.

A Loan Officer in North Carolina

> *Regulatory agency:* North Carolina Commissioner of Banks (COB), Mortgage Lending Division
>
> *Contact info:* www.nccob.org/NCCOB or call (919) 733-0589
>
> *Type of license:* Loan officer

Requirements

Education

Prior to applying for a license, you must:

- Complete an eight-hour mortgage lending fundamentals course. Applicants must successfully complete this course within three years preceding the date of application for a North Carolina mortgage loan officer license.

- Pass the North Carolina Mortgage Loan Officer Test within 90 days preceding the date of the application. The North Carolina Office of the Commissioner of Banks has contracted with PSI Examination Services to conduct the North Carolina Mortgage Loan Officer Test. PSI can be contacted by phone at (800) 733-9267 or on the Web at www.psiexams.com. PSI provides examinations through seven computer examination centers in North Carolina. The tests are available daily. Exam fee is $100.

There is a requirement of eight hours of continuing education due each year by June 30. A continuing education course may not be repeated within a three-year period with the same education provider. An extensive list of continuing education courses and providers is posted on the states' Web site at www.nccob.com/online/ems/courselisting.aspx?coursetype=1.

Licensing

$50 application fee

$55 credit and criminal background check fee (pay by cashier check or money order only)

$50 annual renewal fee

Note: *Working without a license is a felony in North Carolina.*

Background Check and Fingerprinting
You must enclose the fingerprint card issued by the COB with your application for licensure.

Schools for North Carolina (for Initial Education Requirement)

ADVANCED EDUCATION SYSTEMS
73 Timonium Road
Timonium, MD 21093
(877) 878-3600
www.TrainingPro.com

Course:
An Overview of Lending and the Application Process (8 hours)

CENTRAL PIEDMONT COMMUNITY COLLEGE
PO Box 35009
Charlotte, NC 28235-5009
(704) 330-4678
www.cpcc.cc.nc.us

Course:
Introduction to Loan Origination (8 hours)

FINANCIAL STRATEGIES
690 Pro Med Lane
Carmel, IN 46032
(866) 411-9752
www.MyMortgageTrainer.com

Course:
Financial Strategies Fundamentals (8 hours)

LENOIR COMMUNITY COLLEGE
231 Highway 58 S., PO Box 188
Kinston, NC 28502-0188
(252) 527-6223, ext. 713
www.lenoircc.edu

Course:
NC Mortgage Fundamentals (8 hours)

NC ASSOCIATION OF MORTGAGE PROFESSIONALS
3901 Barrett Drive, Suite 202
Raleigh, NC 27609
(919) 783-0767
www.ncmortgageprofessionals.org

Course:
NC Mortgage Fundamentals
(8 hours)

PAUL DONOHUE PRESENTS
PO Box 780
4527 U.S. Highway 220 N.
Summerfield, NC 27358
(888) 341-7767
www.pauldonohuepresents.com

Course:
Fundamentals of Residential
Mortgage Loan Origination
(8 hours)

A Loan Originator in North Dakota

Regulatory agency: North Dakota Department of Financial Institutions

Contact info: www.state.nd.us/dfi or call (701) 328-9933

Type of license: Loan originator

Requirements
Education
None required for loan originators.

Licensing
None required for loan originators.

A Loan Officer in Ohio

Regulatory agency: Ohio Department of Commerce, Financial Institutions Division

Contact info: www.com.state.oh.us/dfi/ or call (614) 728-8400

Type of license: Loan officer

Requirements
Education
Loan officers must complete six hours of continuing education each year beginning in 2003.

Exam
> $65 fee

Experior Assessments, LLC, is the company that conducts all the testing of loan officers. Contact the company by phone at (800) 741-0934 or on the Web at www.experioronline.com. Loan officers are required to pass a test that consists of 75 multiple-choice questions. The test covers:

- Ohio Mortgage Broker Act and Ohio Mortgage Loan Act
- Mortgage loan programs
- Mortgage loan processes
- Federal mortgage lending legislation
- Mortgage terminology

Licensing
> $100 annual fee

A loan originator in the state of Ohio must be registered. The loan application must be notarized.

Background Check and Fingerprinting
> $35 fee for fingerprinting, which includes a criminal background check

Schools for Continuing Education for Ohio

ADVANCED EDUCATION SYSTEMS
73 Timonium Road
Timonium, MD 21093
(877) 878-3600

Course:
Ohio Mortgage Continuing
    Education Seminar,
    Home Study (6 hours)

**AMERICAN BROKER
EDUCATION SERVICES**
20575 Center Ridge Road #460
Rocky River, OH 44116
(440) 829-8626
Contact: Jim Nabors

Courses:
Home Ownership for the Credit
    Impaired (seminar) (2 hours)
Loan Origination
    Fundamentals (seminar) (2 hours)
Understanding Ohio's MB Act
    (seminar) (2 hours)

**ARLINGTON EXCHANGE
SERVICES, LTD.**
4656 Executive Drive
Columbus, OH 43220
(614) 545-3333
Contact: Theodore Sergakis
www.arlingtontitle.com

Courses:
Fraud Detection & Deterrence
(seminar) (6 hours)
Advanced Loan Officer Training
(seminar) (6 hours)

**C&S TRAINING AND
CONSULTING, INC.**
9224 Rock Rose Drive
Tampa, FL 33647
(800) 266-2414
Contact: Lee Comegys

Course:
Mortgage Broker and
Loan Officer
(seminar) (6 hours)

**CAPSTONE INSTITUTE OF
MORTGAGE FINANCE**
2000 Powers Ferry Road, Suite 2-3
Marietta, GA 30067
(770) 956-8252
Contact: Susan Stromquist
www.capinst.com

Courses:
Fundamentals of Loan Processing
(seminar) (6 hours)
Principles of Mortgage Finance
(seminar) (6 hours)
Procedures for Efficient Closing
and Quality Control (seminar)
(6 hours)
Guidelines for Taking a Detailed
Loan Application (seminar)
(6 hours)

**DAYTONA AREA BOARD
OF REALTORS**
1515 S. Main Street
Dayton, OH 45401-0111
(937) 223-0900
Contact: Nicholas Popadyn, Jr.
www.dabr.com

Courses:
3 Down Payment Assistance
Programs (seminar) (3 hours)
New Immigrant Home Ownership
Opportunity (seminar) (3 hours)
Alternative Financing (seminar)
(3 hours)
Reverse Mortgage Facts
(seminar) (3 hours)

EDWARD D. HAYMAN
28499 Orange Meadow Lane
Orange Village, OH 44022
(216) 695-1184
E-mail: ehayman@adelphia.net

Courses:
Core Real Estate Law
(seminar) (3 hours)
Fundamentals of Predatory
Lending (seminar) (3 hours)

EQUITY RESOURCES
PO Box 5177
25/2 S. Park Place
Newark, OH 43058
(740) 349-7082
Contact: Ed Rizor
www.callequity.com

Course:
Credit Scoring and Sub-Prime
Lending (seminar) (3 hours)

FINANCIAL STRATEGIES
690 Pro Med Lane
Carmel, IN 46032
(866) 411-9752
Contact: Alan Griffin
www.mortgagetrainer.com

Courses:
Processing Power (seminar)
(6 hours)
Mortgage Loan Mastery (seminar
or home study) (6 hours)

GE MORTGAGE INSURANCE CORP.
4898 Cambridge Drive
Dunwoody, GA 30338
(919) 870-2131
Contact: Barry Winovich

Course:
Analysis of the Self-Employed
Borrower (seminar) (6 hours)

HONDROS COLLEGE
4140 Executive Parkway
Westerville, OH 43081
(614) 508-7277
Contact: Lisa Fries
www.hondroscollege.com

Courses:
Mortgage Originations
for the Self-Employed Borrower
(seminar) (6 hours)
A History of Laws Affecting
Mortgage Lending (seminar)
(6 hours)

**INSTITUTE OF PROFESSIONAL
EDUCATION**
93 W. Franklin Street
Centerville, OH 45459
(937) 433-4210
Contact: Diane McCracken

Courses:
Broker to Banker, Closing,
Shipping, and Warehouse
(seminar) (3 hours)
Basic Commercial Mortgage
Loan Training
(seminar) (3 hours)

JAMES R. BITONTE
4004 Riverside Drive
Upper Arlington, OH 43220
(614) 736-8717
E-mail: hud203k@msn.com

Course:
FHA 203k (seminar) (6 hours)

KOSSEL AND ASSOCIATES
5489 Wolfpen Pleasant Hill Road
Suite B
Milford, OH 45150
(513) 831-9725
Contact: Douglas A. Kossel
www.kosassoc.com

Courses:
Understanding the Credit Report
(seminar) (2 hours)
Mortgage Loan Programs
(seminar) (4 hours)
Fair Lending Laws & Predatory
Lenders (seminar) (3 hours)

LICENSE EDUCATION AND COMPLIANCE SERVICES, INC.— PROVIDER #2004014
285 Windsor Drive SW
Columbus, OH 43068
(614) 575-4669
Contact: Glen Littlejohn

Courses:
Introduction to FHA
Lending (seminar) (6 hours)
Alt A-A Loan Origination
(seminar) (3 hours)
Construction/Permanent Lending
(seminar) (3 hours)

OHIO ASSOCIATION OF MORTGAGE BROKERS
5686 Dressler Road, NW
North Canton, OH 44720
(330) 497-7233
E-mail: oamb.org
(*Note:* Courses taken through
the National Association of
Mortgage Brokers *will not be
accepted.*)

Courses:
Shedding the Light on Credit
Scoring (seminar) (4 hours)
Truth-in-Lending (seminar)
(4 hours)
Sub Prime Loan Origination
(seminar) (6 hours)
RESPA (seminar) (4 hours)
Residential Mortgage Lending
(seminar) (6 hours)
Mortgage Brokers Business Ethics
(seminar) (3 hours)
Basic Mortgage Brokering
(seminar) (6 hours)

OHIO MORTGAGE BANKERS ASSOCIATION
2586 Oakstone Drive
Columbus, OH 43231
(614) 891-4242
Contact: Kirk Lawson
www.ohiomba.org

Courses:
RESPA Reform Update
(seminar) (3 hours)
How to Process a Conventional
Loan (seminar) (3 hours)
Intro to Conventional
Underwriting (seminar) (3 hours)
FHA Loan Origination
(seminar) (6 hours)

VA Home Loans (seminar)
  (6 hours)
FHA Processing (seminar)
  (6 hours)

SCHOOL OF MORTGAGE LENDING
800 Bellevue Way NE, 4th Floor
Bellevue, WA 98004
(425) 822-3768
Contact: Susan Williams
www.schoolofmortgagelending.com

Courses:
Analyzing Creditworthiness
  (6 hours)
Conventional Processing (6 hours)
Essentials of Mortgage Lending
  (6 hours)
FHA/VA Lending Basics (6 hours)
New Construction and
  Rehab Loans (6 hours)
Principles of Mortgage
  Lending (6 hours)
Processing for the Approval
  (6 hours)
Regulatory Federal Statutes
  (6 hours)
Standards of Conventional
  Origination (6 hours)
Understanding Title Insurance
  (6 hours)
(Distant learning classes available)

SEAN GILL
881 Middlebury Drive North
Columbus, OH 43085
(614) 946-1094

Course:
Mortgage Brokers Guide to Credit
  (seminar) (6 hours)

STARK STATE COLLEGE OF TECHNOLOGY
6200 Frank Avenue NW
Canton, OH 44720
(330) 966-5455
Contact: Russell O'Neill
www.startkstate.edu

Courses:
Compliance and the Mortgage
  Broker (seminar) (6 hours)
The Mortgage Process
  (seminar) (6 hours)

A Loan Originator in Oklahoma

Regulatory agency: Oklahoma Commission of Consumer Credit

Contact info: www.okdocc.state.ok.us/ or call (405) 521-3653

Type of license: Loan originator

Requirements

To qualify for licensing as a loan originator, you must:

- Be at least 21 years old

- Be a U.S. citizen or legal resident alien

- Not have been convicted of a criminal offense that, as determined by the administrator, directly relates to the occupation of loan originator

- Have at least 18 months of experience as a mortgage originator (must provide proof) *or* pass a mortgage loan originator test

Exam

$150 fee

Testing is daily and must be scheduled 24 hours in advance. Testing times are 9 a.m. and 1 p.m. You can schedule your test online at www.okdocc.state.ok.us.

Licensing

$50 fee

The fee should accompany the loan originator application. License is valid for three years.

A Loan Originator in Oregon

Regulatory agency: Department of Consumer & Business Services, Division of Finance & Corporate Securities

Contact info: www.oregondfcs.org or call (503) 378-4140

Type of license: Loan originator

Requirements

Education

Loan originators are required to take an entry-level course on state and federal laws and rules relating to mortgage lending in this state. Loan originators must complete a certified authority-approved course within six months from the time the department is notified of their employment by a licensed mortgage lender or broker. If the loan originator fails to complete the course within the six-month period, the person may not work as a loan originator until completing the entry-level course and passing the examination. The entry-level course and test can be taken at the Mortgage Lending Education Board, located on the Web at www.oregonmleb.com.

All loan originators are required to fulfill 20 hours of continuing education every two years.

Exam

Loan originators must pass an examination on state and federal laws and rules relating to mortgage lending in this state. This test must be taken within six months from the time the department is notified of the person's employment by a licensed mortgage lender or broker. If the test is not passed within six months, the person may not work as a loan originator until passing the examination.

Registration

All loan originators must be registered with the Department of Consumer & Business Services, Division of Finance & Corporate Securities. A Loan Originator Information Form must be completed.

Schools for Oregon

ADVANCED EDUCATIONAL SYSTEMS, LLC
73 W. Timounium Road
Timonium, MD 21903
(877) 878-3600
www.trainingpro.com

FINANCIAL STRATEGIES
3500 DePauw Boulevard, #3070
Indianapolis, IN 46268

(317) 871-2380
www.mymortgagetrainer.com

PROSCHOOLS.COM
Four locations in Oregon
Local (503) 297-1344 or
    toll-free (800) 452-4879
www.proschools.com
(Online service)

A Loan Originator in Pennsylvania

Regulatory agency: Pennsylvania Department of Banking

Contact info: www.banking.state.pa.us or call (717) 787-3717

Type of license: Loan originator

Requirements

Education
None required for loan originators.

Licensing
None required for loan originators.

A Loan Originator in Rhode Island

Regulatory agency: Rhode Island Department of Business Regulation, Division of Banking

Contact info: www.dbr.state.ri.us or call (401) 222-2246

Type of license: Loan originator

Requirements

Education
None required for loan originators.

Licensing
None required for loan originators.

A Loan Originator in South Carolina

Regulatory agency: South Carolina Department of Consumer Affairs

Contact info: www.state.sc.us/consumer or call (803) 734-2020

Type of license: Loan originator

Requirements

Education
Effective April 1, 2005, to apply for an originator license, you must:

- Have 6 months' experience in residential mortgage lending

or

- Complete 8 hours of continuing education within 90 days of employment

All loan originators must be at least 18 years of age at the time of application.

To maintain the license, 8 hours of continuing education is required.

Licensing
$50 annual license fee

License expires annually on March 31.

Effective January 13, 2005, loan originators are required to be licensed with the South Carolina Department of Consumer Affairs. Use Supplemental Form O to apply for a South Carolina originator's license (available online). It is the loan originator's responsibility to maintain current records (address, current employer information) with the Department of Consumer Affairs.

Criminal Records Check
$25 fee

A Loan Originator in South Dakota

Regulatory agency: South Dakota Department of Revenue & Regulation

Contact info: www.state.sd.us/banking or call (605) 733-3421

Type of license: Loan originator

Requirements
Education
None required for loan originators.

Licensing
None required for loan originators.

A Loan Originator in Tennessee

Regulatory agency: Tennessee Department of Financial Institutions

Contact info: www.state.tn.us/financialinst or call (615) 741-2837

Type of license: Loan originator

Requirements

Education

None required for loan originators.

Licensing and Registration

$100 annual fee

Effective January 1, 2005, employing licensees will be required to register their loan originators with the Tennessee Department of Financial Institutions. Registration is required annually. A loan originator is unable to affiliate with more than one licensee or registrant at a time.

A Loan Officer in Texas

Regulatory agency: Texas Savings and Loan Department

Contact info: www.tsld.state.tx.us or call (877) 276-5550

Type of license: A loan officer is considered an employee (W-2). An independent contractor (1099) would need to obtain a mortgage broker license.

Requirements

Education

You must have 18 months of experience as a loan officer as evidenced by documentary proof of full-time employment as a loan officer with a mortgage broker or banker, or you must successfully complete 15 hours of educational courses approved by the commissioner.

In addition, a loan officer must complete 15 hours of continuing education every 2 years. A list of commissioner-approved course providers is given below.

Exam

$42 fee

A prelicensing exam is administered by an approved designated contractor—promissor. You may contact Promissor by telephone, toll-free, at (800) 275-8246.

The test consists of 75 multiple-choice questions, and you will have two hours to complete the exam. Test center locations can be found on the Promissor Web site at www.promissor.com.

Licensing
    $214 fee

The fee breaks down this way:

    $155 license

    $20 Mortgage Broker Recovery Fund

    $39 background check

The fee to renew a license is $175.

License is valid for two years. Texas law requires a mortgage broker or loan officer licensee to maintain a physical address in Texas.

With your license application you must submit a Loan Officer Sponsor Certification Form that is to be completed by your employing broker. In order for the background check to be completed, you will need to submit a fingerprint card completed by the Texas Department of Public Safety or Sheriff's Department. In addition you will need to submit the Verification and Confirmation Authorization to verify and obtain information on credit, employment status and history, financial condition, legal history and status, and personal and professional background, including any criminal record to determine your eligibility.

Fingerprints
    $17.50 fee

Promissor provides electronic fingerprinting services at the exam center.

Schools for Texas

100% MORTGAGE LOAN ORIGINATION
7216 Creekstone Drive
Sachse, TX 75048
(972) 897-6558
Contact: Jason Harmony

123LOANOFFICER.COM
8313 Southwest Freeway #103
Houston, TX 77074
(713) 774-9899
Contact: Scott Hilton

1-ON-1 LOAN TRAINING
3803 Parkwood Boulevard, #400
Frisco, TX 75034
(214) 618-8060
Contact: Gabriel Moreno

1st CHOICE MORTGAGE PROCESSING TRAINING
10303 Northwest Freeway #256
Houston, TX 77092
(713) 263-8956
Contact: L'Tonya Dowdell

360 TRAINING
200 Academy Drive #170
Austin, TX 78704
(512) 441-1097
Contact: Shelly Rayner

ABOUT SUCCESS REAL ESTATE ACADEMY
3307 Northland Drive, #170
Austin, TX 78731
(512) 407-3434
Contact: Kay Adams or Samantha
  Crisp

ACADEMY OF REAL ESTATE
7619 Montana
El Paso, TX 79925
(915) 779-0096
Contact: Phyliss Goodrich

THE ACADEMY OF REGULATED REAL ESTATE COURSES (TARREC)
PO Box 53065
Lubbock, TX 79453
(806) 797-0769
Contact: Karen Nichols

ADVANCED CAREER TRAINING, INC.
(through Baylor University)
9888 Bissonnet #675
Houston, TX 79925
(713) 270-6061
Contact: James Howze

ADVANCED EDUCATION SYSTEMS DBA TRAINING PRO
73 West Timonium Road
Timonium, MD 21093
(877) 878-3600
Contact: Sentell F. Barnes

ADVANCED PERFORMANCE TRAINING
7924 Skylake Drive
Fort Worth, TX 76179
(817) 514-7306
Contact: Mike Mackey

AGENT CAMPUS
200 Academy Drive, #260
Austin, TX 78704
(512) 441-1097
Contact: Melissa Kleeman

ALL-STAR REAL ESTATE SCHOOL
911 Gemini Avenue
Houston, TX 77058
(281) 480-9995
Contact: Reg E. Brittain

ALLIANCE ACADEMY
13322 Southview Lane
Dallas, TX 75240
(972) 644-6635
(Four different locations in Texas)
Contact: Jerry Rutledge

ALVIN COMMUNITY COLLEGE
3110 Mustang Road
Alvin, TX 77511
(281) 756-3793
Contact: Stacey Chambless

AMERICA'S MORTGAGE CENTER
5115 N. Galloway #302
Mesquite, TX 75150
(972) 270-8100
Contact: Tim Barnett

AMERICAN COLLEGE OF REAL ESTATE, INC.
504 Jose Marti Boulevard
Brownsville, TX 78521
(956) 544-6777
Contact: Sherri Berry

AMERICAN DREAM REAL ESTATE TRAINING
1103 Shadow Bend
Pearland, TX 77581
(281) 648-3969
Contact: Elizabeth Penn Adair

AMERICAN INVESCO MORTGAGE CORP.
13101 N.W. Freeway #120
Houston, TX 77040
(713) 690-5422
Contact: Ray Jones

AMERICAN MORTGAGE INSTITUTE
811 S. Central Expressway #530
Richardson, TX 75080
(469) 767-4356
Contact: Kareem Al-tal

APLUSCE.COM
4001 N. Shepard #227
Houston, TX 77018
(713) 742-5272
Contact: John Parker

APPRAISAL INSTITUTE
424 S. Summit Avenue
Ft. Worth, TX 76104
(817) 336-8787
Contact: Scott Burdette

ATLANTIC AMERICAN FINANCIAL INSTITUTE
1603 Babcock #146
San Antonio, TX 78229
(210) 349-7500
Contact: Anita Dansby-Russell

AUSTIN INSTITUTE OF REAL ESTATE
7801 N. Lamar #F-35
Austin, TX 78752
(512) 453-0900
Contact: Lynn Mortgage

AUSTIN MORTGAGE ACADEMY
9101 Burnet Road, #110
Austin, TX 78758
(512) 339-1826
Contact: Richard Small, Jr.

BOARDWALK SCHOOL OF REAL ESTATE
5810 Waterwalk
Richmond, TX 77469
(281) 633-0696
Contact: Diane Colby-Honerkamp

BROKER COMPLIANCE
3267 Bee Caves Road #107,
PMB 517
Austin, TX 78746
(512) 328-1777
Contact: James D. Russell

BROKERCE.COM
5850 San Felipe
Houston, TX 77057
(713) 825-7930
Contact: Betsy Trice

C&S TRAINING & CONSULTANTS
9224 Rockrose Drive
Tampa, FL 33647
(800) 266-2414
Contact: Lee Comegys

CAPITAL REAL ESTATE TRAINING
7701 N. Lamar #420
Austin, TX 78752
(512) 451-9787
Contact: Rick Knowles

CAPSTONE INSTITUTE OF MORTGAGE FINANCE
2000 Powers Ferry #2-3
Marietta, GA 30067
(770) 956-8252
Contact: Susan Stromquist

CENTER FOR CAREER EDUCATION, INC., DBA REAL ESTATE COLLEGE
1140 Empire Central #520
Dallas, TX 75247
(214) 920-9611
Contact: Dan Hamilton

CENTER FOR FINANCIAL TRAINING
1701 River Run Road, #1103
Ft. Worth, TX 76107
(817) 335-8500
Contact: Karen Vanderwerken

C.E.T.C UNLIMITED, INC. DBA ACADEMIC ALTERNATIVE EDUCATION
2800 W. Kingsley Road
Garland, TX 75041
(972) 271-3151
Contact: Donna Townsend

CHAMPIONS SCHOOL OF REAL ESTATE
550 N. Denton Tap Road
Coppell, TX 75019
(Two locations in Houston and
  one in Dallas)
(972) 316-2020
Contact: Rita SantaMaria

CONTINUING EDUCATION INSTITUTE (CEI)
2001 108th Street, #102
Grand Prairie,
  TX 75050
(972) 975-4234
Contact: James V. Parchman

CREDIT RESOURCES, INC.
13831 Northwest Freeway #200
Houston,
  TX 77040
(713) 460-3367
Contact: Debera J. Phinney

CROSSMARK RESIDENTIAL MORTGAGE
25362 Drennan
Splendora, TX 77372
(713) 898-7096
Contact: John Parker

DAVID HERSHMAN/THE HERSHMAN GRP
PO Box 932
Centreville, VA 20122
(800) 581-5678
Contact: David Hershman

DEL MAR COLLEGE
Multi-service Center
Corpus Christi, TX 78404
(361) 698-1515
Contact: Margaret Edwards

EDUCATION AND TRAINING CORP.
1555 Naperville/Wheaton #202
Naperville, IL 60563
(800) 979-9051
Contact: Karl Matthews

FANNIE MAE CORPORATION
700 N. St. Mary's #1925
San Antonio, TX 78210
(210) 228-3803
Contact: Daniel Lopez

FIESTA CAREER INSTITUTE
2616 S. Loop West #515
Houston, TX 77054
(713) 662-2430
Contact: Christian Ashibuogwu

FINANCIAL STRATEGIES
690 Pro Med Lane
Carmel, IN 46032

(317) 566-0425
Contact: Alan Griffin

FIRST AMERICAN TITLE INS CO OF TEXAS
1500 S. Dairy Ashford #300
Houston, TX 77077
(281) 588-2200
Contact: Benita P. Hester

FREDDIE MAC
8250 Jones Branch Drive MSA52
McLean, VA 22102-3110
(703) 918-8573
Contact: Jim Romero

GATEWAY MORTGAGE GROUP, LLC
7030 S. Yale #700
Tulsa, OK 74136
(918) 712-9000
Contact: J. Whitney Barth

GIANTLION, INC.
904 Riviera
Mansfield, TX 76063
(817) 929-9119
Contact: Lonny Coffey

GLB SERVICES PLLC
3522 Vineyard Drive
Houston, TX 77082
(281) 752-5767
Contact: Gail Brown

GOLD FINANCIAL SERVICES
2900 Mossrock #100
San Antonio, TX 78230
(210) 366-1070
Contact: Arline Walker

GRAYSTONE MORTGAGE BUSINESS SCHOOL
4 West Las Olas Boulevard, #600
Ft. Lauderdale, FL 33301
(954) 525-2935
Contact: Cynthia B. Robinson

GREATER DALLAS ASSOCIATION OF REALTORS
8201 N. Stemmons Freeway
Dallas, TX 75247
(214) 637-6660
Contact: Kathleen E. Terrell

HOUSTON COMMUNITY COLLEGE
3100 Main Street
Houston, TX 77002
(713) 718-5229
Contact: Alex Blinkley

HOWELL CAMPBELL & ASSOCIATES
4100 Spring Valley Road, #203
Dallas, TX 75244
(972) 233-6633
Contact: Francis A. Gomez

THE INSTITUTE OF PROFESSIONAL DEVELOPMENT
7801 N. Lamar Boulevard, #F-35
Austin, TX 78752
(512) 453-0900
Contact: Lynn Morgan

INTEGRITY EDUCATIONAL SERVICES
205 S. Commons Ford Road No. 1
Austin, TX 78733
(512) 402-9300
Contact: Curtis Jordan

L&M MORTGAGE PROCESSING
3274 FM 1960 West #330
Houston, TX 77068
(281) 312-1473
Contact: L'Tonya P. Dowdell or
   Michael T. Dowdell

LAKEWAY TRAINING INSTITUTE
2300 Lohmans Spur #190
Austin, TX 78734
(512) 402-9785
Contact: John A. Copapret

LENDERS TRAINING INSTITUTE
113 N. Batavia Avenue
Batavia, IL 60510
(630) 865-5169
Contact: Jennifer A. Schrank

THE LENDING RESOURCE
8620 N. New Braunfels #529
San Antonio, TX 78217
(210) 737-9477
Contact: Steve Davis

LEONARD-HAWES REAL ESTATE SCHOOL
4100 Midway Drive #1055
Carrollton, TX 75007
(800) 442-4593
Contact: Kim Cagle

LOAN MORTGAGE CONSULTANTS (LMC)
8003 N. Circle Drive
Houston, TX 77071
(832) 541-4238
Contact: Lynn Samuel

THE LOAN OFFICER GUIDE
5847 San Felipe, 17th Floor
Houston, TX 77057
(281) 454-5793
Contact: Fredrick R. Williams

LOAN ORIGINATION TRAINING SCHOOL
2512 Oakland Boulevard #9
Ft. Worth, TX 76103
(817) 536-5328
Contact: Ray Williams, Jr.

LOANS UNLIMITED
12703 Veterans Memorial #108
Houston, TX 77014
(281) 440-8810
Contact: Erick Jones

LONE STAR SCHOOL
1120 Nasa Road, #575
The Woodlands, TX 77380
(281) 335-8073
Contact: Chad Sohrt

MARKETAMERICA MORTGAGE
25231 Grogan's Mill #575
The Woodlands, TX 77380
(281) 210-2001
Contact: Matthew Carlton

MATCHMAKER MORTGAGE
14022 Hempstead
Houston, TX 77040
(713) 462-6663
Contact: Michael Ortega

MCE CONNECTION
219 Driftwood Court
Runaway, TX 76426
(940) 575-2841
Contact: Vernon Slocomb

MILLENNIUM RESIDENTIAL MORTGAGE
5644 Westheimer #256
Houston, TX 77056
(281) 820-4800
Contact: Byron McGough

MOC REAL ESTATE SCHOOL
3110 Tidwell
Houston, TX 77093
(713) 674-8898
Contact: Kathy West

MORTGAGE BANKERS ASSOCIATION
1919 Pennsylvania Avenue NW #202
Kennesaw, GA 30144
(202) 557-2763
Contact: Dan Thomas or
   Jennifer Ridings

MORTGAGE BROKER CONT. ED. SCHOOL
3226 N. Seclusion Drive
Sarasota, FL 34239
(941) 923-1228
Contact: Dick Neary

MORTGAGE DATA SOLUTIONS
705 Bridle Drive
Desoto, TX 75115
(972) 274-1841
Contact: Shirley Miller

MORTGAGE-EDUCATION.COM
2959 Cherokee Street #121
Salt Lake City, UT 84107
(770) 792-6770
Contact: Dan Johnson

MORTGAGE ENTREPRENEUR
507 Reinerman
Houston, TX 77007

(713) 457-6800
Contact: John Cruise

MORTGAGE INSTRUCTIONAL SERV. CORP.
3863 SW Loop 820, #118
Ft. Worth, TX 76133
(972) 470-9900
Contact: Julie Clanton or
Mary Jo Gaustad

MORTGAGE SCHOOL OF TEXAS, INC.
4543 Post Oak Place #107
Houston, TX 77027
(832) 615-5403
Contact: Linda D. Bindhammer

MORTGAGE TRAINING ACADEMY
1370 Pantheon Way #180
San Antonio, TX 78232
(210) 403-3313
Contact: Richard McIlveen

MORTGAGE TRAINING INSTITUTE
4155 E. Jewell Avenue, #908
Denver, CO 80222
(303) 758-9037
Contact: Jon Exley

MORTGAGE TRAINING SERVICES
1650 Sierra Avenue, #202
Yuba City, CA 95993
(530) 751-2071
Contact: Angela Gonzales

MORTGAGE U
30300 Telegraph Road #100
Bingham Farms, MI 48025
(800) 278-0200
Contact: Kathy Wade or Alice Alvey

MY REAL ESTATE SCHOOL
8313 Southwest Freeway #106
Houston, TX 77074
(713) 773-0036
Contact: Nick Will

NATIONAL ASSOCIATION OF MORTGAGE BROKERS
8201 Greensboro Drive, 300
McLean, VA 22102
(703) 610-9007
Contact: Scott Hall

NORTH LAKE COLLEGE
5001 N. MacArthur Boulevard
Irving, TX 75038
(972) 273-3467
Contact: J. Keith Baker

NOVUS PROFESSIONAL
869 E. 4500 South
Washington, DC 20006
(239) 850-2485
Contact: Kris Armstrong

OPTION ONE MORTGAGE CORP.
3 Ada
Irvine, CA 92618
(800) 704-0800
Contact: Wendy Tucker

PARAMOUNT SCHOOL OF REAL ESTATE
10333 Harwin #575
Houston, TX 77036
(713) 995-5626
Contact: Angela Walker

PAUL DONOHUE PRESENTS
4527 US Highway #220 NPOB 780
Summerfield, NC 27358
(888) 341-7767
Contact: Paul Donohue or Joy Soler

PMI MORTGAGE INSURANCE CO.
1009 Magnolia Cove
Buda, TX 78610
(800) 392-2238
Contact: Carla Moore

POWER TRAINING
PO Box 9256
Austin, TX 78757
(512) 451-9112
Contact: Juliana Brock

PURVIS REAL ESTATE TRAINING INSTITUTE
2020 Montgomery Street
Ft. Worth, TX 76107
(817) 738-4669
Contact: Bryan McDonald

QUICKSTART MORTGAGE TRAINING
2192 Canterbury Way
Potomac, MD 20854
(301) 738-7031
Contact: Thomas Morgan

REAL ESTATE COLLEGE
1140 Empire Central #520
Dallas, TX 75247
(214) 920-9611
Contact: Dan Hamilton

REAL ESTATE EDUCATION, INC.
290 Dowlen Road #201
Beaumont, TX 77706
(409) 866-6858
Contact: Eddie Stockton

THE REAL ESTATE SCHOOL OF HOUSTON
1570 S. Dairy Ashford #210
Houston, TX 77022

(281) 556-9567
Contact: Ralph Tamper

ROBINSON REAL ESTATE SCHOOL
5445 Almeda #304
Houston, TX 77004
(713) 663-7363
Contact: Rookie Robinson

ROYALE DYNAMICS
613 W. Main Street
W. Dundee, IL 60118
(847) 551-1046
Contact: Tammy Butler

SAN ANTONIO BOARD OF REALTORS
9110 I.H. 10 West #1
San Antonio, TX 78230
(210) 593-1200
Contact: Ron Smith

SCHOOL OF MORTGAGE LENDING
800 Bellevue Way NE, 4th Floor
Bellevue, WA 98004
(888) 398-6620
Contact: Susan Williams

SIERRA SCHOOLS, INC.
3033 Chimney Rock #105
Houston, TX 77056
(713) 334-1900
Contact: Linda S. Cooper

SUPERIOR MORTGAGE
160 Dowlen Road
Beaumont, TX 77706
(409) 866-7743
Contact: Alison Gonzales

SWEETWATER MORTGAGE COMPANY
908 Town & Country Boulevard, #120
Houston, TX 77024
(281) 970-1082
Contact: Jim Norris

TEXAS ASSOCIATION OF MORTGAGE BROKERS
502 E. 11th Street, #400
Austin, TX 78701
(512) 708-0627
Contact: Xina Ortiz

TEXAS BANKERS ASSOCIATION
203 W. 10th Street
Austin, TX 78701
(512) 472-8388
Contact: Sharon Vakes

TEXAS CONTINUING EDUCATION
PO Box 1330
McKinney, TX 75070
(214) 733-8602
Contact: Stephen Trussell

TEXAS MORTGAGE BANKERS ASSOCIATION
823 Congress Avenue, #220
Austin, TX 78701
(512) 480-8622
Contact: Lisa Vercher

TEXAS MORTGAGE BROKER COMPLIANCE GROUP
2935 Thousand Oaks, Suite 6, #250
San Antonio, TX 78247
(210) 861-9946
Contact: S. Ray Casa

TEXAS MORTGAGE LENDING SCHOOL
7322 South West Freeway #1100
Houston, TX 77074
(713) 981-3235
Contact: Abdul Qayyum

TEXAS VETERANS LAND BOARD
3700 Fredericksburg Road, #241
San Antonio, TX 78201
(512) 699-6192
Contact: Tamara Tapman

TRAININGELEMENT.COM
6500 Hillside Terrace Drive
Austin, TX 78749
(512) 301-5205
Contact: Omer Dossani

T.U. CONTINUING EDUCATION
PO Box 6399
Kingwood, TX 77325
(281) 358-0409
Contact: Bernard H. Zick

TYLER REAL ESTATE COLLEGE
509 W. Dobbs
Tyler, TX 75701
(903) 595-5145
Contact: Harold Grimes

USA TRAINING CO.
8871 Tallwood
Austin, TX 78759
(512) 346-4204
Contact: Sue Decker

A Loan Originator in Utah

Regulatory agency: Utah Department of Commerce, Division of Real Estate

Contact info: www.commerce.state.ut.us/dre/ or call (801) 530-6747

Type of license: Individual licensee

Requirements

To qualify for licensure, you must meet the following requirements:

- Have good moral character

- Have no criminal history (a felony or misdemeanor involving moral turpitude) in the last 10 years

- Have not had a license or registration suspended, revoked, or canceled based on misconduct in a professional capacity relating to good moral character

Education

Effective January 1, 2005, there is an initial education requirement of 20 hours of approved courses outlined by the commissioner. A list of approved prelicensing education providers is given below.

In addition, to renew your license you must complete 14 hours of continuing education.

Exam

$75 fee

Promissor, a national test administrator company, administers the Utah mortgage lender exam. You can reach Promissor by calling, toll-free, (800) 274-7292 or by going to the Promissor Web site at www.promissor.com. An Individual Application Form will be generated by the testing service after successful completion of the mortgage lender exam. The exam consists of two parts: general and state law.

Licensing and Registration
   $200 individual application fee

   $36 Recovery Fund fee

License is valid for two years. The renewal fee is $136.

Background Check and Fingerprinting
   $39 fee

If the exam is taken at one of Promissor's Utah test sites, fingerprints will be taken after the successful completion of the mortgage lender exam. Two fingerprint cards are required. In addition, a Fingerprint Letter of Waiver must accompany the application. Blank fingerprint cards are available through the Division of Real Estate.

Bond
Either an individual licensee must provide a surety bond in the amount of $10,000, *or* the loan originator must provide verification that he or she is an "employee or agent" of an entity that is licensed, in which case the applicant's actions are covered by a surety bond as an employee or agent.

Approved Prelicensing Education Providers for Utah

THE MORTGAGE ACADEMY
42 North 200 East, #3
American Fork, UT 84003
(801) 765-0200
Contact: Lance Miller

**MORTGAGE EDUCATION
CONNECTION**
10653 River Front Parkway, #220
South Jordan, UT 84095
(801) 330-7205
Contact: Melanie or Michael

MORTGAGE EDUCATION PROS
4001 South 700 East, #110
Salt Lake City, UT 84107
(801) 269-2404
Contact: Brendon Cassity

MORTGAGE EDUCATORS
1090 South 1100 East
Salt Lake City, UT 84102
(801) 582-7915
Contact: Fredrick R. Williams

**MORTGAGE TRAINING
SYSTEMS**
676 East Vine Street, #5
Salt Lake City, UT 84107
(801) 270-8394
Contact: Scott Phippen

REPUBLIC MORTGAGE SCHOOL
4516 South 700 East, #190
Salt Lake City, UT 84107
(801) 270-6350
Contact: Gary Nielson

STRINGHAM MORTGAGE SCHOOL
5248 S. Pinemont Drive, #C250
Salt Lake City, UT 84123
(801) 269-8889
Contact: Kevin Swenson

UTAH MORTGAGE EDUCATION
472 West 50 North
American Fork, UT 84003
(801) 756-8226
Contact: David Luna

A Loan Originator in Vermont

Regulatory agency: Vermont Department of Banking, Insurance, Securities & Health Care Administration

Contact info: www.bishca.state.vt.us (click on banking) or call (802) 828-3307

Type of license: Loan originator

Requirements
Education
None required for loan originators.

Licensing
None required for loan originators.

When applying for employment with a mortgage broker, a current résumé of experience will be required, as the mortgage broker is required to submit it to the Department of Banking upon commencement of employment.

A Loan Originator in Virginia

Regulatory agency: Virginia State Corporation Commission Bureau of Financial Institutions

Contact info: www.state.va.us/scc/division/banking/index.htm or call (804) 371-9657

Type of license: Loan originator

Requirements
Education
None required for loan originators.

Licensing
None required for loan originators.

A Loan Originator in Washington

Regulatory agency: Washington Department of Financial Institutions

Contact info: www.wa.gov/dfi/home.htm or call (360) 902-8703

Type of license: Loan originator

Requirements

Education
None required for loan originators.

Licensing
None required for loan originators.

A Loan Originator in West Virginia

Regulatory agency: West Virginia Division of Banking, Mortgage Division

Contact info: www.wvdob.org or call (304) 558-2294

Type of license: Loan originator

Requirements

In the state of West Virginia a loan originator working for a mortgage broker must meet the requirements listed below. However, when employed by a mortgage lender, there are *no* licensing or registration requirements.

Licensing
$150 fee

License is valid for five years.

Include the fee along with the loan originator application and:

- A legible copy of a current driver's license or other photo ID card issued by the federal or state government

- Current résumé, detailing education and mortgage experience and training

- Fingerprint forms

- Background form

- Credit release form

Fingerprints and Background Investigation
$44 fee

Credit and Financial Responsibility
A *minimum* standard FICO score of 575 is required as a threshold to meeting the financial responsibility standard. An applicant whose credit score is lower than 575 (minimum 500) may still be considered for licensing if the applicant submits, within *15* calendar days of receipt of notification of a score at or below 575, an explanation for the score, together with supporting documentation and a detailed description of the plan to improve the applicant's financial position.

A Loan Originator in Wisconsin

Regulatory agency: Wisconsin Department of Financial Institutions

Contact info: www.wdfi.org or call (608) 266-1622

Type of license: Loan originator

Requirements

Education
None required for loan originators.

Licensing and Registration
$250 fee

License is valid for two years.

All loan originators must be registered with the Wisconsin Department of Financial Institutions. A loan originator may work for only one employer at a time. Upon termination of employment, it is the loan originator's responsibility to file an Employment Transfer Form with the regulating department, along with a $20 transfer fee.

A Loan Originator in Wyoming

> *Regulatory agency:* Wyoming Department of Audit, Division of Banking
>
> *Contact info:* http://audit.state.wy.us/BANKING/ or call (307) 777-7797
>
> *Type of license:* Loan originator

Requirements

Education
None required for loan originators.

Licensing
None required for loan originators.

MORTGAGE TERMINOLOGY

actual interest rate   The annual interest rate paid on a loan (sometimes referred to as the *note rate*). This rate is used to calculate the monthly mortgage payments. The actual interest rate is one of two interest rates applied to a mortgage loan. The other is the APR. See *annual percentage rate (APR)*.

adjustable-rate mortgage (ARM) loans   Loans with interest rates that are adjusted periodically based on changes in a pre-selected index. As a result, the interest rate and monthly payment on these loans will rise and fall with increases and decreases in the market. These mortgage loans must specify how their interest rate changes, usually in relation to a national index such as (but not always) U.S. Treasury bill rates. If interest rates rise, monthly payments will rise. An interest rate cap limits the amount by which the interest rate can change—this is an important feature to consider in an ARM loan.

adjustment interval   The length of time between changes in the interest rate or monthly payment on an ARM loan.

alternative documentation   Instead of full income documentation such as full tax returns, some lenders offer alternative documentation such as bank statements.

amortization   Repayment of a loan with periodic payments of both principal and interest calculated to pay off the loan at the end of a fixed period of time.

amount financed   The figure that is used to calculate the APR. It represents the loan amount minus any prepaid finance charges and assumes the loan is kept to maturity and only the required monthly payments are made.

annual percentage rate (APR)   Mortgage interest rate that includes both interest and any additional costs or prepaid finance charges such as prepaid interest, private mortgage insurance, closing fees, and points. The APR represents the total cost of credit on a yearly basis after all charges are taken into consideration. It will usually be slightly higher than the actual interest rate because it includes these additional items and assumes the loan will be kept to maturity. See *actual interest rate*.

application   An initial statement of personal and financial information required when applying for a loan.

application fee   The fee charged by the lender to cover the initial costs of processing a loan application.

appraisal   A written analysis of the estimated value of a property. A qualified appraiser who has knowledge of, experience with, and insight into the marketplace prepares the document. It demonstrates approximate fair market value based on recent sales in the neighborhood and is required on purchases and refinances.

appraisal fee   A fee charged by a licensed, certified appraiser to render an opinion of market value as of a specific date.

assignment   The transfer of ownership, rights, or interests in property by one person, the assignor, to another, the assignee.

assignment recording fee   In many instances, after closing, the lender transfers the loan to a specialized loan "servicer" who handles the collection of the monthly payments. The assignment fee covers the cost of recording this transfer at the local recording office.

assumption   A method of selling real estate in which the buyer of the property agrees to become responsible for the repayment of an existing loan on the property.

balloon mortgage   A short-term fixed-rate loan with fixed monthly payments for a set number of years, followed by one large final balloon payment for the remainder of the principal. Typically, the balloon payment may be due at the end of five, seven, or ten years. Borrowers with balloon loans may have the right to refinance the loan when the balloon payment is due, but the right to refinance is not guaranteed.

bankruptcy   A proceeding in a federal court to relieve a person or a business of certain debts it is unable to pay.

blanket mortgage   A mortgage that covers more than one parcel of real estate.

borrower   One who applies for and receives a loan in the form of a mortgage with the intention to repay.

broker   An individual who brings buyers and sellers together and assists in negotiating contracts for a client.

buydown mortgage   A mortgage loan with a below-market rate for a period of time.

buyer's market   Market conditions that favor buyers. With more sellers than buyers in the market, sellers may be forced to make substantial price adjustments.

call option   A provision of a note that allows the lender to require repayment of the loan in full before the end of the loan term. The option may be exercised due to breach of the terms of the loan or at the discretion of the lender.

caps (interest)   Consumer safeguards that limit the amount that the interest rate on an adjustable-rate mortgage can change in an adjustment interval or over the life of the loan.

caps (payment) Consumer safeguards that limit the amount that monthly payments on an adjustable-rate mortgage may change.

cash-out Any cash received when a borrower obtains a new loan that is larger than the remaining balance of the current mortgage. The cash-out amount is calculated by subtracting the sum of the old loan and fees from the new mortgage loan.

ceiling The maximum allowable interest rate of an adjustable-rate mortgage.

certificate of eligibility Veteran's eligibility for a VA-guaranteed loan. Obtainable through a local VA office by submitting Form DD-214 (Separation Paper) and VA Form 1880 (request for certificate of eligibility).

certificate of title A written opinion of the status of a title to a property, given by an attorney or a title company. This certificate does not offer the protection given by title insurance.

certificate of veteran status FHA form filled out by the VA to establish a borrower's eligibility for an FHA vet loan. Obtainable through a local VA office by submitting Form DD 214 (Separation Paper) with Form 26-8261a (request for a certificate of veteran status).

chain of title The chronological order of conveyance of a property from the original owner to the present owner.

closing The conclusion of a real estate transaction. It includes the signing of legal documents and the disbursement of the funds necessary to the sale of a home or loan transaction (refinance). Also known as *settlement*.

closing costs Costs for services that must be performed to process and close the loan application. Examples include title fees, recording fees, appraisal fees, pest inspection, attorney's fees, taxes, and surveying fees. Also known as *settlement costs*.

commission Money paid to a real estate agent or broker for negotiating a real estate or loan transaction.

commitment　A promise to lend and a statement by the lender of the terms and conditions under which a loan is made.

comparables　Refers to "comparable properties," properties used for comparative purposes in the appraisal process. Comparables are properties like the property under consideration; they have reasonably the same size, location, and amenities and have recently been sold. Comparables help the appraiser determine the approximate fair market value of the subject property. Also known as *comps*.

comparative market analysis　An informal estimate of market value that a real estate agent or broker calculates based on sales of comparable properties.

compound interest　Interest that is calculated not only on the initial principal but also on the accumulated interest of prior periods.

condominium　A real estate project in which each unit owner holds title to a unit in a building, an undivided interest in the common areas of the project, and sometimes the exclusive use of certain limited common areas. The condominium may be attached or detached.

conforming loan　A mortgage loan that meets all the requirements to be eligible for purchase by federal agencies such as Fannie Mae and Freddie Mac. The maximum conforming loan amount is $417,000 for a one-unit property.

contingency　A condition that must be satisfied before a contract is legally binding.

contract of sale　The agreement between the buyer and seller on the purchase price, terms, and conditions of a sale.

conventional loan　A loan that is *not* made under any government housing program. Conventional loans are not subject to the restrictions of government housing programs, such as loan size limits.

conversion clause　A provision in some ARMs that allows the borrower to change an ARM to a fixed-rate loan, usually after the first adjustment period. The new fixed rate will be set at current rates, and there may be a charge for the conversion feature.

convertible ARM A type of ARM loan with the option to convert to a fixed-rate loan during a given time period.

conveyance The document used to effect a transfer, such as a deed or mortgage.

cost of funds index (COFI) An index of the weighted-average interest rate paid by savings institutions for sources of funds, usually by members of the Eleventh Federal Home Loan Bank District.

credit bureau A clearinghouse for credit history information. Credit grantors provide the bureau with factual information on how their credit customers pay their bills. The bureau regularly assembles this information, along with public record information obtained from courthouses around the country, into a file on each consumer.

credit report A report that details the credit history of a prospective borrower and that is used to help determine borrower creditworthiness.

credit score A statistical method of assessing a borrower's creditworthiness. Credit card history, amount of outstanding debt, type of credit used, negative information such as bankruptcies or late payments, collection accounts and judgments, too little credit history, and too many credit lines with the maximum amount borrowed are all included in credit scoring models to determine a credit score.

deed A legal document with which title to real property is transferred from one owner to another. The deed contains a description of the property and is signed, witnessed, and delivered to the buyer at closing.

deed of trust A legal document that conveys title to real property to a third party. The third party holds title until the owner of the property has repaid the debt in full.

default   Failure to meet legal obligations in a contract, including failure to make payments on a loan.

delinquency   Failure to make payments as agreed in the loan agreement.

discount points   See *points*.

document preparation fee   Occasionally lenders will use outside companies to prepare the loan closing documents; this fee covers the cost of this service.

down payment   The amount required up front to purchase a property. This amount will vary depending on the type of loan being obtained, the creditworthiness of the borrower, etc.

due-on-sale clause   A provision in a mortgage or deed of trust allowing the lender to demand immediate payment of the loan balance upon sale of the property.

duplex   A property divided into two living units or residences, generally having separate entrances.

earnest money   A deposit made by a buyer toward the down payment in evidence of good faith when the purchase agreement is signed.

Equal Credit Opportunity Act (ECOA)   A federal law requiring creditors to make credit equally available without discrimination based on race, color, religion, national origin, age, sex, marital status, or receipt of income from public assistance programs.

Equifax   One of the three largest credit bureaus in the United States.

equity   The difference between the current market value of a property and the total debt obligations against the property.

escrow   A transaction in which a third party acts as the agent for the seller and the buyer, or for the borrower and the lender, in handling legal documents and disbursement of funds.

escrow account   An account held by the lender to which the borrower pays monthly installments, collected as part of the monthly mortgage payment, for annual expenses such as taxes and insurance. The lender disburses escrow account funds on behalf of the borrower when they become due. Also known as *impound account*.

escrow agent A person with fiduciary responsibility to the buyer and the seller, or the borrower and the lender, to ensure that the terms of the purchase or loan are carried out.

estimated closing fees An estimate of the fees that must be paid on or before the closing date by the buyer and the seller for services, taxes, and other items necessary to obtain the mortgage. These fees will average between 2 and 5% of the loan amount and vary by lender, property location, and type of mortgage.

Experian One of the three largest credit bureaus in the United States.

express or courier fee On refinance transactions, escrow companies will typically use an overnight courier to expedite the payoff of an existing loan. This fee covers the cost of the courier.

Fair, Isaac and Co. The company that invented credit scoring software.

Fannie Mae Agency that buys loans that are underwritten to its specific guidelines. These guidelines are an industry standard for residential conventional lending.

Federal Deposit Insurance Corporation (FDIC) An independent deposit insurance agency created by Congress to maintain stability and public confidence in the nation's banking system.

Federal Housing Administration (FHA) A federal agency within the Department of Housing and Urban Development (HUD) which insures residential mortgage loans made by private lenders and sets standards for underwriting mortgage loans.

Federal Reserve Board The seven-member board of governors that oversees Federal Reserve Banks, establishes monetary policy (interest rates, credit, etc.), and monitors the economic health of the country. Its members are appointed by the president, subject to Senate confirmation, and serve 14-year terms. Also known as *the Fed*.

fee simple   Absolute ownership of real property.

FHA loans   Fixed- or adjustable-rate loans insured by the U.S. Department of Housing and Urban Development. FHA loans are designed to make housing more affordable, particularly for first-time home buyers. FHA loans typically permit borrowers to buy a home with a lower down payment than that needed for conventional loans. With FHA insurance, eligible buyers can purchase a home with a down payment of as little as 3% of the appraised value or the purchase price—whichever is lower. The current FHA loan limits vary depending on home type and home location.

FICO   The most common credit scoring model used by lenders. FICO scores can range from 350 to 900. According to this model, the higher the score, the less likely the borrower is to default on a loan. Also known as a *Fair, Isaac score*.

filing fees   The amount charged by public officials in a specific area for recording a mortgage and other documents.

finance charge   The total of all interest paid over the entire life of a loan, assuming the loan is kept to maturity.

first mortgage   A mortgage that is in first-lien position, taking priority over all other liens. In the case of a foreclosure, the first mortgage will be repaid before any other mortgages.

fixed rate   An interest rate that is fixed for the term of the loan.

fixed-rate loans   Loans that have interest rates that do not change over the life of the loan. Fixed-rate loans typically have 15-, 20-, or 30-year terms.

float   An interest rate that continues to change, or float, due to market fluctuations.

flood certification fee   Federal law requires flood hazard insurance if a property lies in a flood zone. This fee is to secure a determination of the property to be in or out of a flood zone.

flood insurance Insurance that compensates for physical damage to a property caused by flood. Typically it is not covered under standard hazard insurance.

flood life of loan coverage Flood zone determinations may change from time to time. The fee for flood life of loan coverage allows the lender to track any changes in the property's flood zone status over the life of the loan.

forbearance The act by the lender of refraining from taking legal action on a mortgage loan that is delinquent.

foreclosure The legal process by which a mortgaged property may be sold to pay off a mortgage loan that is in default.

Freddie Mac Agency that buys loans that are underwritten to its specific guidelines. These guidelines are an industry standard for residential conventional lending.

good faith estimate A written estimate of the settlement costs the borrower will likely have to pay at closing. Under the Real Estate Settlement Procedures Act (RESPA), the lender is required to provide this disclosure to the borrower within three days of receiving a loan application.

government recording fee This fee is paid to the local county recording office for the recording of a mortgage lien and, in the event of a purchase transaction, for recording of the deed that transfers title. Fees for recording vary by county and are set by state and local governments.

grace period The period of time during which a loan payment may be made after its due date without incurring a late penalty. The grace period is specified as part of the terms of the loan in the note.

gross income Total income before taxes or expenses are deducted.

guideline ratios There are two guideline ratios used to qualify for a mortgage. The first is called the front-end ratio and is calculated by dividing the total monthly mortgage payment by the gross monthly income. The second is called the back-end ratio and is equal to the total monthly mortgage payment plus the total monthly debt divided by the gross monthly income.

hazard insurance   Insurance that protects the insured against loss due to fire or other natural disaster in exchange for a premium paid to the insurer.

home equity line of credit (HELOC)   A credit line that is kept open and restored as the balance is paid off.

homeowner's insurance   Insurance for the home. Homeowner's insurance is required by all lenders to protect their investment and must be obtained before closing. In most cases, coverage must be equal to the loan balance or the value of the home.

HUD   Housing and Urban Development, the U.S. government department established to implement federal housing and community development programs. HUD oversees the Federal Housing Administration.

HUD-1 Uniform Settlement Statement   A standard form that itemizes the closing costs associated with purchasing a home or refinancing a loan. Also called a 1003.

impound account   See *escrow account*.

index   A widely published rate such as LIBOR, T-bill, or Eleventh District cost of funds index (COFI). Lenders use these indexes to establish the interest rates charged on mortgage loans. Most lenders generally tie ARM interest rate changes to an index. For ARMs, a predetermined margin is added to the index to compute the interest rate adjustment.

initial cap   A consumer safeguard that limits the amount that the interest rate on an adjustable-rate mortgage can change during the first adjustment period. See *Caps (Interest)*.

initial rate   The rate charged during the first interval of an ARM loan.

insurance   The type(s) of insurance required for a loan, such as homeowner's insurance or private mortgage insurance.

interest A charge paid for borrowing money.

interest rate The rate of interest on a loan, expressed as a percentage of 100.

interest rate cap See *Caps (Interest)*.

joint liability The liability shared among two or more people, each of whom is liable for the full debt.

joint tenancy A form of ownership of property giving each person equal interest in the property, including rights of survivorship.

jumbo loan A mortgage larger than the limits set by Fannie Mae and Freddie Mac; a nonconforming loan.

junior mortgage A mortgage subordinate to the claim of a prior lien or mortgage. In the case of a foreclosure, a senior mortgage or lien will be paid first.

late charge Penalty paid by a borrower when a payment is made after the due date.

lender The bank, mortgage company, or mortgage broker offering the loan.

lender fees Fees paid to the lender.

lender processing fee A fee that covers the cost of analyzing a loan application and compiling and packaging the necessary supporting documentation to close a loan.

LIBOR (London Interbank Offered Rate) The interest rate charged among banks in the foreign market for short-term loans to one another—a common index for ARM loans.

lien A legal claim by one person on the property of another for security for payment of a debt.

lifetime (or life) cap See *Caps (Interest)*.

loan application An initial statement of personal and financial information required to apply for a loan.

loan application fee A fee charged by a lender to cover the initial costs of processing a loan application.

loan origination fee A fee charged by a lender to cover the administrative costs of processing a loan.

loan term The period of time between the closing date and the date of the last payment due on the loan, at which time the loan is paid in full.

loan-to-value ratio (LTV) The ratio of the loan amount to the appraised value or the sales price of the property, whichever is less, and expressed as a percentage.

lock or lock-in A lender's guarantee of an interest rate for a set period of time—usually the time between the loan application approval and the loan closing.

manufactured home A factory-assembled residence built in units or sections that are transported to a permanent site and erected on a foundation.

margin The percentage difference between the index for a particular loan and the interest rate charged. This is a number predetermined by the lender.

maximum cash-out The maximum amount of money allowed on a mortgage transaction.

monthly principal and interest (P&I) payment The dollar portion needed to repay the loan each month. It is the sum of the principal and interest. All interest that occurs is calculated on the current balance owing. The principal payment reduces the remaining balance of a mortgage.

mortgage A legal document by which real property is pledged as security for the repayment of a loan.

mortgage banker An individual or company that originates and sometimes services mortgage loans.

mortgage broker An individual or company that arranges financing for borrowers and works as an intermediary between the lender and the borrower.

mortgage insurance Insurance to protect the lender in the case of default on a mortgage loan. Conventional loans require mortgage insurance with loans exceeding 80% of the value of the home.

mortgage loan A loan for which real estate serves as collateral to provide for repayment in case of default.

mortgage note A legal document obligating a borrower to repay a loan at a stated interest rate during a specified period of time. The agreement is secured by a mortgage or deed of trust or other security instrument.

mortgage term The length of time given to repay the loan.

mortgagee The lender in a mortgage loan transaction.

mortgagor The borrower in a mortgage loan transaction.

negative amortization A loan payment schedule in which the outstanding principal balance of a loan goes up rather than down because the payments do not cover the full amount of interest due. The monthly shortfall in payment is added to the unpaid principal balance of the loan.

nonassumption clause A statement in a mortgage contract forbidding the assumption of the mortgage by another borrower without the prior approval of the lender.

note A legal document obligating a borrower to repay a loan at a stated interest rate during a specified period of time. The agreement is secured by a mortgage or deed of trust or other security instrument.

notice of default Written notice to a borrower that a default has occurred and that legal action may be taken.

origination fee A fee charged by a lender to cover the administrative costs of processing a loan.

payment cap See *Caps (Payment)*.

payment schedule A schedule that indicates what the required monthly payment will be throughout the life of a fixed-rate loan.

per diem interest Interest calculated per day. Depending on the day of the month on which the closing takes place, interest will have to be paid from the date of the closing to the end of the month. The first mortgage payment will be due the first day of the following month.

periodic cap A consumer safeguard that limits the amount that the interest rate on an adjustable-rate mortgage can change in an adjustment interval. See *Caps (Interest)*.

PITI An acronym that stands for principal, interest, taxes, and insurance, the components of a monthly mortgage payment.

planned unit development (PUD) A project or subdivision that consists of common property and improvements that are owned and maintained by an owners' association for the benefit and use of the individual units within the project. For a project to qualify as a PUD, the owners' association must require automatic, nonservable membership for each unit owner and provide for mandatory assessments.

points An up-front fee paid to the lender. Each point equals 1% of the total loan amount. Also known as *discount points*.

power of attorney A legal document that authorizes one person to act on behalf of another.

preapproval The process of determining how much money a prospective home buyer or refinancer will be eligible to borrow prior to application for a loan. A preapproval includes a preliminary screening of a borrower's credit history.

prepaid expenses Taxes, insurance, and assessments paid in advance of their due dates. These expenses are included at closing.

prepaid interest Interest that is paid in advance of when it is due. Prepaid interest is typically charged to a borrower at closing to cover interest on the loan between the closing date and the first payment date.

prepayment Full or partial repayment of the principal before the contractual due date.

prepayment penalty A fee that is charged if the loan is paid off earlier than the specified term of the loan. The amount of prepayment penalty depends on the loan program and applicable state laws. Some states do not allow a prepayment penalty.

prequalification The process of determining how much money a prospective home buyer will be eligible to borrow prior to applying for a loan.

principal The amount of debt, not counting interest, left on a loan.

private mortgage insurance (PMI) Insurance to protect the lender in case of default on a mortgage loan. Conventional loans require PMI if the loan amount exceeds 80% of the value of the home.

property taxes The taxes assessed on the property by the local government (e.g., city, county, village, or township) for the various services provided to the property owner.

purchase agreement Contract signed by the buyer and the seller stating the terms and conditions under which a property will be sold.

real estate agent A person licensed to negotiate and transact the sale of real estate on behalf of the property owner.

Real Estate Settlement Procedures Act (RESPA) A federal law that gives consumers the right to review information about loan settlement costs after applying for a loan and again at loan settlement. The law requires lenders to provide these settlement costs only after application.

real property Land and any improvements permanently affixed to it, such as buildings.

Realtor A real estate broker or an associate holding active membership in a local real estate board connected to the National Association of Realtors.

recording The act of entering documents concerning title to a property into the public records.

recording fee   Money paid to a government agent for entering the sale of a property into the public records.

refinancing   The process of paying off one loan with the proceeds from a new loan secured from the same property.

rent-free   Refers to a borrower who is living with a relative or friend without paying rent. The borrower is considered to be living "rent-free."

right to rescission   Under the provisions of the Truth in Lending Act, the borrower's right, on certain kinds of loans (e.g., a refinance on an owner-occupied property), to cancel the loan within three days of signing a mortgage.

sales agreement   A contract signed by the buyer and the seller stating the terms and conditions under which a property will be sold.

second mortgage   A mortgage that is placed on a property that is already mortgaged and that has rights that are subordinate to the first mortgage.

settlement   See *closing*.

settlement costs   See *closing costs*.

simple interest   The interest calculated on a principal sum, not compounded on earned interest.

single family   Referring to a residence that houses one family.

structural improvements   Any permanent improvement made to a property which is not strictly for decorating purposes. Examples include additions, new flooring, kitchen or bathroom upgrades, new windows, and central air. Swimming pools are considered structural improvements only if they are in-ground and the property is in a year-round warm weather climate.

subject property   The home for which the borrower is applying for the loan.

survey   A bird's-eye sketch of the property that shows the boundary lines of the lot and that details any encroachments between the subject property and that of the neighbors.

survey fee   The fee that covers the cost of the survey.

tax impound   Money paid to and held by a lender for annual tax payments. See also *escrow account*.

tax lien   A claim against a property for unpaid taxes.

tax sale   A public sale of property by a government authority as a result of nonpayment of taxes.

tax service fee   A fee paid by the lender to a third party to monitor and handle the payment of the property tax bills.

term   The period of time that covers the life of the loan. For example, a 30-year fixed-rate loan has a term of 30 years.

third-party fees   Fees paid to a third party for services requested by the lender.

title   A document that gives evidence of ownership of a property. The title also indicates the rights of ownership and possession of the property. Individuals who will have legal ownership in the property are considered "on title" and will sign the mortgage and other documentation.

title company   A company that insures title to property.

title company closing fee   The fee paid to the title insurance company that conducts the closing and handles the transfer of funds among the parties.

title insurance   Insurance that protects a lender against any title dispute that may arise over a particular property.

title insurance premium   In order to determine that a property is properly owned and not subject to any unacceptable liens, lenders require both a search of the local real estate records and a title insurance policy insuring the lender against any defects in title. The title insurance premium covers the cost of the search and the insurance. The cost of title insurance varies both by state and by county.

title search   An examination of local real estate records to ensure that the seller is the legal owner of a property and that there are no liens or other claims against the property.

trade lines The different credit accounts listed on a borrower's credit report.

Trans Union One of the three largest credit bureaus in the United States.

transfer tax A tax paid when title passes from one owner to another.

Truth in Lending Act (TILA) A federal law requiring written disclosure of the terms of a mortgage (including the APR and other charges) by a lender to a borrower after application. The act also requires the right of rescission period.

underwriting In mortgage lending, the process of determining the risks involved in a particular loan and establishing suitable terms and conditions for the loan.

underwriting fee The fee that covers the cost of evaluating an entire loan package, including the credit report and appraisal, to determine whether the loan falls under lender guidelines in order to approve the loan request.

usury Interest charged in excess of the legal rate established by law.

VA loans Fixed-rate loans guaranteed by the U.S. Department of Veterans Affairs. The loans are designed to make housing affordable for eligible U.S. veterans. VA loans are available to veterans, reservists, active-duty personnel, and surviving spouses of veterans with 100% entitlement. Eligible veterans may be able to purchase a home with no down payment, no cash reserve, no application fee, and lower closing costs than other financing options.

variable rate An interest rate that changes periodically in relation to an index.

verification of deposit (VOD) A document signed by the borrower's bank or other financial institution verifying the borrower's account balance and history.

verification of employment (VOE)   A document signed by the borrower's employer verifying the borrower's position and salary.

verification of mortgage (VOM) or rent (VOR)   A document used to verify the mortgage or rent history of a borrower.

waiver   The voluntary relinquishment or surrender of some right or privilege.

walk-through   A final inspection of a home to check for problems that may need to be corrected before closing.

wire transfer fee   Lenders will transmit funds via the inter-bank wire transfer system to escrow in order to conduct a closing. This fee covers the cost of such transfer.

zoning ordinances   Local laws establishing building codes and usage regulations for properties in a specified area. Also known as *zoning regulations*.

Don't Quit

When things go wrong, as they sometimes will,
When the road you're trudging seems all uphill,
When funds are low and the debts are high,
And you want to smile, but you have to sigh,
When care is pressing you down a bit,
Rest, if you must, but don't you quit.

Life is queer with its twists and turns,
As every one of us sometimes learns,
And many a failure turns about,
When he might have won had he stuck it out.
Don't give up though the pace seems slow,
You may succeed with another blow.

Success is failure turned inside out,
The silver tint of the clouds of doubt,
And you never can tell how close you are,
It may be near when it seems so far.
So stick to the fight when you're hardest hit,
It's when things seems worst that you must not quit.

INDEX

ABOUT THE AUTHOR

Originally from New York City, **Darrin J. Seppinni** went to California in 1982 and began his mortgage career. One of America's leading authorities on becoming a loan officer and mortgage broker, Darrin has more than two decades of experience as a top-producing loan officer, manager, and trainer, helping both new and experienced loan officers and mortgage brokers reach their goals by providing them with up-to-date resources, training, and employment opportunities. He is a licensed real estate broker in California and a member of the California Association of Mortgage Brokers and the National Association of Mortgage Brokers.

Darrin is founder of Mortgage Smarts, LLC, an education and training company, which focuses on career and business development strategies that deliver results in one of the most financially rewarding businesses today. He lives in Newport Beach, California.

For more information, visit: www.mortgage-smarts.com; telephone: 800-442-5028 (toll free); or e-mail: darrin@mortgage-smarts.com.